IMBALANCE of POWER

IMBALANCE of POWER

US Hegemony and International Order

edited by
I. William Zartman

Viva Books
New Delhi | Mumbai | Chennai | Kolkata | Bangalore | Hyderabad | Kochi | Guwahati

First Indian Edition 2011

VIVA BOOKS PRIVATE LIMITED

- 4737/23 Ansari Road, Daryaganj, New Delhi 110 002
  E-mail: vivadelhi@vivagroupindia.net, Tel. 42242200
- 76, Service Industries, Shirvane, Sector 1, Nerul, Navi Mumbai 400 706
  E-mail: vivamumbai@vivagroupindia.net, Tel. 27721273, 27721274
- Jamals Fazal Chambers, 26 Greams Road, Chennai 600 006
  E-mail: vivachennai@vivagroupindia.net, Tel. 28290304, 28294241
- B-103, Jindal Towers, 21/1A/3 Darga Road, Kolkata 700 017
  E-mail: vivakolkata@vivagroupindia.net, Tel. 22836381, 22816713
- 7, Sovereign Park Apartments, 56-58, K. R. Road, Basavanagudi, Bengaluru 560 004
  E-mail: vivabangalore@vivagroupindia.net, Tel. 26607409, 26607410
- 101-102 Mughal Marc Apartments, 3-4-637 to 641, Narayanguda, Hyderabad 500 029
  E-mail: vivahyderabad@vivagroupindia.net, Tel. 27564481, 27564482
- Beevi Towers, First Floor, SRM Road, Kaloor, Kochi 682 018, Kerala
  E-mail: vivakochi@vivagroupindia.net, Tel: 0484-2403055, 2403056
- 232, GNB Road, Beside UCO Bank, Silpukhuri, Guwahati 781 003
  E-mail: vivaguwahati@vivagroupindia.net, Tel: 0361-2666386

www.vivagroupindia.com

Published by arrangement with

Lynne Rienner Publishers, Inc.
1800 30th Street, Suite 314
Boulder, Colorado 80301
USA

ISBN : 978-81-309-1535-7

Published by Vinod Vasishtha for Viva Books Private Limited, 4737/23, Ansari Road, Daryaganj, New Delhi - 110 002. Printed and bound by Raj Press, R-3, Inderpuri, New Delhi - 110 012.

S0000 / S0810

To Matthew Alexander Zartman,
may his world be in a better shape

Contents

Acknowledgments

I am grateful to the contributors to this work for their insights, their patience, and their willingness to revise their chapters in response to the reviewers' comments. I am as usual grateful to the Blaustein Foundation for its support of the Conflict Management Program and in particular for its support of this project. I am also grateful to Adam Correia, who carefully compiled the bibliography, and to Isabelle Talpain-Long, who shepherded this project through its long life with her customary skill and grace, putting in extra time and effort to meet the publisher's deadlines.

Above all, I owe an enormous debt of gratitude to Peter Pavilionis, an extraordinary substantive editor who knows his concepts as well as his grammar, and without whom this book would never have seen publication.

1

The Quest for Order in World Politics

I. William Zartman

It does not take much to see that the world is without form, and void, and darkness is on the face of the earth (Genesis 1:2). The Manichaean certainty of the Cold War as a system of world order is gone, and with it one of the two superpowers that held each other in check. Some mourn its passing and find new challenge from new forces of evil, now colored green instead of red. Others see a clash of many colors. But these colorful nightmares tell us little about the shape of the world and the distribution of power within it. After a suitable mourning period for a time when friends and enemies were easily identified and power was measured in isotopic abilities to overkill, it is time to take stock of the new shape of the world, as it stands now and in the foreseeable future.

In this book, eleven authorities on international relations from the United States and beyond have assumed this challenge. The object they observe is seen quite differently by each, even though it bears similarities for all of them. Their visions enrich the debate while at the same time identifying a number of common elements that indisputably form the world on which we sit. Their combined visions also leave a number of uncertainties and loose ends to pursue as the world moves on and the debate clarifies.

Systems of World Order

The buildup and breakdown of order are the basic subjects of political analysis, but they are particularly topical now that the old millennium has crashed in disorder. The search for order is the sign of our times. Both in the world system of states and in the sovereign systems within states, order has broken down, raising challenges to analysis and action. The earlier systems of world order in the twentieth century—the colonial order and the bipolar order—were structured on conquest and conflict, but these orders have dissolved, yielding place to uncertainty. The successor system is not yet evident, and attempts to order interstate relations through such diverse and conflicting concepts as international organization, uni- or multipolarity, transnational regimes, competing culture blocs, or a North-South divide remain inconclusive.[1] Nor is it evident whether the state system rights itself on its own, responding to the accidents of its own structure, or whether agents and policies are required to put the pieces into proper places. Is imbalance stable, or is an equilibrium required?

What has arisen out of this primeval disorder after the epic struggle between the "forces of good and evil" is a primus inter pares, a hegemonic firmament that wavers between a leadership role of world order through conflict management and cooperation on the one hand and a mission aspiration of world order through inspiration and imposition on the other. Yet neither of these views of its role has yet provoked the balance-of-power reaction from other states that rising hegemons are supposed to trigger. The only putative balancer has been an atavistic reaction to change, rising against the state order, cultural impingement, and economic globalization, in the name of a religious call *(da'wa)* deemed immutable.

Similarly, the concept of the state as the highest form of political organization is undergoing tremendous changes, proving its vulnerability to transnational penetration; interlinking domestic forces; and international regimes, laws, and organizations. The concept of sovereignty has been called into question by the secretaries-general of the United Nations themselves.[2] But at the same time the riddled state is expected to regulate more aspects of human activity than ever before while guarding against state and nonstate destabilizers. Extreme forms of authoritarian order, as in apartheid systems in the third world and totalitarian systems in the Second, have given way to institutionalized participation that is unable to preserve order. Some states end up with such a high degree of concentrated power that they implode, consuming the collapsed state and its fragments in their disorder.[3]

Conflict is not necessarily chaos, any more than disorder is the opposite of any particular form of order. Order appears in many, often ostensibly opposite forms: conflict and cooperation, war and peace, liberty and security, oppression and justice, symmetry and asymmetry, and indeed in many other concepts and values found in the chapters in this collection. Moreover, order is what permits inquiry and analysis in any discipline, as it turns data into knowledge; science looks for regularities or orders in events so that theory can serve "to bring order and meaning to a mass of phenomena which without it would remain disconnected and unintelligible."[4] Thus, inquiry into the concept of world order needs to begin with a search for taxonomies of order, in order to address both analytical questions of cause and relationship and normative questions of purpose and preference.

The Concept of Order

Unlike many other concepts of political (and other social) science, the concept of "order" and its meaning do not divide the discipline into great definitional debates. "Order—peaceful coexistence under conditions of scarcity—," wrote Talcott Parsons and Edward Shills, "is one of the very first of the functions imperatives of social systems."[5] Stephen Krasner apparently initially justified his inquiry into regimes as "related to the most fundamental concern of social theory: how is order established, maintained and destroyed," although the most fundamental concern disappeared in the final version, except in Susan Strange's recounting to question it.[6] Order implies a relationship among items based on some principle.[7] It often carries a suggestion of or is even used synonymously with harmony or stability, as in Saint Augustine's definition, "the distribution which allots things equal and unequal, each to its own place," or in a common parental injunction, "Johnny, go put some order in your room."[8] There is therefore, almost unavoidably, a value attached to order, as something the study of politics seeks to discern and the practice of politics seeks to achieve. Ivorian president Félix Houphouet-Boigny quoted Johann Wolfgang von Goethe here, "I prefer injustice to disorder: One can die of disorder, one does not die of injustice," and after his (natural) death his country proved the point.[9]

In its broadest sense, then, order is all understanding, or at least all political understanding, and politics is the search for order. Inevitably, inherently, therefore, when an incumbent system of world order breaks down, as did the bipolar system of the Cold War, and particularly when it breaks down without a predesignated successor, the component pieces engage in a search for a new order. And since they seek not just any order, but order on the global level, that search is purposeful even if not explicit, intense even if not deadly, involving power even if not violent; the search itself serves as part of the new order and its characteristics.

There are four types of decisionmaking procedures that define how order in a society is achieved. The fundamental typology is based on the type of decisionmaking procedures, which, although mixed in reality, are limited in number in their pure form:[10] (1) *authoritative,* commanded from the top of a hierarchical structure, whether executive or judicial, imperial or hegemonic;[11] (2) *coalitional,* composed of subgroups of shifting size in which the largest or strongest part decides for the whole, the most common forms of which are alliance-related and democratic (depending on whether the component unit is a state or a person);[12] (3) *negotiated,* composed of formally equal subgroups operating under the unanimity or unit veto rule, as in international organizations and national institutions; and (4) *inherent or spontaneous,* run by the hidden hand of some external agency or inner force such as the market.[13]

As happens when clear concepts meet the real world, the current international order is a bit of all of the above.[14] Another typology often invoked draws on the relation among the component units, depending on whether they are equal or unequal and whether their relationship is therefore symmetrical or asymmetrical. Yet, in reality there is no equality in international (or probably any political) relations, although this fact is generally at odds with the legal fiction of interstate equality.

Although the concern of this book lies in the international field, the world order system is composed of state units whose domestic orders are relevant to the shape of the global whole. It may be reassuring, or at least hopeful, that democracies do not fight each other, as subsequent chapters discuss (and generally accept), but other systems do, and democracies fight them too, as just one example of the intrastate-interstate linkage.[15]

Power and Order

Most important for this inquiry is the relationship between *power* and *order.* For all its definitional uncertainties, power is the central concept of political science and also the cause of order, whether exercised in authority, coalition, negotiation, or more automatic dynamics. "Politics for us means striving to share power or striving to influence the distribution of power, either among states or among groups within states," Max Weber averred.[16] The fact that that distribution is always asymmetrical to some degree provides the dynamics of politics, within as well as between states. "Inferiors become revolutionaries in order to be equals," Aristotle wrote; "and equals in order to be superiors."[17] Power provides the structure for world order, as order is the structure for power.

The two prominent notions of power—as a relation or as a possession—are linked but also underlie some diametrically opposite understandings. The first notion, power as a relation, is ex post and conclusionary; it can be appreciated only after an event has taken place, and it is dependent on an outcome of an encounter.[18] As a result, it can be added up over time, but is only grossly predictive and specifically inaccurate. More broadly, it is actor-oriented, dependent on the user's will and skill. The second notion, power as a possession, is ex ante and anticipatory; it can be calculated before any interaction, and it assumes (wrongly) that aggregate sources always produce identifiable outcomes. (Common components of power as a possession are shown in Table 1.1.) This notion reads results into structure and subordinates freedom (or at least wisdom) of choice to its structures. Nigeria and South Africa do not (often?) get their way in Africa, where they are the 900-pound gorillas of their continent. Thus, to assume a coincidence between the two notions of power is inaccurate: The United States does not always

Table 1.1 Indicators of National Power

	Military Expenditure[a] (billions of constant 2005 US$)		Population (millions)		Energy Use (10^{15} BTUs)		Gross Domestic Power/Capita (constant 2000 US$)		Iron + Steel Production (thousands of metric tons)	
	2006	1990	2007	1990	2004	1990	2005	1990	2006	1991
United States	528.6	457.6	301.1	250.4	100.4	84.1	37,267	28,263	136,355	123,280
Japan	43.7	39.5	127.4	123.6	22.6	18.3	39,075	33,280	200,489	189,631
UK	59.2	60.6	60.7	57.4	10.0	9.3	26,891	19,647	24,583	22,013
France	53.1	57.5	63.7	56.4	11.2	8.8	23,494	19,181	32,870	19,499
China	49.5	13.2	1,287.0	1,321.8	49.7	27.0	1,449	392	822,949	131,884
Germany	39.9	58.4[b]	82.4	62.2[c]	14.7	11.5[b]	23,906	19,430	77,586	73,199
Russia	34.7	171.0	141.3	290.9[d] 148.3[e]	28.7	59.8[d]	2,445	2,602	122,315	135,254

Sources: Charles Doran, *Systems in Crisis: New Imperatives of High Politics at Century's End* (Cambridge UP, 1991); Stockholm International Peace Research Institute (SIPRI), http://first.sipri.org/non_first/result_milex.php; *CIA World Factbook,* 1990 and 2003; Energy Information Administration, *International Energy Annual 2004* and *International Energy Annual 1998,* http://www.eia.doe.gov/emeu/iea; World Bank, *World Development Indicators 2007* and *World Development Indicators 2003;* International Iron and Steel Institute, *Steel Statistical Yearbook 2003* and *Steel Statistical Yearbook 2001,* www.worldsteel.org/ssy.php.

Notes: a. The SIPRI data set is converted into constant 2000 US$ using average market exchange rates rather than purchasing power parity conversion rates. This significantly understates military expenditure in some countries, especially developing economies such as China and Russia. See the SIPRI website at http://projects.sipri.org/milex/mex_sources.html for details.

b. Federal Republic of Germany.

c. 78.5 million including German Democratic Republic.

d. USSR.

e. Russia.

get its way either, although it is the 9,000-pound gorilla on the world scene. But the debate remains over how often, in what instances, in what way, and with what freedom of policy choice it does get its way.

The next question concerns the way one arrives at a particular order, a matter of importance under system or regime change, whether in the international system mutating from bipolar coalitions to unipolar hegemony or multipolar pluralism or in domestic polities in transition (from authoritarian order presumably to democracy). The domestic question has occasioned a vigorous literature pointing to the importance of power holders negotiating pacts to retain protection, if not position, in the transition.[19] Analysis of the evolution of the international system is limited by the uniqueness of the current case, the only instance of system change without a major war. The United States arrived at a hegemonic position through the exercise of its enormous economic power, and demonstrated to the Soviet leaders their futile pursuit of a confrontation in technological revolutions and military procurement; the latter preferred the consequences of fatigue to suicidal war.[20] The hegemon now finds itself in a predominant position in which its power (as a possession)—its gross domestic power in Seyom Brown's term—is unable to accomplish its goals (as a relationship); hence, its best course of leadership is to assert its power by restraining it, as subsequent chapters indicate, a central question within this book underlying most chapters but addressed directly by Robert Jervis in Chapter 3. What then is power, and what is the order built on it?

Earlier debates over bipolar versus multipolar stability in international politics have turned into a debate over hegemony versus multipolarity, and the ongoing debate over the importance of a hegemon versus a middle power coalition for regional integration and international cooperation continues into the new world order.[21] Although the verdict seems to have tilted in favor of bipolarity and then hegemony over multipolarity as the key to stability, there is a tinge of argument to please the court or acquiescence to the current order of things in the analysis. Unfortunately, a deeper but less satisfying conclusion is, arguably, that any of the three orders is stable if it is played "right": that is, each order contains stability mechanisms of mutual restraint whose use depends on the dominant parties' sense of responsibility (to maintain stability!) and not on any inherent homeostasis. To identify unilateral philosopher kings, bilateral regimes, and the multilateral balance of power as such mechanisms confirms the need for a place for will and skill in political analysis, along with more objective mechanisms and regularities.[22] Such mechanisms offer structural possibilities, but they are not automatic and require will on the part of the agent and skill in the necessary processes to operate.

Although developed polities in general have worked out their institutional structures, developing countries continue to debate the effects of a centralized, if not authoritarian, power structure versus a pluralistic system, whether parliamentarian or dual executive. The most notable enactment of this debate occurred in the early 1990s in the twelve countries of Africa where civil society made the extraordinary move of seizing sovereignty from the authoritarian incumbent in sovereign national conferences (SNC) and drawing up a new social contract.[23] The same question faces other countries in Africa and elsewhere in the Middle East, Asia, and Latin America that feel the same desire for transition from authoritarian rule, even without a SNC. An authoritative order faces the challenge of keeping the father of the nation dynamic and honest, whereas the coalitional order faces the challenges of keeping the coalition stable or the great coalition honest and dynamic, and the negotiated order faces the challenge of participation, recognizing both those who are part of the problem and those who are not part of the problem as legitimate parts of the solution.

Even though democracy is without exception the favored solution to the power-and-order problem, it is used to justify truly democratic, democratizing, and undemocratic orders, and its inevitable abuses and inefficiencies return the analysis to focus on remedies for problems of effectiveness and responsibility. By the same token, its remedial insignificance on the domestic level should give pause to those who would seek to create a "democratic" international order, as Gustav Schmidt discusses below, whether with states or with populations as the component units, where equivalent remedies have yet to be invented, as well as to those who look to democracy without preparation as a quick fix, either from within or from without.

The millennium brought a startling—or refreshing—new angle to the problem of power orders by introducing the prospects of weakened states facing an increasing number of challenges. In internal politics, the need for the state, whatever its power structure, to rely increasingly on cooperation with nonstate actors returns to prominence the concept of civil society as a crucial element in the internal order and an answer to the problems of effectiveness and responsibility. International politics has already begun to grapple, still inconclusively, with the problem of permeable and circumvented sovereignty weakening the fiber of its state system.[24] It also increasingly recognizes the role of nongovernmental organizations in preparing, supporting, and implementing state initiatives. As a result, negotiation—rather than authority or coalition democracy—has become paramount as the decision-making order within the networks, dialogues, regimes, and outsourcing that are needed to tie the pieces together.[25] The state has come back as the heart of political analysis, just in time for the body politic to be subject to invasive surgery and bypasses to overcome its sclerosis.[26] Thus state building (the correct translation of the misused term "nation building") has again resurfaced as a major link in the rise of the nonstate challengers to the state system and a major challenge to the leaders of the world order system, whether for missional or structural reasons, as Gustav Schmidt discusses in Chapter 7.

The Orders of the Day

Scholarship paces events, as it should (despite the claims of external interference through this relationship). After all, there is more scholarship these days on state collapse or democratization than on revolution or monarchy, more on multipolarity than on bipolarity: "Transformations of political discourse in the West have been a function of changing conceptualizations of threat to the existence of political order."[27] Thus, after the collapse of communism and under international anarchy, authoritarian order is generally not at the top of the current agenda for research and debate, whereas the other three forms of order—democratic coalitions, oligarchic negotiation, and inherent, automatic orders—have produced new analysis and concerns. The assertive policy of the United States in the early 2000s restored concern and debate about authoritarian order, if only to put it into perspective.

Order through hierarchy is doubtless the oldest type, but the divine right of kings has passed into history in most places. Even as late as Talleyrand and the rest of the nineteenth century, it was the source of legitimacy in Europe, and in Africa and the Middle East it still is, whether heredity or coup is the source of incumbency.[28] Even democratic systems have retained strong executive institutions, although they are usually balanced by legislatures and (authoritarian) judiciaries in a separation of powers, or checks and balances. Such balancing is characteristic of international orders, global or regional, as will be discussed next, because by definition they exist in international anarchy (i.e., leaderlessness), the very characteristic that makes assertions of leadership tempting for a great power. It is because of this definitional characteristic that unipolarity and too ostentatious assertions of hegemony are viewed with disapproval by other members of the system, and also because no one likes to be an inferior. A second, more focused level of objections derives from the fact that the authoritative state and the others are certain not to share all the same interests, and indeed to possess certain opposite interests because of their positions, a subject of analysis by Kenneth Waltz in Chapter 2 and Charles Doran in Chapter 5. Efforts by the central power to assert a total commonality of interests can only go so far. So hierarchy alone is not the source of order, and it is essential to recognize that the United States (to name names) does not consistently, or even frequently, prevail. Indeed, the current concern is not that the United States will lead the pack but that it will ignore it, scarcely a form of hierarchical order.

Order through coalition has received new emphasis in current concerns about the process of democratization and the evidence that previously nondemocratic orders of governance lack the coalitional fluidity necessary for their immediate transformation into democratic orders.[29] Balance becomes the source of order; a statesman "must perpetuate order, which he does by keeping the multitudinous aggressions of men in balance against one another," Jacques Barzun maintains, echoing Bagehot and Talleyrand.[30] In international politics, order based on the coalition process is an established tradition. The basic mechanism involving a flexible coalition of states wanting to preserve the status quo against a rising hegemon, known as the balance of power or, more recently, balance of threat, is still central to international relations theory, although the concept of power has evolved, as discussed below.[31] If half a century of bipolarity took some of the flexibility out of coalition behavior, both within and among the blocs, two decades of post-bipolar uncertainties have not produced the antihegemonic coalition against the remaining superpower that the theory might have predicted, as Kenneth Waltz points out, probably because the hegemon's political yoke is easy, its economic burden is lightened by a lot of free riding, and its values are widely shared, as Seyom Brown indicates below. US language and behavior, particularly in the first Bush administration of the 2000s, weakened these restraints, leaving much fence mending for the second term and its successors.

In the process, the opposite coalition behaviors of bandwagoning and balking have also come to light as an attractive alternative, particularly for small states.[32] Another new extension has been the analysis of regime building and multilateral diplomacy, theoretically quite different from the generally assumed bilateral character of negotiation, as a matter of managing complexity through coalition.[33] Although basic coalition theory dates from an earlier era, these new uses of the concept have broken out from the simpler assumptions of that theory and require further theoretical expansion and then testing.[34]

Yet even in established democratic orders, ascriptive components such as ethnicity and gender pose problems of voter rigidity.[35] The result is that democracy is no longer analyzed with the primary focus on the individual voter, as in earlier studies, but on aggregated votes. Analysts have repeatedly and variously noted that the presumed egalitarian status necessary for free choice by individual voters is negated by the inegalitarian status of the ascriptive blocs to which they belong and also by status effects on attitudes, participation, and choice, bringing a reexamination of the new relevance of classical solutions to both aspects of the rigidity problem, ranging from proportional representation to gerrymandering.[36]

The rigidity problem has led to other avenues of analysis. The issue of preconditions to democracy is being reexamined.[37] Either socioeconomic development to higher levels of literacy and productivity or economic reform to pluralist economic competition is claimed by some to be a necessary antecedent to competitive political pluralism. Passage from an authoritarian to a democratic order is found to require a negotiated transition of elite pacts to avoid a replication of the authoritarian bloc under new conditions.[38] Ethnic voting blocs must be broken by crosscutting, interest-aggregating parties to avoid the creation of permanent ethnic majorities, yet political parties tend to become vehicles for ethnic voting blocs. As scholars come to the conclusion that there is no best form of democratic constitution,[39] research on democratization devolves into the "puzzle phase"[40] as its focus is drawn to transitional institutional structures, voting regulations and practices, transparency guarantees, and postelectoral implementation. The flaws of simple majoritarian systems are receiving greater emphasis as democracy, at its best, comes to be seen as a coalition process in which all have a share in power.[41] In the legislative arena, coalition voting has been subject to sophisticated statistical and game-theoretical analysis carrying coalition theory to its most developed point, although circumscribed by the conditions of legislatures.[42]

Negotiated orders were the subject of an enormous burst of attention and analysis in the last decades of the previous millennium. Negotiation has been characterized as involving "an initial disorder—the dispute—and an endeavor to reach an order—the settlement."[43] It has long been studied in the uninstitutionalized order of international relations, leaving coalition and authority and their variants as the contending systems of order for domestic politics. If there are signal dates in the real world for a new focus on negotiation, they come from the 1960s—between 1962 in international relations, when the Cuban missile crisis turned superpower military confrontation to diplomatic bargaining, and 1968 in domestic relations, when youth around the world refusing authority sought to negotiate new realities. It was also the time of seminal works that launched the analysis of a form of order different from the others—neither commanded nor divided but based on unanimity between and among formally equal parties about a constructed outcome.[44] The new attention has opened an entirely new area of analysis untouched in previous accounts that dealt only with outcomes—bills, treaties, institutions, states, constitutions—while ignoring the way in which they were achieved.

Negotiated orders have a participatory legitimacy and ownership shared with voted orders but without the necessary losers, and the negotiated order's threefold choice (accept, reject, continue) allows for a positive-sum creativity that the twofold choice of voting and the "no-choice" acceptance of authority do not provide.[45] Negotiation, however, requires recognition of the parties' legitimacy, an ability to accept half a loaf, and a tolerance of ambiguity in decisions that some situations do not permit. Without the tools of negotiation analysis, it would not be possible to investigate many aspects of world and domestic order such as international regimes, labor-management relations, peacemaking and peacekeeping, business deals, and preparation of legislation; yet it is significant that these very issue-areas are the ones where much remains to be done and learned about negotiation.[46]

Thus negotiation can be treated as both a dependent and an independent variable in the search for order. Two questions dominate: "What is the order inherent in or leading to negotiation?" and "What kind of order does negotiation produce?" Negotiation processes follow one of three patterns (or a mix of them): concession/convergence distributive bargaining, which produces zero-sum ("win/lose") outcomes; compensating exchange trading, which produces positive-sum ("win/win") outcomes; or formula/detail integrating construction, which also produces positive-sum ("win/win") outcomes. There is a high correlation of process to outcome, but the determinants of the initial choice are not yet clear.[47]

Among the three, compensating exchanges and integrating construction produce more stable outcomes since distributive bargaining contains an incentive for later rejection by the losing party—Farhang Rajaee's "politics of deliberation and inclusion." Compared to other types of order, institutionalized negotiation orders such as consensus legislation, international regimes, civil society groups, pacted transitions, and institutional amendments, among others, tend to be more creative, more flexible, and more able to handle change.[48] Recent work has reinforced the conclusion that elected orders confirm legitimacy but only as a prerequisite, and that the real work of satisfying cross-cutting majorities and minorities through effective governance is produced by negotiations among the elected parties and their appointed agents.[49]

Most recently, spurred by approaches in other sciences, a new type of order has begun to receive attention, the *spontaneous or inherent order,* or the political equivalent of the market.[50] International political analysts have long claimed the balance-of-power mechanism to be not a policy option but an automatic pattern into which states' actions fall, although uncertainty remains as to whether it is indeed an automatic effect or a voluntary policy coalition (including a balancer).[51] Structuralists, as expressed in Chapter 2 by Kenneth Waltz, see a determinism over policy and role in the power distribution of the system. Social scientists and philosophers have long sought an elegant explanation for order in the form of a natural, self-maintaining equilibrium, but in the postwar era, they have asserted but then disclaimed the homeostatic tendencies of social systems.

Rational choice analysis carries something of an inherent order mechanism under its innocent assumption of rationality, not surprising since rational choice is putatively the political equivalent of market economics (realist theory is less convincing in the same claim in international politics).[52] However, the proposal that the political system (state or international system) is the equivalent of the market, larger than the sum of the parts of rational political actors, does not provide the same convincing insights[53] and has already been co-opted and worn out (if not discredited) by the twentieth century's emphasis on raison d'état, *Staatsmacht,* and eventually the totalitarian state, and the post–World War II recurrent emphasis on world reformist missions. The millennial search continues for a political order that has its own regularities and mechanisms and can be subjected to scientific theory and analysis, independent of the vagaries of human choice.

In the forms of order—coalition, negotiation, the political equivalent of the market, leaving empire aside—the potential is still underdeveloped. Coalition theory has not kept up with its application; negotiation theory is still a matter of many different views of the elephant; and theorists are still searching for the political equivalent of the market.[54] Whether in domestic legislation or diplomatic mandate, coalitions are best subject to theoretical analysis when their components qualify as constituted units with well-determined interests and positions. But when their interests are inchoate and their existence itself the subject of political action, as is most usually the case, even the best analysis becomes inductive or ad hoc. Similarly, negotiation analysis has long been based on an assumption of established positions, bottom lines, and concession/convergence behavior, conditions that allow elegant theory but omit most of the negotiation process and conceive it in unrealistic terms. The political "market" too can only be a process. Important conceptualizations of a political system as a mechanism with explicable and foreseeable consequences, developed in the 1950s and 1960s, have been put on the shelf for the moment, ready for retrieval in response to new questions and new bursts of inspiration.[55]

Concerns About Order

The relation of power to order sets up a further agenda of concerns, some having to do with the dynamics of putative opposites, such as the relation between order and change, and others with supposed synonyms, such as order and justice, or order and legitimacy, or order and law. None is new (what is, in political theory?) but all are of particular concern for the state of world order at the outset of the millennium.

The relation between *order and change* is a continuing concern that the end of the Cold War order has thrown into new prominence, and is taken up in Chapter 4 by Paul Schroeder and Chapter 5 by Charles Doran. Order is not the opposite of change: There is orderly change and the change of orders, as in patterns (or anatomies) of revolution, stages of development, measures of transition, and amendment of constitutions.[56] Thus, the eternal question regarding the relationship between order and change takes on two meanings: the scientist looks for regularities in new clusters of events, the practitioner (including the victim) looks for orderly—that is, if not nonviolent, at least predictable—change.

New subjects of attention for interpretative scholarship on change and order for the beginning of the millennium include interstate systemic transformation,[57] transitions from one type of world order to another,[58] and state collapse.[59] In international politics, the inability of realist theory to explain, let alone predict, the collapse of the bipolar system and the avenues of its succession has raised penetrating questions about its theoretical power and defensive answers about its constrained applicability.[60] In the now-merging areas of interstate and intrastate conflict, the search for nonviolent change has led to the new field of conflict management, resolution, and transformation, which enables investigation of patterns of conflict and ways of channeling violent conflicts into political interaction.[61] Indeed, government itself is conflict management, providing an orderly process of change and mechanism for handling conflict among legitimate demands (and resources) and controlling its potential escalation into violence.[62] The hegemonic order, like past systems of world order, finds itself torn between selective goals of domestic regime change and regime support against change.

Justice is not necessarily *order,* any more than is peace or mercy. Orders are likely to be overtaken by the struggle for justice if they do not already achieve it (Goethe and Houphouet-Boigny notwithstanding), but since the bases of justice themselves change over time, today's just order may be tomorrow's cause for revolt.[63] International politics has looked for order in justice and justice in order on different occasions, for example, as rival organizations seek "peace" versus "peace with justice" in the Middle East. The relationship between order and justice is the subject of Chapter 8 by Farhang Rajaee. Yet neither on the ground nor in the most recent periodic burst of scholarship has a consensual definition of a just order that can stand up to the inevitable changes in criteria been established.[64] For all the travesties that it perpetrated on humanity, communism began as a search for a just order, but order soon became its own criterion, overriding justice, both in its domestic polities and in its regional system. In the case of fundamentalist religious orders (especially Islamist ones), justice is cited as the motivating factor in the imposition of an authoritarian system, with the same inherent deformation as already seen under communism.[65] Whereas after the Cold War the weak hegemonic order may be criticized more for its ineptitude in the pursuit of justice, the Islamist reaction takes on the injustice of the order itself. Since the defeat of world communism and the confrontation with Islamic fundamentalism, democracy has been frequently touted as the way to a just order, although the question plagues the current confrontation as it did the earlier one: Where is justice if the democratic order produces an antidemocratic system?

Order and *legitimacy* are distinct terms, so that "legitimate order" is not a redundancy, any more than the might that makes order makes that order right. Legitimacy, defined as "the right to rule,"[66] can only refer to domestic political orders, where rule occurs and where the analysis asks whether the reigning domestic order is indeed legitimate and how legitimacy is determined. There is still no internal answer, despite some sophisticated polling techniques and rational choice analyses; legitimacy is generally judged from the outside, as commentators look in, and is often distinguished from "legal," the internal measure.[67] The current criterion for awarding legitimacy, both within states and within the international institutions of world order that they comprise, is the presence of democracy, often elusive to definition and discovery. Yet order and legitimacy are not totally independent of each other: Legitimacy contributes to order, but order contributes to its own legitimacy.

In the anarchic international order, legitimacy needs a new definition, perhaps referring instead to the order's right to exist, if not back to the concept of justice itself. In the absence of a direct determination, which is more applicable in domestic polities, investigations relating to legitimacy in an international order necessarily involve questions about the process of its establishment, the allocation of its benefits, and the balance of benefits and responsibilities (see Chapter 5 by Charles Doran and Chapter 10 by Francis Fukuyama).[68] As with justice, the question is not raised about the legitimacy of the hegemonic order but rather about the uses to which that hegemony is put.

The relation between *order* and *law* is less treated in the current debate. In the late 1960s, "law and order" became the designation of the right, the forces against change. For Weber, "The political element consists, above all, in the task of maintaining 'law and order' in the country, hence maintaining the existing power relations."[69] In domestic relations, law is roughly synonymous with order, despite the ideological appropriations of the phrase, but the heated debate is over how much of public and private life needs to be ordered by law. While the provision of private socioeconomic security from the cradle to the grave has been somewhat reduced in many countries, legal regulation of everything from abortion to zebra mussels is viewed by many as overly intrusive and sparks a conservative call for "less government." The answer for many is found in John Locke's assertion of civil society as an order without authority, with the players capable of regulating their own affairs without invoking Hobbes's Leviathan, but the relation between the two—the subsidiarity question—is unclear: Is law needed to regulate what civil society does not, or is civil society needed to regulate what law does not? Yet civil society is an increasingly important subject of inquiry, particularly in regard to the developing countries,[70] where the problem is an alternative not to intrusive government but to lame or privatized government.

In international politics, where there is practically no government at all,[71] the same question is the basis of the dispute between the realists and the liberals over how anarchic the international order is and to what extent state "behaviors" are constrained by regimes, that is, by soft law, institutions, or "principles, norms, rules and procedures."[72] The debate is partially definitional, although the liberal school is better equipped to explain cooperation than its opponent, which is more attuned to conflict. The two also split over law's application in the current asymmetric world order, as highlighted by Gustav Schmidt in Chapter 7: Are the hegemonic law enforcers subject to the same laws, however soft, as the rest of the international community?

The Universality of Order

It is hard to imagine that any of these concerns could be limited to a particular cultural area of the globalized world or would be a worry to only a Western mind. Order itself is universal, and its forms are limited. Each has its advantages and disadvantages, and none is the cultural property of any particular country or region. There may be (or may have been) a Confucian order in China, an Islamic order in Iran, an Enarquic order in France, or a monarchial order in Morocco, but the concept of order is common to them all, and their peculiar characteristics can also be found here and there around the globe. It is hard to compare, analyze, talk of them, or combine them in a global system without using common concepts of order.

Nonetheless, political culture would aver that particular conceptions of order dominate the ethos and practice of large world areas, based on current political systems, historical traditions, predominant religions, and regional configurations, an analysis that both Gustav Schmidt and Farhang Rajaee develop in Chapters 7 and 8, respectively. From this point of view (admittedly generalized and perhaps caricatured), Asia—both East or Confucian and Western or Arabo-Muslim—can be said to favor a centralized, hierarchical political order, as contrasted with the Judeo-Christian Atlantic West, which is characterized by a pluralized competitive order. China and Egypt would be typical of the first; the United States and Europe of the second.[73] The Confucian system dominant in China (and reinforced by the Marxist-Leninist-Maoist ideology) regards hierarchy as superior to competition as an ordering principle, and enlightened authoritarian command is its form of decisionmaking. A deeply inbred fear of social chaos *(luan)* preconditions the Chinese preference for a strong central authority. A strong government is also perceived to be better able to deliver public goods. Its political geography has long been seen in terms of concentric circles, based on the pivotal Middle Kingdom, and indeed the vast country of China has one time zone. Values are in service of the collective and emphasize communal harmony. Foreigners are held separate, socialization into dominant cultural patterns is the main function of education, and political participation is through the single party.[74] Negotiation becomes difficult to practice, and instructive discourse is preferred.[75] Yet on the interstate level, competition is vigorously engaged, state sovereignty strongly defended, and regional autonomy actively asserted, yielding a nonhierarchial and antihegemonic worldview.

Despite very different sources, Arabo-Muslim political culture has remarkably similar characteristics, as seen in Egypt and most other Arab countries. The authoritarian system centered around the leader *(za'im)* is predominant, the single party or at least the dominant party runs the political system, and democracy has a hard time taking hold. If the Arab world is broken up into separate states, the Arab nation and the single Islamic community *(umma)* are idealized and mythologized, and the classical language of the Quran is the standard of civilization and the word of God *(al-Lah).* Egypt is the Mother of the Earth *(masr umm al-duniya),* even if some other Arab states would claim at least paternity. Out of this culture comes the most important current version of the balance of power, a nonstate protest movement that seeks to stop the globalizing world and get off, to return to its own imposed view of orthodoxy. Its nonstate form reflects the nonstate form of globalization and its hydra-formed organization responds to the hegemonic structure of the world order system. Yet it is also an antipluralizing movement, attaching corrupt Muslim governments in the name of Sunni atavism and a return to a golden age. Although in both East and West Asia pluralism is bound to exist, it is conditioned and contained within the centralized authoritarian order.

In contrast, the Atlantic West is characterized by competitive pluralism, multiparty democracy, a multicultural stew in the melting pot, and many time zones.[76] The United States is no more united than its federalism will allow, and European unity takes place only by preserving its multistate system.[77] Where pluralism has to be contained, it is done through binary logic, Manichaean conceptualization between good and bad, black and white, and legal confrontation. France invented and the United States applied the separation of powers within government, and this pluralism has been paralleled historically by the richness of American associational life in civil society.[78] Even where the European monarchial tradition has left a shadow of centralism, it has been eaten away at the edges throughout history by the English barons, German states, Italian (even including papal) tolerance for ambiguity, and French republicanism. This is a negotiated polity par excellence, combined with the elections and coalitions of democracy. Little wonder that the balance-of-power practice and theory came out of this type of state system.

These vignettes can be either dismissed as caricatures or endlessly debated and diagnosed as clashing civilizations, as can no doubt the whole area of political (or any other) culture.[79] Yet there is a lot of literature and discussion behind the general picture of the three cultures that the vignettes present, and they represent a certain consensus about different notions of order in different parts of the world, even in their abbreviated form. From this point of view, it can be argued that there is a dominant pattern of expectations and discourse about appropriate orders in various parts of the world, whatever the exceptions and blurred edges that might exist.

The overriding point, of course, is that these images reflect a common notion of the meaning of order and of the forms it can take, even if elements in that universal typology find different supporting examples from different regions. These different views of the same elephant combine into a single system of world order, larger than the sum of its diverse parts, in which they must find a role, whatever they do at home. In response to the original questions, different regions may answer differently as to which order is preferable, but they enter into the debate on the basis of a common understanding of the orders possible and practiced among massive human collectivities on this earth.

Hegemony and Order

The following chapters join in this debate from nine different points of view. They identify the current system of world order and the position of the United States in it, and in so doing identify its weaknesses and dangers as well as its strengths. To some, the marking characteristic is US hegemony, which determines the type of international order. To others, it is the order itself, larger than the sum of its parts, that determines the role of its components, including the United States. Although the separation between these two approaches is not neat and their overlap is great, this difference in emphasis has been used to divide the analyses into two parts in the following presentation.

Yet each of these approaches is driven by a larger argument over the relation between structure and policy. To some, in both approaches, it is the structure of relations that determines the policies of the component parts, who do only what they can do given their place in the system, whereas to others, states have a wider range of policy choices that determine the structure of the world order system. As in the previous dichotomy, the distinction between the two is not hermetic, and they tend to meet each other coming and going. In fact, as often in purportedly sharp academic debates, the argument is circular, and its two sides are complementary: Where you sit depends to a large extent on where you get on the train. Structure is the result of component elements' choices, which are in turn limited by their place in the structure. The analysis could be termed structural possibilism, in a recognition that human choice cannot be contained in any determinism but is free to exhibit brilliant inventiveness as well as stupid mistakes, in addition to predominant regularities.[80]

The four chapters in the first part of the book focus on US hegemony in the international order. The first two chapters center their analyses on the concept of power and its operation within the system of world order. Starting from the fact of US predominance, Kenneth Waltz shows how the hegemon will adopt dominant policies, although it has a choice between preemption, on the one hand, and deterrence and containment, on the other. Faced with the hegemon, the others will seek to keep it in check. Yet, they will be ineffective for the very reason that impelled their attempt at balancing. Robert Jervis, in Chapter 3, is not so sure. In a world order characterized by both wars and security communities, hegemonic policies are inherent in the position of the predominant state. Such policies are understandably inherent in the international power structure, but they are not inevitable. Structure need not preempt choice, and indeed the feedback from the choice of prevention (or rather preemption) over deterrence has a profound effect on the next round of choice.

The next pair of chapters emphasizes the importance of choice over structure from very different angles. Both, like the preceding pair of authors, see the urge to domination inherent in the US position of power. In Chapter 4, historian Paul Schroeder examines the historical record to analyze the policies adopted by predominant states in their choice between hegemony and empire (loosely construed). Hegemony is equated with leadership in a multiparticipant, even if not multipolar, system, whereas empire means overextension, exhaustion, and ultimately betrayal of predominance's responsibilities. The historical record shows that the outcome of imperial pursuit is not only policy failure but a return to hegemonic leadership to recoup systemic predominance. The system rights itself at some cost. In Chapter 5, Charles Doran, a quantitative systems analyst, throws doubt on the entire notion of hegemony. No actor, no matter how powerful, is able to impose its policies on the international system, but it can adopt policies that shorten or prolong its predominant position in the power cycles. It cannot overwhelm putative balancing coalitions, but it can gather a coalition around itself, a multilateralism of the willing, that tempers both the single dominance and the countervailing structure.

The chapters in Part 2 focus on the world order system as the context for the hegemon, reversing the emphasis of the first part while maintaining the same elements. In Chapter 6, Seyom Brown sees US hegemony as embedded in a polyarchic field of actors in competition for resources and support. Their classically predicted balancing and bandwagoning around the hegemon is joined by a third policy of balking when the first two become ineffectual. This array of choices structures the system and leaves the hegemon with policy choices of its own (empire, unilateralism, isolationism, and leadership). In Chapter 7, Gustav Schmidt presents a view from within the Atlantic security community but from Europe. Separate policy choices, different definitions of security, and special emphases on welfare mean that the hegemon's coalition partners have a rising role to play in determining the ruling order. Their imperfect community also means that the global order is really a confederation of regional order, a new texture that other analyses have passed over.

The next two chapters see the international order as one of globalization, although again of very different natures. For Farhang Rajaee in Chapter 8, the global order takes the shape of a no-polar world of nonstate as well as state players constituting a single multicultural civilization formed and regulated by the information revolution. Where the previous state system was dominated by a search for security, the ensuing system is challenged by the demands of justice. As the new order develops, its participants, no longer just states but humanity, face the classical alternatives of tyranny, rebellion, or civility, mirroring choices posed in previous chapters but in a different form. To Michael Klare and Peter Pavilionis in Chapter 9, globalization is characterized instead by a competition for scarce resources, conducted by states for their populations as well as for their own security needs. The structural challenge is constituted by demand outpacing supply, in which the various members of the previously identified orders all face resource inadequacies. Policy choices to avert conflict are technical and specific rather than systemic.

The final window on the unfolding shape of the world is opened by Francis Fukuyama in Chapter 10, who echoes the inadequacy of both an institutionalized order and a counterbalanced unipolar order to deal with characteristic conflict. These conflicts are topped by the dual threat of the ultimate nongovernmental organization, the terrorist balancer of the globalized superpower, and the superempowerment conferred by the potential availability of weapons of mass destruction. The answer, still unfolding, comes in the shape of institutions that contain hegemonic leadership and combine the requirements of legitimacy and power needed for a new and stable system of world order.

The contemporary debate, as it develops in these chapters, is not over differences in the sorts of world order that succeed the Cold War bipolarity or over a competition between regional or cultural models for the global system. The contributors quickly come to agreement over the nature of the hegemonic world order, with some slight disagreement over precisely what name to give it. But thereupon, they debate whether policies and relations within that system are the result of automatic mechanisms of power structures inherent in the hegemonic order, as realism would indicate, or whether they are the result of the goals and ultimately the whims of the hegemonic states and their leaders, framed by normative impulses and institutions as liberals would hope or by public opinion as constructionists aver. Although the answer takes on a partisan as well as an academic tone during presidential campaigns, it is crucial for an understanding of the future, as is the underlying goal of the debate in this collection.

For if the policies of the postbipolar hegemonic era are a structural consequence, there is little leeway (other then rhetorical) in its future. A balance of power among states may eventually materialize, delayed beyond the currently analyzed reasons by the common need to face the *nonstate* balance of power that brooks no allies and threatens all who ride the tide of globalization. But the opposition of lesser states is merely a structural phenomenon, an occupational hazard; the hegemonic position itself is a lightening pole for envy, cynicism, and jealousy—the Venus Envy Complex. The hegemon cannot long rely on self-restraint as the mode of its leadership, and its crusades against evil states (before they become empires) for the democratic salvation of their peoples are measures of its stature. The debate, then, is only about verbiage, the packaging, not the content. In this view, ideology (and history) is not banished by realism but is inherent in it. A state's policies and means are always in balance, as Walter Lippman told us long ago.[81]

But if the policies of the hegemon and the bystanders are actor-determined, the scope for alternatives is wide, even if not boundless, limited only (and enabled) by secondary structural characteristics, by the institutions the actors accept, or by the public opinion they court and shape. The debate in this view is directly about policy directions and about the pursuit or abdication of ideational (or "missionary") goals offering wide options. These options may include the speed and decisiveness of response to world conflicts, the purposes of power, the choice and use of allies, the use and acceptance of institutions, and the tone of the message from the hegemon. They could also include a shift to a focus on transnational dangers, from disease to terrorism, or a refocus on the implications of new measures of gross national power (such as oil) in the place of power-structural determinism. In this view, realism provides no guide as to what may or even can happen, although liberal institutionalism and constructivism only indicate additional inputs. But the following chapters agree that the options will not include the renunciation of the hegemonic role and the responsibilities that go with it. Such is the nature of the imbalance of power—the ever-uncertain system of world order.

Notes

1. Han Sung-Joo, ed., *The New International System.*
2. Boutros Boutros-Ghali, *An Agenda for Peace;* Kofi Annan, Ditchley Foundation Lecture XXXV, Ditchley House, UK, June 26, 1998.
3. I. William Zartman, ed., *Collapsed States.*
4. Hans Morgenthau, *Politics Among Nations.*
5. Talcott Parsons and Edward Shils, *Toward a General Theory of Action,* p. 180.
6. Susan Strange, "Cave! Hic Dragones," p. 345.
7. Hedley Bull, *The Anarchical Society,* p. 3; Stanley Hoffmann, *Conditions of World Order,* p. 2.
8. Augustine, *The Political Writings,* p. 144.
9. In Aristide Zolberg, *Creating Political Order,* p. 42.
10. Aristotle, *Politics;* Robert Goodin, "Structures of Political Order"; Oran Young, "Regime Dynamics," pp. 98–101; Lewin, Lippitt, and White, "Patterns of Aggressive Behavior in Experimentally Created 'Social Climates'"; Robert Dahl, "Hierarchy, Democracy, and Bargaining in Politics and Economics."
11. Juan Linz, "Totalitarian and Authoritarian Regimes."

12. Guillermo O'Donnell and Philippe C. Schmitter, *Transitions from Authoritarian Rule.*

13. Friedrich von Hayek, *The Fatal Conceit,* pp. 307–309.

14. Aristotle, *Politics;* Raymond Aron, "The Anarchical Order of Power," pp. 44–45.

15. Immanuel Kant, "Perpetual Peace."

16. Max Weber, "Politics as a Vocation," p. 78.

17. Aristotle, *Politics,* Book V A II §3, p. 242.

18. R. H. Tawney, *Equality;* Robert Dahl, "The Concept of Power"; J. W. Thibaud and H. H. Kelley, *The Social Psychology of Groups.*

19. Guillermo O'Donnell and Philippe C. Schmitter, *Transition from Authoritarian Rule;* Valerie Bunce, *Do New Leaders Make a Difference?*

20. Richard Smoke, *War.*

21. Gunnar Sjöstedt, "Asymmetry in Multilateral Negotiation Between North and South at UNCED."

22. Roger Kanet and Edward Kolodziej, eds., *The Cold War as Cooperation.*

23. I. William Zartman, ed., *Governance as Conflict Management.*

24. Gene Lyons and Michael Mastanduno, eds., *Beyond Westphalia;* Francis Deng et al., *Sovereignty as Responsibility;* Gareth Evans and Mohamed Sahnoun, eds., *The Responsibility to Protect.*

25. Maryann Cusimano, *Beyond Sovereignty;* Harold Saunders, *A Public Peace Process;* Wolfgang Reinicke, *Global Public Policy.*

26. Dietrich Rueschemeyer, Peter Evans, and Theda Skocpol, eds., *Bringing the State Back In.*

27. Pasquale Pasquino, "Political Theory, Order, and Threat," p. 19.

28. Michael Schatzberg, *Big Man in Africa.*

29. Samuel P. Huntington, *The Clash of Civilizations;* Guillermo O'Donnell and Philippe C. Schmitter, *Transitions from Authoritarian Rule.*

30. Jacques Barzun, "Bagehot or the Human Comedy," p. 204; Jean Orieux, *Talleyrand ou le Sphinx Incompris,* pp. 249, 295, 396.

31. Hans J. Morgenthau, *Politics Among Nations;* Stephen M. Walt, *The Origins of Alliances;* Henry Kissinger, "False Dreams of a New World Order," *Washington Post,* February 26, 1991.

32. Stephen M. Walt, *The Origins of Alliances.*

33. Oran Young, *International Cooperation;* I. William Zartman, *International Multilateral Negotiations;* Fen Osler Hampson, *Multilateral Negotiations;* Andreas Hasenclever, Peter Mayer, and Volker Rittberger, *Theories of International Regimes;* Bertram I. Spector and I. William Zartman, eds., *Getting It Done;* John Odell, *Negotiating the World Economy.*

34. William Riker, *The Theory of Political Coalitions.*

35. Alexis de Tocqueville, *De la démocratie en Amérique;* John Stuart Mill, *On Liberty.*

36. Seymour Martin Lipset, *Political Man;* Lani Guinier, *The Tyranny of the Majority.*

37. Seymour Martin Lipset, "Some Requisites of Democracy."

38. Juan Linz and Alfred Stepan, *Problems of Democratic Transition and Consolidation;* Richard Rose, William Mischler, and Christian Haerpfer, *Democracy and Its Alternatives;* Guillermo O'Donnell and Philippe Schmitter, *Transitions from Authoritarian Rule;* I. William Zartman, ed., *Tunisia.*

39. Krishna Kumar, ed., *Post-Conflict Elections, Democratization, and International Assistance,* p. 54.

40. T. S. Kuhn, *The Structure of Scientific Revolutions.*

41. Arend Lijphart, *Democracy in Plural Societies;* Donald Horowitz, *Democratic South Africa?;* Donald Horowitz, *Ethnic Groups in Conflict.*

42. L. S. Shapley, "A Value for N-Person Games"; J. F. Banzhaf, "Weighted Voting Doesn't Work"; Steven J. Brams and P. J. Affuso, "Power and Size: A New Paradox."

43. P. H. Gulliver, *Disputes and Negotiations,* p. 21.

44. Thomas Schelling, *Strategy of Conflict;* Fred Charles Ikle, *How Nations Negotiate;* Richard Walton and Robert McKersie, *A Behavioral Theory of Labor Negotiations.*

45. Fred Charles Ikle, *How Nations Negotiate.*

46. M. Smith, "The European Union and a Changing Europe"; G. Casper and M. M. Taylor, *Negotiated Democracy.*

47. Richard Walton and Robert McKersie, *A Behavioral Theory of Labor Negotiations;* Robert Axelrod, *Conflict of Interest;* Robert Axelrod, *The Evolution of Cooperation;* I. William Zartman, ed., *The Negotiation Process;* Lynn Wagner, *Problem-Solving and Bargaining in International Negotiation;* P. Terrence Hopmann, *The Negotiation Process and the Resolution of International Conflicts;* John Odell, *Negotiating the World Economy.*

48. Robert Keohane and Joseph Nye, *Power and Interdependence;* Oran Young, "Regime Dynamics"; Anselm Strauss, *Negotiations;* Guillermo O'Donnell and Philippe C. Schmitter, *Transitions from Authoritarian Rule.*

49. Krishna Kumar, *Post-Conflict Elections.*

50. Thomas Schelling, *Arms and Influence,* chap. 4; Friedrich von Hayek, *Rules and Order;* Morton Kaplan, *New Approaches to International Relations.*

51. Hans Morgenthau, *Politics Among Nations;* Kenneth Waltz, *Man, the State, and War.*

52. Kenneth N. Waltz, *Theory of International Politics,* pp. 88–93; Mancur Olson, *The Logic of Collective Action;* Robert Bates, *Toward a Political Economy of Development.*

53. Donald Green and Ian Shapiro, *The Pathologies of Rational Choice.*

54. Regarding negotiation theory, see the well-known story about the blind wise men who were asked to describe the elephant. Each returned with a simile based on the part of the animal he grabbed (an elephant is a rope, said the tail-grabber; an elephant is a tree, said the leg-holder; an elephant is a hose, said the trunk man; etc), whereupon the king (who could see) said that the elephant is all these things.

55. David Easton, *A Systems Analysis of Political Life.*

56. David E. Apter, *Choice and the Politics of Allocation,* pp. 19–21.

57. Charles Doran, *Systems in Crisis;* Torbjørn Knutsen, *A History of International Relations Theory;* Robert Gilpin, *War and Change in World Politics.*

58. Samuel P. Huntington, *The Third Wave;* Robert Dahl, *Polyarchy;* Guillermo O'Donnell and Philippe C. Schmitter, *Transitions from Authoritarian Rule;* G. Casper and M. M. Taylor, *Negotiated Democracy;* I. William Zartman, ed., *Collapsed States.*

59. Shmuel N. Eisenstadt, *Modernization;* Samuel P. Huntington, *Political Order in Changing Societies;* I. William Zartman, *Collapsed States.*

60. John J. Mearsheimer, "Back to the Future: Instability in Europe After the Cold War"; Daniel Deudney and John Ikenberry, "Soviet Reform and the End of the Cold War"; Alexander Dallin, "Causes of Collapse of the USSR"; John Lewis Gaddis, "International Relations Theory and the End of the Cold War"; Friederich Kratochwil, "The Embarrassment of Changes"; Richard Ned Lebow, "The Long

Peace, the End of the Cold War, and the Failure of Realism"; Edward Kolodziej, "The Pursuit of Order, Welfare and Legitimacy."

61. Paul Pillar, *Negotiating Peace;* I. William Zartman, *Elusive Peace;* Jacob Bercovitch, I. William Zartman, and Victor Kremenyuk, eds., *Handbook of Conflict Resolution.*

62. Adam Przeworski, *States and Markets;* I. William Zartman, ed., *Governance as Conflict Management.*

63. Hedley Bull, *The Anarchical Society.*

64. John Rawls, *A Theory of Justice;* Brian Barry, *Theories of Justice;* John Elster, *Local Justice.* See also I. William Zartman et al., "Negotiation as a Search for Justice."

65. Ahmad Moussalli, ed., *Islamic Fundamentalism.*

66. Regarding the right to rule, see Harold Lasswell and Abraham Kaplan, *Power and Society,* p. 133; regarding legitimacy, see D. Beetham, *The Legitimation of Power.*

67. Ronald Rogowski, *Rational Legitimacy.*

68. C. von Haldenwang, "The State and Political Regulation."

69. Max Weber, "Politics as a Vocation," p. 91.

70. Augustus Richard Norton, ed., *Civil Society in the Middle East;* regarding "lame or privatized government," see Thomas Callaghy, *The State-Society Struggle.*

71. James Rosenau and E. O. Czempiel, eds., *Governance Without Government.*

72. Stephen Krasner, *International Regimes;* Andreas Hasenclever, Peter Mayer, and Volker Rittberger, *Theories of International Regimes;* Bertram Spector and I. William Zartman, *Getting It Done.*

73. This is the other side of the same coin as discussed by Amartya Sen and not in contradiction with his position; Sen, *Development as Freedom,* chap 10, esp. pp. 244–248. I am grateful to Guy Olivier Faure of the Sorbonne for useful suggestions in this area.

74. June T. Dreyer, *China's Political System;* Lucian Pye, *The Mandarin and the Cadre;* Kenneth Lieberthal, *Governing China;* Alastair Iain Johnston, "Cultural Realism and Strategy in Maoist China"; Kenneth Pomeranz, *The Great Divergence.*

75. Guy Olivier Faure, "Negotiating Joint Ventures in China"; Lucien Pye, *Chinese Negotiating Style.*

76. E. L. Jones, *The European Miracle;* Kenneth Pomeranz, *The Great Divergence.*

77. Richard L. Walker, *The Multi-State System of Ancient China.*

78. Alexis de Tocqueville, *De la démocratie en Amérique.*

79. Samuel P. Huntington, *The Clash of Civilizations.*

80. Harold Sprout and Margaret Sprout, *Environmental Possibilism.*

81. Walter Lippman, *US Foreign Policy.*

Part 1

US Hegemony

2

The United States: Alone in the World

Kenneth N. Waltz

In this chapter I concentrate on how international political conditions and changes in them shape national behavior and affect international outcomes. I take the United States as a case in point. A nation's foreign policy impulses are shaped by its external experiences. The impulse to isolation and its counterpart, the inclination to act unilaterally, are normal ones for any state. Except when it needs help or protection, a state prefers that it not be entangled with others, for to be entangled means to be influenced, limited, compromised, and occasionally duped. Early American statesmen—notably Alexander Hamilton and John Jay—keenly appreciated the advantages of isolation and the possibility of realizing those advantages.[1]

In the colonial period, every time European countries went to war, America was drawn into an imperial war in the new world, usually with little profit. If America became united as an independent country while Europe remained divided, the former would be able to insulate itself from the latter's quarrels. Because European states would have to continue to watch each other warily, no state would be able to turn westward and direct all its military force against the United States. Under those circumstances, the United States was able to follow a quite consistent policy of isolation for more than a hundred years, from the early nineteenth century onward. In its origin, isolationist policy was situationally based and situationally explained. A century's happy experience turned an appreciation of US good fortune into a feeling of moral superiority. In coming to believe that the United States remained aloof from the power-political games of the old world because it was enlightened and uplifted, the policy of isolation became an ideology.

The principal elements of the ideology, and the ways in which it was formed during a century of isolation, can be stated in summary form. Though all men are born equal, some men are rich and others are poor. This apparent contradiction is eliminated by defining equality, as liberals of the eighteenth and nineteenth century did, in purely legal terms. Americans generally accepted the definition. Those unequal in material goods or in capabilities remain intrinsically equal. Absence of established rank in a land of golden opportunity gave meaning to the definition domestically. It was applied internationally as well. Because US foreign policy experiences generally involved dependent states, an egalitarian international ideology easily developed. When small and weak states deal with large and strong ones, the former are conscious of the power in the relation, and the latter are not. With power left out of the equation, national and international experiences combined to establish the US conviction that foreign policy is an extension of, and that international relations are dependent upon, what states are like internally. All causes are seen as clustering at the level of the state, and the international political system becomes a dependent variable. Only through this view could national self-determination be seen as a fundamental principle of foreign policy and as the necessary basis of a proper world order.

So deeply rooted is the US ideology that it informs policies that at the surface are sharply opposed. Beneath the contrary foreign policies of Woodrow Wilson and Herbert Hoover, to take the most striking example, lay a common conviction. Both Wilson and Hoover looked at the world and saw evil rife in it. Hoover concluded that we must isolate ourselves in order to develop the unique virtues of the new world free of contamination from the old one. Wilson concluded that we must act to change the world. As he put it, "No injustice furnishes a basis for permanent peace. If you leave a rankling sense of injustice anywhere, it will not only produce a running sore presently which will result in trouble and probably war, but it ought to produce war somewhere."[2] Through their contrary policies, both Wilson and Hoover renounced old-fashioned, European-style diplomacy and power politics They agreed that the United States could not live in the world as it was.

Neither World War I nor World War II did much to change the basic US view of the world. In both those wars, US enemies could be personified in the characters of their rulers, of Kaiser Wilhelm II, Adolf Hitler, Benito Mussolini, and Hideki Tojo. To our good fortune, moreover, the czar abdicated in March 1917, just in time to permit us to declare war in April of that year without thereby joining a coalition having czarist Russia as one of its principal members. In World War II, we tried to turn Stalin into "Uncle Joe," an aspiring democrat whose application of the admirable provisions of the constitution adopted in 1936 was delayed by difficult conditions at home and abroad. In both wars, we could think of ourselves as fighting authoritarian or totalitarian states in the name of justice and democracy. Whether we were also fighting for reasons of security, whether there was an element of power politics in our policy, was a question that the lineup of forces permitted us to avoid.

How are the habits and assumptions of US foreign policy reflected in policies after 1945? At the conclusion of World War II, the US impulse was to bring the troops home and disband the military, as it had done following victory in the first one. It did so with breathtaking speed and then found that the choice was not a free one. The United States was not able to behave in a world of two great powers as it had behaved in a world of many great powers. Either it led the way in opposing the Soviet Union, or nobody did. The culture of US foreign policy did not suddenly change. Change in foreign policy behavior was produced instead by the abrupt shift of the structure of the international political system from multipolarity to bipolarity. The extent of the change is illustrated by the unprecedented policies the United States adopted: aid to Greece and Turkey, the Truman doctrine, the European Recovery Program, the Atlantic Defense Treaty, the formation of the North Atlantic Treaty Organization (NATO), intervention in the Korean War, and the subsequent dispatch of two divisions to Europe—all of which occurred in a mere six years between 1945 and 1951.

Dwight D. Eisenhower remarked that if, after the reconstruction of Western Europe, the United States continued to keep troops in Europe, then US policy would have failed. NATO was intended to protect Western Europe only until it got back on its feet. Eisenhower, when president, was willing to consider nuclear weapons for Europe in order to make it militarily self-sufficient and restore the United States to normalcy.[3] Old national impulses lingered, but international conditions worked against them. External necessity prevailed over internal preference.

Great victories produce euphoria in the countries that win them. This happened after the first two great victories of the twentieth century and especially after the third one—the US victory in the Cold War. As the ancient Chinese seer, Sun Tzu, said, the most impressive victories are those won without fighting. The prior preparation and the disposition of forces are so impressive that the adversary succumbs without fighting.[4] Sun Tzu aptly described the way the Cold War ended.

Many people, liberals and constructivists especially, thought that with democracy extending its sway, with interdependence tightening its grip, with international organizations smoothing the way to peace, with leaders and people learning that war does not pay, international politics would be transformed. We all know now that international politics has not been transformed. The world remains anarchic; states still have to take care of themselves as best they can. But the world has significantly changed. The change was not produced by the forces and factors mentioned. Instead, the new order of the world was made by one event: the weakening and subsequent disappearance of the Soviet Union. The political reform of the Soviet Union was not accomplished by aspiring democrats but by old-line communist apparatchiks. Nor did interdependence have anything to do with it. The Soviet Union was never part of an economically interdependent world. International institutions are not independent actors but are subject to the wills, and dependent on the resources, of their stronger members. They hardly did anything to bring the Soviet Union down. And far from a newly enlightened leadership renouncing power politics, Gorbachev expressed the wish to see the Soviet Union "enter the new millennium as a great and flourishing state."[5]

Think of what could not have happened had the number of great powers not been reduced to one. With a strong Soviet Union in the background, the United States could not have launched a headlong invasion of Iraq in 1991 for fear that the Soviet Union would act to protect its client state. But then there would have been no war in Iraq because a strong Soviet Union would not have permitted Iraq to annex Kuwait. Germany could not have been reunited. NATO could not have been extended eastward. Yugoslavia would not have broken apart. Even terrorist activity would have been muted. Before the decline and fall of the Soviet Union, weak states and disaffected people could hope to play one superpower against the other. Now the weak and disaffected are on their own. Unsurprisingly, they lash out at the one remaining great power as the symbol and the agent of their suffering. One can easily add to the list of international outcomes caused or made possible by the change in international political structure.

Never since Rome has one country dominated its world as the United States does now. Moreover, militarily it seeks to make the gap between itself and any potential competitors so wide that no one will even try to catch up. In 2000, the United States outspent the next eight big spenders on defense; the 2003 military budget exceeded the spending of the next twenty-five countries, and now militarily the United States handily outspends the rest of the world combined.[6]

What are other countries to think? When Caspar Weinberger was President Ronald Reagan's secretary of defense, and we were as usual overestimating the Soviet Union's defense expenditures, a journalist asked him why the Soviets were spending all that money on their military. He replied, "World domination, it's that simple."[7] The United States is acting now as we wrongly thought the Soviet Union was then. When other countries look at the United States, they see a country without a military challenger in sight spending far more on its military than it did at the height of the Cold War. They see a country that specializes in singling out weak countries it does not like and beating them up, a country that fights wars of choice rather than wars of necessity. In two decades, the United States invaded Lebanon, Grenada, Panama, Iraq, Afghanistan, and Iraq again. President Reagan implied that we got into Grenada just in the nick of time to save the

US medical students held hostage. He was right about the nick of time. Grenada would soon have freed the students, and Reagan would have lost the casus belli needed to redeem him after his costly Lebanese fiasco. Frederick F. Woerner, the general who would have commanded the invasion of Panama, accepted early retirement rather than lead troops into an unnecessary war.[8] The administration of George H. W. Bush called the war "Operation Just Cause" even though it flagrantly violated international law, including the charter of the Organization of American States, of which the United States was a principal sponsor. The first Iraq war had some justification, as did the war in Afghanistan. The reasons for the second Iraq war, as many surmised in advance and we all now know, were illusory.

Before invading Iraq, George W. Bush claimed the right to launch preemptive attacks against countries that it felt intended to do something nasty to somebody.[9] Let us hope that other countries do not follow the example.

This behavior makes one wonder whether recent policies are aberrational, that is, unrepresentative of usual behavior and explicable mainly by the cast of characters currently in power, or whether they are in the historical mainstream. We can answer the question by looking at the behavior of the United States where it has long been dominant: namely, in the Western Hemisphere. For over a century, the United States has intervened in Central and South America where and when it chose. Its behavior can hardly be described as modest and forbearing.

Emphasizing the effect of international conditions on states' behavior leaves open the question of how much difference is made by the internal disposition of states and how much by the structure of international politics. Obviously, states matter and international conditions matter, but which matters more? The answer varies with conditions. Some states kick harder against structural constraints than others do. Some international structures constrict actors more tightly than others do. Anyone who had not noticed this could hardly fail to see it as the world moved from bipolarity to unipolarity. In a bipolar world, two states check and balance each other. In a unipolar world, checks on the behavior of the one great power drop drastically. Unipolarity weakens structural constraints, enlarges the field of action of the remaining great power, and heightens the importance of its internal qualities. An international system in balance is like a political system of checks and balances. The impulses of a state to behave in arbitrary and high-handed fashion are constrained by the presence of states of comparable capability. An international system in which another state or combination of states is unable to balance the might of the most powerful is like a political system without checks and balances. With depressing predictability when rulers establish their dominance, the result is arbitrary and destructive governance that works for the benefit of the governors rather than the governed.

Ideally, a benevolent despot is able to fashion the wise policies that the compromises of democracy impede. Similarly, imperial countries, superior to those they rule, may claim to aim at uplifting the natives but seldom produce that result. Disparity of power spawns despotic rule at home and abroad.

We know what to expect at home when checks and balances weaken, and we should know what to expect abroad. François Fénelon, who lived from 1651 to 1715, was a French theologian and political adviser and one of the first to understand balance of power as a general phenomenon rather than merely as a particular condition. He argued that a country disposing of greater power than others do cannot long be expected to behave with decency and moderation.[10] His theorem is well illustrated by such powerful rulers as Charles V, Louis XIV, Napoleon, and Kaiser Wilhelm II. There was not necessarily something wrong with the character of those rulers or of their countries. At a minimum, it was a surplus of power that tempted them to arbitrary and arrogant behavior.

Given the perils of unbalanced power, why has a new balance of power been slow to form? Formation of a new balance is slowed or hastened by two main forces. Mild and moderate behavior by the state at the top will slow it; arbitrary and arrogant behavior will hasten it. Under the present circumstances balancing should proceed apace, but there are difficulties. First, the materials for balancing are not ready to hand. In the old days, victory in major war always left enough great powers standing to make a new balance of power through realignment among them. In bipolar and unipolar worlds, realignments are impossible. In a unipolar world the making of a new balance depends on one or more major powers lifting themselves to great power status. The wider the gap in capabilities between the one great power and the others, the longer it will take to close it. The gap is now immense.

Particular conditions also work decisively against balancing in the short run. Despite its plentiful resources, Europe does not constitute a political unit able to act in the arena of foreign and military policy. The ghastly experiences of Germany and Japan in the first half of the twentieth century make them reluctant to step forth. China, though growing rapidly, still has a long way to go. Moreover, the one great power left is better able than any other country to dispense favors and to impose pain. Under the circumstances, some countries try to curry favor, while others offer limited resistance.

Signs of balancing have nevertheless appeared. The first stage of balancing occurs when weaker states begin to edge away from the stronger ones, criticize them roundly, and fail to assist in their endeavors. To its apparent surprise, the United States is now going through what is in fact a normal process.

Conclusion

The conclusion is in two parts. In the first part, I ask why in recent years the United States has deemphasized deterrence and containment in favor of preemption and fighting wars. In the second part, I answer this question.

Why Drop Deterrence and Containment?

With the Soviet Union gone, the United States no longer faces a threat to its security. As General Colin Powell said when he was chairman of the Joint Chiefs of Staff: "I'm running out of demons. I'm running out of enemies. I'm down to Castro and Kim Il Sung."[11] To Cuba and North Korea, the present administration added a couple of others—Iraq, Iran, and perhaps Syria—all of them poor, weak countries. President Bush and his lieutenants say again and again that containment and deterrence no longer work. Their assertion is a strange one. Through the long years of the Cold War, the United States was able to contain and deter strong adversaries—the Soviet Union, which had thousands of nuclear warheads, and China, later, with hundreds. The United States clearly can contain and deter strong states, but supposedly not weak ones.

Why not? Consider deterrence first. Les Aspin, when he was chairman of the house Armed Services Committee and shortly before he became President Bill Clinton's first secretary of defense, claimed that rogue states are hard to deter and may well be undeterrable. Yet the rulers of rogue states share one striking characteristic: They are survivors. Kim Il Sung had to be carried out in a box. Muammar Qaddafi has long been with us. They survive under difficult conditions at home and abroad. They are troublesome and nasty. Yet they have a keen ability to find the line that, crossed, would bring their regimes to an end. They stop short of calling down upon themselves the wrath of the mighty. Even Saddam Hussein, the worst calculator of the lot, lasted for a quarter of a century. Rulers of rogue states may seem irrational or simply crazy, but if they were undeterrable, they would have awfully short careers. One marvels at the peculiar notions our governors entertain.

Now, however, we have to worry about terrorists. Rulers of states have everything to lose. Terrorists have nothing to lose and are of unknown location. As we have always known, they cannot be deterred. Yet the world has managed to live with them. Now, however, we are told that "the world has changed, developments in technology have given small groups of people the kind of destructive power once only available to national governments."[12] True, terrorists can steal instruments of destruction or acquire them in other ways, but they cannot arm themselves on a scale that even minor states achieve. Whether we think of the Tamil Tigers, Hamas, or Al-Qaida, terror is the weapon of the weak. Terrorists cannot destroy the social fabric of strong states or threaten their national security.

The thought that terrorists may get weapons of mass destruction is a frightening one. The fear is that a country getting or making such weapons may turn some of them over to terrorists. For two reasons states, including rogue states, are unlikely to do this. A country working long and hard to develop deliverable chemical or biological weapons will not lightly give them to others. Certainly, this is true of the most effective and destructive weapons, nuclear warheads. A country providing weapons of mass destruction to terrorists knows it may be discovered—or blamed, even if not discovered—should the weapons be used. The United States would then have a reason—or an excuse—to retaliate. After all, the United States attacks countries for lesser reasons. States possessing weapons of mass destruction have to be careful lest they bring about their own destruction.

Despite contrary claims, deterrence continues to work when applied to the rulers of countries. It also reduces the chances of terrorists gaining weapons of mass destruction. Deterrence reduces one's worries without eliminating them.

What about containment? When President George W. Bush remarked that "containment no longer works as far as I'm concerned," he was right in one sense. Containment of the United States clearly does not work for any state possessing only conventional weapons. The United States can be contained only by states having a second-strike nuclear force, a condition that whets countries' appetite to have one.

Containment of the strong may be difficult, but the United States managed it for decades. Containment of the weak is easy. Consider supposedly undeterrable, uncontainable Iraq. Aside from US power, Iraq had nowhere to go. With military forces in the early 2000s less than half as strong as they were ten years earlier, Iraq faced Iran to the east with three times the population and five times the gross domestic product (GDP). To the north it faced Turkey with three times the population and ten times the GDP. And to the west lay Israel, the strongest military power in the Middle East. Iraq was deterred and contained. It was bottled up. Yet President Bush persisted in saying that "Saddam Hussein was a danger to the world."[13]

Weak states operate within narrow margins. Inopportune acts, flawed policies, and mistimed moves may have fatal results. In contrast, strong states can be inattentive; they can afford not to learn; they can do the same dumb things over and over again. More sensibly, they can react slowly and wait to see whether the apparently threatening acts of others are truly so. They can be indifferent to most threats because only a few, if carried through, can damage them gravely. They can hold back until the ambiguity of events is resolved without fearing that the moment for effective action will be lost. The Bush administration nevertheless claimed that it had to strike Iraq before it could put (nonexistent) weapons of mass destruction to dastardly use. Deterrence and containment served much better in the old days than preemption does now.

The Behavior of Powerful States

The US government lives on myths of its own making. With no opponents of worthy stature, it continues to arm and fight and extend its influence and control. It populates the world with its bases and maintains more than 200,000 troops abroad even when not fighting.

"One reads about the world's desire for American leadership only in the United States," a British diplomat remarked. "Everywhere else one reads about American arrogance and unilateralism."[14] Why, given the favored position the United States holds in the world, is it so rambunctious? The simple and persuasive explanation is a negative one: the absence of external impediments. One may easily believe that the Soviet Union would have extended its sway beyond Eastern Europe in the absence of effective opposition. One may also easily believe that the United States, which moved into most parts of the world not dominated by the Soviet Union, would have extended its political grip even farther afield if the Soviet Union had not been in the way. As soon as it no longer was, the United States expanded smartly. Americans apparently believe in only the first part of the old cry, "resolute in war; magnanimous in victory." The United States persists in extending NATO eastward into what was once the Soviet's sphere, indeed into what was once its sovereign space. The forward thrust of NATO was the doing of the United States; Europeans showed little enthusiasm. And once the action began in Afghanistan, the United States quickly moved its military bases into the countries that were once the Soviet Union's southern Asian republics, thus nearly completing the encirclement of both Russia and China. President Bush proposed placing missile defenses in Poland and the Czech Republic while adding Ukraine and Georgia to the long roster of NATO nations. France, Germany, and some other NATO members voiced their opposition, but President Bush inexplicably insisted that Ukraine's membership "is in the interest of every member in the alliance and will help advance security and freedom in this region and around the world."[15] The expansion of the United States seems extraordinary until one recalls the similar behavior on a lesser scale of powerful countries throughout history. Fénelon's implied prediction proves to be right again.

We need not ask what the new world order, highly touted by the first President Bush, will be like. We live in it. When the Soviet Union collapsed, the United States became both the principal manager of conflicts in the world and the principal creator of them. No state or combination of states can provide a counterweight to the United States. The United States is truly alone in the world.

Notes

1. About a quarter of the *Federalist Papers* are concerned with foreign affairs in important ways.
2. Reprinted in Joseph Tumulty, *Woodrow Wilson as I Knew Him,* p. 274.
3. Marc Trachtenberg, *A Constructed Peace.*
4. Sun Tzu, *The Art of War,* pp. 77, 79.
5. "Succession in Moscow: First Hours in Power, Gorbachev in His Own Words," *New York Times,* March 12, 1985, p. A16.
6. Editorial, *New York Times,* February 10, 2003, p. A22.
7. Andrew Rosenthal, "Pentagon Report Softens Soviet Menace," *New York Times,* September 28, 1989, p. A6.
8. Discussion with General Woerner; Richard Halloran, "US Military Chief Is Replaced in the Central American Region," *New York Times,* July 21, 1989, p. A5.
9. A preemptive strike is made because another country is about to strike you. A preventive war is fought because an adversary is becoming strong enough to threaten you sometime in the future. "Prevention" was what Bush meant, but "pre-emptive" is the more politic term.
10. Quoted by Herbert Butterfield, "The Balance of Power," p. 140.
11. "Cover Story: Communism's Collapse Poses a Challenge to America's Military," *US News and World Report* 3, no. 16 (October 14, 1991): 28.
12. Alexander Stille, "What Is America's Place in the World Now?" *New York Times,* January 12, 2002, p. B7.
13. David E. Sanger and James Risen, "President Says Report on Arms Vindicates War," *New York Times,* October 4, 2003, p. A1.
14. Quoted in Samuel P. Huntington, "The Lonely Superpower," p. 42.
15. Quoted in Steven Lee Myers, "Bush Backs Ukraine's Bid to Join NATO, Despite Putin's Objections," *New York Times,* April 2, 2008, p. A6.

3

An Empire, But We Can't Keep It

Robert Jervis

People are prone to believe that they live in a unique era, often one that is a turning point. But I think that our era really is unique and that we are living through a transition. More specifically, there are four new elements—each significant in itself—that, as they interact, will create a new world. These are the security community among the most developed countries, the war on terrorism, the war with Iraq, and the general US stance that can be summarized as the Bush Doctrine. The latter, partly a product of the first three, has set the United States on an ambitious course to reshape the world. Both the need to protect itself against new dangers and the perceived opportunity to bring democracy and peace to unruly parts of the globe are leading to the pursuit of unprecedented hegemony, but one that cannot be sustained. With significant setbacks if not failures and the election of a new president, the policy will change. Retraction is always a difficult operation, however. It is far from clear whether a coherent new strategy will be developed to replace it, and the rest of the world will not forget that the United States is capable of moving in unexpected and undesirable directions.

The Four Elements of a New World Order

The Security Community

Throughout history, war and the possibility of war among the great powers has been the motor of international politics, not only strongly influencing the boundaries and distribution of values among them but deeply affecting their internal arrangements and shaping the fates of smaller states. Being seen as an ever-present possibility produced by deeply rooted factors such as human nature and the lack of world government, this force was expected to continue indefinitely. But I would argue that war among the leading great powers—the United States, the states of Western Europe, and Japan—will not occur in the future, and indeed is no longer a source of concern for them.[1] The absence of war among these states would itself be a development of enormous proportions, but the change goes even further because war is not even contemplated. During the Cold War, peace was maintained, but it was due to the fear that if the superpowers did not take care, they would indeed fight.

Now, however, the leading states form what Karl Deutsch called a pluralistic security community, a group among whom war is literally unthinkable (i.e., neither the publics nor the political elites nor even the military establishments expect war with each other).[2] No official in the security community would advocate a policy on the grounds that it would improve the state's position in the event of war with other members. Although no state can move away from the reliance on war by itself lest it become a victim, the collectivity can do so if each forsakes the resort to force.

Security communities are not unprecedented. But what is unprecedented is that the states that constitute this one are the leading members of the international system and so are natural rivals who in the past were central to the violent struggle for security, power, and contested values. Winston Churchill exaggerated only slightly when he declared that "people talked a lot of nonsense when they said nothing was ever settled by war. Nothing in history was ever settled except by wars."[3] Even cases of major change without war, such as Britain yielding hegemony in the Western Hemisphere to the United States at the turn of the twentieth century, were strongly influenced by security calculations. Threatening war, preparing for it, and trying to avoid it have permeated all aspects of politics, and so a world in which war among the most developed states is unthinkable will be a new one. To paraphrase and extend a claim made by Evan Luard, given the scale and frequency of war among the great powers in the preceding millennium, it is a change of spectacular proportions, perhaps the single most striking discontinuity that the history of international politics has anywhere provided.[4]

Two other major states, Russia and China, might fight each other or a member of the security community. But these countries lack many of the attributes of great powers: their internal regimes are shaky, they are not at the forefront of any advanced forms of technology or economic organization, they can pose challenges only regionally, and they have no attraction as models for others. They are not among the most developed states, and I think it would be fair to put them outside the ranks of the great powers as well. But their military potential, their possession of nuclear weapons, and the size of their economies renders that judgment easily debatable, and so I will not press it. Rather I argue that the set of states that form the security community are not all the great powers, but all the most developed ones.

International politics within the security community. In previous eras, no aspect of international politics and few aspects of domestic politics were untouched by the anticipation of future wars among the leading powers. As Charles Tilly put it: "Over the millennium as a whole, war has been the dominant activity of European states." Much will then change in the security community.[5] In the absence of these states amalgamating—a development that is out of the question outside Europe and unlikely within it—they will neither consider using force against one another nor lose their sovereignty. There will then be significant conflicts of interest without clear means of resolving them. The states will continue to be rivals in some respects and to bargain with each other. Indeed, the shared expectation that disputes will remain peaceful will remove some restraints on vituperation and competitive tactics. The dense network of institutions within the security community should serve to provide multiple means for controlling conflicts but will also provide multiple ways for a dissatisfied country to show its displeasure and threaten disruption.

The fact that the situation is a new one poses challenges and opportunities for the leading powers. What goals will have highest priority? Will non-military alliances form? How important will status be, and what will give it? Bargaining will continue, which means that varieties of power, including the ability to help and hurt others, will still be relevant. Threats, bluffs, warnings, the mobilization of resources for future conflicts, intense diplomatic negotiations, and shifting patterns of working with and against others all will remain. But the content of these forms will differ from those of traditional international politics.

Politics within the security community may come to resemble the relations between the United States and Canada and Australia that Robert O. Keohane and Joseph Nye described as complex interdependence: extensive transnational and transgovernmental relations, negotiations conducted across different issue areas, and bargaining power gained through asymmetric dependence but limited by overall common interests.[6] Despite this pathbreaking study, however, we know little about how this kind of politics will be carried out. As numerous commentators have noted, economic issues and economic resources will play large roles, but the changed context will matter. Relative economic advantage was sought in the past in part because it contributed to military security. This no longer being the case, the possibilities for cooperation are increased. States will still seek economic benefits for themselves, but will care about whether others are gaining more than they are only if they believe that it can produce political leverage or future economic benefits. The range of cases in which the latter is true is now thought to be fairly small, however.[7]

Even though force will not be threatened within the security community, it will remain important in relations among its members. During the Cold War the protection the United States afforded to its allies gave it an added moral claim and significant bargaining leverage. Despite the decreased level of threat, this will be true for the indefinite future because, militarily, Japan and Europe need the United States more than the United States needs them. Although the unique US ability to lead military operations like those in the Persian Gulf and Kosovo causes resentments and frictions, it also gives it a resource that is potent even—or especially—if it is never explicitly brought to the table.[8]

Four possible futures. Even within the contours of a security community, a significant range of patterns of relations are possible, four of which can be briefly sketched.

The greatest change would be a world in which national autonomy would be further diminished and the distinctions between domestic and foreign policy would continue to erode. Medieval Europe, with its overlapping forms of sovereignty rather than compartmentalized nation-states, which might dissolve because they are no longer needed to provided security and can no longer control their economies, is one model here. Although most scholars see the reduction of sovereignty and the growth of the power of nongovernmental organizations as conducive to peace and harmony, one can readily imagine sharp conflicts between those with different views of the good life (for example, business interests, labor, and environmentalists) or between those calling for greater centralization to solve common problems and those advocating increased local control. But state power and interest would in any case greatly decrease, and the notion of "national interest," always contested, would become even more problematic.

A second world, not completely incompatible with the first, would be one in which states in the security community play a large role, but with more extensive and intensive cooperation, presumably produced and accompanied by the internalization of the interests of others and stronger institutions. Relations would be increasingly governed by principles, laws, and persuasion rather than by more direct forms of power, a change that could benignly spill over into relations outside the security community. Although bargaining would not disappear, there would be more joint efforts to solve common problems, and the line between "high" and "low" politics would become even more blurred.

In this world, the United States would share more power and responsibility with the rest of the security community than is true today. Although the second option is popular with scholars, at least as likely is a continuation of the present trajectory in which the United States maintains hegemony and rejects significant limitations on its freedom of action. National interests would remain distinct, and the United States would follow the familiar pattern discussed below, in which ambitions and perceived interests expand as power does. Consistent with the ongoing concern with competitive advantages, both conflicts of interests and the belief that hegemony best produces collective goods would lead the United States to oppose the efforts of others to become a counterweight, if not a rival to it. Other members of the security community would resent having their interests overridden by the United States on some occasions, but the exploitation would be limited by their bargaining power and the US realization that excessive discontent would have serious long-term consequences. So others might accept these costs in return for US security guarantees and the ability to keep their own defense spending very low, especially because the alternative to US-dominated stability might be worse.

The fourth model also starts with a US attempt to maintain hegemony, but this time the burdens of US unilateralism become sufficient to produce a counter-balancing coalition, one that might include Russia and China as well. Europe and Japan might also become more assertive because they fear not US domination but the eventual withdrawal of the US security guarantee. In this world, much that realism stresses—the clash of national interests, the weakness of international institutions, maneuvering for advantage, and the use of power and threats—would come to the fore, but with the vital difference that force would not be contemplated and the military balance would enter in only indirectly. It would be a strange mixture of the new and the familiar, and the central question is what ultima ratio will replace cannons. What will be the final arbiter of disputes? What kinds of threats will be most potent? How fungible will the relevant forms of power be?

Outlining these possibilities raises two broad questions that I cannot answer. First, is the future essentially determined, as many structural theories would imply, or does it depend on national choices strongly influenced by domestic politics, leaders, and accidents? Second, if the future is not determined, how much depends on choices the United States has yet to make, and what will most influence these choices?

The development of the security community and these possibilities predate the dramatic changes in the world since 2001. The latter are the subject of the rest of this chapter, but even though they have overshadowed the importance of the security community in the mind of many people, we should not lose sight of the fact that, in the broader perspective, peace among the leading powers is a more far-reaching change in international politics than is terrorism, the war with Iraq, and Bush's dramatic new foreign policy. In fact, the US policies would not have been possible had it faced the danger of war with a peer state.

The War on Terrorism

The second new element defining our era is the war on terrorism. It is often said that "everything has changed after September 11," "this is the end of the post–Cold War era," and "the world will never be the same." Many foreign policy pronouncements from US leaders start by declaring that "Almost any discussion of American foreign policy today must begin with the events of September 11th."[9] Nevertheless, we should be skeptical about some claims that have been made about how the terrorist attacks have reshaped the world, in part because the extravagant claims seem to emanate only from Americans.

Perhaps terrorism is such a scourge that the nations of the world will unite against it, just as most countries pull together internally if they are attacked. The Bush administration argued that this is what should happen, seeing the conflict as one of civilization against evil that must trump all differences. In the past, nations put aside old conflicts when faced by an even more pressing common enemy, as Britain and the Union of Soviet Socialist Republics (USSR) finally did in their struggle against Nazi Germany. But most countries do not see terrorism as posing a threat of this magnitude, although a serious biological or nuclear attack might change their view. Even if few countries support Al-Qaida, many use forms of terror to advance their own goals. If the struggle were against terrorism rather than anti-American terrorism, countries like Syria, Iran, and even Pakistan would have to forgo many of their most valued objectives. And if the enemy is anti-American terror, there is even less reason for countries to unite against it, although the United States does have powerful incentives to deploy.

I do not deny that 9/11 has altered many countries' positions. The changes in Russian foreign policy and Russia-US relations since September 11 have been dramatic but also inconsistent. Russia initially embraced a high degree of cooperation with the United States, largely on US terms. It not only endorsed the US response in Afghanistan but facilitated it by not opposing a US military presence in Central Asia, an area previously seen as a Russian sphere of influence. Even more startlingly, Putin accepted the US renunciation of the antiballistic missile (ABM) treaty and an arms reduction agreement that closely followed US preferences. In return for a greater role in the North Atlantic Treaty Organization (NATO), Putin dropped his opposition to further eastward expansion of that organization. What he needed was US support for his regime, full acceptance into the ranks of Western countries, and help in rebuilding the Russian economy. For these goals, US support was necessary. This stance was not permanent, however. The combination of US support for the "color revolutions" around Russia's borders, the floundering in Iraq, and the revival of the Soviet economy (built to a large extent on higher oil prices), led to a reassertion of Russia's role as a great power and opposition to US hegemony. Although cooperation in targeted operations against terrorism is still likely, it is clear that common interests on this issue will not produce harmony between the two countries.

Relations between the United States and the People's Republic of

China (PRC) also have changed. Before September 11, the Bush administration said that China was the greatest menace to world peace. This discussion has ceased, and for its part the PRC has been quick to point out that it staunchly opposes terrorism throughout the world, especially in the Muslim province of Xinjiang. But I doubt that this common interest will prove sufficient to override the conflict over Taiwan and other issues.

The most important change has been in US foreign policy, which Bush took on a different course from what it was under Bill Clinton and from the direction that he had established before September 11. Although Clinton's foreign policy was far from consistent, it displayed a serious commitment to multilateralism, meaningful consultation with allies, concern with preventing humanitarian disasters, and support for peacekeeping operations. Bush took a different stance in his campaign and his first year in office. He and his colleagues argued that the United States often had to act on its own, that military force should be used only to protect vital interests, and that the burden of humanitarian interventions should be left to others. The Defense Department and its ideological allies were pushing to withdraw US peacekeepers from Bosnia, Kosovo, and Sinai, and no one in the government thought the United States should engage in nation building.

Policy after September 11 continued and extended some of these elements but altered many others. The resulting Bush Doctrine is the subject of the final section of this chapter, but here I just want to note that Bush's claim that the terrorist attacks changed everything may constitute something of a self-fulfilling prophecy.

The War with Iraq: Fear and Vulnerability

The third element in the emerging security environment is the US war with Iraq. It provides both a bridge to and a disconnect between the war on terror and the more general Bush Doctrine. As I will discuss at the end of this chapter, it was also partly responsible for the doctrine's demise. Although the Bush administration provided shifting rationales for the war and the emphasis changed after the search for weapons of mass destruction (WMD) proved futile, most justifications pivoted on efforts to combat terrorism. The US government argued that overthrowing Saddam Hussein's regime would send a powerful message to the world in general and the Middle East in particular that seeking WMD and disturbing world order would not be tolerated, and the government also claimed that the war would make other regimes less likely to support terrorism. According to the administration, there were links between Saddam Hussein and Al-Qaida, and even if they were not solid, only overthrowing the regime could guarantee that they would not develop. Tyrants and terrorists have a natural affinity in hating the United States and rejecting the rule of law. As Bush said before the war, "Saddam Hussein is harboring terrorists and the instruments of terror, the instruments of mass death and destruction."[10] To critics, the links between tyrants and terrorism stem largely from *Sesame Street* thinking—they both begin with the letter "T." Both are indeed antithetical to Western values of democracy and individualism, but they do not go together.[11] In this view the war against Iraq was a distraction from the war on terror. Even more importantly, the war is a marvelous recruiting device, fueling anti-American fervor and generating innumerable new terrorists.

But even if those criticisms are correct, the overthrow of Saddam Hussein is a link between the war on terrorism and the broader changes in US foreign policy (see the next section of this chapter). As Bush put it in his introduction to his 2002 *National Security Strategy* document, "The gravest danger our Nation faces lies at the crossroads of radicalism and technology."[12] Although many members of the administration wanted to overthrow Saddam before 9/11, I do not think they would have prevailed without these attacks. What converted many people, including the president, was the new sense of vulnerability and the associated redefinition of US security. Threats and dangers that could be tolerated if not ignored before now seemed existential menaces. The United States could not be safe at home unless it reached out to suppress enemies abroad.

A clue to why Bush changed his views can be found in one of the few lines that brought applause in Bush's Cincinnati speech of October 7, 2002, and that shows the powerful psychological connection between September 11 and the drive to depose Saddam: "We will not live in fear." Taken literally, it makes no sense. Unfortunately, fear is often well founded. Bush's statement also ignores the fact that attacking Saddam increased the chance of his using WMD against the United States, if he had any. What it indicates is an understandable desire for a better world, despite that fact that the United States did live in fear throughout the Cold War and survive quite well. But if the sentence has little logical meaning, the affect it displays is an understandable fear of fear, a drive to gain certainty, an impulse to assert control by taking strong action. It would be a mistake to try to characterize this as rational or irrational; it just is, and provides a powerful impetus to behavior.[13]

This reading of Bush's statement is consistent with my impression that many people who opposed invading Iraq before September 11 but altered their positions afterward had not taken terrorism terribly seriously before the attacks (and this includes George Bush). As a result, these events greatly increased their feelings of danger. As Bush put it in his Cincinnati speech: "On September 11th, 2001, America felt its vulnerability." It is no accident that this sentence came between two paragraphs about the need to disarm Iraq. Three months later, in response to a question at the joint press conference with Tony Blair accusing him of always wanting to invade Iraq, Bush replied: "Prior to September 11, we were discussing smart sanctions. . . . After September 11, the doctrine of containment just doesn't hold any water. . . . My vision shifted dramatically after September 11, because I now realize the stakes, I realize the world has changed."[14] The claim that some possibilities are unlikely enough to be put aside lost plausibility in face of the obvious retort: "What could be less likely than terrorists flying airplanes into the World Trade Center and the Pentagon?" During the Cold War, Bernard Brodie expressed his exasperation with wild suggestions about military actions the USSR might undertake: "All sorts of notions and propositions are churned out, and often presented for consideration with the prefatory words: 'It is conceivable that. . . .' Such words establish their own truth, for the fact that someone has conceived of whatever proposition follows is enough to establish that it is conceivable. Whether it is worth a second thought, however, is another matter."[15] A worst-case analysis is now hard to dismiss.

The fact that no one can guarantee that an adversary with WMD will not use them means that fear cannot be banished. Psychology plays an important role here because people place a high value on certainty and are willing to pay a high price to decrease the probability of a danger from slight to none.[16] Bush's choice of words declaring a formal end to the organized combat in Iraq was telling: "This much is *certain:* No terrorist network will gain weapons of mass destruction from the Iraqi regime."[17] Although administration officials exaggerated the danger that Saddam posed, they also revealed their true fears when they talked about the *possibility* that he could use WMD against the United States or its allies. At least some of them may have been insensitive to the magnitude of this possibility; what mattered was its very existence.

Concomitantly, people often feel that uncertainty can be best eliminated by taking the initiative. As Bush put it in his letter accompanying the submission of his *National Security Strategy* document, "In the new world we have entered, the only path to peace and security is the path of action," and in the body of the document he declared: "The greater the threat, the greater is the risk of inaction."[18] In the past, a state could let a potential threat grow because it might not turn into a major menace. Now if one follows this cautious path and the worst case does arise, the price will be prohibitive. Subsequent statements by Bush, some of them spontaneous, underlined this point: "We learned a lesson [from September 11]: the dangers of our time must be confronted actively and forcefully, before we see them again in our skies and in our cities"; and again, "Saddam Hussein is a threat to our nation. September 11 changed the strategic thinking, at least as far as I was concerned, for how to protect our country."[19]

The Bush Doctrine

The fourth element of the new world is the Bush Doctrine, of which the invasion of Iraq is a manifestation. In a sharp break from the president's views before September 11, he enunciated a far-reaching program that sees US vital interests implicated throughout the world. More specifically, the Bush Doctrine involves a strong belief in the importance of a nation's domestic regime in determining its foreign policy; the related judgment that this is a time of great opportunity to transform international politics; the perception of great threats that can be defeated only by new and vigorous policies (most notably preventive war); a willingness to act unilaterally when necessary; and, as both a cause and a summary of these beliefs, an overriding sense that peace and stability require the United States to assert its primacy in world politics.

Democracy. Bush and his colleagues see the world at a crossroads. The current system is much better than any that has preceded it, but it is a halfway house because it is a mixed system of democracies and nondemocracies. Bush is a "second-image" thinker, to use Kenneth Waltz's terminology: he believes that a state's foreign policy is the product of its domestic regime.[20] Lasting peace, stability, and prosperity will only come about through a transformation of other states and societies into liberal democracies, respecting individual rights, law, and their neighbors. To the cynical argument that the US position is mere rhetoric, I would reply, first, that rhetoric does have consequences and, second, that although Bush has not pushed undemocratic US allies as hard as he might, he has pushed them harder than any of his predecessors. The unfortunate course of the war in Iraq has led him to back off a bit, but the change in US policy is not to be dismissed. Indeed, a commitment to democracy appears to have been responsible for two highly consequential decisions. First, it appears that it was Bush himself who overturned the Pentagon's plans for installing Ahmad Chalabi in power in the wake of the US invasion of Iraq on the grounds that imposing a regime would be contrary to democracy.[21] Second, Bush overruled several of his advisers who urged him to support postponing Palestinian elections in January 2006 because Hamas was likely to win. According to one account, Bush said that "elections would be good for Hamas. They would have to be responsible."[22] (This is consistent with Bush's earlier claim that the overthrow of Saddam would enable "Palestinians who are working for reform and long for democracy . . . [to] be in a better position to choose new leaders—true leaders who strive for peace."[23])

Bush's position is both pessimistic and optimistic: pessimistic in the assertion that the standard tools of international politics are insufficient to tame tyrannical regimes; optimistic in the argument that democracies will be well-behaved internationally and accept US leadership. Optimism is also prominent in the belief that, with US assistance, democracy can be brought to all other countries. According to the Bush administration, this form of government will thrive when the artificially imposed barriers to it from old autocratic regimes are removed. Democracy does not require demanding preconditions and the prior transformation of society.

The other side of this coin is that as long as many countries are undemocratic, democracies elsewhere, including the United States, cannot be secure. Woodrow Wilson wanted to make the world safe for democracy. Bush extends and reverses this, arguing that only in a world of democracies can the United States be safe. The ringing cry in his second inaugural address—"The survival of liberty in our land increasingly depends on the success of liberty in other lands; the best hope for peace in our world is the expansion of freedom in all the world"—echoed what Secretary of State Dean Acheson said in 1950: "We are children of freedom. We cannot be safe except in an environment of freedom."[24] During the Cold War, the United States vacillated between accepting a heterogeneous world and believing that the USSR would be a threat as long as it was communist, and Ronald Reagan took the Acheson position to heart, although perhaps only when it appeared that the Soviet system might indeed be brought down without triggering a war.

Prevention, not deterrence. For Bush, the great threat posed by terrorism and rogue states cannot be contained by deterrence.[25] Terrorists are fanatics, and there is nothing that they value that we can threaten to destroy; rogues like Iraq accept risk and are accident-prone. Not only deterrence but also defense may be inadequate against terrorists and rogues, especially when the latter are threatening not to attack the United States directly but to coerce its allies. Thus the United States must be ready to wage preventive wars,[26] to nip problems in the bud by attacking adversaries before they gain the ability to menace US interests, and to act "against . . . emerging threats before they are fully formed," as Bush puts it.[27]

Bush and his colleagues believed—or perhaps I should say felt—that Saddam could dominate the region if he acquired nuclear weapons. In one way, this stance showed not a lack of faith in the basic idea of deterrence but rather a healthy—or unhealthy—respect for Iraq's ability to deter the United States from protecting its allies or from rolling back any Iraqi attack on them.[28] Both Saddam Hussein and US friends in the region would not think that US power could shield them. Thus deterrence would operate, but the United States, not Iraq, would have been deterred.[29] Indeed, here and in policy toward North Korea and Iran, the administration's policy implies that the United States is easy to deter.

The administration's doubt that Saddam could have been deterred was in part a reflection of a general skepticism about deterrence, especially pronounced among conservatives, that during the Cold War produced the search for multiple nuclear options, the goal of equaling if not surpassing the USSR at every level of violence (what was known as escalation dominance), and the desire for defense in many forms, most obviously ABMs. It also reflects the legacy of September 11 in the form of the feeling that nothing can be ruled out as totally implausible. Deterrence can fail; therefore it cannot be relied upon.

Those of us who still believe in the policy of deterrence do not see the need for preventive actions and contend that many threats are exaggerated or can be taken care of by strong but less militarized policies. Libya, for example, once the leading rogue, withdraw from the axis of evil. Bismarck called preventive wars "suicide for fear of death," and although the disparity of power between the United States and its adversaries means this is no longer the case, the argument for such wars implies a high degree of confidence that the future will be bleak unless one undertakes them, or at least the belief that this world will be worse than the likely one produced by the war.

Prevention is not a new element in world politics, even if Dale Copeland's important treatment exaggerates its previous centrality.[30] Israel launched a preventive strike against the Iraqi nuclear program in 1981, during the Cold War the United States gave serious thought to attacking the USSR and the PRC before they could develop robust nuclear capabilities, and the Monroe Doctrine and US westward expansion in the nineteenth century stemmed in part from the desire to prevent any European power from establishing a presence that could menace it.[31] The United States was a weak country at that time; now the preventive war doctrine is based on strength and on the associated desire to ensure the maintenance of US dominance.

In the current context, this policy faces three large obstacles. First, by definition, the relevant information is hard to obtain because it involves predictions about threats that reside sometime in the future. Thus although in retrospect it is easy to say that the Western allies should have stopped Hitler long before 1939, at the time it was far from clear that he would turn out to be such a menace. No one who reads Neville Chamberlain's speeches, let alone his presentations to his cabinet, can believe that he was a fool. In some cases, a well-placed spy might be able to provide solid evidence that the other had to be stopped, but in many other cases—perhaps including Nazi Germany—even this would not be sufficient because leaders do not themselves know how they will act in the future. The Bush Doctrine implies that the problem is not so difficult because the state's foreign policy is shaped, if not determined, by its domestic political system. Thus knowing that North Korea, Iran, and Syria are brutal dictatorships tells us that they will seek to dominate their neighbors, sponsor terrorism, and threaten the United States. But although the generalization that states that oppress their own people will disturb the international system fits many cases, it is far from universal, which means that such shortcuts to the assessment process are fallible. Second and relatedly, even information on capabilities and past behavior may be difficult to come by, as the case of Iraq shows. Although much remains unclear, the United States and Britain not only publicly exaggerated but also privately overestimated the extent of Saddam Hussein's WMD program.

Third, unless all challengers are deterred by the exercise of the doctrine in Iraq, preventive war will have to be repeated as other threats reach a similar threshold. Doing so will require sustained domestic if not international support, which is made less likely by the first two complications. The very nature of a preventive war means that the evidence is ambiguous and the supporting arguments are subject to rebuttal. To return to the pre–World War II case, if Britain and France had gone to war with Germany before 1939, large segments of the public would have believed that the war was not necessary. If it had gone badly, the public would have wanted to sue for peace; if it had gone well, public opinion would have questioned its wisdom. The unfortunate course of the war in Iraq has generated great skepticism about the quality of US intelligence, the administration's honesty in using such information, and the wisdom of moving too quickly.

Unilateralism. Preventive war is linked to the fundamental unilateralism of the Bush Doctrine since it is hard to get a consensus for such strong actions and since other states have every reason to let the dominant power carry the full burden. Unilateralism also has deep roots among the members of the Republican Party who do not hail from the Northeast, was well represented in the Reagan administration, draws on long-standing US political traditions, and was part of Bush's outlook before September 11. Of course, some assistance from others was necessary in Afghanistan. But that war should not be mistaken for a joint venture. In order to gain support, the United States agreed to overlook the lack of democracy and human rights in its new friends and to provide them with significant financial assistance. But it did not bend its policy to meet their preferences. Indeed, in stressing that the United States is building coalitions in the plural rather than an alliance (the mission determines the coalition, in Rumsfeld's phrase), US leaders have made it clear that they will forgo the participation of any particular country rather than compromise.

The past administration defended its actions but did not explain its general stance. I think the most principled, persuasive, and perhaps correct defense is built around the familiar argument about the difficulty of procuring public goods. As long as leadership is shared, very little will happen because no one actor will be willing to shoulder the costs and the responsibilities. "At this moment in history, if there is a problem, we're expected to deal with it," is how Bush explains it. "We are trying to lead the world," is how one administration official put it when the United States blocked language in a UN declaration on child health that might be read as condoning abortion.[32]

That view is not entirely hypocritical: many of the countries that endorsed the Kyoto Protocol had grave reservations about it but were unwilling to stand up to strongly committed domestic groups. Indeed, true consultation is likely to produce inaction, as was true in 1993 when Clinton favored the policy of "lift and strike" in Yugoslavia (i.e., lifting the arms embargo against Bosnia and striking Serbian forces). But because he was unwilling to move on his own, he sent Secretary of State Warren Christopher to ascertain European views. This multilateral, democratic procedure did not work because the Europeans did not want to be put on the spot, and in the face of apparent US indecision they refused to endorse such a strong policy. If the United States had informed the Europeans rather than consulted them, they probably would have gone along; what critics call unilateralism is in fact effective leadership.

US hegemony. The final element of the doctrine, which draws together the others, is the establishment of US hegemony, primacy, or empire.[33] There are no universal norms or rules of how international politics is to be conducted.[34] Order can be maintained only if the dominant power behaves quite differently from the others. Thus, one reason the administration is not worried that the US preventive war doctrine or attacking Iraq without the endorsement of the Security Council will set a precedent for others is the assumption that the dictates that apply to others do not bind the United States. Similarly, the United States sees no contradiction between expanding the ambit of nuclear weapons and planning to employ them even if others have not used WMD first, on the one hand, and a vigorous antiproliferation policy, on the other. Indeed, the Bush administration believes that US security, world stability, and the spread of liberalism require the United States to act in ways others cannot and must not.

Although many observers—myself included—were taken by surprise by this turn in US policy, we probably should not have been. It is consistent with (but perhaps not determined by) standard generalizations about international politics and the US place in the world. The United States now has a greater share of world power than has been true for any other state since the beginning of the state system and is not likely to lose this position anytime soon.[35] Before Bush's presidency, the United States took the role of the world's leading power, using a mixture of carrots and sticks and pursuing sometimes narrower but often broader conceptions of US interests.[36] The United States generally acted with others, made compromises to secure their support, and committed itself to multilateral consultation if not multilateral decisionmaking. Indeed, Clinton, and George H. W. Bush before him, worked very hard to maintain large coalitions. Most scholars approve of this mode of behavior, seeing it in the general public interest and the best, if not the only, way for the United States to secure desired behavior from others, minimize the costs to itself, and most smoothly manage a complex and contentious world.[37] But the choice of this approach was indeed a choice, revocable upon the appearance of changed circumstances and different leaders. The structure of world power meant that there was always a possibility that the United States would act on its own and in its own interest.

Until recently, however, it did not seem clear that the United States would in fact behave in a highly unilateral fashion. The new US stance was precipitated, if not caused, by the interaction between the election of George Bush, who brought to the office a more unilateral outlook than his predecessor and his domestic opponents, and the terrorist attack. Bush's transformation after September 11 may both parallel his earlier religious conversion and owe something to his religious beliefs, especially in his propensity to see the struggle as one between good and evil. There is reason to believe that just as his coming to Christ gave meaning to his previously aimless and dissolute personal life, so the war on terrorism has become not only the defining characteristic of his foreign policy but also his sacred mission.[38] Although we can only speculate on what President Al Gore would have done, my sense is that he probably would have invaded Afghanistan but would not have proceeded against Iraq, nor would he have moved away from treaties and other arrangements over a wide range of issues. To some extent, then, the current assertion of strong US hegemony may be an accident.

But I also think it was an accident that was waiting to happen. There are structural reasons to have expected a large terrorist attack at some point. Not only had Osama bin Laden attacked US interests abroad, but it was clear that he sought to strike the homeland. More generally, as Richard Betts has argued, terrorism is the obvious potent weapon of weak actors against the dominant state.[39]

Even without terrorism, both internal and structural factors predisposed the United States to assert its dominance, although not necessarily to sustain it. I think external factors are more important, but let me touch on internal ones. It is almost a truism of the history of US foreign relations that the United States rarely, if ever, engages in deeply cooperative ventures with equals.[40] The structure of the US government, its weak party system, its domestic diversity, and its political traditions, all make sustained cooperation difficult. It would be an exaggeration to say that unilateralism is the US way of foreign policy, but there certainly is a strong pull in this direction.

More important, the United States may be acting like a normal state that has gained a position of dominance. Thus it is not entirely surprising that many of the beliefs mustered in support of US policy toward Iraq parallel those held by European expansionists in earlier eras.[41]

There are four facets to my argument. First and most general is the pillar of realist thinking that power is checked most effectively and often only by counter-balancing power. It follows that states that are not subject to severe external restraints tend to feel few restraints at all. With this as one of his driving ideas, Waltz saw the likelihood of current behavior from the start of the post–Cold War era:

> The powerful state may, and the United States does, think of itself as acting for the sake of peace, justice, and well-being in the world. But these terms will be defined to the liking of the powerful, which may conflict with the preferences and the interests of others. In international politics, overwhelming power repels and leads others to try to balance against it. With benign intent, the United States has behaved, and until its power is brought into a semblance of balance, will continue to behave in ways that annoy and frighten others.[42]

Parts of the Bush Doctrine are unique to the circumstances, but it is the exception rather than the rule for states to chose the path of moderation when they do not expect others to force them to do so.[43]

Second and relatedly, states' definitions of their interests tend to expand as their power does.[44] They can pursue a whole host of objectives and goals that were out of reach when the state's security was in doubt and all efforts had to be directed to primary objectives; they can seek what Arnold Wolfers called "milieu goals."[45] The hope of spreading democracy and liberalism throughout the world has always been a US goal, but the lack of a peer competitor now makes it more realistic—although perhaps not very realistic—to actively strive for it. Seen in this light, it is not so much the special circumstances in other countries that have produced the Bush administration's perception that this is a time of great opportunity, but rather the enormous resources at US disposal.

Third, increased relative power often brings with it new fears. The reasons are both objective and subjective. As Wolfers notes in his classic essay, "National Security as Ambiguous Symbol," the latter can diverge from the former.[46] In one manifestation of this, as major threats disappear, people psychologically elevate ones that were previously seen as quite manageable.[47] Indeed, people now seem to be as worried as they were during the height of the Cold War despite the fact that a terrorist or rogue attack, even with WMD, could cause only a small fraction of World War III's devastation. But there is more to it than psychology. A dominant state acquires an enormous stake in the world order and interests spread throughout the globe. Many countries are primarily concerned with what happens in their immediate neighborhoods; the world is the hegemon's neighborhood, and it is not only hubris that leads it to be concerned with anything that happens anywhere. In the era of European colonialism, the historian John S. Galbraith explored the related dynamic of the "turbulent frontier" that produced the unintended expansion of colonialism. As a European power gained an enclave in Africa or Asia, usually along a coast or river, it also gained an unpacified boundary that had to be policed. This led to further expansion of influence and often of settlement, which in turn produced a new area that had to be protected and a new zone of threat.[48] There were few natural limits to that process. There are not likely to be many now.

The fourth facet can be seen as a broader conception of the previous point. As realists stress, even states that find the status quo acceptable have to worry about the future.[49] Indeed, the more an actor sees the current situation as satisfactory, the more it will expect the future to be worse. Psychology plays a role here too: prospect theory argues that actors are prone to accept great risks when they believe they will suffer losses unless they act boldly. The adoption of a preventive war doctrine may be a mistake, especially if taken too far, but it is not foreign to normal state behavior, as I noted earlier, and it appeals to states that have a valued position to maintain. However secure states are, only rarely can they be secure enough, and if they are currently very powerful, they have strong reasons to act now to prevent a deterioration that could allow others to harm them in the future.[50]

All this means is that the United States cannot readily be considered a status quo power. Its motives may not be selfish, but the combination of power, fear, and perceived opportunity lead it to seek to reshape world politics and the societies of many of its members. The world cannot stand still: without strong US intervention, the international environment will become more menacing to the United States and its values, but strong action can increase its security and produce a better world. In a process akin to what I have elsewhere described as the deep security dilemma, in order to protect itself the United States in impelled to act in a way that will increase or at least bring to the surface conflicts with others.[51] Even if the prevailing situation is satisfactory, it cannot be maintained by purely defensive measures.

Conclusion

The existence of a security community among the leading powers, the salience of terrorism, the preventive war on Iraq, and the Bush Doctrine are new elements in world politics. Where they will take us is uncertain, and that indeed may depend in part on unpredictable events such as economic shocks, the targets and success of future terrorist attacks, and the characteristics of the leaders that arise through diverse domestic processes. But I suspect that we will need more rethinking of our basic concepts than I have been able to do here.

The US overthrow of Saddam Hussein, however, already makes clear the links between preventive war and hegemony, which is much of the reason for the opposition at home and abroad. In parallel, the rocky course of the subsequent political reconstruction shows the vulnerability of the larger project. Bush's goals are extraordinarily ambitious, encompassing the defeat of terrorists and tyrants and seizing the opportunity to remake not only international politics but recalcitrant societies as well, which is seen as an end in itself and a means to US security. The United States will be infringing on what adversaries (if not the United States) see as their vital interests. Coercion and especially deterrence may be insufficient for these tasks; these instruments share with traditional diplomacy the desire to minimize conflict by limiting one's own claims to interests that others can afford to respect. States that seek more are likely to need brute force and preventive war (which gives some of us additional reasons to question the goals themselves). The belief that Saddam's regime would have been an unacceptable menace to US interests if it had developed nuclear weapons may then tell us not only about the model of deterrence that Bush and his colleagues reject but also about the expansive definition of US interests that they hold.

Indeed, the war is hard to understand if the only object was to disarm Saddam or even remove him from power. The danger was simply too remote to justify the effort. But if changing the Iraqi regime was expected to bring democracy and stability to the Middle East, discourage tyrants and energize reformers throughout the world, and demonstrate that the United States was willing to provide a high degree of what it considered world order whether others support it or not, then, as part of a much larger project, the war made a kind of sense. Those of us who find both the hopes and the fears excessive, if not delusional, agree with the views expressed by the great British statesman Lord Salisbury in the Eastern Crisis of 1877–1878: "It has generally been acknowledged to be madness to go to war for an idea, but if anything is more unsatisfactory, it is to go to war against a nightmare."[52]

From the start, skeptics doubted that the project could succeed. Domestically, US political institutions and traditions are not conducive to it.[53] Americans do not think of themselves as imperialists, like to be liked, and resist prolonged projects that do not show convincing signs of success. Looking abroad, many countries may move to acquire nuclear weapons because they fear US attack (Iran), feel they need to match the armaments of new nuclear powers in the region (Egypt), or worry about US steadfastness and wisdom (Japan). What a proliferated world would look like is subject to fierce debate, but the obvious expectation is that it would reduce the US ability to project its influence throughout the globe. Although the security community is likely to last, it too will feel the stress.

Of course, a great deal depends on the outcome in Iraq (and on a possible clash with Iran). Even if it turns out fairly well, the costs have been so high that domestic opinion is not likely to support additional adventures of this kind for some time to come. Although US involvement in the world is too broad and too deep to make isolationism a real alternative, a considerable drawing back is not only possible but likely. The Bush doctrine then will have had a short life, but it will have left a major scar on US policy. It is interesting that none of those seeking to succeed him embraced all aspects of Bush's policy. Rudy Giuliani outdid the president in his general bellicosity, but not in his enthusiasm for promoting democracy. John McCain called for staying in Iraq and has more than matched Bush in threats against Iran, but his previous record on intervention is quite inconsistent, and he has promised to consult much more with allies. For their parts, Senators Hillary Clinton and Barack Obama have heavily criticized Bush in general and the war in Iraq in particular, with the latter promising to remove all combat forces within sixteen months of taking office in January 2009. But President Obama is different from candidate Obama. Elected on a platform of bringing change to America, he skillfully avoided presenting a foreign policy vision. He cannot, however, escape a heavy foreign policy agenda, although he may well want to. Clearly, he opposes much of the Bush Doctrine and, at least initially, he will have ready partners abroad. He has also spoken of the need to promote democracy; and cramped realism, a narrow conception of American national interests, and the ability to shape the world do not fit with his style and what we can discern of his outlook. He will face difficult choices about priorities and how ambitious a policy he wants to pursue. The context is particularly difficult because public opinion is preoccupied with economic challenges and the Republican opposition is likely to be unforgiving of errors or even of controversial choices.

Woodrow Wilson said that both nationalism and internationalism called for the United States to join the League of Nations: "The greatest nationalist is the man who wants his nation to be the greatest nation, and the greatest nation is the nation which penetrates to the heart of its duty and mission among the nations of the world. With every flash of insight into the great politics of mankind, the nation that has that vision is elevated to a place of influence and power which it cannot get by arms."[54] Wilson surely meant what he said, but his great certainty that he knew what was best for the world was troubling. Iraq leaves the United States less certain and, perhaps, more humble, as Bush advocated in the 2000 campaign.[55] But how will the United States find its way in the new world?

Notes

Sections of this chapter are drawn from Robert Jervis, *American Foreign Policy in a New Era*.

1. See John Mueller, *Retreat from Doomsday*. Also see Emanuel Adler, "Europe's New Security Order"; John S. Duffield, "Transatlantic Relations After the Cold War"; James M. Goldgeier and Michael McFaul, "A Tale of Two Worlds";

Robert Jervis, "The Future of World Politics"; Michael Mandelbaum, "Is Major War Obsolete?"; Martin Shaw, *Global Society and International Relations;* Max Singer and Aaron Wildavsky, *The Real World Order;* Richard H. Ullman, *Securing Europe;* Stephen Van Evera, "Primed for Peace."

2. See Karl W. Deutsch et al., *Political Community and the North Atlantic Area.* Also see Emanuel Adler and Michael Barnett, eds., *Security Communities;* Matthew Melko, *Fifty-Two Peaceful Societies.*

3. Martin Gilbert, *Winston S. Churchill,* pp. 860–861.

4. Evan Luard, *War in International Society,* p. 77.

5. Charles Tilly, *Coercion, Capital, and European States, AD 990–1990,* p. 74.

6. Robert Keohane and Joseph Nye, *Power and Interdependence.*

7. Marc L. Busch, *Trade Warriors;* Paul Krugman, *Rethinking International Trade.*

8. For a related debate about the fungibility of military power, see Robert J. Art, "American Foreign Policy and the Fungibility of Force"; Robert J. Art, "Force and Fungibility Reconsidered"; David A. Baldwin, "Force, Fungibility, and Influence."

9. Stephen Hadley, "Remarks to the Council on Foreign Relations," February 12, 2003, Washington, DC. Vaclav Havel said in 2003: "Americans are fond of saying, 'The world changed on September 11.' But what has changed is America. The extraordinary moral self-righteousness of this Administration is quite surprising and staggering to Europeans." Quoted in Eric Alterman, "USA Oui! Bush Non!" *The Nation,* February 10, 2003, p. 14.

10. White House, "President Bush Outlines Iraqi Threat," October 7, 2002, Washington, DC, p. 3.

11. For a good discussion, see F. Gregory Gause III, "Can Democracy Stop Terrorism?"

12. White House, *The National Security Strategy of the United States of America,* p. ii.

13. A minor illustration of the power of fear was the closing of a New York subway station when a first-year art student taped to the girders and walls thirty-seven black boxes with the word "fear" on them, an unlikely thing for a bomber to do: Michael Kimmelman, "In New York, Art Is Crime, and Crime Becomes Art," *New York Times,* December 18, 2002. For a study of how people's willingness to sacrifice civil liberties is affected by their level of fear of a future attack, see Darren Davis and Brian Silver, "Civil Liberties vs. Security"; Leonie Huddy et al., "The Politics of Threat"; Leonie Huddy et al., "The Consequences of Terrorism."

14. "President Bush Meets with Prime Minister Blair," White House Press Office, January 31, 2003, http://www.whitehouse.gov/news/releases/2003/01/print/20030131.

15. Bernard Brodie, "The Development of Nuclear Strategy," p. 83.

16. Daniel Kahneman and Amos Tversky, eds., *Choices, Values, and Frames.*

17. "Transcript of President Bush's Remarks on the End of Major Combat in Iraq," *New York Times,* March 2, 2003, emphasis added. Bush used a similar formulation three months later: see White House, "President Meets with Small Business Owners in New Jersey," June 16, 2003, Washington, DC.

18. White House, *The National Security Strategy of the United States of America,* pp. ii, 15; also see "In the President's Words: Free People Will Keep the Peace of the World," *New York Times,* February 27, 2003; "Bush's Speech on Iraq: 'Saddam Hussein and His Sons Must Leave,'" *New York Times,* March 18, 2003; Tony Blair's statement quoted in Emma Daly, "Both Britain and Spain Dismiss Offer on Iraq Missiles," *New York Times,* March 1, 2003.

19. "President Discusses the Future of Iraq," White House Press Office, February 26, 2003, http://www.whitehouse.gov/news/releases/2003/02/print/20030226; "Excerpts from Bush's News Conference on Iraq and Likelihood of War," *New York Times*, March 7, 2003. The latter presentation is filled with statements linking the terrorist attacks with the need to disarm Iraq, which may have been partially attributable to the need to build public support for the war.

20. Kenneth N. Waltz, *Man, the State, and War.*

21. James Risen, *State of War,* p. 133.

22. Craig Unger, "From the Wonderful Folks Who Brought You Iraq," *Vanity Fair,* March 2007, p. 302.

23. Speech to the American Enterprise Institute, February 26, 2003. For a general discussion of the administration's optimism about the effects on the Middle East of overthrowing Saddam, see Philip Gordon, "Bush's Middle East Vision."

24. George W. Bush, "Second Inaugural Address," January 20, 2005, Washington, DC; Acheson is quoted in John Lewis Gaddis, *Strategies of Containment,* p. 106. During the Cold War, international politics scholars and US policymakers vacillated between believing that the United States could be secure and the international system could be stable despite being composed of heterogeneous units and that only homogeneity would bring with it safety; homogeneity was generally sought, but heterogeneity was accepted, albeit often grudgingly.

25. It is no accident that the leading critic of Cold War deterrence thinking, Albert Wohlstetter, trained and sponsored many of the driving figures of the Bush administration, such as Paul Wolfowitz and Richard Perle.

26. Calling this aspect of the doctrine and our policy against Iraq "preemptive," as the Bush administration does, is to do violence to the English language. No one believed that Iraq was about to attack anyone; rather the argument was that Iraq and perhaps others were terrible menaces that eventually would do the United States great harm and should be dealt with as soon as possible, before the harm was been inflicted and while counteractions could be taken at reasonable cost.

27. White House, *The National Security Strategy of the United States of America,* p. ii.

28. The latter is the topic of Barry Posen's important counterfactual probing of how the United States might have responded to the Iraqi invasion of Kuwait in 1990 if Iraq had possessed nuclear weapons: "US Security Policy in a Nuclear-Armed World, or: What If Iraq Had Had Nuclear Weapons?"

29. Richard Betts presciently noted this problem in "What Will It Take to Deter the United States?" For the argument that with the US use of nuclear weapons deterred, Saddam Hussein could have used his conventional forces to attack his neighbors, see Edward Rhodes, "Can the United States Deter Iraqi Aggression?" For an analysis of the structurally related problem of deterring an attack on Taiwan by the People's Republic of China that reaches a more optimistic conclusion, see Robert Ross, "Navigating the Taiwan Strait"; also see Thomas J. Christensen, "Posing Problems Without Catching Up." Elsewhere, I have discussed what the actors expected from nuclear weapons and what effects they have seem to have had in the Kargil crisis between India and Pakistan in Robert Jervis, "Kargil, Deterrence, and IR Theory."

30. Dale Copeland, *The Origins of Major War;* also see John J. Mearsheimer, *The Tragedy of Great Power Politics.* For important conceptual distinctions and propositions, see Jack Levy, "Declining Power and the Preventive Motivation for War"; and for a study that is skeptical of the general prevalence of preventive wars but presents one example, see Jack Levy and Joseph Gochal, "Democracy and

Preventive War." Randall Schweller argues that democratic states fight preventively only under very restrictive circumstances: "Domestic Structure and Preventive War"; Schweller notes the unusual nature of the Israeli cases. For a review of power transition theory, which in one interpretation is driven by preventive motivation, see Jacek Kugler and Douglas Lemke, *Parity and War.*

31. Marc Trachtenberg, *History and Strategy*, chapter 3.

32. Quoted in Bob Woodward's interview with Bush in the *Washington Post,* November 19, 2002; quoted in Somini Sengupta, "UN Forum Stalls on Sex Education and Abortion Rights," *New York Times,* May 10, 2002.

33. Paul Schroeder sharply differentiates hegemony from empire, arguing that the former is much more benign and rests on a high degree of consent and respect for diverse interests: "The Mirage of Empire Versus the Promise of Hegemony?" I agree that distinctions are needed, but at this point both the terms and US policy are unclear. I have a soft spot in my heart for primacy because it has the fewest connotations, and ten years ago I argued that the United States did not need to seek primacy (at least I was sensible enough to avoid saying whether the United States would be sensible): Robert Jervis, "The Future of World Politics"; Robert Jervis, "International Primacy."

34. It was only after World War I that even lip service was paid to the concept that all states had equal rights. The diplomatic documents of the nineteenth century make clear that even if small states are given some consideration, they can be treated in ways that would be unthinkable for a great power.

35. William Wohlforth, "The Stability of a Unipolar World"; Stephen Brooks and William Wohlforth, *World Out of Balance.* See also Kenneth N. Waltz, "Contemporary Conflict in Theory and Practice." The well-crafted argument by Robert Kudrle that the United States does not always get its way, even on some important issues, is correct, but I think it does not contradict the basic structural point: Kudrle, "Hegemony Strikes Out."

36. Michael Mastanduno, "Preserving the Unipolar Moment"; also see the exchange between Mark Sheetz and Mastanduno in *International Security* 22 (Winter 1997–1998): 168–174.

37. See, for example, G. John Ikenberry, "After September 11"; Ikenberry, *After Victory;* John Gerard Ruggie, *Winning the Peace;* Joseph Nye, *The Paradox of American Power.*

38. For a perceptive analysis, see Frank Bruni, "For President, a Mission and a Role in History," *New York Times,* September 22, 2001.

39. Richard Betts, "The Soft Underbelly of American Primacy."

40. See, for example, Jesse Helms's defense of unilateralism as the only way consistent with US interests and traditions: "American Sovereignty and the UN." For a discussion of historical and geographical sources of the moralistic outlook in US foreign policy, see Arnold Wolfers, *Discord and Collaboration,* chapter 15.

41. Jack Snyder, "The New Myths of Empire."

42. Kenneth N. Waltz, "America as a Model for the World?" p. 69; also see Waltz's discussion of the Gulf War: "A Necessary War?" Charles Krauthammer also expected this kind of behavior, but he believed that it would serve world as well as US interests: "The Unipolar Moment"; also see Krauthammer, "The Unipolar Moment Revisited." For a critical analysis, see James Chace, "Imperial America and the Common Interest."

43. Alexander Wendt and, more persuasively, Paul Schroeder would disagree or at least modify this generalization, arguing that prevailing ideas can and have led to more moderate and consensual behavior: Wendt, *Social Theory of International*

Politics; Schroeder, *The Transformation of European Politics, 1763–1848,* and "Does the History of International Politics Go Anywhere?" This is a central question of international politics and history that I cannot fully discuss here, but I believe that at least the mild statement that unbalanced power is dangerous can be sustained.

44. See, for example, Fareed Zakaria, "Realism and Domestic Politics"; Robert Tucker, "The Radical Critique Assessed."

45. Arnold Wolfers, *Discord and Collaboration,* chapter 5.

46. Ibid., chapter 10.

47. John Mueller, "The Catastrophe Quota"; also see Frederick Hartmann, *The Conservation of Enemies.*

48. John S. Galbraith, "The 'Turbulent Frontier' as a Factor in British Expansion"; John S. Galbraith, *Reluctant Empire.* Also see Ronald Robinson and John Gallager, with Alice Denny, *Africa and the Victorians.* A related imperial dynamic that is likely to recur is that turning a previously recalcitrant state into a client usually weakens it internally and requires further intervention.

49. See especially Dale Copeland, *The Origins of Major War;* John J. Mearsheimer, *The Tragedy of Great Power Politics.*

50. Waltz sees this behavior as often self-defeating; Mearsheimer implies that it is not; Copeland's position is somewhere in between.

51. Robert Jervis, "Was the Cold War a Security Dilemma?"; Robert Jervis, "The Remaking of a Unipolar World."

52. Quoted in R. W. Seton-Watson, *Disraeli, Gladstone, and the Eastern Question,* p. 222.

53. For further discussion, see Robert Jervis, *American Foreign Policy in a New Era,* pp. 111–115.

54. "A Luncheon Address to the St. Louis Chamber of Commerce, September 5, 1919," in *The Papers of Woodrow Wilson,* vol. 63: *September 4–November 5, 1919,* ed. Arthur Link et al. (Princeton: Princeton University Press, 1990), p. 33.

55. Quoted in David Sanger, "A New View of Where America Fits in the World," *New York Times,* February 18, 2001.

4

From Hegemony to Empire: The Fatal Leap

Paul W. Schroeder

Most people consider the United States still the leading power in the world, and most of its citizens believe that it should exercise world leadership. The question is mainly what kind of leadership and how to exercise it. In this chapter, I draw on the history of international politics to argue that the United States, even if its position as leader is shaky, still faces a choice between two modes of political leadership, empire and hegemony, that seem similar and are often identified or discussed as synonymous, but differ fundamentally in their nature and effects. The lure of achieving world order and peace through empire is a treacherous mirage, while hegemony presents a path open to these goals. In today's global international system, moreover, it is impossible to pursue policies of empire and of hegemony simultaneously or keep them separate but compatible, as was possible in previous eras, because they now lead in opposite directions and contradict each other. This means that US policy in recent years, especially in Iraq, which I will argue has constituted a bid for empire, has already undermined and continues to undermine the possibility of a useful US hegemony. It has contributed instead to a growth of Hobbesian disorder in the Middle East and the world that the pursuit of a sane hegemony could have avoided.

Asserting this is one thing, proving it quite another, requiring a detailed theoretical argument and extensive historical exposition impossible here. This chapter can only attempt to state the case in bare outline and illustrate it at crucial points with historical evidence and examples. I start by explaining why the distinction between empire and hegemony is not merely a device for formal definition and analysis but reflects a concrete set of choices or alternatives in history leading to different outcomes. I further try to show why the pursuit of empire within the current international system has proved counterproductive and destructive, whereas hegemony remains compatible with that system and is often needed for it to function and endure.

Any such argument from history, however, whether it is extensively developed or cursory and fragmentary as it will be here, is unlikely to be considered seriously by the advocates of the current US policy. They instead continue to dismiss historical arguments as irrelevant for policy today because history itself has changed drastically since September 11, 2001. According to this view, the most serious threats to the United States and the so-called free world today, consisting of international terrorist organizations, radical ideologies and movements subject to no law or moral restraints, rogue regimes, and the danger of weapons of mass destruction coming into the hands of rogue states and terrorist organizations and movements, are so different from those confronted by the old international system that they cannot be met by its traditional diplomatic and military measures, rules, and procedures. The main current dangers arise not from sovereign states with regular governments, but can come from anywhere and must be fought everywhere and nowhere in particular, necessarily by proactive and preventive means and weapons. The old international system, with its emphasis on state actors and its legalistic rules, simply obstructs the appropriate response and has to be circumvented, discarded, or replaced with something better. In addition, the military power and margin of superiority held by the United States today is so much greater than any other power's has ever been; the ability of the United States to project that power globally with great speed and devastating effect is so unprecedented; and the economic global reach and soft power given the United States by its attractive material culture and widely envied political and social institutions and values are so effective in penetrating other countries and societies that limits placed on US action by the old rules no longer apply.[1]

My response is that this argument has already been refuted by events. The US bid to win the so-called global war on terror and promote world order and peace by creating a Pax Americana kind of empire, a project proclaimed with the Bush Doctrine in 2002 and launched with the invasion of Iraq in 2003, is not merely fated to fail ultimately, as some observers, including me, predicted before the project was begun.[2] It has already failed; a majority of Americans have recognized this long after it had become apparent to the rest of the world. The Obama administration is not likely to continue this failed venture and redouble the reckless gamble of its predecessor, further undermining stability in the Middle East, the position the United States holds in the world, and world peace. It is also unlikely to acknowledge failure and abandon the venture, choosing instead to redirect US goals, strategy, and tactics. Meanwhile, there is one surprising and hopeful aspect to this melancholy story: the old international system, attacked from opposite sides by the Bush administration and its neoconservative allies in the United States and by revolutionary forces of various kinds, radical Islamist and other, has so far survived the onslaught and proved itself more resilient, resourceful, and valuable in the crisis than even ardent proponents like me expected.

The Empire/Hegemony Dichotomy as Concept and in History

Now to try to put a little historical flesh on these assertions. For reasons of space, the argument must be sketchy, apodictic, and apparently dogmatic. Qualifiers like "It seems to me" or "In my opinion" should therefore be assumed in much of what follows.

Both empire and hegemony are slippery terms, often defined in misleading or vague, excessively broad ways blurring or obliterating the difference between them. That is especially true with "empire" and "imperialism." A central, essential element of empire, however, can be identified: the ability of one organized community to exercise political control over another organized community different from and separate from it, making the former the final locus of decision and authority in central political decisions for the community under its rule. Obviously, many elements can go into the acquisition and exercise of that kind of imperial authority—military and economic power, scientific and technological prowess, culture, religion, ideology, ethnicity, and so on. Nonetheless, the essence of empire lies in the possession and exercise of political control over a foreign community.

Less obvious but equally important is the fact that empire need not involve *direct* political control and administration by one unit over another, and historically has not for the most part. Most empires, ancient and modern, have existed as *informal* or indirect empires (i.e., indirect control exercised by the imperial power through local authorities in a particular region without having to govern it directly, based on and derived from its recognized paramountcy).[3] This kind of informal and indirect control, of which there are many ancient and modern examples, still constitutes genuine empire because (and so long as) final authority and decisionmaking power in critical political matters rests with the imperial authorities.[4]

The term "hegemony" is also slippery and problematic as currently used in international politics. One difficulty is that the revisionist Marxist sociologist Antonio Gramsci's definition of hegemony as cultural dominance functioning as an instrument of class rule has become standard in sociology and other social sciences and has come to dominate popular usage, thus contributing to the common identification of empire and hegemony.[5] Both the theory and the history of international politics, however, require a different understanding of the term. Hegemony in international history and politics does not mean, like empire, the possession of final political authority over another community. It means the possession and exercise of clear, acknowledged leadership and superior influence by one unit within a community of units *not* under a single authority.[6]

Thus a hegemon is in principle first among equals. An imperial power rules over subordinates. A hegemonic power is one without whom no final decision on crucial issues can be reached within the system, whose task and responsibility it is to see that necessary decisions are reached. An imperial power can finally impose its decision if it chooses, and must do if seriously challenged or it will cease to be an empire.

True, this distinction, like most such distinctions in social and political life, is not airtight but one of degree, like the differences between warm, hot, and boiling. As will be argued later, hegemonic powers can become empires and are regularly tempted to do so. There are also instances in which empires devolve or attempt to devolve into hegemonic structures (the British Empire into the Commonwealth, the French Empire into the Union Française, the Soviet Union into the Commonwealth of Independent States, the US informal empire in Latin America into the good neighbor policy and the Organization of American States, etc.). But the very fact that each can evolve into the other shows that the distinction is more than merely verbal or a matter of degree, and has important implications for the international system.

In systemic terms, hegemony as here defined is compatible in theory and practice with the workings of the modern international system (usually called, somewhat misleadingly, the Westphalian system), one made up of autonomous coordinate units (mainly states) regarded as juridically equal in status, rights, and obligations, though vastly unequal in size and power. Empire is not compatible with such a system. Whatever the leaders of empires may claim, empires cancel that essential juridical equality between all the units and the autonomy that goes with it.[7] The fundamental principles of empire and of a genuine international system of independent states mix like oil and water.

The difference extends to functions. Empires function to rule, to establish the final locus of authority in one center. Hegemony functions essentially to manage, to maintain some degree of order and decisionmaking capacity within a system of dispersed authority. Empire means the negation of balance within the system, both that of a sustainable balance of power and a balance in other elements equally important for a stable international system, namely, a desirable or at least tolerable balance in the distribution of rights, status, privileges, duties, responsibilities, and honor. Hegemony, in contrast, is fully compatible with equilibrium in both areas and is often necessary to achieve and maintain it.[8] Empire tends by nature toward exclusive, final control and cannot be shared or exercised in partnership or in common. To be sure, colonial territory can be parceled out and divided up among imperial powers, but only if the respective parcels are clearly marked, each controls one, and each honors the agreement.[9] Hegemony, however, can readily be shared and exercised in common, and often works better when so shared and exercised in either equal or unequal partnership. One can sensibly speak about hegemonies shared between two, three, or even more members (e.g., the hegemony of the great power Concert of Europe in the nineteenth century, Franco-German hegemony in the Common Market, NATO hegemony after 1985, etc.).[10]

This distinction between empire and hegemony, far from being abstract or academic, reflects lived and perceived reality and practice in history since the beginnings of the modern international system in the sixteenth century. The difference between policies of empire and hegemony has repeatedly made a critical difference in outcomes. Empires, both traditional and modern, can work for a considerable time, prove stable, and produce and maintain order—but only in premodern, noninternational settings outside or alongside an international order. They produce such order essentially by imposing stable governance and law on areas either too little governed and organized or too mired in chronic, uncontrolled violence and war to enjoy peace and stability. However, once stable autonomous polities have evolved and been organized within an international system such as the one that has developed from its Western European origins to the global system of today, attempts to create order within that system or impose a new order upon it through empire regularly produce disorder, instability, and war. Hegemony, however, can promote peace and systemic stability and has often done so. In fact, the absence of a hegemonic power or the failure of actual or potential hegemons to exercise hegemonic leadership where and when it is needed can be and frequently has been an important cause of systemic breakdown and war.

I do not mean that the effects of hegemony are automatically beneficial or those of empire always and everywhere harmful. Austrian hegemony in Germany and Italy after 1815, for example, arguably was harmful on balance, its repressive and regressive political effects too high a price to pay for the international stability and peace it promoted. Napoleon's military-colonial empire, in contrast, had major stimulating and progressive aspects in parts of Western Europe, though overall it led to escalating tyranny, exploitation, and war. Other examples could be cited. The central point is simply that hegemony can exist and operate within an international system of independent states and help sustain it, and empire cannot.

These sweeping generalizations can only be illustrated here by a few leading instances. First, one can cite crucial points in history at which leaders of states that already enjoyed potential or actual hegemony within the existing international system or could have tried for it chose (consciously or subconsciously, willingly or under perceived necessity) to seek empire rather than hegemony. These bids for empire, one should note, did not usually or necessarily involve attempts to gain direct rule over their opponents by annexation or conquest; as noted earlier, most empire historically has not required that. What they did involve was various efforts to secure and exercise that power earlier defined as the essence of empire: the power to make and enforce decisions in other countries on issues regarded by other authorities and peoples as under their jurisdiction, critical to their autonomy and rights within the prevailing order. There could be many diverse reasons and motives behind these bids for empire, ranging from momentary impulse and personal predilection to perceived strategic or political necessity or religious and ideological commitment. Yet the imperial ventures shared two things in common. They all ultimately failed, thereby ruining whatever chances the empire seekers and their governments had to sustain a durable hegemony within the system, and they promoted instability, wars,. and in some instances the breakdown of the entire system.

What follows is a list of some major historical instances in which hegemonic leaders who arguably were in a position to preserve and enjoy hegemony for a substantial period of time instead chose to make bids for empire. The brief and incomplete list is intended only to show how their policies involved a choice between empire and hegemony, as defined here, and led to the kinds of results I have indicated.

Charles V, the Holy Roman Emperor, and German Lutheran Princes and Cities, 1521–1552. In this case, the bid for empire grew out of Charles's view of his political and religious duties and prerogatives as emperor and his determination to defend Christian unity and orthodoxy in the German empire against Lutheran heresy.[11] The German princes and free cities joined in the Smalcald League did not challenge the emperor's constitutional suzerainty and hegemony as their elected overlord, but regarded this policy as an attack on their historical rights to control public worship and religion within their own domains—in short, as empire rather than hegemony. The result was that after two minor wars, Charles was compelled to accept failure in his attempts to suppress heresy or prevent a schism in the church. Rather than sanction this himself, he abdicated as emperor, and the religious divisions in Germany, though kept within bounds for about sixty years through a political and religious truce between the parties, subsequently led to war again in 1618.

Philip II of Spain and the Magnates of the Netherlands, 1560s. Here the issue, though similar, involved Philip's determination to exercise direct and full political and religious authority over subjects who, though initially loyal to his authority, believed that he was usurping long-standing political and religious rights and privileges guaranteed to them by the king's oath of office.[12] Once again, Philip's choice was one essentially between empire and hegemony and resulted in a revolt and series of wars lasting off and on for eighty years. It ended in Spain's concession of independence to the northern Netherlands (the United Provinces) and helped undermine Spain's position as a world power.

Ferdinand II as Holy Roman Emperor and the German Estates in the Thirty Years' War, 1618–1635. Here the decisive issue was Ferdinand's determination to respond to a Protestant, mainly Calvinist revolt in Bohemia by not merely suppressing the political revolt against his rule as king of Bohemia but also wiping out Protestant heresy entirely, or at a minimum reducing it to harmless dimensions and ultimate extinction.[13] It was part of his attempt, supported by some other Catholic princes and by Spain, to apply to the entire Holy Roman Empire of which Ferdinand was only the elected suzerain the religious policy he had followed in his Austrian Habsburg hereditary lands—this despite the fact that most German Lutheran princes had not supported the Bohemian-Palatine revolt, remained loyal to the existing imperial constitution, and were willing to accept a political-religious settlement that would recognize traditional imperial authority, stabilize the religious status quo in Germany, and thus end the fighting. This choice by Ferdinand of empire over hegemony, urged by some of his religious and political advisers, resulted eventually, despite initial Habsburg-Catholic victories, in alienating even some Catholic princes worried about their autonomy, calling new outside forces (Lutheran Denmark and Sweden and Catholic France) into the fray against the emperor, and prolonging a war that ravaged Central Europe and ultimately undermined the emperor's authority.

Louis XIV of France and His Bid for "Universal Monarchy," 1665–1715. Louis's quest for empire defies any brief summary. Suffice it to say that during his long reign (1660–1715), Louis had many opportunities to consolidate France's natural hegemonic position in Western Europe through alliances, subsidies, and judicious territorial acquisitions and fortifications.[14] Some of his political and military advisers repeatedly urged him to exploit them. Instead, his actions convinced even would-be allies that his policy was one of endless conquest and political and religious despotism (the latter illustrated by the revocation of the Edict of Nantes) that threatened the "liberties of Europe" (i.e., the independence of other states). The resulting series of European wars ended in partial French defeat, the exhaustion of France, and Louis's own admission at the end of his reign that he had gone too far in pursuit of military glory and unchallenged European supremacy.

Charles XII of Sweden in the Baltic After 1702. Again, no summary of the story is possible here.[15] The central point is that a war that began as a struggle by Charles to defend the existing Swedish empire in the Baltic and surrounding region against a coalition organized by Czar Peter of Russia turned into an aggressive imperialist effort by Charles to defeat and subjugate all his enemies, ending in his defeat and death, the exhaustion of Sweden, the end of the Swedish empire, and the rise of a new imperial threat in the Baltic from czarist Russia. Whether Charles could have established a peaceful hegemony after his initial victories is unclear (though his predecessor Charles XI had enjoyed one); what is certain is that he did not try for it.

These choices of empire over hegemony in early modern Europe, as well as others that could be mentioned, are admittedly not as clear-cut as one might wish. The lines between empire and hegemony were then blurred by the undeveloped condition of the early modern states system, in which the locus and extent of authority were often unclear and instances of mixed sovereignty and overlapping jurisdictions were commonplace. Still, they illustrate how bids for empire even then clashed with the development of the international system and promoted instability and war. Modern bids for empire have been more obvious and deliberate, and prove the point with little need for elaboration or demonstration.

Napoleon, for example, had many chances between 1801 and 1814 to convert his conquests in Europe into durable French hegemony over western and central Europe. Certain of his supporters, most notably his foreign minister Prince Talleyrand in late 1805, repeatedly suggested plans for achieving it. Many of the satellite states he created or enlarged in Germany and Italy had leaders loyal to him, ready to accept French leadership for their own purposes. Even countries unfriendly toward France, such as Spain or the Dutch Republic, contained important leaders and groups who wanted to accept French hegemony for the sake of the peace, security and modernization it could bring. Most important, all the other great powers in Europe who fought against Napoleonic France, including Britain, were at various times ready to recognize Napoleon's military invincibility on the Continent and live with French hegemony.[16] What essentially kept France from consolidating its victories into durable hegemony was Napoleon's character—his refusal to renounce conquest and exploitation, his insistence on an ever-expanding military-colonial empire.

The same thing is even more obvious with Adolf Hitler, who had a program for empire far more explicit, deliberately chosen, and brutal than Napoleon's. After the Munich agreement in 1938, Germany was clearly hegemonic in continental Europe; no power including the other great powers wanted at that point to challenge German hegemony. Germany's eastern neighbors from Finland to Greece were not only afraid to oppose Germany but in many instances looked to it for economic recovery and protection against the Soviet Union. Britain and France had accepted German leadership in Central and Eastern Europe. Joseph Stalin, as ever most concerned about defending his personal dictatorship against possible internal enemies, dreaded another war and defeat like 1914–1918 that would overthrow his regime. Nothing stood in the way of durable German hegemony save Hitler and the ideology, regime, and movement he led. He explicitly and totally rejected mere hegemony in Europe as useless; only the worst and most brutal form of empire would do.

In the latter stages of World War II, Stalin had ample opportunity and considerable incentive to try to build a durable Soviet hegemony over the greater part of Europe. The Western allies took for granted that the Soviet Union's enormous wartime sacrifices and the power it had displayed in breaking the back of the German army and liberating most of Europe entitled it to an extensive security zone and dominant sphere of influence in all of Eastern and much of Central Europe. Even states within that security zone historically hostile to Russia, such as Poland and Hungary, accepted this reality so far as international politics was concerned and only hoped to preserve their internal independence. Some states, like Czechoslovakia and Bulgaria, welcomed the idea of close relations with the Soviet Union under its protection. Marshal Tito in Yugoslavia not only accepted Stalin's general leadership of the world communist movement but pursued a domestic agenda and ideology more Stalinist than Stalin himself. By the end of the war, there were some in the United States and Western Europe calling for resistance to a possible Soviet threat, but there was no organized movement or capacity for one. The West was far too divided, exhausted, and (save for the United States) weak to pose any challenge to Soviet leadership in its sphere. The obstacle to Soviet hegemony, as everyone knows, was Stalin himself—his inability to be satisfied and secure merely through having friendly, dependent countries as allies on Russia's western frontier (the kind of glacis policy that czarist Russia had pursued for centuries). Stalin could only consider a neighbor as friendly if it was tightly under his control (i.e., he had to have empire).

Everyone knows what choosing empire over hegemony led to in these cases. In 1814–1815, it caused Napoleon's ultimate downfall and put an end not only to his French empire in Europe but to any real chances for durable French hegemony in Europe for the rest of the century.[17] Hitler's bid for a Thousand Years' Reich lasted a scant twelve; the unprecedented devastation and atrocities it caused ended Germany's history as a great independent military power once and for all. Stalin's empire proved more durable, sustained mainly by military power and the ruthless suppression of opposition and dissent, but the Soviet Union never became really stable, either at home or in its satellite territories, or overcame the fatal flaws in its original conception that led to its collapse in the 1980s.

Many realist international relations theorists, especially so-called structural and offensive realists, have a simple explanation for all this. They ascribe it to international anarchy and the competitive search for security—proof that weaker states threatened by hegemonic powers normally and of necessity balance for security against them and usually defeat them in the long run. But even these thumbnail historical accounts show that this interpretation is historically untenable. In all the above cases, with the possible exception of that of Charles XII of Sweden, what caused these imperialist ventures to fail was not the resistance of various smaller states to hegemony by greater ones, but their rejection of empire. They usually accepted and often welcomed leadership and protection from a hegemonic power, only to resist, often late and reluctantly, when the hegemonic power was perceived (in most cases correctly) as no longer content with exercising acknowledged leadership and superior influence within a community of autonomous equals but clearly seeking imperial control over them.

The central point that hegemony, unlike empire, is compatible with an international system is reinforced by numerous cases in which, when a particular leader or government decided to seek hegemony rather than empire (even if that choice was forced on them by necessity or appeared the only rational policy available), their choice helped them stabilize their position and promoted peace. Following are some examples.

Charles V's successors as Holy Roman Emperor, especially Ferdinand I and Matthias, were able to maintain their imperial positions and leadership under difficult circumstances even while religious wars were raging in other parts of Europe, especially France and the Low Countries, by accepting a religious truce and not pushing religious issues to a confrontation.[18]

Cardinal de Richelieu and Jules Mazarin, as prime ministers in France from 1624 to 1660, achieved an impressive leading position for France in Europe through war and diplomacy.[19] Yet even as they pushed French prerogatives and claims very far, they carefully avoided laying claims to empire, presenting France instead as the champion of religious and political liberties in other countries (e.g., the estates of the German empire). Doing so gave France the commanding position in Europe inherited by Louis XIV that his brand of imperialism ultimately undermined.

As ruler of Habsburg Austria and Holy Roman Emperor (1658–1705), Leopold I adopted a policy of carefully managing the German estates in the Reichstag rather than trying to dominate or control them. Thereby he succeeded both in restoring much of the prestige and authority of the emperor in Germany lost in the Thirty Years' War and in enlisting German help for Habsburg causes (notably in the second Ottoman Turk siege of Vienna in 1683), thus helping Austria to emerge as a European great power in its own right during his reign.[20]

Britain and France after the Peace of Utrecht in 1713 deliberately cooperated as leading powers in compelling restive states aggrieved at the peace settlement, principally Spain and Austria, to accept their terms and thereby to maintain a fragile peace and the so-called balance of power. This was shared hegemony, not empire.[21]

As first minister of France in the 1730s, Cardinal Claude Fleury rejected the urging of other bellicose French leaders to take advantage of opportunities they saw for France to destroy its hereditary enemy and rival Austria, thereby giving France unchallenged supremacy in Western Europe.[22] Fleury opted instead for sparing Austria and making it a kind of junior partner in a French-led program of peace and hegemony. When Fleury's rivals led France into an aggressive imperialist course of attempting to break up Austria in 1741, it not only expanded a local Austro-Prussian war into a great European one, but quickly led to French defeat and the abandonment of this plan in favor of pursuing another version of French hegemony under the Marquis d'Argenson.

* * *

If these instances of choosing hegemony over empire are unfamiliar to nonspecialists, more recent history contains instances both better known and more compelling. The victorious allies who defeated Napoleon in 1814 and again in 1815 deliberately chose in the Vienna Settlement to establish a peace based on various kinds and spheres of hegemony rather than empire.[23] After Prussia's brilliant victories in 1864, 1866, and 1870–1871, Prince Bismarck deliberately chose to found Germany's security from 1871 to 1890 on a labile, carefully restrained, and managed half-hegemony in Europe rather than further conquest and military supremacy.[24] The most obvious and impressive example is also the most recent: the US option for hegemony in Europe and the West during the Cold War, in contrast to the Soviet choice of empire in its sphere, made a critical difference in the ultimate results.

This argument is further strengthened by important instances in which the absence or failure of hegemony (i.e., the refusal or inability of actual or potential hegemonic powers to exercise leadership and fulfill the needed hegemonic managerial functions in critical situations) promoted the breakdown of the system and resultant disorder and war. Two illustrations will have to suffice. In the era following the Seven Years' War (1756–1763), the fact that one hegemon, Great Britain, withdrew from most European affairs to concentrate on reorganizing its empire, while the other, Russia, ruthlessly exploited its dominant position in Eastern Europe for territorial expansion against Poland and the Ottoman Empire, contributed greatly to promoting the wars, international crimes (the partitions of Poland), and revolutionary instability that led to a generation of general systemic war from 1787 to 1815.[25] More obvious still, in the interwar era of 1919–1933, the victors in World War I, the United States, Britain, and France, either declined to fill the hegemonic roles required to ensure general security throughout the system or in trying to do so contradicted and frustrated each other's efforts.

The same picture holds for Britain and the United States in the vital arena of international economics and is one major explanation for the disaster of the Great Depression.[26]

Even if some of these individual historical instances can be debated, the overall conclusion is clear. Empire can conceivably work reasonably well for purposes of governance and stable order outside the modern international system, even alongside it, but not within it. It is incompatible with a genuine international system composed of autonomous units. The pursuit of empire attacks and undermines any such system, creates disorder, instability, and conflict within it, and ruins the chances for the empire-seeking power or powers to enjoy a durable and tolerable hegemony within the system.

Why Is This Distinction Relevant Today?

It is possible, of course, to accept the distinction between empire and hegemony as a historical generalization and deny its relevance for the current world situation and US foreign policy today. Many do; at least four different sets of reasons are commonly given for deeming it irrelevant. Briefly summarized, they are: (1) Both the world and the position of the United States in it have changed so radically that the old international system, its rules, and historical examples and generalizations like this are obsolete. (2) The United States did not seek empire, in Iraq or anywhere else; the war was and still is a war of liberation, waged to end tyranny; defend against international terrorism and other threats; spread liberty, democracy, and a market economy; and help to peacefully transform the Middle East and other parts of the world. (3) Whatever the motives and character of the US initiative originally were, subsequent events and developments have drastically changed them; the bid for empire (if there ever was one) is effectively over. Now that even the administration basically hopes only to get out of Iraq with some dignity and honor and to leave behind a country that can govern and defend itself, it is irrelevant and distracting to worry about whether the original motives and aims were imperialist or not. (4) The overriding concern now should not be whether the war was justified or its motives aggressive-imperialist or what caused the present difficulties, but the fact that the war has now become an integral part of the struggle against Islamic radicalism and jihadism, the most dangerous element in the general terrorist threat to the United States and the world. This makes the Iraq war one that the United States cannot escape, abandon, or afford to lose and renders irrelevant the debate over what led the United States into it. The only serious question is how to prevail in Iraq as the current central battleground in a wider conflict.

Plainly these four lines of argument do not fit together very well, either as a defense of the original US policy or as a prescription for the current one. They all reject the empire-versus-hegemony case made here as irrelevant, for different, partly contradictory reasons. The first says it is irrelevant because all previous history is; the second, because US policy and the war in Iraq were never imperialist; the third, because whether they were or not, the United States is now only trying to get out; and the fourth, because why the United States got in makes no difference now—it must stay and win. I am reminded of the lawyer who defended a client being sued because his dog attacked a neighbor, who argued in his defense that (1) the attack never happened; (2) the dog was provoked and acted in self-defense; (3) the neighbor's injuries were trifling; and (4) his client did not own a dog. Nonetheless, each deserves some answer on the issue of relevance.

The best one to start with is (2), the denial that US policy in Iraq constituted a bid for empire, and the best response is not to try to prove by historical comparisons and analogies that it really was. However plausible a case might be made (and it would be easy to refute the president's assertion that the whole world knows that the United States never fights wars of conquest), historical arguments of this sort can always be denied, dismissed, or shunted aside, and the effort to make it would be distracting. Nor is the best response, at least for me, another argument that other, real motives for going to war were hidden under the justifying rhetoric of self-defense, liberation, and democracy. If existing arguments along this line made by real experts in current politics in Washington and the Middle East have not convinced people, I as a historian surely cannot. Instead I would like to point out an elemental fact of international politics. The decisive criterion for judging the real character of policies and of wars that result from them is not the reasons given by those who launch them or even the aims and motives they might subjectively feel and more or less genuinely profess, but rather what the actions involved in the policy leading to war objectively mean within the system of international politics (i.e., what they actually represent as moves within an ongoing game of action and response, and how they concretely affect the international system and the other players within it). Intentions and motives are important in interpreting history, but for judging the fundamental nature of a policy or decision, its actual systemic impacts and results, immediate and longer-range, are decisive.[27]

For the United States in this instance, it means that when one country, without having been attacked or overtly threatened by another, chooses to invade and conquer that country for the purpose of overthrowing and replacing its government and then occupies it for an indefinite period with the aim of determining the kind of government, social system, and economic system that conquered country will have, who will govern it, who will control its natural resources, and what alignments and positions that foreign government will take in regard to vital regional and international questions;

when in addition that invading country rejects international supervision of its actions and essentially insists on controlling the process and the outcome unilaterally, that course of action ipso facto constitutes a bid for empire—informal rather than formal empire, perhaps, but empire all the same.

On this score, it also does not matter whether the advocates of war were sincere or insincere in professing noble aims and disinterested purposes, or how the policy was publicly justified and how the public responded to that justification. None of this is decisive in determining whether a policy was imperialist; the question of the sincerity and genuineness of reasons and motives is often impossible to answer and relatively unimportant. Historically, most imperial ventures and acquisitions have not arisen simply either from deliberate design or from accident and contingency, but usually out of policies and actions chosen for a mix of reasons; the critical point is that the objective became that of acquiring empire. It happened in this instance with the United States, both the government and the people. As often in history, it is probably less important and enlightening to ask what motives and aims drove the United States forward and why they did so, and more important to inquire what restraints should have held it back and why they failed to do so; to concentrate, in other words, not on what caused the United States to choose the course of empire, but on what failed to stop it. But in any case, it is essential for Americans to recognize once and for all that it did choose empire.

The other three arguments—(1) that the argument over empire versus hegemony, like lessons from earlier generally, does not apply to the post-9/11 world; (3) that whether or not the war was a bid for empire, the bid has failed and the effort has been tacitly abandoned, making the warnings against empire outdated and irrelevant; and (4) that debating the war's origins and initial character and purposes is futile and debilitating now that it has merged into a wider struggle that the United States and its allies must fight and win—can be addressed more or less together, even though they diverge and in some ways contradict each other.

Here too the best response is to point out important facts about international politics, historical and current, that they miss. No historian should expect historical evidence, analysis, and analogies to convince people that their strongly held views about recent and current events and future prospects are wrong, especially on so heated an issue as the war in Iraq. History is not suited for that. It cannot offer a single unified and unchallengeable interpretation of the past, much less predict the future. But where history can make a vital contribution to public policy is by performing another task, triage. Armed with some serious knowledge and a sound sense of history, things arguably missing in Americans in general and this administration in particular, one can separate out of the welter of opinions, analyses, and policy options proffered in the public sphere the relatively few that are within the bounds of historical possibility, and by this triage help concentrate attention on those relatively few policy analyses and choices that are rationally defensible.

I hope—probably with the incurable optimism of the incorrigible rationalist—to do such a useful job of triage here, showing that certain premises in arguments (1) and (4) and in a different, lesser way in (3) can be shown to exceed the bounds of historical possibility and that conclusions and policy recommendations based on them should be discarded.

Both arguments (1) and (4) say essentially the same thing: the world has changed so drastically since the late twentieth century and the threats obvious since 9/11 have grown to such dimensions that the United States cannot afford either to be inhibited in its responses by the cumbersome legalistic rules and procedures of the old international system or to accept failure and defeat in Iraq. In short, the United States must prevail in Iraq and in the global war on terror regardless of the rules and whatever the cost. Leave aside here the arguments made by current analysts that these supposedly apocalyptic threats have been exaggerated for partisan purposes,[28] or that US policy has already failed in Iraq, so that continuing it will only make things worse.[29] Let me instead try to draw on history for an answer.

The historical argument here, though it involves comparison and analogy, accepts—indeed, insists—that there have been profound changes in the world's international order and even deeper ones in its economic, social, ideological, and political orders over recent decades. But it cites these changes along with earlier ones in the mid-twentieth century as precisely the main factors that make the Bush Doctrine delusional and unworkable and the US invasion and occupation of Iraq doomed from the outset to long-run failure. It agrees that the global scene has been altered drastically by terrorism and other factors, but claims that these changes are just what make the Bush administration's attempt to revive late-nineteenth to early-twentieth-century imperialist assumptions and act upon them futile and counterproductive, while at the same time they make a rapid return to the late-twentieth-century international order more imperative than ever.

The way to show this, as often holds for historical analysis, is to pose the basic question differently. Instead of debating, as virtually all the current discussion does, just where, when, and why the US venture in Iraq went wrong and what better decisions and measures might have made it succeed or could still enable it to do so, let us ask, "Have any similar ventures in the Middle East succeeded in the past, and if so, what made their success possible?" That question might enable us to escape the endless and futile search for particular decisive errors or turning points and fix on certain general, minimal requirements for success.

Here is where history ought to be useful. If it cannot show exactly why this current venture failed or even prove decisively that it has, it could conceivably provide analogous instances of durable success in the past and analyze what made that success possible and whether those conditions are replicable today. Hence, the particular questions to ask are: "Are there historical examples that indicate the general conditions under which the United States might, starting in 2003, have succeeded in conquering Iraq, restoring order, setting up a government it approved, and then leaving the country to be governed by local administrators, retaining only a small military presence to keep the new government from falling into dangerous hands and to protect US strategic interests? Are there historical examples of prevailing conditions and circumstances in international politics that might have enabled the United States to persuade or compel other members of the international community to accept this outcome of US victory and dominance in Iraq and the region as permanent and legitimate, so that some of them would even help the United States maintain that dominant position? Can history further indicate under what conditions this durable US success in Iraq could help transform the region politically, ideologically, and economically in ways favorable to US interests and acceptable to other major actors in the world? In other words, are there historical instances in which the sort of project the United States undertook in Iraq and still pursues today has enjoyed durable success, indicating what basic conditions might have led or might still lead to US success in this one?"

There certainly are. The two best examples are the successful British suppression of an Arab revolt in Iraq in 1919–1921 and subsequent control of the country, and (my favorite choice here) the British success in occupying and controlling Egypt from 1882 to 1936.[30] The basic story, greatly oversimplified, can be sketched as follows: The British military intervention in Egypt and occupation in 1882 that turned Egypt into a de facto British colony until 1936, developed in a far more hesitant, bumbling fashion, with much less deliberate intent at military conquest and occupation, than that of the United States in Iraq. But analogous motives and fears lay behind it. The chief British concern was strategic (control of the eastern Mediterranean Sea and the route to India through the Suez Canal), but with it also went broader ones—Islamic jihadism already raising its ugly head in the Sudan, dislike of French and other European interference and competition in Egypt and the rest of Africa, and fears for British prestige and the security of the empire, especially in India with its large Muslim territories, should Muslim Egyptians succeed in resisting British pressure.

In any case, when the British government finally decided to go in to restore order in Egypt for the benefit of British strategic security and European bondholders, Prime Minister William Gladstone (like George W. Bush) needed to believe that he had good moral reasons for acting. He found them principally in the menace posed by the leader of the Egyptian resistance, Colonel Ahmed Urabi of the Egyptian army, whom the British denounced as a potential tyrant and terrorist and falsely blamed for atrocities committed against Europeans and Egyptians. Though many in the British government understood that the real reasons were strategic and imperial, the official justification for the venture was to liberate Egypt and restore law and order. Gladstone's long-standing and subjectively genuine slogan of "Egypt for the Egyptians" remained the ostensible British goal.

As with the US experience in Iraq, military victory over the Egyptian forces proved swift and easy, and superficial order was restored in Egypt relatively readily and quickly (unlike in Iraq) because the British enjoyed the aid of a subservient head of state and a Europeanized professional and commercial class willing to serve their new masters. The man placed in charge of Egyptian affairs, Evelyn Baring (later Lord Cromer) was experienced and efficient, the Egyptian authorities for whom British officials served as advisers proved mostly compliant, the Egyptian masses turned out to be inert and apolitical rather than nationalist as feared, and the financial burdens of the British occupation and of protecting British and European financial interests in Egypt and British imperial and strategic interests in the Suez Canal and East Africa were borne by a wretched but powerless Egyptian peasantry.

Thus the internal problems in taking over Egypt were successfully managed. International complications proved more difficult, but ultimately through showing sufficient resolve, the British triumphed—first ignoring France's pressure to regain its former role in the so-called dual control of Egypt, then ignoring and violating Britain's own repeated promises to evacuate Egypt, next using Egyptian forces and treasure to help conquer the Sudan in 1898, then facing down the French in a confrontation in the Sudan immediately thereafter, and finally making a favorable deal with France in 1904 over Morocco and Egypt. All that enabled Britain to shake off the remaining international restrictions on its financial control of Egypt imposed by European bondholders and the international Treasury of the Ottoman Debt that supervised Egypt's debt payments. Thus Britain, despite signs of growing Egyptian restiveness, which were especially evident in 1907, remained in control of Egypt before World War I at little or no cost to itself, and used that control to help it bring most of East Africa from the Cape of Good Hope to Cairo into the British Empire, making friends with France against Germany in the process.

These great successes were possible without provoking an international conflict only because of Britain's especially favorable position within the international system, which at the time maintained general world peace. In the 1880s, Prince Bismarck, Germany's chancellor and the most powerful statesman in Europe, used the Egyptian question for his balance-of-power purposes but would not allow a European war to develop over it or other colonial questions. After his fall in 1890 the continental great powers became locked in a great competition for world power and continental security that Britain was able to exploit for its imperial purposes. This special British advantage, however, was either ignored by British leaders and the public or, if noted, accepted as the natural order of things. The imperial success was ascribed to Britain's power and wealth, the special, universally admired virtues of British imperial authorities and of the British people and their political system, and Britain's indispensable role as leader of the international system. Thus Britain's imperial venture in Egypt proved a great success, outlasting even World War I and promoting a further major expansion of the empire in the Middle East in its aftermath.

This British experience, then, provides us with a good historical recipe for achieving a durable, successful US informal empire in Iraq and the Middle East. The secret is simple: restore the general conditions prevailing in the Middle East and the world during the late nineteenth and early twentieth centuries. That is, eliminate nationalism among Iraqis and Arabs, or at least reduce it to an inchoate, unorganized proto-nationalism; eliminate militant radical Islamist movements and regimes (as the British destroyed the Sudanese one with a British-led Egyptian army in 1898); abolish Iraq and other independent Arab states in the Middle East, returning them to their pre-1914 status as loosely governed backward territories and parts of decaying regimes (the Ottoman Empire and Persia) offering easy prey for Western imperialism; eliminate Israel as a powerful Jewish state established in the midst of Arab lands and perceived as their common enemy and a tool of the United States; eliminate the United Nations, the North Atlantic Treaty Organization, the European Union, and all the other international and transnational institutions and organizations that now interfere with empire building; eliminate the existence and influence of radio, TV, the Internet, and other means of mass communications; eliminate the educated middle and professional classes in the region; reverse the globalization of industry, commerce, science and technology, and culture that has occurred throughout the twentieth century; and finally, restore the general international competition in alliances, arms, and imperialism prevalent in pre–World War I Europe, so that the United States would now find intense rivalries between other great powers it could exploit for its purposes—do these small things, and a similar US venture today might well succeed.

Those who believe that the US strategy toward Iraq and the Middle East could have succeeded with better planning and execution or can still succeed by these means, and those who dismiss the constraints of the existing international system as quaint and obsolete in the face of recent global threats, thus are guilty of precisely what they accuse opponents of doing: living in the past. Out of their reckless ignorance both of the actual conditions in the region and of the historical preconditions for success in any such venture, and their arrogant confidence that US power, resolve, and virtue would sweep away every obstacle, the Bush administration and its followers have led the United States in Iraq and the Middle East not into a bold, forward-looking effort to create a brave new democratic world, but into an attempted revival of late-nineteenth-century imperialism—an imperialism that could succeed for a time then (with ultimately devastating consequences) only because of conditions special to that era, long since vanished and now impossible to imagine reproducing.

Those who defend position (3) are in one respect more realistic. They recognize that the Iraq venture has failed and want it ended with whatever damage limitation is feasible. They conclude, however, that this failure makes further discussion of whether the venture was a bid for empire a useless distraction from the important task, that of getting the United States out of Iraq with a whole skin. That argument, however, is also problematic on practical and historical grounds. It ignores or at least fails to answer the claim made by many that the United States cannot get out of Iraq with a whole skin without a victory and dare not try to do so, since Iraq has now become an inseparable part of a bigger, more fateful struggle that would become much worse and more dangerous if the United States withdrew from Iraq before achieving a satisfactory settlement.

This claim, though it is obviously an attempt by those responsible for the war to escape blame for its consequences and is often made in exaggerated and alarmist fashion, cannot simply be dismissed as empty or foolish. A US withdrawal at a time when the Iraqi government and society are threatened by dissolution and civil war would undoubtedly risk making sectarian violence worse. It could further increase Iran's influence in Iraq and the region, might lead to full-scale civil war, and could possibly promote international conflict and war (e.g., through Turkish armed intervention in northern Iraq, pro-Sunni interventions by Saudi Arabia and others, a Saudi-Iranian conflict, or Sunni-Shiite conflict in other countries). Other ripple effects on terrorism, oil supplies, the world economy, and Muslim-Western relations in general are possible—all this besides at least temporary damage to what remaining prestige and credibility the United States possesses.

This makes the impasse seem complete and hopeless. The United States cannot stay in Iraq with any hope of real success, not only because the occupation has been fatally compromised by manifold failures in planning and execution but even more because the whole enterprise was a bid for nineteenth-century-style empire structurally impossible and unthinkable in the twenty-first century. Every effort to achieve success in it therefore must make things worse in the long run. The United States cannot get out of Iraq, however, because the immediate side effects of withdrawing would be worse than the current problems of staying on and would not extricate it from the wider struggle but drag it further in.

Here, at this point of impasse, the other half of the "empire versus hegemony" argument kicks in. This chapter has focused so far on the "mirage of empire," emphasizing the futility, destructiveness, and structural impossibility of the US bid for it. The other side, the promise and necessity of hegemony, now offers an answer—not a clear, bright, confident one, but the only one available—to the impasse that bid has created. The way out lies in changing the main objective away from either (1) getting out of Iraq and stopping the ongoing loss of US and Iraqi lives and treasure and other collateral damage, or (2) staying on and somehow, anyhow, managing to win the global war on terror by more of the same methods used thus far. Neither of these courses is possible; both are self-stultifying. Instead, the United States needs deliberately to focus its aim on a third alternative: regaining its former position of hegemony in the international community, now gravely compromised and damaged, because recovering that position, necessary and valuable per se both for the United States and the international system, is also the only means likely to help it escape from the morass in Iraq and achieve a sanely defined success (not military victory) in the global war on terror.

Are there historical examples that illustrate and support the notion that a country involved in a war or prolonged struggle that it was not losing but that offered no way to victory or a negotiated exit on tolerable terms, might be able to solve the dilemma by changing its central goal and priority away from the simple alternatives of victory or abandonment of the war to hegemony—that is, to achieving leadership in a coalition genuinely dedicated to reaching joint goals based on consensus?

Yes, there are: the United States did so at certain junctures during the Cold War, and Britain did so vis-à-vis the United States in 1940–1941 before the US entry into World War II. The clearest example, which I will briefly discuss, is the policy Britain followed in the latter stages of the Napoleonic wars, especially in 1811–1814.

As noted, the dilemma the United States faces now is that it can neither win the Iraq War nor get out of it by negotiation. It faces no immediate danger of defeat, but the war's political and economic burdens and costs at home and abroad continue to grow exponentially, at the same time as the consequences of quitting or accepting failure appear intolerable. It was the dilemma that confronted Britain in a vastly more dangerous form from June 1807 on. Its situation was in some respects even worse than in June 1940. Napoleon had just defeated France's last remaining continental foe, Russia, and had drawn Russia over to France's side in the Peace of Tilsit, leaving Britain completely isolated. The British still controlled the seas and could capture colonial prizes and at least hold their own in the economic war waged between Britain and France and its continental empire. But they could make no serious dent on that French empire even after Spanish and Portuguese resistance to Napoleon's takeover in Spain and Portugal gave the British a toehold there. The popular view is that Britain only needed to hold on until a new coalition against Napoleon arose on the continent, provoked by his insatiable ambition, aggression, and exploitation. This view is highly misleading. Austria did rise in 1809, was crushed again, lost all strength and heart for another contest, and joined Napoleon's camp. Prussia was firmly under the French heel, as was all of Western Europe. Even Russia, though it grew restive and broke with Napoleon, feared taking Napoleon on alone, and when its attempts to recruit allies for defense against France failed badly in 1811, the Russian government tried hard to avoid war with France. By 1811, war-weariness was spreading in Britain; the burdens of wartime debt, popular unrest, and industrial and economic problems were growing more serious; further triumphs at sea and overseas seemed pointless; and no real ally was in sight. Even when Napoleon attacked Russia against the advice of almost all his civilian and military advisers, Britons could not be confident that Russia would win or survive. The United States, in contrast to 1940, posed an additional threat, exploiting Britain's difficulties to wring concessions from it and make its own territorial gains, and in 1812, in one of the supreme acts of folly in US history, actually joining the war on the side of Britain's enemies.

How then did Britain finally manage to win? Grit, staying power, determination, economic and naval strength, and some good generalship were all important, without doubt. It also profited from great good luck in the form of Napoleon's fatal strategy in Russia, the ensuing destruction of the Grand Army, and a subsequent unexpected rising that brought Prussia back into the war and enabled Russia to pursue the war into central Europe. Yet all this would not have been enough for final victory had not the British also changed their own strategy. Slowly and painfully, they learned lessons from their first three failed coalitions against the French Republic and Napoleonic empire in 1793–1807 and changed the basic character and style of their war effort. Until 1807 Britain had fought this war against France, as it had others, in the usual British way of war in Europe: using diplomacy, alliances, loans, and subsidies to build continental coalitions that would fight France on the continent with their armies as Britain's proxies, while Britain concentrated on defeating France and its allies at sea, destroying its commerce, and picking up colonies, trade, and strategic strong points round the world. This strategy generally paid off for the British, giving them major naval victories and colonial prizes that cemented their control of all the world's sea lanes, but on the Continent the strategy failed disastrously and created bitter resentment and distrust among Britain's erstwhile allies in Europe.

From 1807 on, Britain's war strategy and tactics changed gradually from those of empire (i.e., exploiting the strategic vulnerability of France's continental neighbors and compelling them to fight and lose while Britain profited) toward hegemony. That meant British leadership based on a genuine British commitment to a common cause with war aims and a strategy jointly defined, as well as British readiness to make an all-out effort and great sacrifices in Europe itself: not simply to win the war for victory's sake, but also to meet the particular war aims and security requirements of its allies in the coalition, regardless of whether these aims benefited Britain or not. Put too simply but accurately enough, British strategy in the final victorious coalition switched gradually from empire building (waging war simply to defeat France and expand the British Empire) to hegemony (leading a wartime coalition that would found a lasting European general peace). The story is far too complicated to relate here, but every aspect of British policy in the final coalition—military, fiscal, economic, and above all political and diplomatic—reflects this fundamental change and helps account for the coalition's success in war and peace.

How this model applies to the US situation in Iraq should be fairly obvious. The basic point has been made by political and military analysts over and over: the United States cannot succeed in Iraq, Afghanistan, and the region until it ceases to go simply for military victory—as if that alone would solve everything—and becomes leader of a genuine coalition, military and political, working for common goals jointly debated and agreed on. The Baker-Hamilton Iraq Study Group's recommendations, assiduously ignored by President Bush, stressed above all the critical necessity of enrolling more Iraqis and all of Iraq's neighbors, including Iran and Syria, in the attempt to stabilize and unite Iraq, and to do so by reconciling all the legitimate needs and requirements of the different groups and countries. Such advice and much more like it simply calls for benign, sensible US hegemony—leadership in a coalition of (this time) the genuinely willing—willing not because they have been pressured or bribed into participating, but because they are persuaded and pulled into cooperation by the prospect of really being heard on the goals and purposes of the coalition, and actually advancing their particular interests as part of a general solution.

It is impossible here to discuss in detail how this goal of recovering US hegemony could be pursued, either in Iraq and the Middle East or the world. One can point to certain prerequisites. The United States would have to disavow frankly and clearly the attitude of "My way or the highway" that has pervaded its approach from the outset. It would have to admit, without groveling about it, that the venture has failed and promise it will not be repeated. It will have to stop using stupid, insulting arguments to justify continuing the war, such as the claim that the war in Iraq is worth it because so long as the terrorists are being fought there they will not come to the United States. What that argument, factually false and foolish per se, clearly implies is that Americans do not care if this war makes life hell for Iraqis, destabilizes the whole Middle East, threatens the regimes of Iraq's neighbors, some of them US allies, and heightens Arab-Muslim outrage and alienation from the West, increasing the danger of terrorism in Europe and elsewhere—just so long as it makes Americans feel safer for now at home. The United States, in sum, will have to get over its remarkable self-absorption and start seeing itself more as others see it, to have any chance of recovering its former leadership.

It is also impossible to predict confidently that even such a good faith effort under new leadership (an obvious prerequisite) would succeed. In more pessimistic moments I fear that the US potential for a beneficial leadership in international affairs has already been fatally compromised by this venture and other follies; at others I feel there is a reasonable chance it could be restored over time and work tolerably well. What one can say with assurance is that a quest for recovery of its former kind of hegemony is the only way to go. For that belief there is striking evidence, astonishingly neglected, in the story of the Iraq venture itself. Almost everyone looks to that story to find what went wrong, leading to failure and disaster, and who was responsible. Few examine the story to see who had it right, whose judgment and recommendations now stand vindicated by events, whose actions, individual and institutional, pointed in the right direction and should have been followed. Everyone, for example, now concedes that the US claim that Iraq had weapons of mass destruction was wrong and argues about why the mistake or deception occurred and who was responsible. No one seems to recall that at that time US allies at the UN, along with Hans Blix and the other UN arms inspectors, had it right. Their judgment was that Iraq might possess some such weapons and might be trying to get more, but that since they did not know for certain and needed more time to find out, the international community should exhaust all other means of finding out and dealing with the problem before using military force. That was sound policy. The United States rejected it.

Similarly, most Americans have now learned that the use of military power to effect regime change, even when that power is overwhelming, technically sophisticated, brilliantly applied, and apparently successful, cannot in itself solve basic political problems but can easily create new ones and make existing ones worse. No one now notices or recalls that many Europeans and others knew this all along and said so, but were brushed aside. These same people also knew and said further that conventional deterrence and containment could work and was actually working in Iraq. Here too they were right and the US government was wrong.

What all this means is that had the United States acted in 2003 as a genuine hegemon in the international community, willing to consult its allies and other vitally interested parties, to listen to their counsel, and to consider their interests in order to achieve a real consensus, this whole tragedy might have been avoided. Cleaning it up now will be very difficult and messy, if it is possible at all, but sane hegemonic leadership within the international community is the only possible road for the United States to follow. A good initial step would be recognizing the empire-versus-hegemony distinction, abjuring further attempts at empire, and acknowledging frankly that the United States failed to act as a responsible hegemon in this instance.

Notes

An earlier version of this chapter appeared as "The Mirage of Empire Versus the Promise of Hegemony," in Paul W. Schroeder, *Systems, Stability, and Statecraft. Essays on the International History of Modern Europe,* edited and with an Introduction by David Wetzel, Robert Jervis, and Jack S. Levy (New York: Palgrave Macmillan, 2004), pp. 297–305.

1. Some examples of arguments for unipolar US world supremacy are Charles Krauthammer, "The Unipolar Moment Revisited"; William Kristol and L. F. Kaplan, *The War over Iraq;* and Robert Kagan, *Of Paradise and Power.* A much more ambitious and outwardly impressive attempt to ground both the US world military and political supremacy and the emergence of what the author calls a "market state" in history is P. Bobbitt, *The Shield of Achilles.* For a critique of the work as history, see Paul W. Schroeder, "A Papier-Maché Fortress.

2. Paul W. Schroeder, "The Risks of Victory: An Historian's Provocation"; Paul W. Schroeder, "Iraq: The Case Against Preemptive War."

3. This was clearly the case with the second British Empire in the late eighteenth, nineteenth, and early twentieth centuries, for example. The famous "imperialism of free trade" thesis of Ronald Robinson and John Gallagher in *Africa and the Victorians* was and remains controversial at many points, but the recognition that British ascendancy in Africa, India, and elsewhere at its height was mainly a matter of informal but recognized dominance, and that the empire actually passed its peak when international competition compelled the British to change to formal rule, has not been overturned. For an excellent analysis and survey of the controversy, see W. R. Louis, ed., *The Robinson and Gallagher Controversy.* For the best introduction to the massive subject and its literature, see W. R. Louis, ed., *The Oxford History of the British Empire* (5 vols.); on "informal empire" see especially vol. 3, *The Nineteenth Century,* edited by Andrew Porter, pp. 8–9, 170–197. For the relative decline of the British Empire in the era of new imperialism as informal empire gave way to more formal rule, see M. Beloff, *Imperial Sunset;* Ronald Hyam, *Britain's Imperial Century, 1815–1914.*

4. To illustrate: Yugoslavia was part of the Soviet satellite empire in Eastern Europe until 1948, when under Marshal Tito it successfully resisted Soviet authority and broke free. Hungary remained part of the empire; its attempt at independence was crushed in 1956. So long as the British were able to keep their chosen ruler of Afghanistan in power in the First Afghan War (1839–1842), Afghanistan was part of the British Empire, as was much of India. When the British were expelled, Afghanistan remained loosely within the British sphere as a buffer against Russia but was no longer under British imperial control.

5. For example, see N. J. Smelser and P. B. Baltes, eds., *International Encyclopedia of the Social Sciences,* pp. 6642–6650; A. G. Johnson, ed., *The Blackwell Dictionary of Sociology,* pp. 141–142. C. J. Nolan, *The Greenwood Encyclopedia of International Relations* is not very helpful on hegemony (vol. 2, pp.

699–700) but rightly stresses political control as the essence of imperialism. So does the famous authority on the structure of empires Shmuel N. Eisenstadt, "Empires," pp. 41–49.

6. The best discussions of hegemony within the modern international system have gained little attention in the Anglo-American literature, perhaps because they come from German historians (Heinrich Triepel, E. R. Huber, and Rudolf Stadelmann) in the Nazi and immediate postwar era, though the basic ideas they present are much older. For a good brief discussion of the relation between hegemony and balance (Gleichgewicht), see O. Brunner, W. Conze, and R. Koselleck, eds., *Geschichtliche Grundbegriffe,* vol. 2, 968–969. For the importance and value of hegemony in political economy, see Robert Gilpin, *The Political Economy of International Relations,* and Charles Kindleberger, *The World in Depression, 1929–1939.*

7. Two examples: Following the British conquest and occupation of Egypt in 1882, Egypt remained technically an autonomous province of the Ottoman Empire with certain residual rights of suzerainty belonging to the sultan. Officially, the British were there only to advise the Egyptian government, and the British government even used the Egyptian government's claims to ownership of the Sudan to carry out a conquest of the Sudan in 1898 with the aid of Egyptian forces and resources (though subsequently denying the Egyptians any control over the Sudan). No one was fooled as to who really ruled Egypt under this arrangement, which also applied in various ways to other parts of the British Empire. Similarly, the Soviet Empire after 1945 included not merely ostensibly sovereign and independent communist states behind the Iron Curtain, but supposedly independent republics within the Soviet Union itself, some of whom had seats in the United Nations. Once again, no one was fooled. Nor were many outside the United States deceived by the absence of formal US rule in Latin America, especially the Caribbean, into denying the reality of US empire through much of the nineteenth and twentieth centuries.

8. R. Stadelmann's definition of hegemony as "guided balance" ("gelenktes Gleichgewicht"—see note 6, above) often applies in history. For example, the relative stability and peace of the Bismarckian era in Europe (1871–1890), frequently attributed simply to the operation of the balance of power, actually would have been impossible without what Andreas Hillgruber aptly described as a labile German half-hegemony and Otto von Bismarck's skillful use of that half-hegemony to devise and impose expedients for managing European crises (Andreas Hillgruber, *Bismarcks Ausenpolitik*). Two excellent accounts of this are Klaus Hildebrand, *Das vergangene Reich,* and G. F. Kennan, *The Decline of Bismarck's European Order.*

9. Again, examples are easy to find: the breakdown of Anglo-French dual control in Egypt (1875–1882), leading to heightened tension and imperial competition in Africa and elsewhere and a serious crisis in 1898, only healed by a clear delimitation of spheres in 1904; or the Anglo-Russian partition of Persia into spheres of influence in 1907, which worked badly and was breaking down by 1914 despite the two powers' shared interest in excluding and blocking Germany, because each side believed the other was interfering in its exclusive sphere and the intervening neutral zone or illegitimately expanding its control. For the Anglo-French contest, see G. N. Sanderson, *England, Europe, and the Upper Nile, 1882–1899.* For the Anglo-Russian one, F. Kazemzadeh, *Russia and Britain in Persia. 1864–1914.*

10. For an example of how dual and shared hegemony can work, I argue in my book *The Transformation of European Politics, 1763–1848,* that peace and stability in the Vienna era (1815–1848) is best explained by the existence and operation of an overall Anglo-Russian shared hegemony in Europe (Britain's in Western Europe and Russia's in Eastern Europe), complemented by the subhegemonies in Central Europe

and Italy enjoyed by Austria and Prussia. France, the great power that felt excluded from its legitimate share of influence in Spain, Italy, and Germany, felt injured and threatened by this even though no serious territorial question, economic stake, or concrete military threat was involved.

11. A. Kohler, *Karl V: 1500–1558.*

12. G. Parker, *The Grand Strategy of Philip II.*

13. R. Bireley, *Religion and Politics in the Age of the Counterreformation;* J. Burkhardt, *Der Dreissig-Jährige Krieg.*

14. F. Bosbach, *Monarchia Universalis;* A. Lossky, *Louis XIV and the French Monarchy.*

15. M. Roberts, *The Swedish Imperial Experience, 1560–1718.*

16. I make the case for this in Paul W. Schroeder, *The Transformation of European Politics.*

17. The attempt by Napoleon's nephew Napoleon III in the 1850s and 1860s to revive French leadership in Europe was nothing like the military imperialism of his uncle. It consisted instead of a series of ill-conceived and badly coordinated initiatives that ended in creating new rivals for France (Italy and Prussia-Germany), alienating possible allies (Britain and Austria), and bringing both Napoleon III and his empire down in disastrous defeat in 1870.

18. A. Kohler, *Das Reich im Kampf um die Hegemonie in Europa, 1521–1648.*

19. K. Malettke, *Frankreich, Deutschland, und Europa im 17 und 18 Jahrhundert;* P. Goubert, *Mazarin.*

20. H. Duchhardt, *Altes Reich und Europäische Staatenwelt, 1648–1806;* A. Schindling, *Die Anfänge des immerwährenden Reichstags zu Regensburg;* K. O. von Aretin, *Das alte Reich,* vol. 1, *1648–1684.*

21. D. McKay and H. M. Scott, *The Rise of the Great Powers, 1648–1815;* J. H. Plumb, *Sir Robert Walpole;* J. Black, *British Foreign Policy in the Age of Walpole;* J. Black, *Natural and Necessary Enemies.*

22. P. Vaucher, *Robert Walpole et la politique de Fleury.*

23. Paul W. Schroeder, "Did the Vienna Settlement Rest on a Balance of Power?"

24. There are many excellent treatments of this, but the best short analysis remains Andreas Hillgruber's *Bismarcks Ausenpolitik.*

25. H. M. Scott, *British Foreign Policy in the Age of the American Revolution;* Isabel de Madariaga, *Russia in the Age of Catherine the Great;* M. G. Müller, *Die Teilungen Polens.*

26. S. Marks, *Illusion of Peace;* Kindleberger, *The World in Depression.*

27. A historical illustration: Napoleon, in engineering the overthrow of the Bourbon dynasty in Spain, installing his own puppet ruler, and sending in his army to occupy Spain in 1808, may genuinely have believed that he was conferring great benefits on Spain and the Spanish people—an end to a feeble, corrupt regime and ruling house; modernization; efficient government; economic revival; liberation from superstition, clericalism, and backwardness; and the like. Though Napoleon's real motives are almost impossible to determine, some Spaniards at the time undoubtedly saw French leadership as a source of enlightenment and reform and were willing to collaborate with a pro-French regime. None of this makes any difference in deciding on the character of this Napoleonic venture. It was by definition imperialist, as the whole Napoleonic adventure in Europe was, and Spanish resistance to it turned the venture into a savage colonial-imperialist war.

28. John Mueller, *Overblown.*

29. For example, Thomas E. Ricks, *Fiasco.*

30. The reason for preferring the latter is that although the Iraq case looks more similar to the present one, it is harder to describe British policy in the Middle East then as a durable success. The occupation of Iraq and especially the connected British administration of its mandate in Palestine were always a burden for Britain, rather than an overall asset, and became increasingly troublesome in the 1930s when other strategic concerns grew more urgent.

5

Statecraft Today: Regional Predicaments, Global Conundrums

Charles F. Doran

Warrants

1. The structure of the international system is competitive and plural, not hegemonic. In particular, no actor (hegemon) is capable of imposing its will on matters internal to the central system of the principal powers.

2. World politics is dynamic; hence power and statecraft are dynamic. Power cycle theory unites the structural (state and system) and behavioral (power and statecraft) aspects of world politics in its single dynamic of power and role. It explains the evolution of systems structure, as well as the concerns of statecraft, via the cyclical dynamic of state "relative" rise and decline.

3. Foreign policy role is the behavioral component of statecraft over which states fight and may find compromise. It is the medium of exchange, or bargaining currency, whereby structural change can be assimilated and world order legitimized. Territorial security itself is nonnegotiable.

Static Versus Dynamic Analyses of World Order

An article by Kenneth Waltz in 1964 on the alleged stability and durability of the bipolar system, together with the critiques and extensions that followed by Karl Deutsch and David Singer, Richard Rosecrance, George Liska, and many others, established a new paradigm of international relations in which the international system itself was argued to determine the stability of world politics.[1] More specifically, the *type* of international system, for example, bipolarity versus multipolarity, was argued to determine the *degree* of world order.

For a variety of reasons, bipolarity was said to be more stable (more peaceful) than multipolarity. Even more incredible for the readers of the time, the bipolar system was thought to be durable (it would last until the end of the century). Systems seemed to be solid, static entities, and therefore durable. The idea that the type of international system would determine the degree of world order was extrapolated from thinking about the balance of power as process. Process occurs inside systems, contributing to the identity of each system. If a balance of power system could determine stability, then so could other systems. Especially important, this paradigm created what is largely a top-down explanation for world order. Different configurations of top-down power within each system chiefly defined the system. That the structure of the system appeared unchanging gave plausibility to the argument that it could determine political stability. The preeminent conclusion was that differences in systemic type were responsible for the varying degrees of stability associated with each static system.

I have proposed a different interpretation of major war and its causation, emerging out of a dynamic understanding of world politics known as power cycle theory.[2] As indicated in the prefatory warrants, power cycle theory rejects the top-down structural assumption that only the leading actor determines world order. And, in contrast to the view that the type of system determines the degree of world order, I propose that the type of system is not the key to understanding the breakdown of world order. At maturity, each system has its own mechanism of world order. There is a sense of assuredness about the direction of power trends and hence confidence in strategic assessment of future security and role. Given this sense of political predictability at maturity, each type of system is about as stable as every other type of system. Each system has its own techniques of order-maintenance and its own equilibrium. But structural change undermines the equilibrium. Adjustment is at its most difficult even as it is most necessary. Disorder ensues during and because of structural transformation.

Structural change thus precedes and causes the change in political stability. Structural change causes war, not the other way round. States move up and down their power cycles in a single dynamic of state and system. Each power cycle includes points of nonlinear change, points where an abrupt, massive, and unpredictable inversion from the prior trend occurs, where the "tides of history" shift for state and system. At these critical points, where political uncertainty is at a maximum, where everything changes structurally and diplomatically, and where the very identity of the members of the central system may be in doubt, the probability of major war is highest.

Power cycle theory thus shifts focus from the type of system and the amount or degree of world order to the period between the collapse of one system and the emergence of a new system (systems transformation). Systems transformation is defined as that interval in which a number of major states pass through critical points on their respective power cycles at about the same time in history. It is this movement between systems where the danger of war is greatest. It is systems transformation that is responsible for the most massive forms of political instability and the largest wars—world war. Why?

This uncertain interval between systems is a problem because the rules of order-maintenance with respect to the new, emergent system have not yet been well established. Old, unresolved problems of world order, long dormant, come to the surface during systems transformation and must be confronted. Yet, old foreign policy roles can no longer be counted on. The old guidelines no longer apply. At issue is the capacity to act in foreign policy. The legitimacy of the new system is still in question. Will statecraft fracture amid the ensuing disequilibrium of massive structural change?

Thus I am not at all surprised at the degree of warfare today. Moreover, since one pole of the bipolar system (the Soviet Union) collapsed, leaving the other pole (the United States) extant, the United States is endowed with military capability substantially greater in amount than that of its competitors and allies. Whether such capability is greater than that required for the role that the United States is expected to assume is unknown, for this new system is still untested. Though not essentially unstable, the system in its present phase is quite turbulent. How will it deal with the unresolved problems of world order? Maturity of system cannot be expected to occur immediately, since the system is emerging from one of the greatest systems transformations in its history, the transformation away from bipolarity where things were done so very differently.

Leadership Within the International System

The Static Interpretation

According to the static, neorealist understanding of world politics, bipolarity ended in 1991 and a new system emerged called unipolarity or, more ambiguously, "hegemony." The logic of this analysis seemed unimpeachable. If two poles constitute bipolarity, and one of them (the Soviet Union) disappears or is transformed, then what is left must be a single pole, or unipolarity. By elimination, all other possibilities apparently have been negated. Given the absolute increases in US military power between 1985 and the present, and the reductions in manpower and military spending in Russia, Europe, and Canada, the notion of hegemony appeared more and more plausible. No one could match US military might. The old static system was bipolarity; the new static system was labeled US hegemony.

The Dynamic (Power Cycle) Interpretation

In contrast to the static, neorealist interpretation, the dynamic interpretation emphasizes two considerations. First, the change between systems is not instantaneous; it takes time to evolve from one type of mature international system to another. Moreover, uncertainty is great. The question is, how uncertain and how unstable is the process of systems transformation from bipolarity to the new emergent system?

Second, the argument that, when one pole of the bipolar system (the Soviet Union) collapses, unipolarity inevitably emerges as the only possible alternate systemic outcome is incorrect. Because international politics is dynamic, many other things could have changed, and did change, in the interim between 1991 and the present that altered the nature of the resulting structure. Europe continued to unify and enlarge. China continued to ascend its power cycle incrementally. Japan began to reconsider its security situation. Other governments such as India (nuclear weapons) and Brazil (trade) adopted policies with an impact on the central system. The onset of a new form of international terrorism, and of virulent Islamic fundamentalism, swept parts of the Middle East. The new, static structure of the international system may or may not have reflected these changes. The dynamic power cycle approach was indubitably sensitive to these alterations and nuances of structural metamorphosis.

Rather than documenting all the changes each state in the central system has undergone in the last decade, I here briefly summarize the changes affecting the US power cycle, which are perhaps sufficiently instructive of the character of this structural transformation.

The level of power. In keeping with the static view, the dynamic view holds that the United States in terms of level of power, both economically and militarily, is by far the strongest actor in the system. But in sharp contrast to the static view, the dynamic view holds that the United States peaked in (overall) relative power terms around 1970, and in the 1980s entered nascent, slow, relative decline. Some slippage occurred despite the reality that the United States remained first in overall level of relative national capability.

The trajectory of power. An analyst might therefore rightly conclude that the trajectory of US relative power was trending downward, although at what rate is still open to question. However, what is not in question is that by the 1990s a number of things happened to alter both the trajectory and the rate of change in US power, strikingly so. Remember that one must think about this dynamic as a ratio in which the power of State A (here, that of the United States) is in the numerator, and the power of State A plus the power of the other states in the central system is in the denominator. Two large changes took place, monumentally affecting the trajectory of US relative power.

First, in the denominator of the US power ratio, the collapse of the

Soviet Union did transfer a great deal of power to the United States since it was the only other actor in the system with global reach, and therefore the only actor with the capacity to employ fully this transfer. Second, in the numerator of that ratio, two changes of importance occurred. The legacy of the Reagan military buildup, financed by borrowing from the most efficient capital market in the world (combined with the advantage that the world used the US dollar as its key currency), drove absolute US military power upward. Also, the information revolution, notwithstanding its "bubble" character, and the reform of US corporations toward greatly enhanced efficiency, suddenly increased US overall total factor productivity and economic growth. The combined effect of change in both the denominator and numerator of the power ratio meant that US power reversed its decline of the prior decade, a remarkable achievement.

In sum, by the beginning of the twenty-first century, the trajectory of US power was higher than was expected, based on a straight-line extrapolation from the data points of the 1980s. Since the power cycle is a fitted curve, the new data points tugged the slope of the power curve upward. Relative US capability now appeared to have recovered, if not to the levels of 1965–1970, at least to a level that was more positive. The trajectory of US power had shifted. What was the effect of all of this dynamic structural change on US foreign policy behavior and attitude?

What we know historically about governments that have undergone such a far-reaching, abrupt shift in power trajectory is that they acquire a new optimism about their foreign policy role. They become buoyant, if not euphoric, about their place in the system and their prospects. They are prepared to assume foreign policy risks that they would not have assumed given their earlier downward relative power trajectory.

According to this dynamic interpretation of the changes on the US power cycle, the decision to assume new major responsibilities in Afghanistan and in Iraq following the shock of the attacks on September 11, 2001, is not at all surprising. That many foreign policy analysts would interpret US power to be that of a hegemon *capable* of doing almost anything in world affairs, also is not unanticipated—although, as I argue below, it is not a theoretically valid conception of this or any international system since its origin.

In any case, change in the US relative power trajectory induced the United States to once again assume a larger foreign policy role, notwithstanding the reality that the United States had already peaked in relative power terms in the latter half of the twentieth century. The newer, higher trajectory of US relative power encouraged the United States to strike out aggressively against terrorism and against a hostile ideology in Iraq, even though the preemptive character of that fight was not comprehensible to certain other governments. The uptick in US power encouraged the United

States to act militarily and gave it confidence in the Middle East with respect to a very encompassing vision of what was needed to sustain world order. Was this vision too assertive? Did the United States have the economic capability and the political endurance to try to rebuild an entire region of the Middle East in its own image, and all alone? To what extent was this action a "legitimate" foreign policy role?

The United States and Hegemony

Is the United States a hegemon? Although each of the propositions, yes or no, can be wrong, they cannot possibly both be right. If one is right, the other must be wrong. But which is which?

The Claim That the United States Is a Hegemon

That is a claim upon which both the critic of "US hegemony" and the proponent insist. Charles Krauthammer urges the United States to take advantage of the "unipolar moment."[3] William Wohlforth holds that the system is unambiguously unipolar.[4] Paul Kennedy, in the *Financial Times,* argues that the United States is the most powerful state since the Roman Empire. Chris Layne writes that the United States is so powerful that its membership in the North Atlatnic Treaty Organization (NATO) "perpetuates US hegemony" and serves to "thwart European strategic and diplomatic independence."[5] Niall Ferguson implores the United States to transform this hegemony into true empire.[6] Assuming US hegemony as fact, some analysts argue in support, others in criticism.

The Claim That the United States Is Not a Hegemon

Kenneth Waltz notes that Iraq should not be used as an indicator of US military prowess since, militarily, Iraq's expenditures were approximately 1 percent as large as those of the United States, and Iraq was only one-half as powerful as it once was in 1991.[7] Evidence persuasively presented elsewhere is that Iraq was already in relative decline by the time of Saddam's invasion of Kuwait.[8] Moreover, John McCain and others suggested in late summer of 2003 that additional US troops, and troops from other countries, were needed in Iraq beyond the more than 100,000 that were already deployed there. The decision in the summer of 2007 to commit to a "surge" of increased troop deployment in one last attempt to restore order in Iraq before a more complete handover of power reflects tactical necessity. But the counter-argument is heard that a continued deployment would strain the US military presence elsewhere in the world.[9] The administration of George W. Bush also requested new multinational military support from the United Nations. The amount the United States is currently spending on the military security of Iraq vastly exceeds the oil revenues obtainable annually from Iraq. Independent of these Iraq-related considerations, economic studies have shown that the United States is borrowing at an overall rate that is not sustainable.[10] These economists say that either the US government must significantly reduce expenses or find new revenue.[11] Otherwise, future generations will be swamped by debt.

* * *

How can these two hugely divergent interpretations of US power and foreign policy role be reconciled? Both cannot be right. If the United States is a hegemon, it does not need to worry about the problem of finding UN troops to multilateralize the operation in Iraq. It does not need to concern itself with the gap between financial costs and receipts in Iraq. It does not need to agonize over intergenerational debts that within decades are expected to outstrip receipts by $44 trillion.[12]

Conversely, if these challenges are genuine and recognizable, then why is US power being described in such extravagant terms? If the United States is a very large but ordinary power facing limits on its capacity, not so much on its capacity to defend itself and its allies but on its capacity to impose its conception of politics on recalcitrant rogue states and otherwise to act as a hegemon—then why are so many analysts exaggerating its capabilities? Perhaps this puzzle, about whether the United States is or is not a hegemon, does have an answer.

Leadership Is Not Hegemony

It goes without saying that if important action is to be taken in the present international system, the United States must take that action. The United States must not just resort to vetoing the actions of others. It must take a positive lead.[13] But taking the lead, and attempting to act like a hegemon, are two very different kinds of roles.[14] Much confusion exists, for example, regarding multilateralism and unilateralism.

For one thing, hegemony—that is, acting alone (unilateralism) despite the preferences of most of the other leading governments in the system—requires huge military and economic power, and a lasting and iron will. The concept of hegemony goes beyond Leopold von Ranke's notion of a "great power" that must be able to "stand alone," for that merely implies the capacity to prevail militarily in defensive terms against any and all comers.[15] Hegemony implies that the actor can in military terms impose its will on issues involving the active projection of force when others disagree. A contested military intervention is an illustration of this principle. Hegemony implies even more in power terms than this. It implies that the government undertaking such ventures has the political stamina and the economic wherewithal to maintain order and to restore the material basis of a society after intervention has occurred.

Historically, every effort at hegemony has started as military intervention to right wrongs and to establish new order. Initially, for instance, Napoleon was greeted in the German provinces as a liberator. Beethoven would dedicate the *Eroica* symphony to Napoleon the hero and the liberator. But very soon the isolated interventions became a military campaign. A balance of power rose up against the "liberator" who in the eyes of opponents had become an occupier. By that time, Beethoven had torn up his dedication.

Every effort at hegemony has also met ruinous failure, failure, that is, for the would-be hegemon, and indeed horrible desolation for the other members of the system who became locked in a war to oppose hegemony.[16] On no fewer than six occasions of catastrophic systems transformation has the world been convulsed in the largest and most extensive of wars. During each of these intervals of history, these wars followed simultaneous passage through points of nonlinearity when everything changes in structural terms in the power cycles of a number of the preponderant states.[17] The history of the modern state system can describe the outcome of these terrible intervals as a "success" in that the decentralized nation-state character of the system has been maintained. Universal empire of the sort that was Rome has been eluded. But the price in human and material terms attached to victory has been prodigious on behalf of that decentralization and pluralism.

In reflecting upon the future of world order, we must consider how a mature, long-term equilibrium can emerge. First, according to Hans Morgenthau, one of the most common mistakes in statecraft is, out of fear, to mistake "a policy of the status quo for a policy of imperialism."[18] But if other governments mistake an effort by a state with the greatest power in the system to be that of imperialism, this misperception will evoke a reaction.[19] In instances of imperialism or even perceived imperialism, the most likely reaction is coalition formation and a triggering of the balance of power. The balance of power can be consciously implemented. Otherwise, as in the fall of 1939, in the face of overt aggression, the response will be automatic. John Owen asks why the balance of power has not shifted against the United States.[20]

The answers are several. First, threat and power are different; both must be present to elicit balance. For some in Europe and Asia, the democratic liberalism associated with the US image helps to soften any sense of threat. None of the major powers feels that its interests are sufficiently threatened by US military preponderance to take part in a full-fledged balancing effort. Second, William Wohlforth, Robert Kagan, and others are correct that the disparity of military difference between the United States and its nearest competitor is large and not easily bridged. But power is complex, involving will, societal unity, ideology, and differences in what money is spent on, in strategy, and in tactics, all of which may offset gross power differences in strictly financial terms. Third, the process of balancing is arcane and may be ongoing, in a nascent way, without widely being perceived as such.

Normally, balancing works in stages. First, the other members of the system refuse to cooperate with the state they think threatens them. Next, they quietly begin to subsidize proxy states with sub-rosa military assistance to be used against the interests of the predominant state. (In a September 2003 visit to Bush's Texas ranch, Putin reminded his listeners at a press conference that Russia could have chosen the course of subverting the effort in Afghanistan and Iraq but did not. Was this a threat?) They form an explicit coalition or alliance against the state they fear. Finally, if all else fails as a deterrent, they may put military force into the breech to oppose directly the state they suspect of military imperialism. What skeptics regarding the balance of power forget is that the defensive use of power is much easier to employ than the projection of power.[21] What they must understand is that in the face of aggravated imperialism, the balance of power will balance.

The second reason the balance of power has not shifted against the United States has to do with what kind of relationship is likely to emerge in the twenty-first century between the changing structure of the international system and world order. Over time, from the power cycle perspective, the much smaller states at the bottom of the central system, such as China and India, will take power share away from the much bigger states at the top of the system. This has already happened to Japan, forcing it to peak in relative power terms. Through power diffusion, actors can take power share away from a dominant state or states. Hence, power share will once again continue to shift away from the United States as well.

Thus, to maintain world order while not triggering a balance of power against itself, the United States must sustain a coalition around itself. Accomplishing that will take great persistence and skill. As the century proceeds, the task will become more difficult. As the equality of the great powers becomes more pronounced, a true multipolar system will in time begin to form.

Meanwhile, three monumental questions confront statecraft today: Can the great alliance systems composed of NATO on one wing of the United States and Japan on the other wing be preserved? Can the current unipolar system reach maturity in which the United States learns to work with other governments to establish a kind of equilibrium of power and foreign policy role that is regarded as legitimate by the leading members of the international system? Can the United States and other like-minded governments cope with the state-supported terrorism and the proliferation of the weapons of mass destruction—chemical, biological, and nuclear—in such a fashion that the very foundation of this new order can be preserved?

Pluralism Contra Hierarchy

The hegemonic leadership conception of world order is the most prevalent alternative to the balance of power in the recent literature. Finding some support in the earlier writings of E. H. Carr, a number or academic writers argue that each peaceful period of history is characterized by the "hegemony" of a single state—a Pax Britannica or a Pax Americana—that creates and maintains the system of rules and benefits.[22] Bertrand Russell's vision of future peace invokes such a notion: "The preponderant Power can establish a single Authority over the whole world, and thus make future wars impossible."[23] However, this depiction of international politics simply does not correspond to historical reality. Ludwig Dehio, for example, wrote of repeated attempts at hegemony, not realized hegemony.[24] In fact, a single power never in the past established "Authority" in the central system of states (whatever may have happened outside the central system, among colonies, and so on), nor could it today.

Worse, as Joseph Nye observes, the hegemonic thesis exaggerates the sense of present decline for principal states that are led to believe in some now-lost mystical past in which they alone established the rules of trade or of world order.[25] It also inflates the hostility and the aspirations of potential rivals (see next section), who are encouraged to dream of singular predominance. In a word, these notions of hegemony distort.

At least since the Holy Roman Empire under Charlemagne, no individual state dominated any international system. On the contrary, power has always been shared. Four and one-half centuries ago, a full century before Thomas Hobbes and probably with more societal impact, John Calvin warned of the dangers of tyranny and of world empire. "No person is competent to rule the whole earth." The pretensions to universal empire, thought Calvin, were "utterly absurd."[26] Pluralism is the very gist of the modern state system. Single states could control regions or peripheries. Britain and later the United States employed navies for localized peacekeeping and to ensure freedom of movement on the high seas. However, this is a far cry from military predominance in the central system where the essence of world order is determined.

Indeed, all the major wars have been fought to preserve national autonomy and the decentralized character of the nation-state system. As indicated in the previous section, aggressors, made abruptly aware of their decline during systems transformation, have struck out against others in an attempted hegemony and have been beaten back by force. Hence, the hegemonic theories assert just the opposite of reality. States coalesce in opposition to attempted hegemony, not in response to an effort to defend purported hegemony. Hegemony and the idea of the balance of power, indeed of pluralism, are utterly at odds. In the conduct of diplomacy, it is well to remember this dynamic and the limits of coercive power.

Hence, the notion of hegemony, at its structural and policy essence, attempts to reorganize systems along the lines of hierarchy.[27] "Anarchy"—the decentralized nature of the system that corresponds to a pluralism of actors and relations—would be exchanged for a more rigid top-down kind of systemic organization. In such a hierarchical system of organization, State C at the bottom of the system is made dependent upon State B at the regional level. And State B at the regional level is made dependent upon State A, the hegemon, at the top of the central system of states. This hierarchical form of organization is regarded by proponents as more stable than a system of balance among pluralistic units contending for a foreign policy role. Control is the theme of hierarchical organization. How much power is required to sustain such a vertical structure of political control has never been estimated, either historically or contemporarily, since such a vertical hierarchy has never existed in the history of the modern state system.

The only place where hierarchical organization of the type imagined for systems-wide hegemony has actually existed is within the great colonial empires. Hence the attribution to Britain of hegemony in the nineteenth century applies to its colonial empire, but not otherwise. The proponents of hegemony confuse the existence of hierarchy and hierarchical organization within the colonial spheres with the existence of inequality (mere hierarchical order) within the central international system. They confuse mere hierarchical ordering with hierarchical organization. Hierarchical organization has never existed within the central international system, the core of which for most of the modern period since 1559 at least has been located on the continent of Europe. Never has any single country—not the Hapsburgs, not Louis XIV, not Napoleon, and certainly not Britain—dominated the Continent in hegemonic terms.

Hence the attempt to create structural hierarchy would be a struggle to transform the horizontal, pluralistic, decentralized nation-state system into something that it is not and never can be. Hierarchy and pluralism are antithetical. A study of the cycles of state power and role reveal that the changing structure of the system itself operates against the assumption of a hierarchy of power and role and in favor of an understanding based on a perpetual, dynamic competition among nations.

Imbalance of Power

Every international system contains an imbalance of power across states, less or more. In the present international system, the problem is not that the

United States has too much power and that other states have too little. If anything, in economic terms the United States is struggling to do the things in security, the fight against terrorism, foreign assistance, and economic reconstruction that other states envision for it, encourage, and expect. The key is not a problem imposed by the existence of an imbalance of power per se across states. The key is in how foreign policy role is defined relative to power.[28]

The problem for contemporary world politics is that some members of the European system aspire to a larger foreign policy role than their current power justifies. This European unhappiness with its present role is illustrated by the desire of the France of Jacques Chirac to "handcuff" US power so as to try artificially to bolster its own. It is illustrated by the opinion poll results in Germany that reveal that 70 percent of the respondents would like the European Union (EU) to become a "superpower." The problem for Europe (and therefore for the system) is that its military capability is very far from measuring up to its lofty aspirations for foreign policy role. Frustration results.

For world order to be regarded as "legitimate," and for any associated frustration to be at a minimum, the key is that the resulting array of state power levels and foreign policy roles must over time be in (dynamic) equilibrium. Despite membership in a central system that inevitably, at every point in time, is highly unequal in terms of power, do states acknowledge the existence of an overall equilibrium of power and foreign policy role across the membership? Is that equilibrium of power and role capable of overcoming the mere fact of an imbalance (difference) of power among states? A hypothesis offered here is that either continental European power must increase in absolute terms, or its role aspirations must decrease.

Protest over the Iraq Intervention

Because the role adopted by the United States was allegedly seen as illegitimate by states such as France, Germany, Russia, or Canada, the US intervention in Iraq was controversial. The US intervention in Liberia and the French intervention in the Democratic Republic of Congo were seen as legitimate by the other members of the Group of Eight, for example, partly because of diplomatic circumstance, partly because of geography, and partly because of the alleged stakes involved (i.e., the absence of oil), whereas Iraq met none of these criteria. Likewise, the multilateral approach to diplomacy involving North Korea, though highly uneven as to initiative and influence, was seen as legitimate largely because of the multiple participants and the apparent lack of force involved. Imbalances of power are a reality. How foreign policy role is therefore distributed across these imbalances is key.

Why a number of leading governments protested so vigorously the actions of Britain and the United States in Iraq is a pertinent question. Because, potentially, so many other competing explanations exist to account for the protest of these largely European governments, the claim of illegitimacy must be scrutinized carefully.

First, it is well to recognize that Britain *and* the United States both contributed substantial forces and together planned and staged the intervention. It was conspicuously not an action by the United States alone, belying the accusations that the United States was an out-of-control hegemon acting by itself, a rogue state of sorts.

Second, the matter of oil cannot be hidden or disregarded. If Iraq had not possessed the second-largest known pool of oil in the world, France, Germany, and Russia might have adopted a much less critical posture toward the Anglo-American intervention. These governments were perhaps less concerned about the legitimacy of the intervention, or about foreign policy unilateralism, than they were about being shoved out of a lucrative oil market that under the prior Iraq government they had enjoyed and undoubtedly expected in the future to enjoy. That Britain and the United States were home to a number of prominent oil corporations did not lessen this oil-based criticism, however misplaced in a global market these fears of exclusion are.

Third, whether the goal of the intervention (i.e., replacing Saddam Hussein with a more open government) or the means (i.e., preemption) was more odious to these governments is not clear. That Saddam Hussein's government itself was hardly politically legitimate surely ought to have had a bearing on this matter of legitimacy of international roles, though there is no evidence that the political legitimacy of his regime ever figured into discussions of the intervention by the critics. Preemption as a doctrine certainly met deep resistance from many circles, and with justification, if preemption qua doctrine was conceived of as a foundation of world order rather than just as an isolated act of self-help. But whether the European opposition was founded more on a rejection of the means of the Iraq intervention or of the ends remains uncertain.

Fourth, much prescient opposition to the intervention had little to do with any of the so-far-assessed criteria of judgment and much more to do with the anticipated low likelihood of success, not of the military intervention itself, but of the broader goals of the intervention involving the proposed democratic transformation of the society and of the capacity to maintain order and unity and to govern in a post-Saddam regime. For these experts, the delta between the Euphrates and the Tigris Rivers was rocky ground indeed for planting the flower of democracy. If these latter aspects of the intervention were not successful, whatever the merits of intervention per se, the overall intervention could not be regarded as a success. Yet whatever doubts the European opponents of the Iraq intervention may have had, these operational criticisms did not seem to register in the critical statements of the governments. They preferred to remain on the moral high ground of conviction that the military element of the intervention was unjustified.

Fifth, according to some analysts, international legitimacy of roles had less to do with French objections than fear that the United States, with its appeals for foreign policy support, was undermining the political legitimacy of the European Union. The US intervention was hateful because it exposed fissures in the European Union that France and Germany preferred to think were not there. According to these analysts, President Chirac exchanged trans-Atlantic unity for intra-European unity. His was a calculated strategic choice in which anti-Americanism was the principal lubricant. Resentment of the US intervention occurred because it had caused him so much trouble regarding preservation of the myth of foreign policy unity inside Europe (if not inside France, where the bonus of the strategy was that the French electorate adored his expression of anti-Americanism). President Nicolas Sarkozy adopted a much more acceptable tone in noting that the arrogance of the condemnation was misplaced, without denying a difference of view regarding the wisdom of the intervention.

Sixth, if legitimacy of international role is the primary justification for the European critique, then the more than titular support of Spain, Poland, Australia, and quite a number of other governments must be considered. How many governments must record their vote before legitimacy is legitimacy, is a puzzling question. But to the extent that a number so record their support for intervention, the legitimacy of the resulting interventionary role must be regarded at least as partial.

In sum, so many competing explanations exist regarding why a number of the leading governments in the system opposed the Anglo-American intervention in Iraq that the hypothesis of "illegitimacy" must be submitted to deeper scrutiny. Is the role of the United States in terms of world order and the role of other governments in support of that order illegitimate? Is power and role within the international system out of sync and therefore problematic for international political equilibrium? These are the questions to which we will return.

Unilateralism, Multilateralism, and Foreign Policy Role

Hegemony and unilateralism, while superficially attractive when looked at in terms of flexibility and the ease to act, also possess very high opportunity costs in terms of what is lost to, or given up by, the government pursuing such action. Hegemony and unilateralism also possess very high opportunity costs in terms of foreign policy role.

Over long periods of time, changes in role tend to follow changes in power. In the short term, many aberrations may occur in foreign policy role relative to power. For example, although Prussia was much the smallest and poorest of the European great powers, Frederick the Great rarely missed an opportunity to try to assert the Prussian role on the European stage. Conversely, the United States in 1885 was probably the equivalent in raw power to any nation in Europe, yet the United States continued to follow the admonitions of George Washington's Farewell Address and the Monroe Doctrine and "stayed out of European quarrels."[29] But at least in a well-equilibrated system—and even in some like the early-twentieth-century international system that are not—these aberrations tend to average out in the longer term.

When hegemony is sought, whether or not power and role are in sync, the opportunity costs associated with foreign policy role are sharply etched. If the leading actor in the system tries to behave like a hegemon and do all the heavy lifting itself, other governments are likely to believe that it is acting only in its own interest and not primarily or significantly in the interest of worldwide order.[30] Because it has assumed a foreign policy role not in conjunction with their preferences but despite their preferences, they will interpret the leading actor's role to be that of self-interest. To them, unilateralism looks like self-interest rather than community-wide interest. They may be forgiven if they assume that the reason the leading state neglected to include them in the initial decisionmaking about an intervention, for example, was that the foreign policy objective at stake seemed to correspond more to the leading state's interest rather than to their own.

If power and role are in sync, and the leading actor embarks on a controversial intervention unilaterally, that actor will be accused of arrogance. If power and role are not in sync, role substantially exceeds power, and the state carrying out the intervention is unable to do so successfully or without the eventual support of other governments in some capacity, the state will be looked upon as imprudent and as having overreached itself. Moreover, the other major powers will scarcely be in the mood to offer much assistance, for example, in terms of help with peacekeeping.

In contrast, multilateralism, whatever its shortcomings in terms of decisiveness and immediacy, contains the advantage that the roles of the various major powers look consonant. Each government, of course, will have its own interest in shifting the outcome of the debate. But multilateralism possesses the advantage that the leading state, even though it will exercise preponderant influence over the outcome, will be seen as acting in the interest of the global community and not just in its own idiosyncratic preference.

Europe

Britain practiced the same policies throughout the nineteenth century in a strategy dubbed "splendid isolation." Britain sought to influence politics on the Continent by associating itself with a coalition, usually the weaker coalition, so as to discourage aggression and therefore to prevent a land war on the Continent that Britain was unprepared to fight. This strategy also fit well with British naval strength that could be used most successfully on the margins of the central system between mother country and colonies. Far from dissociating itself from politics in the central system, as the term "splendid isolation" might suggest to the unwary reader, this strategy involved very active and very sensitive monitoring and alliance interaction.

Given that the United States finds itself in a very similar place on its power cycle, American conservatives see this former British policy as meaningful for the kind of foreign policy that the United States should be following in Asia and the Middle East today. A strategy of modified deterrence fits nicely with an overall balance of power strategy, even in an age of proliferation of weapons of mass destruction.[31]

Europeans, regardless of political party or ideological affiliation, fall into two categories: those who think of their own policies as an extension of European Union interests (e.g., Gerhard Schroeder and Jacques Chirac), and those who think of their foreign policy as essentially an extension of the individual nation-state (e.g., Tony Blair, Jose Maria Aznar, Silvio Berlusconi, Nicolas Sarkozy, and Angela Merkel). Thinking about foreign policy as an extension of European Union interests almost necessarily inflates the aspirations of the policymaker regarding the role a government believes it should and can play in world politics. More particularly, thinking in terms of Europe-wide foreign policy encourages the policymaker to believe that the United States should take that policy far more seriously than if it were offered only as the foreign policy of an individual state. And should that policy clash with US policy, the European policymaker who conceives of foreign policy in Europe-wide terms is likely to be far more perturbed with the United States if it seems to be going its own way. There will be much more of a propensity to brand the US approach as "unilateral" if the policymaker is thinking of its own foreign policy as "Europe-wide" than if the policy were merely an expression of its own national will.

To the extent that the Western analyst thinks in liberal terms of concerts of cooperating democracies, the notion of a European-wide foreign policy seems to fit right in.[32] Building a concert ought to be easier if the base for such a concert has already been constructed in Europe.[33] Inevitably, however, the concert approach is likely to be characterized by lowest common denominator thinking because that is the only way such a policy can be "concerted." The concert approach, partially for reasons of strategic preference, partially for reasons of political necessity, will also be more response-oriented than initiative-oriented. The concert approach, especially among democracies, lends itself better to deterrence (because of the need to find consensus) than to the more controversial policies of either preemption or preventive war.

A balance of power approach can work at either level, the nation-state or the European level.[34] But the outcome of the Iraq debate reveals that for trans-Atlantic relations, much is at stake in balance of power terms. In the jocular-yet-earnest reference by Secretary of Defense Donald Rumsfeld about "Old Europe" and "New Europe," the US side and the European side were exchanging not so much blows but visions. At some point in the events leading up to the Anglo-American decision to intervene in Iraq, President Chirac decided that to save a united Europe and his relationship with Germany, he had to sacrifice trans-Atlantic relations and his association with the United States. We do not know how labored and painful this decision was for him and his government. France is one of two quintessential "balance of power" states in contemporary world politics. When circumstances shift, France may become the United States' most vocal ally. Not so then. That the decision to oppose was similar to the US decision in Suez in 1956 opposing the Anglo-French-Israeli intervention in Egypt against Gamal Abdul Nasser regarding the Suez Canal is clear. Whether the French-German decision to sacrifice trans-Atlantic relations for intra-European unity is as climatic for world politics as the US Suez decision cannot yet be determined. The Suez decision ended the European empire in the Middle East. Will the French-German decision begin an Anglo-US empire east of Suez, ending broad-based trans-Atlantic cooperation? That is unlikely.

But in another sense the French-German decision was definitive. On matters of foreign policy outside Europe, the two governments will act together; their ties with the United States are less strong. If "blood [kinship] is stronger than water," France and Germany were confirming their new kinship. By elimination, their relationship with the United States, across the ocean, is that only of water, much weaker.[35] Britain, this time, confirmed just the opposite expression of kinship in its relationship with the United States. The English Channel once again is a mightier barrier than the Atlantic Ocean when it comes to English relations with the Continent, at least on matters of worldwide diplomacy involving the remnants of the British Empire. Prime Minister Gordon Brown has sought a more intermediate role once again for British diplomacy.

Looking to the future, the central question is, would the United States continue to support European integration, or had these events so soured US confidence in Europe that it would turn against the European project because it saw the project as less about peace, security, economies of scale, and greater economic efficiency, and more about brutal power politics in which Europe would conceivably make a bid for a full and equal role with the United States on the world stage, including a security role? Which role would the United States see for Europe, and how would the United States respond to European integration given that perception; as a sympathetic if somewhat chastened supporter or as a disappointed and increasingly adamant opponent?[36]

With whom the European interlocutor is talking determines the answer. For the liberal, the answer is simple and quite emphatic. Although each democracy possesses its own interest, on important matters of security and foreign policy they ought to act together as a concert. A single democratic Europe is no different than a Europe of many democracies. European integration is and always has been in the US interest for reasons of common security and global prosperity. For the liberal, nothing has changed.

For the US neoconservative, the question about the US perspective toward European integration is really beside the point. Because of internal divisiveness, Europe is never really going to achieve a single foreign policy and defense policy. Given fundamental differences of national interest, according to the neoconservative, each government will jealously cling to its own foreign policy autonomy. Poland is an illustration.

No country in Europe is more aware of its trade and commercial dependence on the European Union for its future economic viability than Poland. Yet like other Central European states, Poland has just undergone a most wrenching century. First it was invaded twice by German armies. Then it was trampled upon and occupied by the Soviet Union for more than four decades. Squeezed between two hugely powerful states, Germany and Russia, Poland looks outward to the United States as the moderator and source of long-term security. Poland and other states with similar interests want the United States to remain in Europe because they do not believe that France will ever be able to put together a European-only framework of security that is durable and completely reliable.

Given these realities, the European Union will be of importance in economic matters, although the neoconservative tends to see these negotiations too as a matter of bargaining between coalitions. Just as the global system is composed of shifting coalitions of states, with the United States at the center, so Europe on foreign policy matters looks like a region composed of discernable coalitions of states that will vary their allegiance depending upon the issue at stake. Regarding the "European role" in world politics, the US neoconservative sees not so much a single role, as roles that will vary and change as the structure of the system changes and as each specific problem of security is redefined.

For the US conservative, the matter of the US perspective on European integration is once again quite different. The US understanding is likely to be shaped in large part by the chosen actions of the Europeans. On the one hand, the conservative observes that the needs of economic efficiency and economies of scale have long since been met by the Group of Eight (Canada, France, Germany, Italy, Japan, Russia, the United Kingdom, and the United States) or by the Group of Twelve (which actually consists of thirteen countries: Australia, Belgium, Canada, France, Germany, Italy, Japan, Netherlands, Spain, Sweden, Switzerland, United Kingdom, United States). The Fifteen or the Twenty seem like overkill. But the conservative also sees the difference between the European Union of increasingly unified, efficient, and productive economic actors, and a NATO of an approximately similar number of states that is principally responsible for security in the North Atlantic. When the conservative lifts the phone, to paraphrase Henry Kissinger, he still hears no answer with respect to security from Brussels. He must phone Berlin, London, or Paris. That does not mean that Berlin, London, and Paris do not talk to each other about common security interests, yet seemingly these common interests often stop at the continental edge.

For the conservative, the role that Europe (read: some circles in France) expects of Russia is intriguing. A Europe united with Russia on security matters in opposition to the United States would of course be quite a factor in world politics. But the conservative does not rush to judgment regarding the likelihood of such an arrangement. Russia is and always will be as much an Asian power as it is a European power. Given this geographical and strategic necessity, its interests are always going to be much broader and more bifurcated than those of Europe. At the end of the day, for the conservative, the interests of the United States and Europe look at least as consonant as the interests of Europe and Russia, or, for that matter, of the United States and Russia. But more important, from the perspective of the conservative, Europe's relations with the United States will unavoidably be governed by global priorities and politics at the highest levels of statecraft worldwide.[37] Neither actor will jeopardize these broad and deep interests easily or recklessly (certainly Germany will not) regarding short-term gains, or controversial regionally based policies in the Gulf, for or against. Depending on how far the cooperation over defensive missile systems goes, with changes of government in each capital, Iraq will recede in importance under the shadow of more strategic issues of cooperation.

Power cycle theory is perhaps helpful in addressing the problems with Europe. The UN Security Council inspections debacle over Iraq in March 2003 is a useful case study of these problems. A gap exists between the foreign policy role sought by at least some European governments, expressed in particular by France, and the power that these governments possess to carry out this role. In contrast to the organic evolution of almost every state power cycle, the power cycle traced by the European Union is a kind of constructed cycle. It is built block by block, state by state, over time. Huge misunderstanding results between the systems view of what European power is, and therefore what its proper role should be, and the view, for example, of France.

France in this period claims equality with the United States with regard to EU economic power. The United States too could synthesize groups of countries around itself in arrangements such as the North American Free Trade Agreement to demonstrate the heft of its bargaining leverage. But this would take discussions to ludicrous lengths. Better to accept plausibility regarding the comparative bargaining equality among Japan, the United States, and the EU in trade and financial matters.

But Europe, however configured, is not the equivalent of the United States in military and security matters. Yet France and to some extent Germany would like to assert a foreign policy role that is exactly the equivalent of the US role. These governments deny that their status is any different from US status in decisions regarding international security. The superficiality of the Security Council veto only reinforces the depth of the misunderstanding. Iraq was thus the occasion that served to expose the gap between European power and their aspirations for a European foreign policy role in terms of decisionmaking authority in international security matters.

As the (purportedly) largest economic actor in the world, however, the European Union has increasingly adopted the perspective of a proponent of hegemony in trade and financial matters. It is trying to copy in economic matters what it perceives the United States is doing in strategic military matters. Indicating to the world that the EU and the EU alone will decide whether agriculture will be put on the international bargaining table, for example, France and Germany have unilaterally extended the terms of the Common Agricultural Policy regarding agricultural subsidy out to the year 2113. Likewise, the EU has decided that it will be the sole arbiter of whether genetically modified seeds, and processed food made from plants grown from such seeds, will be admissible as goods that (according to the rules of the World Trade Organization) can be traded internationally.

What is the impact of this European effort to act hegemonic regarding its agricultural policies?[38] The evidence from the Doha Round speaks for itself. While the Japanese continued to coddle their rice farmers, and the Americans demanded irresponsible subsidies for their sugar producers and cotton farmers (commodities that third world farmers can efficiently produce), the last set of demands by the EU drove the third world representatives out of the negotiations in self-righteous rage. The presumptuous European demand for the third world to accept new rules on investment, government procurement, competition, and trade facilitation in this setting destroyed the negotiations for the Doha Round in Cancún. Arrogant behavior is often reciprocal.

As the United States appears to claim the right to decide alone the rules for military intervention, because it is the biggest state militarily, so the

European Union appears bent on emulating this posture in trade and commerce. As the purportedly largest economic actor in the world, the EU claims that its preponderance makes its views on economic matters legitimate internationally. The parallel contradiction in the notion that other leading states ought to be excluded from important issues of statecraft in either the economic sphere or the military sphere thus becomes apparent.

Hence the other leading actors in the international system will continue to reject the notion that the United States by itself should decide all matters of world order. Having a leading role in determining the rules of world order is quite different from having an exclusive right to determine how, when, and where military intervention should be allowed to occur or should be mandated and upon what principles. What is being tested is the proposition that "other great powers in the system *prefer* management of the international system by a single hegemon as long as it's a relatively benign one."[39] The danger with this kind of talk is that it will be used against the United States in every possible propaganda tirade in the UN General Assembly and elsewhere. Worse than talking softly and carrying a big stick, by far, is talking loudly and, in the end, carrying a small stick.

Iraq also caused two other revelations of a tragic flaw in the European decisionmaking architecture: First, France worried that because of the quasi-pacifist stance of some members of the German population, Germany was in danger of being left isolated and alone. Echoes of Alleingang (going it alone) resonated in the ears of some European diplomats. Thus Paris bound itself to Berlin. Second, an early sample of opinion on Iraq showed that the ideal of a single, unified European foreign and defense policy was quite possibly just a myth. As Gustav Schmidt has shown, there has always been benign competition in the foreign and economic policies of the various European and North American governments.[40] But this competition has remained secondary to larger cooperation on all important matters of international security since at least the 1956 Suez Crisis.

In the minds of some observers, France (in contrast to the UK, Spain, and Italy) chose to sacrifice transatlantic security for European security. Indeed, these same observers (e.g., British foreign minister Jack Straw, in remarks to Parliament) suspect that France deliberately made the decision some time after the passage of the seventeenth resolution on Iraqi inspections (Resolution 4331) to use political opposition to the United States to rally European support so as to try to regain a sense of common European foreign policy purposiveness.

Asia

The United States projects an image on security in Asia that looks to be, and is, in the interests of all of Asia. It accomplished that by working with China, Japan, and South Korea to convince North Korea to negotiate multilaterally. China and Japan, moreover, have been made to feel that they have a responsibility for their own security.

When China is given a legitimate role in the North Korea negotiations, it is much less likely to attempt to negotiate behind the back of the United States, thus undermining whatever bilateral agreement the United States and North Korea might in isolation be able to patch together. In this sense, role brings with it responsibility. A nuclear-armed North Korea is a problem for China, because such a North Korea will likely elicit a response of nuclear armament from Japan, and a nuclear Japan, with all the sophistication of command and control that such a country can muster, could become a huge problem for China. With multilateralism, China has a large role in determining that North Korean nuclear acquisition is stopped and thus prevents a far more aggravated form of proliferation (at least in its own estimation) from occurring.

Multilateral participation enables Japan to realize that it is not on the outside, but is very much on the inside, of negotiations with North Korea. Japan is able to assess the prospects for success in the negotiations and the role that it may be expected to play to ensure that success. It will feel less dependent on the United States, thus comforting its electorate, while at the same time estimating more realistically the size of the challenge in getting North Korea to relinquish its nascent nuclear arsenal. When the time comes to exchange resources for guarantees, the Japanese government will be in a stronger position to make material demands on its electorate.

South Korea is made to realize that any outcome on the peninsula is an outcome that must satisfy the interests of all of Asia and not just its own and Washington's. Nor will the South Korean electorate be allowed to drift into simplistic anti-Americanism. South Koreans will more fully begin to appreciate that a nuclear North Korea is a problem not just for Seoul, but for Tokyo, and therefore for Seoul's relations with Tokyo.

All this is possible only when the various governments in Asia realize that the United States is not going to negotiate alone or on behalf of its own interests only. Given a multilateral approach in which each government has a role, each government unmistakably realizes that a successful outcome of negotiations depends upon its own input and its own commitment.

On the matter of North Korea's "going nuclear," what is remarkable is the closeness of the interests of the United States, Japan, China, and South Korea. Nor, standing in the wings, are Europe and Russia opposed to a collective outcome either. Multilateralism means that, concerning the other major actors, the United States is not going to "pull their chestnuts out of the fire" and then be blamed for having insufficiently taken the global interest into account. Tailoring a role for each country in the negotiations is arduous, but such shaping of multiple roles binds the players to a single, eventual outcome. In the meantime, tenacious multilateral diplomacy, combined with the realities of technological limitation in North Korea, may yield positive results.

But in the end, the question will be, will multilateralism fail where perhaps a tougher bilateral initiative might have succeeded?

Formation of Preferential Coalitions Between and Among Democracies

With the end of the Cold War, ideological walls came tumbling down. But did that mean that governments thought more punctiliously in terms of interest and power considerations (realism), or that moral norms became more persuasive (liberalism), or that large political ideas became more of a preoccupation (constructivism)? Little evidence supports these contentions. Instead what surfaced, especially among the advanced-industrial democracies, was a comparatively new form of *preferential coalition formation* between and among governments. Often driven by political party ideology and identification (such as between conservative parties or between liberal parties in different countries), this form of coalition formation sometimes also crosses party lines. That happened between the administration of George W. Bush, with its neoconservative leadership, and the government of Tony Blair, under its moderate Labor Party orientation.

The intensity of cross-government meddling and tinkering is greatest at election times, when one government seeks to enhance the electoral chances of a "like-thinking" political party abroad, or to hinder the chances of another political party with an opposed agenda from gaining office. So far, this political intervention has taken the form only of public statements or attempts to use the media in a way that is favorable or detrimental to a government or to the opposition party leadership within another country. No movement of campaign funds has occurred, which, in any case, would probably be construed as illegal by the recipient country, if not by the donor. The best way to trace preferential coalition formation is in terms of highly interactive pairs of countries such as the United States and Canada, or the United States and Israel, or Germany and France.

One of the best tests with respect to whether preferential coalition formation is occurring is when a very strong set of working relationships between two governments is confronted by an electoral change in one of them. For example, President Bill Clinton and Prime Minister Jean Chretien of Canada enjoyed a close working relationship that changed abruptly when George W. Bush became president; the rupture continued even when a change in the Liberal Party leadership took place with Paul Martin replacing Chretien. In another example, the Democrats and the Israeli Labor Party tend to think alike, and the Republican Party and members of the Likud

Party tend to share assumptions about both global and local politics. Although President Chirac leaned toward conservative politics, and Chancellor Schroeder headed the Social Democratic Party of Germany, they forged a close working relationship that carried over both to leadership within the EU and transatlantic relations.

A kind of natural experiment occurs with every election. At issue in foreign policy is not only what items will appear on the foreign policy agenda, nor how the new personalities will interact. For in reality, the interaction between governments often has less to do with the personal chemistry of the leaders than with deeper issues of values, objectives, and strategies that surround them politically in terms of advice and party priorities. For example, when Brown replaced Blair, the interaction with George W. Bush altered perceptively, notwithstanding the continuing British commitment to NATO's role in Afghanistan, largely because the priorities within the British Labor Party made themselves felt in the conduct of British foreign policy. Perhaps the largest shifts of atmosphere occurred when Christian Democratic Union leader Merkel replaced Schroeder as chancellor of the German government. Yet intraparty and interparty constraints on the foreign policy conduct of the Merkel government meant that the degree of actual coordination of policy with Washington was often limited. Likewise, a remarkable flip-flop of style and foreign policy substance occurred with the emergence of the Sarkozy government in Paris.

From a theoretical perspective, the analytic task is to generalize about the bilateral and multilateral consequences for foreign policy of these preferential coalitional arrangements, especially abrupt changes in the coalitional makeup that might foretell alternations of policy outcome. Then the task is to code and collate these coalitional orientations so as to be able to empirically test some of the hypotheses concerning international politics in the twenty-first century. A primary hypothesis might be that preferential coalitional arrangements may take priority over actual balance of power considerations among the democracies because security matters have been taken care of through more formal interaction and means.

Conclusion

From the static perspective on international relations (which was the predominant academic and policy view during most of the latter half of the twentieth century), the United States often was construed as a hegemon. After bipolarity collapsed, this simple, almost intuitive image of the international system posed the United States at the top of a rather rigid structure, in which all other states were ranked in a kind of hierarchy beneath the hegemon, very distant from its lofty height and virtually incapable of affecting it or its interests.

But from the dynamic perspective, international relations looks not only more complex but more subject to nuance and to crucial structural change, affecting all the leading actors, including the United States. European critics of the United States like to use the double entendre, *hyper-puissance,* to characterize the role. The United States is not just a superpower but a hyperpower with too much capability. But looked at from the vantage point of Japan, and many other states today, US power is barely sufficient to meet its ascribed and assumed foreign policy role. Japan, for example, once thought by some to challenge the United States for a leadership role, clearly peaked in its power cycle and entered a long, flat plateau in the 1990s, as nearby China began to soar at the bottom of the central system, taking power share away from Japan.[41] As far as Japan is concerned, the United States is not so much a hegemon as an indispensable but none-too-robust counterweight to the vast alterations of power and role taking place in Asia.

So, if by hegemonic behavior is meant the will and capacity to control the entire international system through hierarchy and force, then from the dynamic, power cycle perspective of international relations, the United States is not a hegemon. Still the most powerful actor in the system by a wide margin, the United States in the 1970s and 1980s nonetheless had entered a nascent, relative decline. By the 1990s, the pace of that decline had slowed considerably and had, in some important ways, been reversed. These developments very much altered the face of US power. Perceptions of US power changed substantially. The effect of this sudden tempering of US decline was to impart a new confidence—even assertiveness—to US foreign policy, not an uncommon response historically, according to the evidence of power cycle analysis, by governments that have found themselves in quite similar structural circumstances. In an era when the Soviet Union no longer menaced Western security, the new confidence would affect the nature of US foreign policy conduct, especially in central Asia.

From the perspective of some analysts, "nonpolarity," which is not quite the same as "multipolarity," is the static rubric under which the next phase of international politics will evolve.[42] Nonpolarity presumably is as much a commentary on whether governments are polarized around power or ideology as it is on whether a big disparity of power exists between the largest state in the system and its contemporaries. If nonpolarity is the condition of international relations today, the explanation for the lack of ideological polarization is that governments like China and Russia are too busy with their tasks of international development to mount a challenge to the systemic leadership. The lack of a visible power disparity is a legacy of continued involvement in two wars on the part of the United States in Iraq and in Afghanistan and devaluation of the US dollar. In the central system, where as elsewhere a continued inequality of power exists, non-polarity implies plurality and balance among the leading actors in the central system.

From the perspective of world order, the most important index of alteration in the underlying structure is any change in the continuing presence of US armed forces worldwide, notably in Japan and South Korea, in the Middle East, and in Europe.[43] The most important countertrend is the growing Chinese presence in Africa, more recently in Latin America, and in naval port facilities along the maritime routes to Asia.

For whatever reason, because of pressure from within the United States to withdraw, or similar pressures from previously supportive host governments, this distribution of capability and force structure is subject to buffeting and interactive tension. The background to all of this is the changing position of governments on their respective power cycles and the changing foreign policy role that the governments expect or are in a position to claim or acquire. Today only one country possesses a role involving a truly global reach, but by the mid-twenty-first century there will be others.

An underlying anxiety for a large number of states regarding foreign policy issues connects past and present. That anxiety is the impending peak in the world supply of "easy oil" and the impact this event could possess for the economic vitality of any and all oil importers. At present, everything is connected to the future supply of oil: trade deficits, security burdens, the fight against global warming, food prices, and the future of transportation. The volatility in the short-term price of oil merely accentuates an energy reality that has been long in the making but that now, for many countries, is inescapable. Governments will spend hundreds of billions on attempted security or on traditional energy imports, and almost nothing on serious investment in energy research and development that is essential for a genuine solution to the oil dilemma and therefore to all of the other interrelated policy problems. Although serious effort in all the advanced-industrial countries to achieve the fruits of such innovation has been tardy and too anemic, the answer in the end will be found both on the supply and demand sides in technological innovation.

Seen from the dynamic perspective of international relations, the United States does not seek a unilateral increase in its foreign policy role. It is struggling to sustain the role of order maintenance that it has unavoidably inherited from the twentieth century. With itself in a leading and cardinal, though not imperious or domineering role, it seeks to exercise a "multilateralism of the willing." It is constrained very much by costs, both financial and human, that very few other actors are, apparently, willing to share.

Notes

1. Karl W. Deutsch and J. David Singer, "Multipolar Power Systems and International Stability"; Richard N. Rosecrance, "Bipolarity, Multi-polarity, and the Future." In fairness, a number of conceptions of world order with a static face had already been around for some time, in particular the brilliant chapter in the Ph.D. dissertation by Morton Kaplan, and the similarly impressive Ph.D. dissertation by Kenneth Waltz, both published. But nowhere did the static paradigm of system make as great a mark in strategic circles as did the 1964 article.

2. Charles F. Doran, "Power Cycle Theory and Global Politics"; Charles F. Doran, *Systems in Crisis.*

3. Charles Krauthammer, "The Unipolar Moment."

4. William Wohlforth, "The Stability of a Bipolar World."

5. Christopher Layne, "Casualties of War: Transatlantic Relations and the Future of NATO in the Wake of the Second Gulf War."

6. Niall Ferguson, "Hegemony or Empire?"

7. Kenneth Waltz, Letter to *Foreign Affairs,* p. 193.

8. Andrew Parasiliti, "The Causes and Timing of Iraq's Wars: A Power Cycle Assessment."

9. "A Divided House Denounces Plan for More Troops," *New York Times,* February 16, 2007.

10. "Hidden Dangers," *Economist,* August 2, 2003, p. 65.

11. "Reassessing the Fiscal Gap: Why Tax-Deferred Saving Will Not Solve the Problem," http://www.brookings.edu/~/media/Files/rc/articles/2003/0728budgetdeficit_auerbach/20030714.pdf; Jagadeesh Gokhale and Kent Smetters "Fiscal and Generational Imbalances: New Budget Measures for New Budget Priorities," www.aei.org/docLib/20030723_SmettersFinalCC.pdf.

12. Jagadeesh Gokhale and Kent Smetters, "Fiscal and Generational Imbalances," p. 13.

13. Joseph Nye has bracketed the crucial notion of leadership by warning of a "declinist" mentality in *Bound to Lead,* and then, in his more recent book, of a too strongly unilateralist mentality. Joseph Nye, *The Paradox of American Power.*

14. Stephen E. Lobell, *The Challenge of Hegemony.*

15. Leopold von Ranke, *Leopold Ranke.*

16. Charles F. Doran, *Politics of Assimilation;* Arthur A. Stein, "Introduction"; G. John Ikenberry, *After Victory;* Dale C. Copeland, *The Origins of Major War.*

17. Daniel S. Geller, "Material Capabilities: Power and International Conflict."

18. Hans Morgenthau, *Politics Among Nations,* 1st ed., p. 45.

19. Robert Jervis, *Perception and Misperception in World Politics.*

20. John M. Owen IV, "Transnational Liberalism and US Primacy."

21. See Stephen Van Evera, *Causes of War,* pp. 14–34. Consider also, Randall L. Schweller, "The Twenty Years' Crisis, 1919–39: Why a Concert Didn't Arise"; for a full discussion of the significance of threat as an intermediate variable between power and war, see Stephen M. Walt, *Taming American Power.* A series of articles in *International Security* in the summer of 2005 nicely explored the notion of "soft balancing" and why it did or did not emerge as an effective counterweight to "the hegemon." Likewise, this question is examined in Jack Levy, "What Do Great Powers Balance Against and When?". But in every instance, the argument comes back to the basic notion that power in the absence of threat is not alone sufficient to evoke a major effort to put force into the balance equation.

22. E. H. Carr, *The Twenty Years' Crisis, 1919–1939.*

23. Bertrand Russell, *The Impact of Science on Society,* pp. 106–107.

24. Ludwig Dehio, *The Precarious Balance;* for a fine contemporary explanation of how domestic politics in democracies can overwhelm foreign policy calculation, see Randall Schweller, "Unanswered Threats: A Neoclassical Realist Theory of Underbalancing."

25. Joseph S. Nye Jr., *Bound to Lead.*

26. Quote from John Calvin in William J. Bouwsma, *John Calvin,* p. 208.

27. Each of the following theories of international politics builds upon the notion of hierarchy: George Modelski, "The Long Cycle of Global Politics and the Nation-State"; A. F. K. Organski and J. Kugler, *The War Ledger;* Robert Gilpin, *War and Change in World Politics;* William R. Thompson, *On Global War*. For a contrast with the hierarchical assumption of these theories and that of pluralism and equilibrium, see Franz Kohout, "Cyclical, Hegemonic, and Pluralistic Theories of International Relations on War Causation."

28. Alexander Wendt, *Social Theory of International Politics,* p. 228. Wendt importantly observes that most neorealist writing has neglected the concept of foreign policy role. Power cycle theory, however, makes foreign policy role equal with power. Wendt argues that role is not only a "unit-level phenomenon" but notes that "the sovereignty of the modern state is recognized by other states." Power cycle theory has always argued that for role to be *legitimate* it must be recognized by other states (Doran, *Systems in Crisis,* pp. 30–40, 100–101). What makes role a systems-level phenomenon is that when role is acknowledged by a number of states, it becomes embedded in the system whether it emerges primarily from the state, from other states, or from state interaction. Wendt insists that a state may not be able to escape a role as part of the state's "identity." But equally, other states see the new role as *obligation* (such as to defend a subordinate ally) that they expect the state in continuing fashion to assume.

29. For a quantitative presentation on the economic side, see Angus Maddison, "The Nature of US Economic Leadership: A Historical and Comparative View."

30. For an excellent discussion of foreign policy belief and preference, see Andrew Moravsik, "Taking Preferences Seriously: A Liberal Theory of International Politics." Robert Keohane and Lisa L. Martin ("The Promise of Institutional Theory") argue that institutions in conjunction with power matter. Such institutions codify preferences. The process of imbedding value is thoroughly discussed in John Gerard Ruggie, "International Regimes, Transactions, and Change: Embedded Liberalism in the Postwar Economic Order"; the classic treatment of perception and misperception is Robert Jervis, *Perception and Misperception in International Politics.*

31. See Lawrence J. Korb, *A New National Security Strategy in an Age of Terrorists, Tyrants, and Weapons of Mass Destruction,* "Speech Two: US Power for Deterrence and Containment," pp. 58–76. What is needed, however, is a truly revised strategy of deterrence for the age of nuclear-state proliferation, not the old concept of deterrence applied to new circumstances.

32. Richard Rosecrance and Arthur A. Stein, "The Theory of Overlapping Clubs."

33. Charles A. Kupchan and Clifford A. Kupchan, "The Promise of Collective Security."

34. John Mearsheimer has an acute understanding of why in most systems comparative equality of power is more stabilizing than destabilizing. See John J. Mearsheimer, "Back to the Future: Instability in Europe after the Cold War."

35. Should the United States engage or retrench, asks Stephen A. Walt in

"Beyond bin Laden: Reshaping US Foreign Policy." Could NATO survive withdrawal of US troops from European soil, even with off-shore capability in place?

36. Henry S. Farber and Joanne Gowa, "Polities and Peace." To the extent that Farber and Gowa are correct that most of the evidence for the democratic peace occurs in the Cold War period, disentangling the effects of bipolarity and of cooperation among democracies becomes key. That is also why the institutionalization of the EU is so important, as a counterweight to historical tendencies, and why the EU countries and the United States need each other. See also Edward D. Mansfield and Jack Snyder, "Democratization and the Danger of War"; David E. Spiro, "The Insignificance of the Liberal Peace."

37. Robert J. Art, "Why Western Europe Needs the United States and NATO."

38. Bruce Russett and John Oneal, *Triangulating Peace,* pp. 184–196. These scholars find that there is no empirical evidence that hegemony (to the extent that it has existed historically) has mitigated conflict. Presumably, this conclusion is valid in international trade as well as in international politics. See also Brian Pollins, "Global Political Order, Economic Change, and Armed Conflict."

39. John Lewis Gaddis, "A Grand Strategy of Transformation," p. 52.

40. Gustav Schmidt and Charles F. Doran, *Amerikas Option fuer Deutschland und Japan.*

41. Charles F. Doran, *Systems in Crisis,* pp. 220–236.

42. Richard Haass, "US Foreign Policy in a Nonpolar World."

43. Kent Calder, *Embattled Garrisons.*

Part 2

International Order

6

Adapting to the Evolving Polyarchy

Seyom Brown

A wide gap has developed between standard views of the post–Cold War international system as "unipolar" and the reality of a highly diffused system in which few, if any, international actors are firmly aligned with the United States. In the emergent structure of power, allies on one issue, characteristically, are adversaries on other issues, and today's closest coalition partner may be tomorrow's determined rival. The concept of *polyarchy* is both a better descriptor and predictor of the contemporary volatility of world politics than is either *unipolarity* or *multipolarity*.

US economic and military primacy, contrary to early post–Cold War expectations, has not translated into an ability to make others dance to Washington's tune. It is true that efforts by the United States to invoke its military and/or economic prowess as a trump card are rarely opposed by direct counterbalancing (since the United States would likely win any major contest in material prowess) or even by "soft balancing." Instead, US hegemonic assertiveness has been generating indirect stratagems for opposing US demands, or "balking." Moreover, countries are diversifying their security and economic dependency relationships to reduce the bargaining power of the United States. Nor is "soft power" able to fill the gap between unipolar expectations and the polyarchic realities. Proponents of the soft power thesis exaggerate the extent to which the US model of democracy, free markets, and materialistic culture is admired and can be relied on to persuade others to accept Washington's leadership. Negative foreign attitudes toward the United States are not simply reactions to specific US policies or to misinformation that can be corrected by "public diplomacy." In some communities the anti-US attitudes are the product of deeply ingrained cultural differences with what is perceived to be the American lifestyle.

Simply to protect its immediate interests in the emergent polyarchic system, the United States will have to rely less on command and more on bargaining in which Washington does not hold all the high-value cards. But to advance the security and well-being of its people for the longer term, the United States will have to adopt a policy of "higher realism"—a credible demonstration (in action, not just rhetoric) that in pursuing its national interests it is animated by the need to serve, via mutual accountability arrangements with other countries, the essential *world* interests of conflict control, poverty alleviation, environmental protection, human security, and mutual respect for cultural differences.

The Unipolar Illusion

In the early 1990s, seeing one of the two power centers of the Cold War bipolar system collapse, its sphere of control in Eastern Europe disintegrate, and its satraps around the world left without a big-brother military ally, many analysts, policymakers, and pundits deduced that the successor system, as long as the power of the United States remained intact, was *unipolar.*[1] With a defense budget greater than the combined military budgets of the next fifteen countries, the United States fielded the strongest and most technologically sophisticated forces in the world, sustained military deployments in over 100 countries, and maintained a strategic nuclear arsenal of over 6,000 nuclear warheads.[2] The gross national product (GNP) of the United States, running well over $10 trillion a year, was almost 30 percent of the world's combined GNPs.[3] And although the government spent only a very small percentage of the country's GNP on official development assistance (one of the lowest percentages of the countries in the Organization for Economic Cooperation and Development), it still amounted to a larger absolute amount of foreign aid than was provided by any other country.[4]

Fused with the neo-Wilsonian conceit that the United States had been chosen by history to bring peace to the world by spreading democracy and economic freedom, such military and economic primacy became both driver and justification for an often imperious foreign policy. Indeed, for some influential policymakers and analysts, unipolarity was not only a descriptive concept but a normative good that must be sustained.

Pax Americana Visions

The conviction that the security and well-being of the people of the United States required international peace and security, and that this in turn required the United States to take the leading role in enforcing world law and order, was gaining support in the US policy community and the populace even before September 11, 2001. From the perspective of many high officials (dominant in the Clinton administration, and increasingly prominent in the Bush administration), the fact that the country's contemporary global vocation involved enormous trade with and direct investment in other countries meant that the international peace and security interests of the United States must now encompass the domestic political situations of countries around the world—the stability of their governments and their capacity to sustain the law and order necessary for conducting market-oriented commerce. If the United States could induce other global and regional powers to share the burdens of maintaining such a world order, all to the good, but if the others faltered due to lack of capability or will, the United States in its own self-interest must be prepared to take on the tasks, even if that meant becoming "the world's policeman" (a term officially rejected but nonetheless descriptive).[5]

In light of this expanded scope of US global "security" interests, the United States in the 1990s found it increasingly difficult to remain aloof from the interethnic conflicts that flared up in many states now freed from the disciplining presence of a colonial power or the attentive control of one of the Cold War superpowers. Initially attempting to write off most internal wars as insufficiently threatening to US vital interests, Clinton officials by the middle of the decade were by and large persuaded that a range of at least "*important* interests" was often at stake—important enough even to warrant the use of force to sustain them.[6] The interests now worth fighting for included not only the security of US economic investments in various countries embroiled in violence, but also the rescue of collapsing states to save them from takeover by neighboring states or political movements hostile to the United States; and the prevention of genocide and related forms of interethnic warfare deeply offensive to the American people. Moreover, the swelling sea of homeless refugees escaping from brutal or failed states was perceived as a potential threat to the political stability and economic well-being of the United States and its primary economic partners. This expanded definition of interests whose protection might require the use of US military power was increasingly featured in official statements of the Clinton administration in parallel with statements tightening the criteria for US participation in United Nations peacekeeping actions.[7] "If we have to use force," explained Secretary of State Madeleine Albright, "it is because we are America! We are the indispensable nation, and we see further into the future."[8]

The interventionist Pax Americana disposition had become dominant in the Clinton administration by the end of the 1990s. It was ridiculed by Republicans in the 2000 election but was reincarnated in the new national security imperatives embraced by the Bush administration in the wake of September 11, 2001, and by the experience of the war against Al-Qaida and the Taliban in Afghanistan. The safety and well-being of the United States were held by the Bush administration to be crucially dependent upon the success of the worldwide battle against terrorism—a battle that this country was singularly capable of leading. As articulated by Vice President Dick Cheney,

> America has friends and allies in this cause, but only we can lead it. Only we can rally the world in a task of this complexity. . . . The United States and only the United States can see this effort through to victory.
>
> This responsibility did not come to us by chance. We are in a unique position because of our unique assets, because of the character of our people, the strength of our ideals, and the might of our military and the enormous economy that supports it.[9]

The expectation of a twenty-first-century world safe for globally expanding US commerce and investments, residually backed up by overwhelming US military superiority, draws on the model of nineteenth-century Pax Britannica. Britain, with its technologically advanced and ubiquitous navy, not only aspired to "rule the waves" but to foster a free-trading global economic system highly favorable to the industrially superior and raw-material-importing country. The champions of Pax Britannica held that what was good for England was good for the world, since free markets and global commerce, protected by the Royal Navy, would "lift all economic boats," as the Adam Smith/David Ricardo predictions of product specialization on the basis of comparative advantage were at last permitted to materialize. They convinced themselves, falsely as it turned out, that as long as Britain was willing to absorb the costs of protecting free international commerce and of correcting temporary disequilibria produced by open global competition, most of the other countries would join the free trade bandwagon and accept British hegemony.[10]

The contemporary US unipolarists were no less idealistic than their British progenitors. Those who saw economic globalization as a prime engine of world peace and prosperity argued, along with Charles Kindleberger, that the liberal economic trading and monetary systems were the underpinning of world order and stability and that they required the leadership of a hegemon willing to take on the economic and political burdens of maintaining the liberal system.[11] Those unipolarists who saw the *political/ideological* characteristics of nations around the world as the principal determinants of international peace and security also regarded continuing US primacy, particularly in the military sphere, as the indispensable condition for facilitating and sustaining the needed regime changes. The main purpose of the administration's new military buildup, strategies, and transformation, averred the Bush administration's 2002 national security strategy paper, was to "create a balance of power that favors human freedom."[12] This, in the president's words, was the country's new "forward strategy of freedom," justified by the proposition that "in every region of the world, the advance of freedom leads to peace."[13]

Although John F. Kerry's 2004 presidential election campaign criticized the elevation of preemptive and preventive force options to the level of doctrine, it did not challenge the Bush statements of the expansive purposes of US national security policy, nor did it advocate a scaling down of defense expenditures or a reduction in US overseas military deployments.[14] This was hardly surprising, as most of the foreign policy experts in the Kerry advisory entourage were high officials in the Clinton administration, responsible for the professed strategy of "enlargement" and the oft-repeated "indispensable superpower" claim.

During George W. Bush's second term, "realist" counters to the Pax Americana hubris in post–Cold War US foreign policy surfaced primarily within the Republican Party elite who were closely associated with the administration of George H. W. Bush—close associates of the former president such as James Baker and Brent Scowcroft. Democratic leaders increasingly criticized the administration's conduct of the Iraq War, and by the 2008 presidential primaries were pledging to bring most US troops back home by the end of 2009. Except for pledges to restore a multilateral thrust to US actions abroad, including cooperation in combating global warming, there were hardly any defections from the Clintonian neo-Wilsonian ethos. Again, that was unsurprising, given the gravitation of most of President Bill Clinton's former top foreign policy and national officials into the advisory entourages of the two leading candidates for the Democratic nomination.

Getting Real

True, the United States, the only remaining superpower, is the most influential single actor, and its cooperation or opposition can often determine the fate of policies and programs of others around the world. But being the only superpower is not the same as having power over most others in the system. Some forms of power—military, economic, ideational, or the power that comes from diplomatic and political skill—may be more or less usable vis-à-vis some actors in the system than others.[15] These various types of power are often neither fungible nor additive into a kind of gross national power that when posed against the power of another state will overcome its resistance, like a magnet pulling on a piece of metal.[16]

In other words, *super* power does not simply translate into *polar* power, in the sense of the impact exerted by the United States and the Soviet Union during the Cold War. The bipolarity of the Cold War system inhered not just in the existence of two countries more powerful than any of the rest, but also in the massive gravitational pull (geostrategic and ideological) by each superpower on the others.[17] Each superpower's influence over the international behavior of its allies and clients was so great that it was indeed appropriate to regard the whole system, except for the determinedly nonaligned countries, as in a condition of two-sided polarization.[18]

Ironically, since the demise of its superpower rival, the United States has been less able to influence other nations to accede to its will than during the Cold War, even when applying its putative hegemonic weight—benignly by providing economic, security, and prestige benefits to those who cooperate, or coercively by applying punitive economic or political sanctions or wielding military power. Except in certain specifically defined post-9/11 counterterrorism projects, "bandwagoning"—jumping aboard the US coalition—has not been a typical response to Washington's hegemonic posturing.[19] Rather, as became evident after the US failure to gain United Nations Security Council backing for Operation Iraqi Freedom, many influential actors in the international community, including countries the United States used to count on as loyal allies, are resisting being pushed around or bought off when their interests, values, or grand strategies diverge from those of the hegemon. As will be argued below, such resistance—sometimes in the form of open and direct opposition, even forming a coalition to balance the power of the United States, but more often than not by balking at US demands—can be expected to increase in the decades ahead.[20]

The Anachronism of Great Power Multipolarity

If not the hegemonic peace postulated by the unipolarists—a world in which the United States, like an omnipotent regent, dispenses rewards and threatens sanctions to maintain order among its otherwise unruly wards—what about a revival of the traditional system of great power alignments, power balancing, and concerts? Perhaps there can yet be a "multipolar" equilibrium among the great powers, analogous to the multipolar systems of the past, in which power balancing among a number of major states (possibly five, but as many as a dozen) was the key to international stability or a breakdown of world order and peace.[21]

The emerging twenty-first-century geopolitical reality, however, looks quite different from traditional multipolarity. Only two contemporary "great powers" are potential imperial aggressors capable, in theory, of pursuing and consolidating the kind of regional hegemony that the United States and others would feel compelled to resist: China, if it resorts to military means to take over Taiwan and to implement its claims in the South China and East China seas, could provoke a countervailing alliance response.[22] And possibly Russia, once again wracked by internal turbulence and hypernationalist reactions, if it attempts to reassert control over former Soviet-controlled areas, could well activate a response from the North Atlantic Treaty Organization (NATO) in the West and/or a coalition of Asian nations in the East. Much less plausible is the revival of a Japanese quest for regional hegemony; yet if defensive security considerations (in response, for example, to North Korean provocations) and a resurgent nationalism prompt Japan to convert its hefty "self-defense" forces into an all-purpose military, and particularly if it develops its own nuclear arsenal, future Japanese confrontation with China or Russia could escalate to levels that would seriously threaten overall peace and security.[23] The European Union, which if further consolidated could be considered a great power, could progressively intensify both its economic and diplomatic rivalry with the United States. Yet such economic and political conflicts as do emerge between the EU and the United States are highly unlikely to escalate to the level of threats of force, let alone war, unless preceded by some fundamental discontinuities in world politics.[24]

The sources of internationally destabilizing actions are more likely to be middle powers such as Iraq and Iran (the latter perhaps trying to exploit the triangular conflict in Iraq among the Kurds, Shiites, and Sunnis to its advantage, or actually deploying nuclear weapons) or an outbreak of full-scale war between Pakistan and India over Kashmir or between Israel and its neighbors. The greatest worry vis-à-vis North Korea may be an implosion of its governing regime resulting from an inability to satisfy the basic needs of its people, in which case both its international marketing of nuclear weapons components and its temptation to raise diversionary tensions with South Korea or Japan are potentially serious threats to international peace and security. Other failed or failing states—like Zimbabwe, Sudan, Somalia, Bangladesh, or Afghanistan (if current counterinsurgency and stabilization efforts collapse), or Kosovo after the departure of NATO security forces—could also catalyze dangerous regional instabilities.[25] Moreover, the entire system can be destabilized by wars initiated and conducted by nongovernmental actors, such as violent political movements, terrorist networks, and criminal syndicates.

In the system maturing before us, the precipitating events more than ever are likely to come in a variety of forms besides the movement of military forces across borders: terrorism, subnational and transnational ethnic wars, failed domestic political systems, collapsing economies, contraband in weapons and drugs, ecological disasters.[26] Rivalries or concerted action among the great powers might be important in exploiting or countering various of these threats to international peace and security, but more often than not, the sources of war and peace will lie elsewhere than in the great power competition.

In short, in contrast to the great power multipolar systems of the past, there are now a much larger number and variety of actors, state and nonstate actors, who can shake up the system. The major threats to system equilibrium are not primarily territorial expansion, tipping the balance of power through the addition or subtraction of allies, or dramatic augmentation of one or another of the great powers' military capabilities. Opposition to a great power's policies that one does not like will rarely take the form of power balancing through the formation or tightening of countervailing alliances. More likely, opposition will come as irritating, even defiant, acts of noncooperation—the *balking* diplomacy that is one of the hallmarks of polyarchy.

The Emergent Polyarchy

In the emergent structure of world politics, the United States finds itself embedded increasingly within a polyarchic field of actors: nation-states, terrorist networks, subnational groups, transnational religious groups, multinational enterprises, and global and regional economic and security institutions.[27] Many of these communities and organizations have partially overlapping constituencies for whose loyalty and support they often compete. And very few of these entities—whether states or nonstate actors—are unidirectionally aligned in their major international relationships, either with one another or with the United States.[28]

Cross-Pressured Countries and Crosscutting Alliances

The polyarchic cross-pressures make for fickle friendships and adversarial relationships, in which today's ally may be tomorrow's enemy and vice versa, depending on the issue at hand. The fact that many NATO countries and members of the 1990–1991 Gulf War coalition were bitterly divided in 2003 over how to deal with Saddam Hussein was less an anomaly than an expression of the evolving polyarchic system.

Whereas the Cold War system featured a high degree of congruence between primary security communities, trading blocs, and ideological coalitions, the polyarchic system characteristically features a good deal of incongruence. The partners in the North American Free Trade Agreement (NAFTA), Canada, Mexico, and the United States, are at odds over how to deal with difficult countries in the Western Hemisphere, such as Cuba, Venezuela, and Bolivia. Many of the NATO countries differ significantly from the United States on Israeli-Palestinian issues. Even the closest US political ally, Britain, is visibly in disagreement with Washington over major world order issues—namely, the International Criminal Court and international controls on the production of greenhouse gases. Cultural and ideological allies, such as Sweden and Finland, may be in serious dispute over navigational and fishing rights. Countries engaged in joint military projects (Russia and the former Soviet states in Central Asia, for example) may have major differences over fighting terrorism, the location and ownership of petroleum pipelines, and combating the traffic in drugs. Allies on global environmental issues (say, India and China) are frequently at odds on questions of human rights.[29] The cross-pressures also operate at the transstate level, with some sectors maintaining and institutionalizing cooperative interaction with particular sectors in countries toward which other sectors are hostile—an increasingly evident feature in the thickening relations in Asia among the Japanese, the South Koreans, and the Chinese.

Such cross-pressures, and the volatility of alignments and antagonisms, make it difficult to form and sustain reliable alliance commitments and collective security arrangements for dealing with potential threats from one's adversaries. The prospect of looser, less dependable, and shifting alliances has been affecting US military planning and procurement in the direction of a military posture that will give national command authorities the maximum array of attack and defense options that can be applied regardless of allied cooperation or concurrence.[30] Publicly released planning documents continue to affirm that "a secure international system requires collective action" and that "we are strengthening security relationships with traditional allies and friends [and] developing new international partnerships."[31] Meanwhile, programs for enhancing long-range transportation and heavy airlift reflect a determination to reduce reliance on long-term foreign base arrangements for pre-positioning military equipment and troops. The advances in remote-sensing, stand-off delivery of attacks, and rapid airlifting of equipment and troops into zones of combat both reflect and reinforce the reduced reliance on allies dictated by the politics of polyarchy.[32]

The awareness in foreign capitals that the US military has been moving in this direction only deepens tensions with Washington. These developments in turn confirm the concern among US strategists that in future conflicts allies may be less forthcoming than in the past when it comes to providing forward bases and overflight rights, and even crucial intelligence, let alone contributing combat units. Despite the resignation of Secretary of Defense Donald Rumsfeld and the failure of his lean-and-mean strategy for victory in Iraq, US grand strategy is progressively premised on the need for the United States to be able to pursue its national and global interests with very few allies or even without allies.

This is not your father's anarchic state system, however. The "anarchy" of the traditional system was by comparison quite stable and predictable. National leaders could by and large control what went on within their jurisdictions and reliably commit their countries to alliances in order to counter the power of their aggressive adversaries. In the polyarchic system, there are many more loose cannons capable of generating havoc in the system, destabilizing governments as well as international peace and security arrangements—not only Osama bin Laden but transnational entrepreneurs and pirates of weapons, high-tech knowledge, and illicit substances (such as A. J. Khan and Pablo Escobar). In addition, multinational corporations and even individual billionaires can, by shifting of resources in and out of countries, affect who gets what, when, and how in world politics.

Polyarchy is not without conflict-moderating features. The dense transnational networks of interdependence and multiple and diverse relationships of groups and countries in at least the industrialized regions mean that international adversaries are likely to have economic partners and/or ethnic "brothers" and "sisters" in the population and societies against which they are in conflict. These crosscutting attachments can work as a brake on efforts to generate the total nation-to-nation hostility required to mobilize domestic support for war. But these same characteristics mitigate against durable and credible international alliances and effective global or regional collective security organizations that can deter war.

Bandwagoning, Balancing, or Balking

In this emergent polyarchy, continued assertions of hegemonic primacy by the United States are less likely than in previous international systems to generate the typical *bandwagoning* or *balancing* responses. Some actors will, of course, jump on board the US bandwagon, fearful of alienating the still powerful superpower and seeking the positive benefits of loyal support. But as Tony Blair in England and Prime Minister José Maria Aznar of Spain each discovered, bandwagoning often proves to be highly unpopular with nationalist constituents. Others—for example, governments catalyzed by Islamist resentments—may try to "balance" the power of the United States—benignly, through anti-US coalitions in international forums and discriminatory commercial blocs; or dangerously, through conspiring to harass and play havoc with Americans and their assets around the world.

More likely, however, are *balking* strategies by governments or political leaders, when caving in to the United States can embarrass them with their constituents but refusing to go along can enhance their legitimacy, and when frontally opposing the insistent hegemon (even by what some analysts are calling "soft balancing") can incur high material costs.[33] Various balking strategies—ranging from refusing to cooperate to initiating complicated rounds of bargaining to taking determined postures of nonalignment—have come into prominence, including[34]

- refusing to cooperate in some specific policy, not out of any profound philosophical or geostrategic interest but simply in order to get the United States to offer more to gain one's cooperation (Mexico's often irritating objection to US policies on global security issues appears to be of this sort, being more a stratagem to leverage Washington to move Mexico's way on trade and immigration issues);
- refusing to agree to a specific request because to agree would be risky domestically, not out of any motive to balance or delegitimize US power (e.g., Turkey's refusal to allow US forces to come through its territory in Operation Iraqi Freedom);
- finding ways to indicate that one is not completely in the pocket of

the United States (such as the Polish government's decision to terminate its deployment of troops in Iraq while accepting the deployment of components of US antimissile systems on its soil);

- insisting on subjecting US demarches to authorization by multilateral forums in which US influence will be diluted (the French and German strategies for reining in US policies toward Iraq);
- pursuing a grand strategy of diversifying one's dependency relationships and thus enhancing one's bargaining position overall (much of what is going on in Central Asia on the part of the former Soviet republics in reaction to US efforts to turn them into more permanent military allies);
- not cooperating fully with US demands, even in the security field, because of commercial/economic motives, not necessarily out of a calculated strategy to be difficult (e.g., French, Chinese, and even Israeli international sales of nuclear power items that could be converted into weapons components, as well as general arms sales to governments against US wishes);
- engaging in cross-sector "linkage" diplomacy against the United States (such as China's favoring Airbus over Boeing in retaliation for anti-Chinese positions by the United States in the human rights forums);
- open, publicly manifested disagreement with the wisdom of US policy (such as NATO members' refusal to put Ukraine and Georgia in the queue for membership in the alliance) by governments who know they won't be coercively sanctioned by the United States, even though US leaders are irritated.

Such balking strategies, given the crosscutting relationships in the emerging polyarchy, are becoming a standard feature of international diplomacy. They were by no means absent from Cold War diplomacy ("nonaligned" countries like India and Indonesia developed them into a high art form); but the disappearance of the Cold War imperatives championed by the United States for containing the rival superpower has created a more permissive environment for balking. The danger is that balking will be confused with belligerent balancing—stimulating mutual recriminations and escalating what were only tough bargaining encounters into zero-sum confrontations.

Alternative US Responses

It is no longer sensible—if, indeed, it ever was—for Washington to operate on hubristic unipolar assumptions of a twenty-first-century Pax Americana benignly flowing from the country's unparalleled economic and military primacy. But neither is it realistic or prudent to gear up for a century of competitive multipolar and war-provoking imperialisms, lest the United States by such anticipatory arming and proactive counter-balancing inadvertently confirms the hypothetical "tragedy of great power politics."

What, then, are the alternatives? There are four plausible contenders:

1. Pax Americana with teeth—the neoconservative, neo-Wilsonian policy of interventions—multilateral if possible, unilateral if necessary, peaceful if possible, with force if necessary—to stabilize and democratize violence-prone societies around the world;
2. Traditional realism—a more patient response to polyarchic complexities, avoiding intrusive involvement in areas of instability and chaos that do not substantially affect US vital interests, and relying mostly on the sovereignty-respecting diplomacy of state-to-state bargaining rather than political and military interventions to resolve disputes;
3. Neo-isolationism, avoiding entangling multilateral commitments, resisting globalization trends that limit US self-sufficiency, washing our hands of the world's great unwashed, and making this country once again a "city on a hill" that knows what it wants for itself but does not try to actively convert others to the American way; and
4. Higher realism—melding vital US interests with essential global security and humanitarian interests while embracing the political, economic, and cultural *diversity* of world society and, at the same time, championing global norms, rules, and processes of mutual international accountability (binding on the United States as well as others) for managing the deepening interdependence of peoples.

Pax Americana with Teeth

This ambitious policy affirms that it is the nation's destiny to lead the world in countering today's polyarchic threats to world order: rogue states that flout their international obligations; transnational terrorists, and states that sponsor or harbor them; and failed or failing states. The strategy assumes that it may not be enough to attempt to militarily *deter* such governments or movements from hostile acts against the world, or to dissuade them with carrot-and-stick diplomacy from grossly mistreating or neglecting their own people. It may require going to war to effect a change in regime, as in the deposition of the Taliban in Afghanistan and Saddam Hussein in Iraq. It may require "humanitarian intervention" with major military force, as in Bosnia and Kosovo. And it may require preventive military action to disarm irresponsible countries or movements of weapons of mass destruction.

Pax Americana with teeth casts the United States as standing for purposes beyond the perpetuation of its own primacy. But it risks establishing global commitments that cannot be sustained without a degree of investment of US material resources, and potentially of military manpower, that is politically unsustainable at home. As the achievements fall far short of the promises, there may be a backlash of cynical reactions around the world to US professions of global responsibility and leadership: allegations of double standards and hypocrisy as the resource crunch compels a highly selective policy that favors some countries over others. The likes of Hugo Chavez of Venezuela, Mahmoud Ahmadinejad of Iran, and Osama bin Laden would only be encouraged to increase their vilifications of the United States. And former US Cold War allies would be resentful of Washington's continuing presumptions of omnipotence and omniscience despite the polyarchic realities.[35]

Traditional Realism

From the perspective of traditional realism,[36] the response to the emergent polyarchy should be a patient US foreign policy—dealing with particular challenges as they arise, but selectively, while according priority to preventing an attack on the homeland and preserving access to foreign sources of oil.[37] Recognizing that most disputes the United States has or is likely to have with other countries do not, and need not, jeopardize the irreducible US national interest (the physical security of the citizenry, the country's economic well-being, and its basic constitutional system),[38] post–Cold War realists tend to favor a statecraft of bargaining rather than hegemonic diktat, backed up, however, by unambiguous military superiority to discourage others from escalating disputes with the United States to the level of violence.[39]

The traditional realists caution that the United States should use its power prudentially, not expend it in futile attempts to run the whole system. Nor should Washington intervene in the domestic affairs of other countries unless vital US national interests require regime change. Any such overriding of state sovereignty should have the widest possible international writ of approval, be situation-specific, and be designed only to secure peace—not to prescribe and impose a particular political or economic way of life.

The problem with the traditional realist response is that it is long on what the United States should *not* attempt to do, yet short on what can and should be done to counteract the chaos and often violent eruptions in the emerging polyarchy. It has no vision of system transformation, let alone global governance, for ameliorating the looming threats to human security and well-being posed by global warming, extreme poverty, terrorism, and the further spread of weapons of mass destruction.[40]

Neo-isolationism

The growing national backlash against the blood and treasure costs of the neoconservative venture in Iraq and the upsurge of anti-Americanism around the world provide a receptive context and attentive audiences for the arguments of today's isolationists. The foreigners don't want us, so let's come home.[41] Intellectual expression of the isolationist impulse—the flip side of the impulse to transform the world in the image of the United States (the former a reaction to the inability to meet the latter goal)—has been voiced in a spate of post-9/11 books and articles inveighing against the alleged disposition of those who ran US foreign policy to establish a global imperium.[42]

More than a temporary reaction against the ascendant neoconservative/neo-Wilsonian globalism, neo-isolationism has deep roots in the nationalist and populist soil of the country. Politicians ask why any sacrifices should be borne to make the world safe for US investments, when these are the investments of the very multinational firms that are transferring jobs and productive facilities to other countries. The new isolationism also has cultural sources and expressions, some quite openly xenophobic, of hostility toward the one-world, global market, open-borders, liberal-immigration approach perceived to be diluting the "American way of life" and undermining the country's role as a "city on a hill" to be envied and eventually emulated by others.[43]

The isolationist response to polyarchy, like the Pax Americana response, is one of *non*-accommodation to the contemporary world disorder. Instead of trying to police and reform the outside world, the United States should do a better job of insulating itself from economic, physical, and cultural viruses. The neo-isolationists would apply new electronic technologies (which the globalists praise as finally allowing the dream of an integrated world market to be realized) to the securing and strengthening of borders and barriers against the free ingress of goods and people—not simply as part of the war on terrorism but also to keep out the carriers of societal dissipation and corruption.

Global technological and economic integration has matured too far, however, and benefits too many sectors of American society, for the isolationist response to polyarchy to appeal to more than a minority of the electorate, let alone to become the official US worldview. Yet because of their concentration in particular electoral districts, the intensity of some of their grievances, and the seniority of their representatives in the House and the Senate, neo-isolationists can often seriously constrain and inhibit policies they regard as too internationalist.

Higher Realism

I call the fourth of the alternative responses to the emerging polyarchy "higher realism." Like traditional realism, it holds that US foreign policy must give priority to the vital *national* interests of the country—securing the homeland against physical attack; sustaining the economic well-being of the American people and preserving their basic liberties—and that the grand strategy for serving these national interests must be consistent with both US resources and the international distribution of power. But higher realism differs from traditional realism's tendency to discount the nonmaterial components of power and the importance of international institutions and norms.

A higher realist foreign policy would be based on the recognition of how inextricably bound up with *world* interests—with the security and well-being of people everywhere—US national interests have become. But it would reject the Pax Americana hubris that what is good for the United States is ipso facto good for the world.

Higher realism regards the enhancement of international accountability norms and institutions (a rule-based global system)—even though they may at times constrain the United States from acting with complete flexibility—as necessary for the country's long-term security and well-being.[44] It understands how US military superiority and economic primacy, and the will to invoke them at times coercively, remain essential components of US power for securing the country's national interests; but it also insists on the importance of subjecting the coercive use of US material power to widely accepted standards of legitimacy.

Higher realism contends that the well-being of the people of the United States requires a determined effort to reduce the vast amount of poverty and disease in the world. And it requires that the United States take a leading role in forging global cooperation to preserve the planet's temperate climate and to husband its scarce resources and natural ecologies.

Higher realism supports the evolution of political systems based on the informed consent of the governed and respect for human rights. But it opposes attempting to universalize the American way of life as *the* way of organizing society and to project it onto the world's culturally diverse nations. Rather, both as an end in itself, consistent with the continuing e pluribus unum experiment that is the essence of the United States, and because otherwise US foreign policy will generate increasing hostility, the United States should be a champion, not an adversary, of a culturally and religiously diverse world.

Under these premises, the United States would be generally supportive of efforts by distinct cultural communities around the world to practice their own ways of life and to devise their own political and economic systems, and would refrain from intervening to compel them to emulate the US or other "Western" models. This does not, however, preclude interventions, legitimized by a broad international consensus, to counter genocide and other crimes against humanity as defined in the statute of the new International Criminal Court. Nor should such forbearance prevent the

United States from engaging in internationally authorized peacekeeping or conflict control operations where they are required to prevent an eruption of violence.

More than the other three alternatives, the foreign policy of higher realism provides a proactive and constructive adaptation to the emergent polyarchy that is consonant with fundamental US interests and values. The problem with this prescription, however, lies in the difficulty in generating sufficient domestic public and even elite support for the long-term international community-building policies that, in the absence of a dramatic threat to the security and well-being of the American people, are not obviously required for servicing immediate and tangible interests of the country.[45]

Conclusion

The United States is at a historic juncture when a fundamental shift in worldview is required to make US foreign policy consistent with the evolving structure of world politics. Expectations of a unipolar world need modification if the United States is to develop a foreign policy that will be both effective and command international respect. The emerging geopolitical reality also looks quite different from traditional multipolarity. Instead, the United States, the world's only superpower in terms of the standard economic and military metrics of power, must pursue its interests in an increasingly *polyarchic* global system, in which influential actors capable of significantly frustrating US purposes include other nation-states of various sizes, terrorist networks, subnational groups, transnational religious groups, multinational enterprises, and global and regional institutions.

Notes

Some of the material in this chapter is adapted from Seyom Brown, *Higher Realism: A New Foreign Policy for the United States* (Boulder, CO: Paradigm, 2009).

1. An early and widely cited expression of the unipolar thesis was Charles Krauthammer, "The Unipolar Moment." See also Michael Mastanduno, "Preserving the Unipolar Moment."

2. Assessing the data, Stephen G. Brooks and William C. Wohlforth in "American Primacy in Perspective," observed, "No state in the modern history of international politics has come close to the military predominance these numbers suggest."

3. World Bank, *World Development Indicators Database,* September 2004.

4. Ibid.

5. An early indication that the Clinton administration was defining the post–Cold War role of the United States this ambitiously was National Security Adviser Anthony Lake's highly publicized speech of September 25, 1993, announc-

ing a new global "strategy of enlargement" (to supplant the strategy of containment), featuring the active promotion of "new democracies and market economies" and the "liberalization of states hostile to democracy and markets." Text in US Department of State, *Dispatch* 4, no. 39 (September 27, 1993). "Enlargement," so defined, became the philosophical underpinning of a succession of basic foreign policy speeches and papers of the administration, including the comprehensive national security strategy papers issued in 1995 and 1999, respectively, that contemplated the use of force on behalf of the enlargement imperatives: White House, *A National Security Strategy of Engagement and Enlargement* and White House, *A National Security Strategy for a New Century.*

6. The administration defined "important interests" as those that, while not affecting our national survival, "do affect importantly our national well-being and the character of the world in which we live." White House, *A National Security Strategy of Enlargement and Engagement,* p. 12.

7. Presidential Decision Directive 25 (White House, May 1994).

8. Madeleine Albright, interview on NBC *Today,* February 19, 1998.

9. Remarks by Vice President Dick Cheney before the Council on Foreign Relations, February 15, 2002 (available at www.whitehouse.gov/vicepresident/news-speeches).

10. Paul Kennedy, *The Rise and Fall of the Great Powers;* Jack Snyder, *Myths of Empire;* and Niall Ferguson, *Empire.* See also Timothy J. McKeown, "Hegemonic Stability Theory and Nineteenth-Century Tariff Levels in Europe."

11. Charles Kindleberger, *The World in Depression, 1929–1939.* For additional discussion of how the characteristics and role of hegemonic powers affect the prospects for peace and war, see Robert Gilpin, *War and Change in World Politics.* See also Stephen Krasner, "State Power and the Structure of International Trade."

12. White House, *The National Security Strategy of the United States of America.*

13. President George W. Bush, Remarks on the Twentieth Anniversary of the National Endowment for Democracy, November 2, 2003 (text in the *New York Times,* November 6, 2003).

14. Indeed, it was the Bush administration itself that announced in August 2004 a major "realignment" of troop deployments to take place over the next decade, involving substantial reductions of US forces in Europe and South Korea.

15. Such understanding of the various dimensions of power and their varying utility in different situations was a lesson learned, sometimes painfully, by US leaders in prosecuting the Cold War. See Seyom Brown, *The Faces of Power.* See also Joseph P. Nye, *Soft Power.* Remarkably, many of today's policymakers and analysts apparently need to be taught this lesson for the first time.

16. For an exposition of the power "fungibility" notion, see Robert J. Art, "American Foreign Policy and the Fungibility of Force."

17. In the academic literature on international systems, there is no agreed-upon definition of the "polar" suffix in the bipolar, multipolar, unipolar typology. Thus, Kenneth N. Waltz in his *Theory of International Politics,* pp. 161–193, used it simply to designate the *number* of powerful states in a system, whereas Raymond Aron in his *Peace and War,* pp. 125–149, compared systems divided into two *camps* (bipolar) with systems with numerous power centers (multipolar), some of which may operate as coalitions, and some of which may be states standing apart from any coalition. Standard contemporary textbooks reflect the confusion. For example, Joshua Goldstein's *International Relations,* pp. 98–99, says that "In a multipolar system there are typically five or six centers of power, which are grouped into

alliances. Each state participates independently and on relatively equal terms with others. . . . A bipolar system has two predominant states or two great rival alliances. . . . [A] unipolar system has a single center of power around which all others revolve."

18. Even most of the professedly "nonaligned" countries tilted rather obviously to one side or the other during most of the Cold War: for example, Egypt toward the Soviet Union, Mexico toward the United States. India, widely regarded as the leader of the nonaligned movement, though never really taking orders from Moscow, also tended to take the Kremlin's side in many Cold War disputes.

19. For an analysis of the "bandwagoning" phenomenon, see Randall Schweller, "Bandwagoning for Profit."

20. In *The Origins of Alliances* Stephen Walt found balancing to be more prevalent than bandwagoning; in his most recent study of reactions to US hegemonic assertiveness since the end of the Cold War, *Taming American Power,* he finds very little balancing and (as will be discussed below) more selective and indirect strategies such as balking for opposing the United States.

21. John Mearsheimer, *The Tragedy of Great Power Politics.* For the pre-Napoleonic multipolar system, see Edward V. Gulick, *Europe's Classical Balance of Power.* For the functioning of multipolarity during the nineteenth century and up to World War I, see Henry Kissinger, *Diplomacy,* chapters 4–7.

22. For discussion of China's evolving grand strategy, see David Shambaugh, "China Engages Asia"; and Evan S. Medeiros and M. Taylor Fravel, "China's New Diplomacy." See also Thomas Christensen, "Posing Problems Without Catching Up"; and Robert Sutter, "Asia in the Balance."

23. For analysis of Japanese interests and capabilities, see Michael J. Green, "Japan Is Back" (a review of *Japan Rising* by Kenneth Pyle). On the prospects for a resurgence of Sino-Japanese "great power" rivalry, see Kent E. Calder, "China and Japan's Simmering Rivalry"; see also "Special Report on China and Japan: So Hard to Be Friends," *Economist,* March 26, 2005, pp. 23–25 (US edition).

24. Despite the title, the unlikelihood of anything stronger than benign clashes of interest and competition between the United States and the EU is the message of Philip H. Gordon and Jeremy Shapiro's book, *Allies at War,* and all other serious analyses of post–Cold War transatlantic relations.

25. See Robert Rotberg, ed., *When States Fail.* On the international escalatory potential of the failing-states crises in East Africa, see John Prendergast and Colin Thomas Jensen, "Blowing the Horn."

26. Seyom Brown, *New Forces, Old Forces, and the Future of World Politics.*

27. The term "polyarchy" was coined by political scientist Robert Dahl in *Polyarchy: Participation and Opposition* to describe requisite structures and processes of well-functioning democracies. As applied here to the world scene, the term comes closer to denoting what its etymology conveys: a political system, which could well be quite chaotic, run by numerous diverse actors. World polyarchy differs from *anarchy,* however, which in its classic meaning—the absence of government—as applied to world politics describes a system in which sovereign states are the essential actors and there are no supranational actors with enforceable authority over the states. Polyarchy, as conceptualized in this chapter, while including significant nonstate, subnational, and transnational actors in addition to national governments, also comprehends regional and universal institutions with supranational authority. The term was first used in this way by Seyom Brown, *New Forces in World Politics.*

28. Richard N. Haass presents a similar characterization of the emergent international system in "The Age of Nonpolarity."

29. Cross-pressures on and within the US- and Soviet-led alliances did exist during the Cold War, of course—most dramatically in the 1956 British-French-Israeli military assault on Egypt, which surprised and angered the Eisenhower administration, followed by France acquiring its own nuclear arsenal; and in China's unilateral expansionary moves against Taiwan and on the Sino-Indian border (crises in which the Kremlin failed to back Beijing against US threats), leading to China's development of its own nuclear weapons in the 1960s. But during that era such defections from superpower control were widely recognized as having the potential to collapse the constraints the bipolar system provided against the outbreak of a planet-destroying World War III. By contrast, in the emergent polyarchy, although there are fewer disincentives to alliance defection and unilateral action, the likelihood is remote that such moves, even if they precipitate local war, will engulf the whole system in another world war.

30. For the interactive effects of the new technologies and alliance relations, see Lawrence Freedman, *The Revolution in Strategic Affairs;* and Seyom Brown, *The Illusion of Control,* especially pp. 78–104.

31. US Department of Defense, *The National Defense Strategy of the United States of America.*

32. Thus the call in the US Department of Defense *2001 Quadrennial Defense Review Report* for "the capability to send well-armed and logistically supported forces to critical points around the globe, even . . . to locations where the support infrastructure is lacking or has collapsed," p. 43.

33. For advocacy of the concept of "soft balancing," see Robert A. Pape, "Soft Balancing Against the United States"; and T. V. Paul, "Soft Balancing in the Age of US Primacy." Criticisms of the usefulness of the concept were featured in the same *International Security* issue by Stephen G. Brooks and William C. Wohlforth, "Hard Times for Soft Balancing"; and Keir Lieber and Gerard Alexander, "Waiting for Balancing." The debate—largely over the semantics of the terminology rather than over the substance of the phenomenon—was carried on in the correspondence section of the Winter 2005–2006 issue of the journal in letters from Robert J. Art, Brooks and Wohlforth, and Lieber and Alexander, vol. 30, no. 3, pp. 177–196.

34. Other analysts have also observed the prominence of what I call "balking." John Ikenberry, focusing on the reactions of the "great powers," finds that "today, strategies for coping with a preeminent America tend to fall in between these [bandwagoning and balancing] extremes." He divides these coping responses into two types: "strategies of resistance" and "strategies of engagement." The resistance strategies include "buffering" (to reduce the direct influence of the United States by inducing it to deal with the issue at hand through multilateral institutions or processes), "baiting" (creating such multilateral venues despite US reluctance to participate in them, thereby making it politically harder for the United States to oppose one's positions), and "bargaining" (offering or withholding cooperation with the United States in exchange for US responsiveness to one's preferences). The engagement strategies involve working with the United States in ways that create a degree of US dependence on one's cooperation that will discourage the United States from exploiting or taking one for granted. John Ikenberry, "Strategic Reactions to American Prominence: Great Power Politics in the Age of Uncertainty," Report to the National Intelligence Council, 28 July 2003 (available at http://www.dni.gov/nic/confreports_stratreact.html). Similarly, Stephen Walt sees a range of strategies being pursued by other countries (great powers and lesser powers) to deal with the overbearing hegemon. On the one hand are strategies of "accommodation," including quid pro quo agreements in which the United States agrees to support the lesser

country's local interests; personal "bonding" by one's leaders with US leaders (i.e., Blair with Bush) so as to bring home some payoffs for one's constituents; and "penetration" of the US political system by mobilizing active lobbies (e.g., US supporters of Israel) to obtain advantages for one's country. On the other hand are strategies of "opposition"—apart from balancing—such as "delegitimation" (portraying US policies as in violation of international law or norms), "blackmail" (threatening unwanted actors to extract concessions), and "asymmetric" responses (terrorism being the starkest example). Walt, *Taming American Power.*

35. David Skidmore, "Understanding the Unilateralist Turn in US Foreign Policy."

36. Classical realism and its various neorealist offshoots are here lumped together under the heading "Traditional Realism" since, for purposes of the present analysis, their common basic assumptions about the anarchic international system and the preoccupation of the system's principal actors (the leading nation-states) with the international distribution of coercive power distinguishes this worldview from the others, including what I call "higher realism." Although the so-called offensive realists (à la John Mearsheimer) may differ in some of their analytical premises and policy prescriptions from the so-called defensive realists (à la Robert Jervis), the response to polyarchy sketched in this section flows from their shared insistence that the parameters of world politics in any era, and therefore the range of rational foreign policy alternatives for a country like the United States, is largely defined by the relative coercive power of the major states vis-à-vis one another.

37. See, for example, Robert J. Art, *A Grand Strategy for America.* Art also gives high priority to preventing "great power Eurasian wars and, if possible, the intense security competitions that make them possible," and therefore also recommends a continued substantial deployment of US forces in Europe and Asia. Other realists are somewhat more restrictive in their selection of US interests worth fighting for and of the military implications. Thus, Stephen M. Walt, in *Taming American Power,* argues against continuing to maintain substantial deployments of US troops in Europe and Asia during peacetime and instead advocates a strategy of "offshore balancing."

38. The concept of the "irreducible national interest" is developed in Seyom Brown, *The Faces of Power,* pp. 3–4.

39. Barry Posen suggests that a US military capable of maintaining command of the oceans, outer space, and air space above 5,000 meters is sufficient to support a realist, even hegemony-preserving, foreign policy. Command of these global "commons" areas means that the United States can credibly threaten to deny their use to others, and that others would lose a military contest if they attempted to deny any of the commons areas to the United States. See his "Command of the Commons."

40. The "constructivist" school of international relations, criticizing the realist view as static, is all in favor of system transformation—but perhaps too optimistically, in their assumption that a sufficient density and intensity of interactions among actors can lead to system transformation. See, for example, Alexander Wendt, "Anarchy Is What States Make of It"; and Dale Copeland, "The Constructivist Challenge to Structural Realism."

41. Six years after President George H. W. Bush, victorious in the Gulf War to expel Saddam Hussein from Kuwait, proclaimed an end to the "Vietnam syndrome," *International Security* published as its lead article a strongly articulated argument for pulling US military forces out of Europe and out of Asia, and substantially scaling down the US military presence, particularly of its ground forces, in the Middle

East. The end of the Cold War, the article contended, made these very expensive deployments anachronistic. The authors were not urging economic disengagement from the world or political indifference to violations of human rights. The only justification for a continuation of US global military engagement, however, would be "some new ambitious strategy—to prevent war everywhere, to make everyone democratic, or to keep everyone else down. But if Americans simply want to be free, enjoy peace, and concentrate more on problems closer to home, the choice is clear: it is time to come home, America." Eugene Gholz, Daryl G. Press, and Harvey M. Sapolsky, "Come Home, America."

42. See, for example, Chalmers Johnson, *The Sorrows of Empire:* John B. Jusis, *The Folly of Empire;* and Ivan Eland, *The Empire Has No Clothes.*

43. The publication of Samuel P. Huntington's *Who Are We? The Challenges to American National Identity* can be viewed as a sign of the contemporary market (perhaps growing) for intellectual and social science justifications for the new isolationism.

44. Some analysts who at least claim previous realist credentials are now supporting this view. Thus, John Ikenberry urges the United States to champion and participate in the building of a global "constitutional" order in which "power is exercised—at least to some extent—through agreed-upon institutional rules and practices, thereby limiting the capacities of states to exercise power in arbitrary and indiscriminate ways or use their power advantages to gain a permanent advantage over weaker states." G. John Ikenberry, *After Victory,* p. 19. And Richard Haass argues that the increasingly "integrated" world of the twenty-first century requires institutions to constructively manage the integration. The foreign policy debate, he writes, "ought not to be whether to choose unilateralism or multilateralism, but how to choose wisely among the various forms of the latter, that is, when to turn to the UN as opposed to other standing clusters of states, alliances, regional groupings, contact groups, or ad hoc coalitions of the willing. The guiding principle should be to aim for forms of cooperation that are as broad and as formal as possible—and to choose narrow (less inclusive) and informal forms of cooperation only as required." Richard N. Haass, *The Opportunity,* p. 200. For a conceptual scholarly analysis of the various means (and difficulty) of enhancing international accountability processes and institutions, see Ruth W. Grant and Robert O. Keohane, "Accountability and the Abuses of Power in World Politics."

45. As put by one sage analyst, "a dominant power like the United States is apt to find multilateral cooperation restraining. Possessing extensive policy options—including unilateralism, bilateral arrangements, or temporary coalitions—it can often afford (at least in the short term) to bypass consultations, enforce its will, or absorb the costs of acting alone." Stewart Patrick, "Multilateralism and Its Discontents."

7

Primacy and Other Ways of Shaping World Order

Gustav Schmidt

The heat of the controversy between Washington-London and Paris-Berlin[1] about the right strategy for disarming Iraq marked the revealing moment—it brought the contestation between two mindsets into the open: whether "it is much better to engage 'our' enemies in their backyard than in ours, at a time and place of our choosing and not theirs"[2] (i.e., preemptive military intervention), or whether political-diplomatic efforts must be applied to what is perceived as a political challenge or provocation (i.e., preventive diplomacy). Do the differences reflect ways of perceiving threats or indicate a deeper political and social divide ("values gap")? How can we explain the ideological confrontation between the Big Four of what we used to call the West and the consequences of such a contest for a security order in the twenty-first century?[3] What principles are going to prevail in world politics? The US thrust in using its unprecedented military power to subdue the centers of violence, particularly in the (larger) Middle East, in order to safeguard its homeland security?[4] Or the French-German insistence that especially the *hyper-puissance* has to abide by the authority of the law, resting in the hands of the UN Security Council (UNSC)?[5]

Is the transatlantic security community a matter of the past, because "old Europe" refuses to admit that the hate-infused use of force against the Western world by Islamist terrorists calls for new standards and methods to make the world safe for democratic order? Must a doctrine of preemptive strikes replace the policy of containment, because the frontal attack of Islamist terrorism blurs the boundary between civilian and military targets and thus per se denies the foundations of humanity? Or is the international security community, centered on the UNSC, willing and capable of adapting international law to the new threats to security, just as it had developed the doctrine of humanitarian intervention in response to the challenges of failed states, ethnic cleansing, and mass murder of political opponents?[6]

The latter, however, has no legal basis in the UN Charter. Correspondingly, Russia and China threatened to impose a veto to prevent humanitarian intervention against Serbia, claiming that the successor to Yugoslavia had all the rights of a sovereign state to act at its pleasure in all parts of the realm. The infringement of human rights led to the clash over the North Atlantic Treaty Organization's (NATO's) self-mandated intervention in Kosovo. In the Kosovo crisis, Britain and France shared the moral burden with the United States, justifying the use of force to stop Slobodan Milosevic's crusade against the Kosovo-Albanians. At about the same time (throughout 1998 and early 1999) but concerning Iraq, France parted company with the United States and Britain in enforcing disarmament and joined Russia in demanding the end of sanctions and restoration of Baghdad's full sovereignty. The French government disputed the argument that Iraq provided an example of the proliferation of weapons of mass destruction. Hence, President George W. Bush's brand-naming Iraq, Iran, and North Korea as the "axis of evil" provoked Paris on the one hand to question the sanity of the US intermingling of the "war on terrorism" with a war to change the Iraqi regime, and on the other hand dismissing Bush's argument that regime change in Iraq would facilitate peacemaking between Israel and the Palestinians. Instead, the world must urge Israel to accept a Palestinian state, which would induce the Arabs and Islamists to stop violence. Washington's claim that Arafat and then Hamas as well as Saddam Hussein must go, so that peace and democracy could get a chance, was countered by statements that US imperialism and Israeli occupation were the real culprits and must be subjected to multilateralism and international law.

In the competition of name-calling, President Jacques Chirac and Foreign Minister Dominique de Villepin of France, with the help of the Schroeder government in Germany, recruited a majority for their point of view. With regard to the substance of new international law, Paris and Berlin were in a dilemma. For one, they stated publicly that the expedient alliance with Russia and China was no basis for the evolution of a new value system; second, they must have been aware that their top military echelon as well as the European Union's (EU's) "security adviser" Javier Solana were strongly convinced of the need to place the fight against weapons of mass destruction at the top of common European defense priorities.[7] Acknowledging the need to address the option of using a preemptive strike is not, of course, the same as the quest for an Iraq-like situation to prove the case, as could be said of some US strategists. The alternative to US precedent-creating imposition of new order in "areas generating and exporting terror" is not simply to insist on formal procedures, but to define first the types of terrorism that the civilized world cannot stand, second the criteria for determining the duties of states with respect to preventing "mass attacks" from their territory on other states, and third the option for the UN and/or its regional organizations to mandate action against infringements of such "new" international security law.[8]

The fact that the Iraq War was the latest demonstration of US exceptionalism raises the questions of (1) whether opposite mindsets are at work or (2) whether both sides take the controversies as tests for doing things their way or (3) both. In support of the second argument, one could refer to the series of conferences at which the Europeans denied the US concessions while showing a willingness to compromise in order to buy Russia's or Japan's vote (e.g., to improve the chances for attaining the quorum required for the inauguration of the Kyoto Protocol). Are US provisos per se objectionable, or were Europeans unwilling to consider views from Washington, partly because they otherwise might have to join the United States in exerting more pressure on China, India, and Brazil with a view to reallocating the costs of international regimes? Is the regulatory competition between the United States and the EU an indicator of self-assertiveness/divisiveness or a stage in the process of agreeing on best available practices?[9]

In support of the first argument, one could refer to the stalwarts of US unipolar moment: Charles Krauthammer, praising the conservative turnaround in US positions, surmised that the Chirac-Schroeder alliance wanted to block the Bush administration's righteousness in order to recover "their" United States from the grip of the Republicans.

> The idea of a new international community with self-governing institutions and self-enforcing norms—the vision that requires the domestication of American power—is the view of the Democratic Party in the United States and of a large part of the American foreign policy establishment. They spent the last decade in power facilitating precisely those multilateral ties to restrain the American Gulliver and remake him into a tame international citizen.[10]

There is no doubt that Chirac and Schroeder aimed at replacing the dominance of US military force projection, attributed to the coalition between offensive liberal strategists (Paul Wolfowitz) and offensive realists (Donald Rumsfeld, Dick Cheney), with the primacy of deliberative processes and political dialogue. The Wolfowitz-Rumsfeld doctrine that the mission should define the coalition (of the willing), rather than permitting a coalition (e.g., NATO) or majority voting (UNSC) to determine the operation, is a reversal of the long-standing secret that Europe wanted the United States to lead as long as the United States moved in the direction the Europeans wanted it to go anyway.[11] Becoming the equal of the United States, at least in economic terms and as a "normative" superpower, the EU and Europeans expected Washington to accommodate their demands, notwithstanding conflicting interests and diverging strategies. Borrowing from Robert Kagan, the dominant view in Europe is "multilateral handcuffing of American power."[12] In reverse, unilateralism is a cry for US emancipation from "foreign" agendas: "Unilateralism simply means that one does not allow oneself to be hostage to others. . . . Coalitions are made by asserting a position and inviting others to join."[13] The clash can be seen as the culmination (breaking) point of the drawn-out battle between French-inspired ambitions either to domesticate the United States or to emancipate "old Europe" from US control, and US aspirations for emancipation from serving French (and British) desires to prevent the resurgence of the German-Russian deal-or-duel situation, so that the former could act freely on the global stage.[14]

The split within the West comprises conflicting interests and antagonistic mindsets that affect the tenets of Western thinking. The first part of this chapter addresses two issues, with a view to locating the difficulties in assessing the nature and the implications of the change(s) in our thinking about world order. First, what new order was emerging during the 1990s? Was there an unspoken assumption that the US unipolar moment was a force for good, that is, some kind of bargain between the other primary powers, in which they accept US military superiority and tolerate Washington's posture that none of them should use its potential to develop into a competing global power, on the one hand, and in which the United States agrees to practice multilateralism and consult them on the other?[15] What difference did the US posture make in the post–World War II and the post–Cold War era? Second, with no state challenging US hegemony, Al-Qaida stepped in. Immersed in thinking in terms of a clash of civilizations, Al-Qaida provoked the United States to launch a crusade against terrorism, calculating that the US government, obsessed by its proven vulnerability, would overreact and thus demonstrate to the world that the United States was the real projector of deadly force. What sort of power do "rogue states" and terrorist networks have?

The second part of this chapter focuses on fundamental changes in European definitions of the notion of security since the 1970s and how they caused a rift with US perspectives. The third part considers whether uniting Europe qualifies as a second pole in restructuring a multipolar world order. What should the Europeans do to and for themselves? Does the comprehensive EU polity, with its all-embracing perspectives, present a persuasive (convincing) example of *effective multilateralism,* so that its devotion to that principle is sustaining the UN's central position in maintaining and elaborating world order?[16] The fourth and final part looks at multipolarity and region-based ways of shaping order as an alternative to the stalemated UNSC-centered agenda for peace.

Thinking About World Order

The basic approach in post–World War II Western political thought about freedom, peace, and security is predicated on the assumption that the remaking of the international system in the image of domestic civil society is best for all. What is "good" for domestic order should become the guide for the conduct of international affairs: "the rule of law" should pervade the domestic and the international levels, with "multipolarity" at the international level corresponding to "pluralism" at the domestic level. The principles and norms defining domestic democratic order should infuse international organizations and regimes, even though the rules and decisionmaking procedures in the latter must pay attention to the asymmetries in power and wealth between nations. Under a state-centered perspective, governments are bound to honor the obligations inherent in their monopoly on the legitimate exercise of force domestically and to demonstrate self-restraint in employing the military as a means of last resort in defending the nation's security. The differences between the schools of thought (e.g., neorealism, liberal institutionalism, interdependence) were profound at the time but became marginal when confronted with the unbundling of territoriality and the changes in the notion of security (this will be discussed below).[17]

Whereas the principle of the state's monopoly on employing force[18] is still upheld in most democratic societies, the principle of non-resort-to-force, enshrined in the UN Charter and anchored in many treaties can—in a strict sense—be and is taken to mean that there exists no legal basis for the UNSC, not to speak of any other international body, to authorize use of force in cases other than those defined in Article 2, Chapters VI and VII.[19] This *reservatio mentalis* is reaffirmed by the publics in Organization for Economic Cooperation and Development (OECD) countries at a time when terrorist networks are reinventing the anarchists' propaganda of the deed and launching frontal attacks against "Westernizers" as a form of just war of liberation. The UN Security Council confirmed the individual and collective right of the United States to self-defense immediately after September 11, 2001. The UNSC did not object to the United States using the UN's doctrine of forming coalitions of the willing as the platform for organizing a worldwide campaign against international terrorism. The permanent members joined the US-led effort on a war scale,[20] each thinking of its own old- and new-style terrorist threats.

The global alliance dissipated when the Bush administration began to link the danger arising from Al-Qaida and its network to the states suspected of proliferation of weapons of mass destruction, especially Iraq. Gaining little support for its interlocking agenda, the United States—first the Pentagon (January 2002) and then the White House (*The National Security Strategy of the United States of America* dated September 8, 2002)—pushed for new visions and missions, asserting that the UN Charter is not suited to meet the challenges to order and security posed by actors who despise rules of international conduct and put their "divine right" above any secular law.[21] From this perspective, the United States postulates that sovereign states must retain the right to respond or even preempt threats to their national security, as they see it. Although other states agree that prompt action is necessary in the case of impending threats to national security, they denied the United States the right to be sole judge in the case of whether Iraq was either likely to attack the United States directly or assist terrorist groups in destroying symbols of US pride. But all agree that states—individually and through collective security or defense organizations—must sustain armed forces capable of fighting terrorism. Are security and defense back to being at the center of foreign policy thought?

What I want to emphasize is that traditional approaches have two tenets in common: (1) No other (supranational/integrative or international) agency has been upgraded to compete with or attempt to substitute for the state in the defense arena; and (2) security rather than peace (especially in the sense of Weltinnenpolitik) is the watchword or yardstick for international cooperation and coordination. In the following list I briefly describe several "traditional" approaches.

• *Neorealism* postulates that states owe their internal and external sovereignty to meeting the standard that they must constantly be renewing their credibility as a guarantor of security and custodian of the rule of law, civil rights, and property rights. As long as states perform to match that trust and obligation, they sustain the principle of nonintervention.

• *Wilsonianism* maintains that the world could be made safe for democracy by exporting its principle of peaceful change at home via public diplomacy and by resolving conflicts between nations in international institutions. The assumption is that interactions within nations are of concern to peaceful democracies, "for they shape how these nations treat their neighbors as well as their own people and whether they are reliable when they give us their word."[22]

• *Interdependence/International regime:* Under the concept of international custodianship, "the state acts in a manner that expresses not merely its own interests and preferences but also its role as the embodiment and enforcer of community norms."[23] The unspoken assumption is a triple set of assessments:

1. The ruling elites (in democracies) are more prone to communicate and cooperate with each other than they are in forging new reform coalitions at home.
2. The "masses" do not see the need for (or are too unskilled to try) developing an equivalent international understanding of their own.
3. The elites aim at international arrangements with a view to re-importing the guiding propositions and pragmatic measures they agreed upon into their domestic order.

The *conditio sine qua non* for the continuous success of international regime building is the ability of participating governments to deliver.[24] But as argument 2 has become obsolete, the vision is stalled. The self-organization of the masses is aiming at demonstrating to elected governments that their mandate no longer implies the power to impose internationally negotiated agreements on the peoples back home.

Hegemonic stability merges the interpretation of the singular historical experience of the United States in the Cold War era—the making of the American age—with general observations elaborated in the aforementioned "theories."[25] The United States acted as a hinge between "free Europe" (i.e., Organization for European Economic Cooperation [OEEC]—Europe rather than simply NATO—and European Economic Community–Europe) and Japan/Southeast Asia[26]—under the notion of security of the West, and between the domains of security/defense matters and international political economy.[27] It should be noted, however, that the US role of security guarantor and controller of (West) Germany's and Japan's reliability as peaceful democracies coincided with US support for the reemergence of Germany and Japan as economic hubs in their regions and the subsequent, even though contentious, acknowledgment of their claim to evolve their own capitalist model, which in turn promoted Bonn's and Tokyo's habit of admonishing the United States to practice sound finance.

The difference, of course, is that the United States pursued multilateral strategies in Europe. It practiced institution building in Europe, following a keen awareness that the American public would accept international involvement but object to both one-sided commitments and entangling alliances. In the "free" Asia-Pacific region, however, competing bilateral—and asymmetrical—contractual links with Japan, South Korea, and Thailand, and American (US and Canadian) backup of British-led (the Colombo Plan) and UN-affiliated (Economic Commission for Asia and the Far East) intraregional frameworks were characteristic of the US engagement. Notwithstanding this difference, it is the fact of US hegemony "that accounts for the explosion of multilateral arrangements."

> The breadth and diversity of multilateral arrangements across a broad array of issue-areas increased substantially after 1945. Quite naturally, therefore, one associates this change with the postwar posture of the US. . . . For American postwar planners, multilateralism served as foundational architectural principle on the basis of which to reconstruct the postwar world. . . . Even for the relatively more liberal United States, the international edifice of the open door had to accommodate the domestic interventionism of the New Deal. . . . The move toward some form of collective security organization . . . had to (strip away) the Wilsonian aspiration that collective security somehow be substituted for balance-of-power politics. . . . Instead, they sought to make the two compatible, so that the collective security mechanism would have a basis in the balance-of-power but also mute the more deleterious effects of balance-of-power politics.[28]

On top of such argument grounded in history, we should note another implication of the notion of US hegemony: The critical factor is the "permissive domestic political environment in the leading power," that is, the fact that the distinctive organizing principles of the world order postures of US governments[29] resonated with the US form of nationalism,[30] and the concomitant advocacy and export of such prescriptions abroad. The affinity of the multilateral world order principles to the "sense of self as nation" is assumed to rest upon the successful experiment of interethnic accommodation at home.

Both the evidence in support of this thesis and the acceptance of US hegemony in the relevant time span raise serious problems, but the arguments bear a sufficient grain of salt such that they can be carried along for the purpose of contrasting one set of distinctive propositions with the current divergence between principles of order at play in the US understanding of the world and the ideas evoked by Europeans for the grounding of world order. What empirical analysis, but no theory, can account for is the difference that personality can make; bluntly speaking, similar to taking away the emperor's new clothes, the situation discloses the flimsiness of the *Lebenslüge* (self-deception), which had hitherto allowed alliance partners to mend fences, and opens the floodgates for recriminations.[31] The Europeans may be willing to accommodate the unique power of the United States, but they react furiously to being accused of bigotry. They are accustomed to living under the umbrella of US power while disputing the US *logic* that the United States, in order to be the guarantor of peace, needs weapons that others do not and should not have.[32]

Rogue States and/or Terrorist Networks

Starting from Susan Strange's application of structural power to both regular states and private command centers like the Mafia, I shall extend this idea further to include both rogue states and terrorist networks.[33] The resemblance between the sources of power of states and of private force-based units should not, however, mask the differences in legitimation and procedure. When applied to the nonstate/statelike organizations, the terms refer to an older, simpler version of the notion of ruling power (Herrschaft). The indicators include

- the acquisition of armaments: for terrorist states and groups, the possession of most dangerous weapons is the big stick that should shock the strong (the United States and its allies) and provide leverage to defeat the will to resist, or at least serve to blackmail the strong into granting the wanted concessions (e.g., North Korea);

- the extraction of taxes from those it pretends to protect;
- the use of violence to ensure obedience within its public-at-large and especially within its ranks;
- the reference to beliefs rooted in society and the claim to loyalty to the head of state, leadership of clans, etc.;
- the proliferation of money power/credit through possession, production, and trade in drugs, arms, human trafficking, forgery, or money laundering;
- the ability to spread but also to control knowledge; the leadership circle uses efficient means of communication to shape the mindset of its followers and to employ propaganda to incite protest movements against foreign governments who are determined to restrict international trade in narcotics, for example; and
- censure to exclude information about the world outside that could change the views imposed by the regime.

In spite of the obvious objections, I would like to submit the proposition that it is weaknesses in state-based structures that influence the ability of the blackmailing powers to distort the evolution of world order principles.[34] Although most of us did and do welcome the functional retreat of the state (e.g., deregulation and privatization), which began in the late 1970s, certain private force-based and force-using units exploited the change in statehood within the OECD to introduce hate-inspired types of violence into international relations, ranging from kidnapping of Western tourists to attacking both civilian and military symbols of US Western societies with the announced intent of causing a massacre and demonstrating the failure of the state to protect its citizens. Their wars know of no borders, no open deployment, no rules of engagement, but aim at record numbers of deaths with one single strike. In response to this new threat to international peace, the UNSC agreed in September 2001 to extend Article 51 to permit states to respond to acts of terror by nonstate actors with resort to the use of force (see UNSC Resolution 1368). But as the resolutions against Israel show, the community of states begs to differ on the appropriate reaction of a state to attacks on its citizens; Israel is admonished to abide by the Geneva Convention of 1949, whereas the international community invents all sorts of excuses why the Palestinian Authority cannot prevent Hamas from bombing civilian targets in Israel.[35] It is not even considered an issue whether member states of the United Nations must be asked to prohibit the appeal to hatred or at least stipulate that authorities must do their best to deny hate-preaching organizations the opportunity to prepare and launch assaults from their soil against *soft* (unprotected) civilian targets located in the territory of the "enemy-state."[36]

Changes in European Notions of Security and Economy

The long-standing dependence of Western Europe's security on the nuclearization of the US (and British) defense guarantee was bound to induce Europeans to search for an enlarged notion of security. With the shift to the stalemate in the contest between the superpowers and the simultaneous improvement in the economic situation of Western Europe compared to the relative decline of US hegemony, the Europeans took the opportunity to assert their share in regime building: to define the rules and to define the *rebus sic stantibus* clauses and the exemptions from the rules.[37] In these disputes, the Europeans emphasized multilateralism and their experience in harmonizing rules or developing common practices. Criticism of US practices became a stock-in-trade; competition and rivalries over access to markets presented examples for proving the case. The expansion of the exchange relationships—in trade, services, investments, capital flows—and the accompanying mutual penetration of the internal markets in the EU and the United States increased the number of occasions for disputes about regulations.

The United States responded in kind but also took advantage of the fact that Europe was fragmented. Even though Germany's attempt to posit civil power versus military power challenged the United States more strongly in intellectual terms, Washington singled out France as the embodiment of mischievous competition in institution building: "France, it seems, would rather be more important in a world of chaos than less important in a world of order."[38] "The Bush administration, playing on its own preference for unilateral action, now portrays France and Germany as the new unilateralists, who obstruct cooperation among the allies and whose minority opposition, if carried through, will push the United States to proceed outside international institutions like NATO and the Security Council."[39]

Insisting on its right to interpret US interests to be sometimes different from those of its partners, the superpower slips into the role of being an ordinary country, too, without realizing that its acting alone or stipulating that it knows what is best for all makes a difference to the fate of multilateral institutions and international organizations. Europeans aiming at "multilateral handcuffing of American power" are countered with US warnings that whoever joins France in setting a premium on strategic partnerships with Russia, China, and India and assembling francophone African countries against the United States with a view to defining world order would force Washington to build coalitions of the willing. As always, the opposition from within the US foreign policy establishment speaks out against the rough-rider approach. Ivo Daalder, director for European Affairs, National Security Council, said, "We are witnessing a fundamental realignment of

US friendships and alliances that goes well beyond Europe. . . . I find it very shortsighted. Our strategic alliances in the past have always had an element of shared values."[40]

Much of the recurring debate focuses on the US redefinition of the assumptions behind established partnerships—namely, that deterrence and containment have become obsolete. The allies considered this shift to mean that to side with the United States would obligate them to become involved in US military assertiveness. That constitutes one focal point of the argument. Unfortunately, the debate misses the other—the fundamental changes in European thinking about how to achieve security and peace in the world and what standards of conduct nation-states should observe. These changes come under two headings:

1. Security with defense left out *(Gewaltfreie Gestaltung des Krisen- und Konfliktmanagements)*.[41]
2. Regulatory competition between a supposedly socially conscious European market economy and American robber capitalism. In milder terms, it reads like this: "Transatlantic relations will inevitably become increasingly competitive and possibly even [adversarial]. . . . People who once saw American power as a benign force may be starting to see us as predatory. Such a loss of international legitimacy for the global superpower would change the world."[42]

The link between the two is that the EU seeks to compensate for its limited projection power under the first (security) heading by asserting the power of its reputation under the second (economic) heading. The question for the United States is whether it is worth its while to comply with Europe's request for institution building, multilateralism, and legislating international law in order to recruit a stock of European goodwill in situations in which the United States might have to act alone (Afghanistan, Iraq, rescuing Taiwan or Israel?), or whether it should stick to its position and take the risk that the Europeans might manage to assemble a majority and thus be able to renege on compromises with the United States (e.g., with regard to the Kyoto Protocol or the Rome Statute that established the International Criminal Court). The question concerning the Europeans is whether they would have acted differently (e.g., in the Iraq crisis) if the US record in the other policy areas had not made anti-Americanism a popular stock-in-trade.

The common denominator of the two changes is the thesis that the EU constitutes a prototype of multiperspectival polity (Ruggie), a security community that

- effectively abolishes resort to force as a means for correcting imbalances of advantage among its member states;
- gives priority to redistribution with a view to leveling up the conditions of life in derelict and disadvantaged regions;
- introduces binding rules for peoples and governments of different member countries alike; and
- has responsibility and competence for the full range of policy arenas (in contrast to all other regional and international organizations, such as NATO, the Organization for Security and Cooperation in Europe, the Association of South-East Asian Nations, the Organization of American States, the International Monetary Fund, the World Trade Organization, etc.).[43]

"In addressing the problem of terrorism, the EU is, on paper, better placed than NATO to have an impact, given its ability to act as an agent of civilian power and coordination as well as its emergent capabilities in the defense sphere as such. If the war against terror requires a multidimensional approach, then the EU has some influence over almost all the relevant dimensions."[44]

These qualities destine the EU to lead in solving international problems.

The First Change in the Notion of Security

The change in the notion of security encompassed two stages. If not by intent, then as a result, the European content in both instances challenged the supposedly dominant current in US policies.[45] In the first stage, around the late 1960s and early 1970s, security was defined as freedom for each society to choose its path of development *(Freiheit der gesellschaftlichen Eigenentwicklung)*. It was a call for emancipation from the American age/American way. The historical background is obvious.[46] What counts is that Europe no longer subscribed to the doctrine of indivisible peace, better known as domino theory, but considered détente to be the best way to manage the East-West conflict in Europe. While the West German government accepted stability and peace in Europe through the divisions of Europe, Germany, and Berlin and while the superpowers engaged in the evolution of rules of conduct for their global contest, the emphasis shifted toward solving the serious economic, financial, social security, and education problems each country faced, even before the oil crises (1973–1975, 1980–1981) increased the dilemmas, but that shift also intensified the differences between the management capabilities of the members of the OECD world. Efforts were concentrated on repairing and reconstructing the international economy. The serious problems in the defense arena were put out of sight; the dilemmas of nuclear strategy were left to the strategic community; the understanding of the problems differed between the few within governments who cared and the "peace movements."[47] This ended the career of Chancellor Helmut Schmidt and gave a lifelong impetus to Genscherism[48] as the ruling elites' response to public anxieties. Hardly anyone in Europe noticed that the United States (under James Schlesinger and Donald Rumsfeld) laid the foundations in the mid-1970s for what by now has become the unprecedented superiority in conventional armed forces projection capability. Attention instead was focused on how Leonid Brezhnev provided the Soviet military with the means to win the strategic arms race, only to exhaust the Soviet Union's resources so that it fell prey a decade later to Reagan's display of US technology and credit power.

The gist of the argument is that the European notion of security covered every aspect of public attention, from job security and the right to work, to social security, to environmental safety, to various sorts of protectionism—everything except defense. It was deemed legitimate for countries like Germany (and Japan), who were called upon by the United States to pull the world economy from the abyss, to stick to their model of sound finance and defend their economic strategies against US intrusions; the German "paymaster" had to volunteer to facilitate compromise within the EU. Enlarging and extending the notion of security had two effects.

- The state's classical function as sole possessor and purveyor of policing and military forces did not matter much with respect to the new security tasks; civil powers create mechanisms and means other than simply repressive force to deal with the public's perception of security goals.
- In the early 1980s, with peace in Europe apparently assured through the US-Soviet balance of strategic deterrence, and by reinventing the doctrine that for Europeans conventional deterrence was an unacceptable alternative to nuclear deterrence, the Europeans saw no need to implement a US-induced NATO long-term defense program.[49] Although relying on the US nuclear umbrella, European allies criticized Jimmy Carter's and Reagan's relaunch of the strategic arms race. Most European countries in NATO, especially Britain during the 1970s and 1980s, experienced structural disarmament.[50]

Even though the mindset began to change in the early 1990s under the impact of the wars in the former Yugoslavia and Europeans resolved to participate in out-of-area conflicts, acknowledging the use of armed forces for collectively legitimated missions, the military capabilities remained relatively paltry. Only France made a virtue of the necessity to decrease Cold War–type conventional forces and restructure part of its military into rapid deployment/joint task forces (since the 1980s). Except for humanitarian interventions, the so-called Petersberg tasks (Western European Union, June 1992), Europe as a civil power dislodged defense needs from its mindset.[51]

The enlarged notion of security mentioned above has become commonplace in Western societies, as did the hope of benefiting from the peace dividend. In all issue areas except defense, preventive action generally constitutes a preferred option. Nevertheless the generic connotations of "Freiheit der gesellschaftlichen Eigenentwicklung" (freedom for each society to choose its path of development) still infuse the Europeans' distrust of the "American way."

For the best examples of how the enlarged notion of security plays out in government policies, I would single out the second Schroeder government (October 2002–September 2005) and the subsequent grand coalition government of Angela Merkel and Frank-Walter Steinmeier. They conceived of war prevention and peacekeeping as multidimensional, comprehensive, and intersecting components of foreign, development, financial, trade, and environmental policy. They also established both a special unit under the auspices of the foreign ministry and the Center for International Peace Missions. Because of the war in Afghanistan, these governments did not neglect the military dimension, but their policy stresses that the role of German troops is restricted to peace support operations, that is, civil and military administration, judicature, and police forces. Secondly, their policy emphasizes the cooperation and coordination of actors such as the UN, donor states, and nongovernmental organizations (NGOs) (i.e., "intersecting multilateralism" is a catchphrase in German and EU terminology). That interaction shapes the conduct of public authorities (both civilian and military) and the segments of society at the central level (capital) as well as on the periphery. Their policy reads like a compilation from the catalogue of conflict resolution studies. The emphasis is on structural prevention, aiming at the medium- and long-term reduction or even dissipation of causes and sources of critical tensions and patterns of confrontation in the reemerging "polity" of failing states. Among the instruments, the war on poverty, sustainable development, disarmament and arms control, and regional integration are considered most important.[52]

The Second Change in the Notion of Security

The second change in the notion of security refers to the marked tendency among European elites to favor enlarging as well as intensifying the binding power of regime codes and of UN resolutions; the International Criminal Court (ICC), the Kyoto Protocol, and their like are esteemed as institutions promoting and enforcing civilized conduct. Top officials, eminent lawyers, and party elites postulate the primacy of the collective security system, whose commonly resolved international norms should constrain the use of military force and prohibit unilateralism.[53] The stance is formulated with a view to handcuffing and domesticating the United States multilaterally.[54] The formula applies to nonmilitary policy areas, too. According to one scholar, "The announcement of . . . Chirac that the Kyoto Protocol would represent the first component of 'authentic global governance' was intended as an insult to the US."[55] It is no wonder that US senators—for example, Chuck Hagel—rejected the Kyoto Protocol Framework Convention on Climate Change (adopted December 1997) asserting that the UN would gain for the first time the power to prescribe how much energy a nation might consume and what sort of energy it had to be; the UN would be empowered to come to the United States and inspect, control, and close down establishments; and US citizens would not be able to do much about it, except to appeal to the International Court of Justice at The Hague.[56]

After observing the Clinton and Bush administrations' resolve to act alone if necessary, EU member states, which are obligated to practice consensus building and diplomatic coaxing in Europolitics, jump at chances to assemble their type of coalition of the willing.[57] Their coalitions would embrace small and middle powers in one case, Russia and China in another, and also NGOs. They always pretend that they are neither ganging up against the United States nor sacrificing their values and beliefs to the promotion of the moral and material aspirations of their partners in majority building.[58]

What is most important about the second change in the notion of security is its insistence on "democratization," in both equality of voting rights for all states and representation of NGO networks at all international lawmaking conferences. Democratization aims at turning the tables on Washington's efforts to spread democracy via embedded power politics, a mixture of Wilsonianism and the doctrine that no rival superpower should reemerge in Eurasia or Asia-Pacific. Instead of the imposing power of the United States, a majority of states have resolved—operating either via international conventions like the Rome Statute establishing the ICC, the Kyoto Protocol, or the Ottawa Convention to ban land mines, or by turning UNSC meetings into a sort of tribunal—to become promoters of new international law. The United States is seen as representing traditional state-centered power politics, seeking to take advantage of the unipolar moment to carry responsibility for the rest of the world without the need to consult the many about how to change the world for the better.[59] As former secretary of state Madeleine Albright maintained, the United States is the indispensable nation that manages to move the world to take effective measures; without US *hyper-puissance,* it would become less likely that international law could prevail.[60] By contrast, European elites and NGOs count on legalization of international politics, egalitarian world society, and progress through the activities of civil society–based organizations.[61] To them, the spread of nongovernmental organizations is a force for good and their existence is so well entrenched that they must be given a voice in envisaging, designing, and defining world order.[62] For the US government, NGOs already exert too much power and should not be treated—at the international level—like peers.[63] The erosion of "statism" and the sovereign rights of state has gone too far.[64] According to John Bolton, former US ambassador to the United Nations, "The notion that the Security Council or any other body could actually dilute American decision-making authority is simply not acceptable."[65] US delegations would threaten nonratification by Congress rather than go along with the doctrine that international rulings (by the World Trade Organization or the ICC) must have precedence over national prescriptions.

In defense of sovereignty, the White House and Congress assert that the leading power must demonstrate its willingness and ability, especially after September 11, to guarantee the peoples' safety (at a cost) and to improve standards of living both at home and abroad. The US government, while inviting NGOs to cooperate in these goals,[66] rejects the new doctrine that civic organizations are already doing many good services (especially in the third world), thus substituting for classical functions of the state.[67] International law, if it codified US moral standards, could become the medium for peaceful progress in the world.

It is telling that the preamble to the Rome Statute lists the common bond and the conscience of humanity as the first terms of reference. Other inspirations come from development and aid policy, the ban on land mines, and so on. Why not extend the lesson, that donors need the engagement of NGOs to change the conditions of life in developing countries for the better, to international affairs in general? Why not urge states, especially the superpower, to acknowledge that each and all of them must submit to the rule of law, which would be the product of international negotiations?[68]

The visible hand of the NGOs should, so to speak, replace the power of the United States in shaping international statutes and rule-making procedures. The overwhelming power of the United States should no longer be the enabling or rejecting factor on the international stage. Instead of (re)turning to hegemonic stability, the world should move forward with dismantling statism and put its trust in promoting the role of civil society–based organizations.[69]

European governments (and others, especially Canada) encourage the new idea of domesticating the United States multilaterally, but do so for their own reasons. They object to the US double standard, in which it establishes a world order, under which the Americans implant their values, standards of conduct, and material interests globally, while reserving the right to act unilaterally in defense of their vital interests or make use of waivers and escape clauses.[70]

It is not yet clear whether a coalition between governments, including all members of the EU, and NGOs would be willing to and capable of repeating the maneuver at Rome where they blocked the US attempt to incorporate a link between the UNSC and the ICC in the statute. Apart from the damage to the US image created by President Bush's undoing of his predecessor's last-minute signature, two problems emerge.

- How to reconcile the doctrine that only the UNSC is authorized to promote humanitarian intervention as a new pillar of international law—and in that context clarify the legal basis for peace enforcement ("robust mandate") and peacekeeping missions—with the privilege of the International Criminal Court to define through its practice the meaning of the items under crimes against humanity and war crimes (Art. 8.2.b.IV)?
- How to justify international law with reference to democratization, if a majority of states pass a statute and establish the ICC, but none of the most populous states—China, India, the United States, Russia, Indonesia, Pakistan—joins the membership? Hitherto, international organizations with a say on central aspects of state sovereignty—defense/military operations (UNSC) and money (the International Monetary Fund)—have been constituted to reflect the asymmetry in what different nations can do. With respect to its own institution building, the EU is continuously evolving weighted voting procedures but maintains the principle of consensus building in politically sensitive issue areas. Neorealism supplies the theoretical basis for such a rationale.

These questions, however, raise another big question. World order hitherto rested on the assumption that what is best practice and valid within democracies must set the standards for international conduct. Now, this transfer of good governance is connected with the message that democracies, particularly the United States, have rejected internally the principle that the rich and wealthy could claim more rights (voting power) in politics than others. Other welfare state societies went further and established the norm—as the basis for redistributive policies—that those citizens who have more should be obligated to pay proportionately more into the public purse. Within limits, this mindset was applied to foreign economic assistance policy. The third world's attempt to anchor the principle in the new international economic order and upgrade the Economic and Social Council into a second pillar of the UN dissipated in the 1980s, but now a coalition of the EU, Canada, other states, and the NGOs have resolved to restore that agenda.

Is, then, international politics, inspired by European governments and NGOs, on the move to turn the caring-state doctrine into a generalized organizing principle of world economic order? Would their success in founding the ICC generate a spillover effect into other areas, starting from the premise that poverty breeds terrorism,[71] hence the urgency for accelerating the quest for a global partnership in development policy? Or would the other premise—that imposing "democracy" (in the sense of Western values) on Arab and/or Muslim states would set the world on fire—lead to a decoupling of democratization (in the sense of regime change) from development assistance?[72] Would this decoupling increase the split between the EU and the United States—the EU objecting to US discrimination against the Mugabes, Hamas, and their likes, the United States demanding a change in the approach to development aid?

The Change in the Notion of Regulatory Competition

There is a tendency in Europe to claim parity with the United States or even to claim primacy over the United States with respect to special agreements made under the auspices of the World Trade Organization, such as financial services. The EU is the equal of the United States in world trade and foreign direct investment. It has been continuously immersed in regime building; its achievements in uniting Europe have been likened to creating a patchwork of regimes by William Wallace.[73]

Europe is now faced with the task of making its legislation and enforcement regarding multinational corporations and small and medium-size enterprises compatible with the rule making and judicial findings of the World Trade Organization. The EU enacted a series of rules on investment and subsidies, government procurement, banking regulations, accounting standards, competition in service industries, and mergers and acquisitions. In this process, the European Commission investigates the worldwide activities and business connections of companies penetrating Euroland markets, exchanges information with the equivalent US agencies, and issues prescriptions concerning mergers and acquisitions, thereby influencing corporate strategies. Having completed the Common Market as a truly internal market and preferential area for all domestic firms, the EU sees its eastern enlargement, association contracts, and series of free trade agreements (with, e.g., Mexico, and Mercosur) as chances to extend its regulatory regimes to the applicants' and partners' economies.[74]

The sprawl of the EU via economic diplomacy is accompanied by protests against US attempts to export its values and rule-making capabilities into Euroland.[75] In response to the challenge of the penetrating power of US companies, especially credit rating agencies, and regulatory standards, members of the European Parliament and advisory councils demand that the EU establish some sort of European Monroe Doctrine.[76]

Due to its enlargement processes, the EU now borders unstable and conflict-prone states. Even though the EU has no experience in handling neighbor-states on the verge of failing on their own,[77] neither the option to invite the US protector back in (as in Bosnia in 1995 or Kosovo in 1999) nor the option to delegate regulation to Russia, which borders on the same range of states, is considered viable.[78] Rather, the EU must, according to former commissioner Chris Patten,[79] test whether its multiperspectival preventive diplomacy and crisis management can expedite peace and reform beyond its proper integration zone of member states. It is hard to believe that the officials' belief in what they assign as tasks in the enlarged EU's backyard is as firm as the coined words about the EU being a supplier of security.[80]

The EU's search for a world order profile is not limited to its near-abroad. Praising the modernity of its political systems, the EU asserts that it must also show the flag as chief architect of global order. "The US is going to have to accept that the Europeans are using clout," an EU official said in Washington. "The global market is not an American market. . . . Europe wants leadership and control of the agenda."[81] Regulatory competition, however, has to have regard for the strategies and concerns of multinational corporations operating on both sides of the Atlantic and in other areas; these actors urge the watchdog agencies to inform and consult each other about the yardsticks and instruments with which the EU and US legislators have endowed them to monitor and control competition. The fact that transatlantic business partners—rather than NGOs—are third actors in the regulatory competition may have a different impact on the outcome of the rivalry-and-partnership relations between the EU and the United States than the alignments between European governments and NGOs on the aforementioned politicized issues (the ICC, the Kyoto Protocol, etc.).

What Europeans Did for and to Themselves

Intra-European Rivalries and Partnerships

The uneasy coexistence of the divisive as well as convergent approaches and interests discussed above not only affects the relationships among the United States, NATO, and the EU, but also intersects intra-European rivalries and partnerships. Although predicated on the doctrines of indivisible security and collectively (rather than nationally) balanced forces, NATO suffered throughout its existence from the fact that neither burdens nor risks were equally shared. The main features of the Cold War and post–Cold War periods were as follows.[82]

- The United States predicated its role as a European power on the reconciliation between France and Germany, notwithstanding the tensions between Paris and Washington because the United States could never do it right from the French perspective. As long as Germany did not copy French assertiveness vis-à-vis the United States and France needed the United States to control the reliability of Germany, the French-US-German triangle got over the tensions within each of the three bilateral relationships. It survived the strains of the Carter and Reagan eras, when the Bonn(e) Entente departed from the indivisibility-of-security doctrine encapsulated in the US version of the "security of the West"/North Atlantic security community. It even survived French attempts to "liberate" Europe from US-NATO dominance, at least until 1998, when the UK and Germany joined the French effort.[83]

• Great Britain aimed at sustaining the presence of the "giant to the West" in Europe: "much as Germans cannot tolerate a truly hostile Russia, so Britons are fearful of potentially absent Americans. If German security in the last resort is about managing the giant to the East, so British security . . . is mainly about managing the giant to the West."[84] Not even at St. Malo in December 1998—where Tony Blair and Chirac agreed to promote a European autonomous defense force—did the British support a position in which a "unifying" Europe would relate to the United States. "The risk of the US becoming frustrated by the incapability of the Europeans" to back diplomacy by credible military forces made British governments engage in European defense and "give a lead" to an autonomous political and military capability for the EU.[85]

• The Federal Republic of Germany (FRG) postulated the need to manage—together with France—relationships with the giant to the East; what the Helmut Schmidt–Valéry Giscard d'Estaing tandem began in the mid-1970s evolved into Genscherism and was continued in Helmut Kohl's lining up support for Boris Yeltsin. The FRG also leaned toward the French interest in, first, relaunching the Western European Union as a security organization for out-of-area tasks and crisis management (EUROCORPS), and then incorporating it into the European Security and Defense Policy, balanced with the self-imposed task of building bridges for the return of France into NATO's military organization.

• France, immersed in Gaullism, asserted that Europe—including Russia as a genuine European power—must regulate its own security affairs; only then could it live in peace.[86] The United States was kept in as a residual power to reassure West Germany against Soviet blackmail and to help France to maintain its post–World War II superior status compared to the FRG; it was assumed that the United States as well as Britain was interested in seeing France be politically stronger than Germany. This offers France the occasion to use Germany against Britain in the EU and against the United States in transatlantic relationships and to invite Russia to complement the EU's role as counterweight to the US hyperpower.

The Dissolution of the 1998–1999 Consensus

It is no surprise that the Blair government sided with the United States in demanding that Europe had to face the Iraqi threat; it is another question whether Blair miscalculated in thinking he could rally Chirac to the cause, and whether Chirac, angry about Blair's challenge of France's primacy in European matters, attempted the political assassination of Blair rather than lending his hand to the ouster of Saddam Hussein.[87] What came as a surprise was that Schroeder, ignoring the fact that he had been roughed up by Chirac at least twice (in March 1999 and December 2000), played "Gaullism" to Chirac in August–September 2002, signaling that he wanted to diminish US influence in Europe and throughout the world and to shape the EU as a counterweight to the United States. Schroeder discarded the two basic tenets of the FRG's foreign policy—respect for the small and medium powers in integrated Europe and the primacy of US-NATO ties—and adopted two traditional French-Gaullist stances: directorate in European affairs and Europeanization of the EU's security and defense postures.[88] One may speculate that he gave in to the temptation to practice left-wing "Wilhelminism"[89] or wanted to demonstrate that he plays in the same league with Vladimir Putin, Jiang Zemin, and Chirac, without, however, noticing that he got nothing in return for his calling the tune for countervailing US arrogance.

More importantly, the German chancellor apparently made up his mind that it would serve him better to ignore at least two central aspects:

- France, due to its self-elected special position in NATO, has no established record for being a supplier of security in and for Europe. This is important because the EU has committed itself to include Turkey, thus moving the "security belt" to the borders of Iraq, Syria, and Iran.[90] The EU is thus adjusting to NATO's membership, but France refused to permit the NATO Council to give the Military Committee the inevitable mandate to formalize the procedure to assist Turkey in case of attack from Iraq.[91] Chirac welcomed Turkey's refusal to allow the United States to build up a second war front as a sign of maturing democracy, but is adamant against Turkey's great power ambitions. In general, France's position is singular because it had developed a rapid deployment force before 1990, but defines its own and EU military missions from a neocolonial, geostrategic, and geoeconomic perspective.[92]
- France and Britain noticed that the Schroeder government was not matching their input into creating a European defense capacity. The Christian Democratic Union–Christian Social Union (CDU/CSU) opposition was correct in stating: "He who dismantles his army cannot expect to get a say in defense matters. He who cannot deliver in military terms, should not request that Europe must speak with a single voice in Defense and Security Policy."[93]

In order to mend the credibility gap, then foreign minister Joschka Fischer started to stick out his neck with an appeal to overcome the chastening Balkan, Kosovo, Afghanistan, and Iraq experiences by putting Europe's money where its mouth is, that is, by allocating substantial resources to achieve a concrete, stronger, and more usable military capability.[94] France and Germany must be aware that in international conflicts the United States could not be left alone to do the military work;[95] developing capabilities for "robust" peace enforcement missions should not be inspired by anti-Americanism. With this volte-face from the key representative of the Green Party and peace movement, the FRG may actually be siding with the French in showing that the aspiration to remain relevant for truly multilateral peace enforcement missions requires either

- a shift in individual government expenditures or—alternatively, as recommended by Fischer—authorizing the EU to raise a special tax to meet the force goals for expeditionary operations; or
- a contract between willing governments to pool the existent military forces into an operational Common European Security and Defense Policy and to underpin this mobile joint task force with the concomitant European collaboration in specifying priorities in the production and procurement of modern combat equipment.[96]

As matters stood in March 2003 (as well as 2008), "the problem is that the military goals which the EU set for itself in 1999—the Helsinki headline goals—though modest enough in themselves, appear now to be increasingly marginal to the immediate needs of the European allies and the transatlantic alliance. . . . the headline goals appear only to offer hope of too little extra capacity."[97] Hence the disparity in military power between the United States and the EU remains and is bound to spark resentments on both sides of the Atlantic. The resentment is ambiguous. On the one hand—and in contrast to the United States—the EU is averse to converting more of its resources into military might and to employing them for pacifying the peripheries of its enlarged realm; on the other hand, Berlin and Paris believe they know the right solution to the problem—and doubt that the United States can do it right—but find it difficult to back up diplomacy by threatening employment of sanctions or "policing missions," partly because the required military and police units are committed elsewhere.[98] Accused of doing too little and too slowly to mold an effective police force in Kabul, the Germans transferred that task to the EU, which faces difficulties of its own in recruiting personnel and equipment for joint management of its external borders.[99] The United States, overstretched in Iraq and Afghanistan, expects that its partners, although not (yet?) willing to replace the combined US military and civil presence with their own capabilities, should at least comply with the US idea of making NATO the anchor of the democracies' stabilization and peace support operations.[100] This version of "robust" West-only "might to make rights" resembles Rumsfeld's coalition of the willing too much and contradicts the German-French basic instinct that Russia and China should not be excluded because they could be called protectors of "evil" rulers but must be engaged in consultations with a view to making deals, however time-consuming the process could be and vague and face-saving the results might be.

Apart from the problem of the capability gap and the question of how long it will take to implement the Common European Security and Defense Policy's plan for autonomous action in coping with the instability in the bordering areas,[101] two other issues are on the agenda. Will the EU restrict itself to the established task of being able to manage one heavy mission (e.g., separation of belligerent forces) and one light mission (humanitarian or noncombatant evacuation operation) simultaneously,[102] or will the lessons of Iraq and Afghanistan jolt Sarkozy, Merkel, and Brown into the posture that the diplomatic front must be complemented by sufficient military capability, so that the United States could never again benefit from Europe splitting itself up?[103]

Sarkozy would only have to liberate France from "military Gaullism" in order to gain credibility as Europe's distinctive security supplier, but the German grand coalition government faces the formidable task of reversing its claim that all that is necessary is *gewaltfreie Gestaltung* (nonviolent arrangement) of conflict management, and instead convincing its rank-and-file as well as the electorate of the soundness of Fischer's appeal that the EU must also become a military actor. In the words of Alain Lamassoure, former French minister for European affairs and member of the European parliament, *Europe* must be willing to do the military *Drecksarbeit* (dirty work), too; Barack Obama took a similar message to Europeans.[104] Likewise, Merkel and Sarkozy have to convince the EU that anti-Americanism cannot and should not be the glue for European unity. In view of the available capabilities on the one hand and the common task of restructuring world order and subduing the appalling force of international terrorism on the other, the EU could only supplement NATO and the United Nations and with it the United States.[105] When the stakes are high, as in Afghanistan, the Germans want to adhere to the terms of Article 7 of the UN Charter with regard to International Security Assistance Force—including responsibility for its Provincial Reconstruction Team (PRT) zone in the north, which Berlin since June 2006 wanted to become a command headquarters. The United States, however, having established its PRT zones under Operation Enduring Freedom (based on Article 51 of the UN Charter) and bearing the brunt—together with British and Canadian armed forces—of combating Taliban and Al-Qaida forces, aimed at extending NATO-led ISAF operations to the embattled south and using the US dual command of ISAF and Operation Enduring Freedom in the arena for more centrally steered dispatches of forces to where the serious battlegrounds are. The Germans suspected that the United States envisions shifting the burden to NATO-ISAF operations in order to reduce its troop commitment in Afghanistan and restructure the military to treat stability operations as a core mission. Identifying France with NATO's mission to stop Afghanistan from again becoming a hub of international terrorism, Sarkozy resolved to deploy a battalion in the US-led regional command east, thus enabling the United States to increase its presence in the south and helping to meet Canada's request that other allies must bear the strain from renewed insurgent violence or it would pull its 2,500 troops out of Afghanistan.

The second and perhaps more disturbing issue is that none of the veto-bearing members of the UNSC is genuinely disposed to put the decisions of multilateral institutions ahead of interests of national security (in their defense and economic dimensions), except that they ensure for themselves a contractual or constitutional right to have the final say.[106] Whenever it came to the test, the Schroeder government—not only with regard to the Iraq question but in many intra-EU matters—did not strengthen the international, that is, supranational institutions. The record of the past also shows that France always insisted—partly because of the constitutional rights of the president and the *problematique* of cohabitation governments—on establishing "head of government" councils as the sole decisionmaking authority in NATO and the EU; if the partners hesitated to follow the French lead or disagreed with France's demands, France opted out (in the case of NATO) or proceeded with second-best stopover mechanisms (in the case of the Economic and Monetary Union).[107] The consequence is that compromises are not allowed to develop a dynamic of their own—a "must" for genuinely effective multilateralism—but are subjected to the proviso that the interpretation of the agreement as well as the decision about taking the next step belong to the national capitals. French insistence that the UNSC must run the show is nothing but a device to ensure that France's handwriting is firmly entrenched in the rulebook.

The task for the incumbent German grand coalition government and post-Chirac France is formidable. They have to renew the compromise about how to reassure the partners in the unstable periphery in the east facing Russia's drive to restore structural power in its former sphere of dominance and at the same time stabilize the Mediterranean periphery against the repercussions of the escalating conflict between Iran/Shiite expansionism and Arab/Sunni assertiveness.[108] Due to its commitments to assist in promoting the rule of law, economic progress, and public services for its many regional and individual partners, the EU, especially France and Germany, are overstretched with respect to satisfying the diverse claims of the "clientele" and balancing their diplomatic, economic, and cultural activities. Since the United States is confronted with similar challenges and engaged in many of the same areas, Germany and France must get their act together while taking care that the United States is neither undermined in its efforts to strengthen the West's position in unstable areas nor taking advantage of the cooperativeness of the Europeans (i.e., marginalizing the EU's presence in such regions).[109] In this respect, Chancellor Merkel is more cognizant of the importance of sustaining US influence, whereas Sarkozy—although friendly toward the United States but vulnerable to the reproach of "Atlanticist obsession"—is seeking to reorient France toward building and expanding national industrial and financial conglomerates and emphasizing the sociocultural and politico-economic differences between a French-inspired Europe and the power-guzzling habits of the United States, which trample on the concerns of others.

Multipolarity and Region-Based Ways of Shaping Order

What we have discussed is whether the European mindset and the everlasting process of uniting Europe qualify the EU as a second pole in reconstructing a multipolar world polity order.[110] The Sarkozy-Merkel coalition, if it copes with the Chirac-Schroeder legacies—the problems of self-inflicted torture of enduring Gaullism and the spurs of German singularization—might for domestic reasons have to depart from their momentary track of strengthening NATO's European pillar.[111] Ironically, the ensuing expenses and the exposure of Europe to security threats as well as the revolt of their publics against European "militarism" may stop them from embarking on the path of the "third option."[112] The latter would make sense anyway only when Britain is reconciled to the project of linking EU resources and the Common European Security and Defense Policy. Britain and Germany were instrumental in establishing (since March 2003) the EU-NATO Capabilities Group, which is to ensure the complementarity, compatibility, and transparency of EU and NATO capability development planning.[113] The question is whether Sarkozy, aiming at a "new Franco-British brotherhood" (as of March 2008) will pursue his ambition for a EU defense force as a complement to NATO and frame the terms and conditions for rejoining NATO's military organization in a sensible way.[114]

Besides, both Paris-Bonn and Washington-London asserted that the courting of Russia, China, and others depends on circumstances (Iraq, Iran, North Korea, Darfur) and should not be perceived as the core of a new value community that would become the workhorse for legislating world order. The self-restraint does not prevent the revival of dissonances. When Frank-Walter Steinmeier elaborated in October 2006 on the Foreign Office's Annäherung durch Verflechtung (rapprochement through involvement) doctrine, the "Atlanticists" in Germany (including Chancellor Merkel) and US commentators warned that engaging Russia under the Putin regime in designing Europe's shape could easily put Germany in opposition to the US desire to relaunch the transatlantic partnership and defend common interests with respect to nuclear nonproliferation (Iran), reciprocity in trade and energy, enforcing UN-mediated solutions for Kosovo and Bosnia, and handling "Kyoto and beyond."[115] After all, the Putin regime demonstrated its intention to pressure the United States to let Russia maximize its influence in Iran and in the EU's eastern borderlands and exploit its oil and gas resources to alter contracts with US companies.

In view of the diminished influence of the United States over events in divided societies (Iraq, Afghanistan, Lebanon, Sudan, Democratic Republic of Congo, etc.) on the one hand and the ineffectiveness of the EU-3 (Britain, France, and Germany) and the United States to exert meaningful pressure on Iran on the other hand, the German, French, and British governments must contribute ideas about a sound status of self-centered and ambitious powers like Iran or Sudan, who disregard rulings of the UNSC and international regime agencies and thereby challenge fundamental assumptions of the principal Western powers to have the UN define what limitations should be imposed on the exercise of sovereign rights by "rogue states." In their quest for *political* solutions, the Europeans are inclined to accept manageable deals that are ambiguous about the obligations of such "wrongdoers." The United States, however, demands that the West should agree on the range of effective sanctions that might induce a change of course and then proceed immediately, whether Russia and China, the other veto powers in the UNSC, would go along.[116]

The EU would have to find out (1) who the other "poles" would be and what value-adding strategies could be practiced with them, and (2) how seriously the others would take the EU's capability to share risks with them and in return to what extent the other poles have regard for the complicated evolution of Europolitics.[117] The question of what states or associations of states qualify as poles is one critical issue.[118] More important in determining what effective multilateralism (the EU's watchword) stands for is the issue of defining the hard core of security that the international community should uphold. It makes no sense to circumscribe the spectrum of measures targeted states are allowed to take to protect their citizens against an array of attacks by international terrorists, when nothing is done simultaneously to codify the activities that must not be tolerated in any environment. It cannot be left to certain governments to make arrangements with proven terrorist groups on the basis that the latter would not display their fatal power and disrupt public life in the tolerating country. The improvement in practical cooperation between homeland security agencies in response to September

11 is something, but it does not affect the different approaches to dealing with hate-generating terror cells or the bigger issue of agreeing on a "responsibility to prevent" doctrine and acting upon it.[119] Separately—and even more damaging—is the shirking of the issue that temporary members of the Security Council such as Syria openly sponsor terrorist organizations.

All of this can be explained and excused with so-called commonsense arguments that the practice of benign neglect is less costly than the incalculable consequences of strictly applying the law to the non-law-abiding successors to the anarchists. This know-nothing attitude of various members of the UN toward the blackmailing power of certain states and terrorist networks makes it very difficult to expect the UN to take steps to prevent the spread of violence. The posture that, apart from the inherent right of states to self-defense, only the UNSC can authorize resort to force to resist threats to international peace, has caused a stalemate between (1) the belief that Article 2 (via a majority of votes in the UNSC) is crucial and (2) the "precedent" that the war in Kosovo and the Iraq War established, that if any veto power threatens or exercises its prohibitive vote then "a coalition of the willing," with references to moral standards enshrined in a series of UNSC resolutions, substitute and implement the substance of the agreed-upon resolutions.

With respect to peace enforcement, it had been easy to say that the use of force in this case was envisaged by the framers of the UN Charter. But can the UN any longer restrict itself to the mission of separating warring parties and urge an early armistice? Or is the UN as the organization of sovereign states obliged to mandate a clear-cut victory against a "party"—like Milosevic's Serbia—claiming a right to "ethnic cleansing"? Can the UNSC extend its vague notions ("international responsibility to protect human life") invented for the justification of humanitarian intervention to mean that it is ready to consider it the duty of the UNSC to define and decide under what circumstances preemptive military operations are appropriate?[120] As a prerequisite, the UN, possibly the Department of Peacekeeping Operations or the new Peacebuilding Support Office, might have to be empowered to develop early warning capabilities, so that "independent" evidence would be at hand and alert the UNSC to a scenario (e.g., Kosovo in 1991) in which it might opt for early coercive diplomatic action.[121] This incidence is mentioned in order to stress the point that too many other suspects or proven worst cases come to mind. Consequently, the UNSC would have had to pass robust mandates by the dozen, at the risk of being short on contributing member states on the one hand or being blamed—like the International Monetary Fund—for making a difficult situation worse on the other.

In view of what happened to UN-mandated missions in the early 1990s and to Boutros Boutros-Ghali's *Agenda for Peace* (January 1992), seeking to deploy peacekeepers without local consent and to turn the attention away from cases affecting Europe to genocides in third world areas, especially Africa, and the disputes about Kosovo and Iraq, I would recommend deemphasizing the focus on the UNSC monopoly.[122] Instead, the advocates of multipolarity should be taken at their word and demonstrate their ability and willingness to

- concentrate on working out a collective security arrangement for their respective regions (on the model of the CSCE Paris Charter on European Security of November 1990 and the revised OSCE Charter of 1999); organizations other than the UNSC, such as the Economic Community of West African States, have already prepared themselves to act in the face of the Security Council's inability or unwillingness to forge a collective response;[123] and
- promulgate norms and rules that define standards of conduct for classes of legitimate action against threats to peace and security, acts of terror, and crimes against humanity.[124]

With respect to peacekeeping missions, the UN has neither clarified the legal basis for peacekeeping in failed and collapsed states nor tackled the problem of what to do about the flaws in the chain of command that discredited UN peace operations.[125] Furthermore, the lessons learned from the missions in Somalia or the Balkans are not universally accepted and hence provide no guidance for what the UNSC can do better next time.[126]

Taking the issues of peace enforcement and peacekeeping together, it may be advisable to bow to the irresistible pressure for a multipolar world order,[127] but at the same time urge the aspirants

- to settle with their neighbors in the region on the boundary of the respective pole areas;[128] and
- conclude a bilateral contract with the UN to ensure (1) the compatibility of terms with the UN Charter and its eventual evolution with respect to defense against acts of terrorism and (2) the primacy of the regional organizations, provided they are based on statutory, collective decisionmaking with respect to coping with crises and conflicts. Similar to the example of regional development banks, the partners in the region could agree on the participatory rights of international members in their collective security arrangement.

Being freed of the sole responsibility for resolving the stalemate, the UNSC might concentrate upon legislating the ground rules for world order that commit states to good governance and outlaw the privatization of the use of force.

Notes

The idea of *primacy* is adapted from Richard Haass, "What to Do with American Primacy?" *Foreign Affairs* 78 (1999).

1. In many respects, French attitudes and postures resemble US patterns about, rather than German approaches to, the role of military power. It is a different matter whether French rulers are true believers in multilateralism/institutionalism or instrumentalize the trend toward *legalization* of international relations in order to outbid the incumbent US government. The customary French revolt against US predominance in European security affairs can be explained as a reaction to the shift in status and prestige since World War II. In 2003, Chirac and Dominique de Villepin enabled France for the first time to gain broad(er) support for its claims that (1) diplomatic venues must be explored to the utmost; (2) all members must get a hearing in UN decisionmaking; and (3) Art. 2 as well as Iraq's sovereignty (not being a "failed state") must take precedence over the Bush administration's volatile interpretations of principles (Art. 1) and the spirit of previous UNSC resolutions. The fact that the "publics" in many European countries are all too willing to let their latent anti-Americanism go wild and take Bush's sayings and doings as an excuse, facilitated the attempt to win the rhetorical battle for France. Public opinion polls, however, demonstrated that the differences between the Americans' and the Europeans' political preferences are less significant than the governments' positions (stances). The main differences between the publics' judgments relate to military expenditures and Israel's "state terrorism."

2. The wording is attributed to British Defense Minister Geoff Hoon; see Michael Clarke and Paul Cornish, "The European Defense Project and the Prague Summit." The doctrine is spelled out in White House, *The National Security Strategy of the United States of America.*

3. I am using the terms "US/Americans" and "Europe/Europeans" in most instances as shortcut notions, without the necessary differentiation and qualifications. I am talking about prevailing trends. For the purpose of illustration, I shall incorporate current news analyses.

4. Lee Feinstein, Senator Hillary Clinton's foreign and security policy adviser, advocated in 2004 a "responsibility-to-prevent" doctrine; Lee Feinstein and Anne-Marie Slaughter, "A Duty to Prevent."

5. Wolfgang Ischinger, German ambassador to the United States, quoted in Michael Inacker, "Ein neues Band über den Atlantik," *Frankfurter Allgemeine Zeitung,* June 16, 2003.

6. Jane Stromseth, David Wippman, and Rosa Brooks, *Can Might Make Rights?*

7. Members of the EU's Military Committee stated in autumn 2002 that the National Security Strategy of the United States was addressing the essential issues. Solana's draft paper was presented to the EU summit at Porto Carras (Greece) in mid-June 2003. It was interpreted as a step to bring the EU debate closer to facing the issue of what to do about the new threats in a globalized security arena. Weapons of mass destruction were identified as a primary target for planning purposes; the defense line is expected to lie "out-of-area"; reaction might become necessary before an attack; North Korea is the one country named as a likely purveyor of military force. The heads of government summit resolved to adopt the final strategy in December 2003.

8. Curt Gasteyger, "Den Sicherheitsrat neu gestalten," *Frankfurter Allgemeine Zeitung,* March 19, 2003.

9. Jens Scherpenberg and Elke Thiel, eds., *Towards Rival Regionalism?;* Craig Parsons and Nicolas Jabko, *With US or Against US?,* vol. 7.

10. Charles Krauthammer, "The Unipolar Moment Revisited," p. 13.

11. The best example is France's support for the increasing deployment of US armed forces as the indispensable means to make Saddam Hussein comply with the step-up in inspections. France wanted a strong Drohkulisse, (credible threat of force) only to argue later that the US buildup indicated nothing but the will to launch a war. From mid-February 2003 onward, French objections to a second (war-empowering) resolution were accompanied by the cynical maneuver to extend the inspections into July–August while expecting the fully deployed allied forces to maintain the Drohkulisse throughout the hot weather period. Being assured of a majority in the UN, Chirac and his flamboyant foreign minister de Villepin wanted to give the impression that the UNSC had to control the US rather than urge Saddam Hussein to go into exile.

12. Robert Kagan, "Power and Weakness."

13. Charles Krauthammer, "The Unipolar Moment Revisited," p. 17.

14. On the deal-or-duel-situation, see Richard H. Ullman, *Securing Europe,* p. 29.

15. Beijing is said to have welcomed the US military presence in Asia-Pacific as a guarantee that Japan could not reemerge as the region's hegemon; NATO's survival is explained with the partners' (including Germany's own) interest in tying "united Germany's" security and defense interests to the West; the diplomacy of the Gulf War in 1990–1991 was seen by many as an illustration of multilateralism at work; George H. W. Bush's call in 1991 for a "new order" was praised by Foreign Minister Joschka Fischer in 2003 as a model for building international order; and so on.

16. Katie Verlin Laatikainen and Karen E. Smith, eds., *The European Union at the United Nations;* Heinz Gärtner and Ian M. Cuthbertson, *European Security and Transatlantic Relations After 9/11 and the Iraq War.*

17. J. G. Ruggie, *Constructing the World Polity,* pp. 195ff.

18. This refers to Max Weber's notion "Monopol legitimen physischen Zwanges" in Max Weber, *Wirtschaft und Gesellschaft,* chapter I, section 17, p. 39.

19. The 2+4 Treaty (also known as the Treaty on the Final Settlement with Respect to Germany, or the Two Plus Four Agreement) embraces a Gewaltverzicht-clausula; the accompanying treaty between the Soviet Union and a "united Germany" (September 12, 1990) came close to old-style benevolent neutrality obligations and was interpreted in French media as diluting German membership in NATO.

20. President Bush, December 7, 2001, www.whitehouse.gov/news/releases /2001/12/20001207-3.html.

21. Mary R. Habeck, *Knowing the Enemy,* pp. 31, 64, 118, 126.

22. President Clinton, "A Strategic Alliance with Russian Reform," April 1, 1993, quoted in Thomas E. Graham Jr., "US Leadership and Domestic Factors in Dealing with Russia During the Clinton Administration," p. 134. That strategy can be perverted into advocating "political assassination" of a leadership that does not suit the head of a "coalition of the willing," as was said of Chirac's blunt veto that must have hurt Blair or Harold Macmillan's and J. F. Kennedy's collusion in early 1963 to get Konrad Adenauer out of office.

23. J. G. Ruggie, *Constructing the World Polity,* p. 198.

24. The high reputation of the Federal Republic of Germany in the Helmut Schmidt and Helmut Kohl eras rested on the capability to deliver.

25. In my interpretation, the span of the Cold War covers the period from 1946 until the late 1960s; Ostpolitik and the US-China accord—among other factors—constitute a different pattern; see my article in N. J. Smelser and P. B. Baltes, *International Encyclopedia of the Social and Behavioral Sciences*, pp. 2194–2200.

26. Gustav Schmidt and Charles F. Doran, eds., *Amerikas Option für Deutschland und Japan.*

27. Gustav Schmidt, "Asia, Europe, North America, and the Asian Capitalist Miracle"; Charles F. Doran, "Power Cycle Theory and Global Politics," p. 70; Peter J. Katzenstein and Takashi Shiraishi, eds., *A World of Regions.*

28. J. G. Ruggie, *Constructing the World Polity,* p. 123.

29. Ibid., pp. 216–219, lists the following: security cooperation by means of more comprehensive and institutionalized arrangements than the traditional system of bilateral alliances; an open door world economy comprising uniform rules of trade and monetary relations together with minimum state-imposed barriers to the flow of international economic transactions; anticolonialism grounded in self-determination; antistatism grounded in individual rights; and the promotion of democracy.

30. The core values of that nationalism are intrinsic individual as opposed to group rights: equality of opportunity for all; antistatism; the rule of law; and a revolutionary legacy that holds that human betterment can be achieved by means of deliberate human actions, especially when they are pursued in accordance with these fundamental values. Ruggie, *Constructing the World Polity,* p. 217fn.

31. Schroeder's entourage justified the chancellor's *uneingeschränkte* (unreserved) "no" to Bush's "adventurism" with reference to Vice President Cheney's explanation of the good causes for regime change in Iraq; the argument ignores that Schroeder's statement (August 3) preceded Cheney's speech (August 26, 2002). Schroeder did not comply with Bush's request to dismiss Justice Minister Herta Däubler-Gmelin for her indirect comparison of Bush's steering toward war with Iraq with Hitler-Germany's unrestrained expansionism; the election was to solve that problem for him.

32. "Being uniquely situated in the world, we cannot afford the platitudes of allies not quite candid enough to admit that they live under the umbrella of American power." From Charles Krauthammer, "The Unipolar Moment Revisited," p. 12; Robert J. Lieber, *The American Era.*

33. Susan Strange, *States and Markets,* chapter 2.

34. The argument that weakness invites terrorists to think that they can act with impunity has been elaborated on by many commentators, for example, Thomas L. Friedman, "Crazier Than Thou," *International Herald Tribune,* February 13, 2002. The fact that a tenet can be employed for "finger pointing" should, of course, not distract from the need to explore the observation and to define the substance and salience of the notion.

35. The problem, of course, is that many countries (e.g., France, Spain, the UK) have developed different strategies to cope with hate-inspired conflicts at home; that "culture" does not allow China to view granting of independence as an option in solving the conflict with "separatist" (ethnic or other) movements; that escalating rhetorical support of the Palestinians' cause is the best available practice to Arab governments to divert domestic criticism, and so on.

36. I am aware that this may appear to question the principle of freedom of speech and that such debates in the United States and Germany follow a different pattern. I also know that US attempts to tie assistance to Egypt or Saudi Arabia to

stopping "hate campaigns" is considered impermissible interference in domestic affairs. However, there is no way to shirk the issue or replace this issue with the issue of political correctness. After all, international relations depend on the principle of reciprocity, including mutual toleration of values.

37. Exemptions have been written in the statute for the General Agreement on Tariffs and Trade (GATT) and are continuously practiced against the background of interdependence and globalization. The outstanding case is the "American" waiver with respect to agriculture (1955). Governments and parliaments need leverage to protect workers in areas affected by international agreements.

38. Michael Mandelbaum, quoted in Thomas L. Friedman, "In Face of Disorder, France Plays Games," *International Herald Tribune,* February 12, 2003: "Most of France's energy is devoted to holding America back from acting alone, not holding Saddam Hussein's feet to the fire to comply with the United Nations."

39. J. Fitchett, "3 Western Pillars Already Shaken," *International Herald Tribune,* February 12, 2003; Lothar Rühl, "Der Dreibund: Alte Chimären und eine neue Balance-Politik," *Frankfurter Allgemeine Zeitung,* February 18, 2003.

40. Ivo Daalder, quoted in James Kitfield, "Alliances Fractured," *National Journal,* March 7, 2003; Ivo Daalder, "Are the United States and Europe Heading for Divorce?"

41. This refers to the European Community's (and then the European Union's) longtime focus on the Common Foreign and Security Policy, *expressis verbis* excluding "defense" (being preserved in the NATO-WEU relationships), and its association with the image of "uniting Europe" as a "civilian power." The formula is my variation of criticism of social history as history with politics left out.

42. Charles Kupchan, quoted in James Kitfield, "Alliances Fractured," *National Journal,* March 7, 2003.

43. The German notion is Querschnittsaufgabe.

44. Michael Clarke and Paul Cornish, "The European Defense Project and the Prague Summit," p. 784.

45. This means that the contrast is not absolute. The linkage between peace and democracy became a topos of speech. The chances for a "harmonization" were overshadowed by at least two factors: (1) The criticism that the vicissitudes of the Clinton administration made US policy appear "to be a problem rather than a solution" (William Hyland); hence Clinton had to engage in damage control for his own doings or omissions and the "interference" of the majority party in foreign and international affairs (Helms-Burton Act, D'Amato Act, pressure to lift the arms embargo on Bosnia-Herzegovina, etc.). The concept of benevolent global hegemony, espoused by William Kristol and Robert Kagan in "Toward a Neo-Reaganite Foreign Policy," projected a moderate version of Republican internationalism to which "Europeans" reacted. (2) US NGOs seem to prefer cooperation at the international level, trusting that the re-import of generalized principles into US politics would ensure greater influence than lobbying Congress and/or administrations. In his address to the General Assembly (September 27, 1993) and in his 1994 State of the Union address, President Clinton developed the notion of "consensual globalization"; the UN or the WTO rather than the United States should take the lead in reducing tensions, ensuring nonproliferation of weapons of mass destruction, protecting human rights, and advancing international trade. See Richard Haass, "What to Do with American Primacy?" pp. 39ff.

46. The Vietnam War and civil disobedience in the United States, Watergate, the critique of Richard Nixon's and Ronald Reagan's destruction of the welfare state, benign neglect of the dollar standard, and so on.

47. The political aspects of the theme are well addressed in Colin S. Gray, "European Perspectives on US Ballistic Missile Response."

48. Hans-Dietrich Genscher was German foreign minister from 1974 until 1992. The positive connotation of Genscherism refers to his belief that, with the de-ideologizing of Soviet policy under Gorbachev, arms reduction and disarmament could mean more security, not less. The Federal Republic of Germany, as the country in mid-Europe, should become the bridge builder between East and West, without losing its status as a reliable NATO ally. The bad connotation rests on his opponents, especially in the United States, who accused him of advocating equidistance between the United States and the Soviet Union or appeasement. Emil J. Kirchner, "Genscher and What Lies Behind 'Genscherism'"; Josef Joffe, "The Secret of Genscher's Staying Power"; Berthold Meyer, "Spannungsreduktion und Vertrauensbildung"; Stephen Kinzer, "Genscher at the Eye of Public Debate," *New York Times,* March 22, 1991; Helga Walter and Brian Crozier, "Appeasement in Our Time: West German Foreign Minister Hans-Dietrich Genscher," *National Review,* June 2, 1989.

49. In 1977, NATO agreed on a program in which European members—in the name of burden sharing—would increase defense expenditures by 3 percent per year over a ten-year period.

50. "Less bang for less money," due to the growing gap between costs for modernizing and introducing new military equipment on the one hand and the increase in inflation rates (or, alternatively, interest rates, because then debt services would eat up revenues).

51. Britain and France are obliged to their out-of-NATO-area treaty commitments. The situation changed in the 1990s, due to the "nonengagement" of the United States in the Bosnian war before 1995. Changes since 1999 are discussed later in this chapter.

52. Stuart Gordon, "Exploring the Civil-Military Interface and Its Impact on European Strategic and Operational Personalities"; Hans-Georg Ehrhart, "Die EU als zivil-militärischer Krisenmanager." The EU borrowed the concept of *civil-military cooperation* from NATO's 2002 concept; its comprehensive approach operates under the name of civil-military coordination (Markus Reinhardt, "Zivil-militärische Beziehungen im Rahmen der ESVP," *Stiftung Wissenschaft und Politik-Berlin,* August 2006. The State Department and the Pentagon developed—since 2005 at the latest—similar concepts, but the implementation is overshadowed by the military operations in Iraq and Afghanistan.

53. French foreign minister Dominique de Villepin, Speech at the International Institute of Strategic Studies, April 1, 2003, *Frankfurter Allgemeine Zeitung,* April 2, 2003.

54. H. P. Kaul and C. Kress, "Jurisdiction and Cooperation in the Statute of the International Criminal Court"; H. P. Kaul, "Internationaler Strafgerichtshof." H. P. Kaul was head of the Law Division in the German Auswärtiges Amt and has been elected as one of the eighteen judges of the ICC. Claus Kreß, "Der Internationale Strafgerichtshof und die USA. Hintergründe der Sicherheitsresolution 1422," *Blätter für deutsche und internationale Politik,* no. 9 (2002):1088–1100. Claus Kreß was head of the German delegation at the Rome Conference. See also Kenneth Roth (Human Rights Watch), "Resist Washington's Arm-twisting," *International Herald Tribune,* September 30, 2002; Andreas Zimmermann and H. Scheel, "Zwischen Konfrontation und Kooperation"; R. Ch. van Oyen, "Der Internationale Strafgerichtshof zwischen Normativität, Machtpolitik und Symbolik."

55. Petra Holtrup, "The Lack of US Leadership in Climate Change Diplomacy," p. 206.

56. Georg Schild, *Die bedrohte Supermacht,* p. 117.

57. Caroline Fehl and Johannes Thimm, "Weltmacht und Weltordnung."

58. Interview with Foreign Minister J. Fischer by Frank Schirrmacher and Christian Schwägerl, *Frankfurter Allgemeine Zeitung,* March 19, 2003.

59. "Sich anschicken, für den Rest der Welt Verantwortung zu tragen, ohne den Rest der Welt zu fragen" (The US arrogates the role to bear responsibility for the rest of the world, without consulting any of the others). Roland Koch, "Im deutschen Interesse. Für eine multipolare Ordnung der Welt," *Frankfurter Allgemeine Zeitung,* December 7, 2002.

60. Ivo H. Daalder and J. M. Lindsay, "Scheidung oder Neubeginn?"

61. Wilfried von Bredow, "Zivilisierungsagentur Strafgerichtshof," *Frankfurter Allgemeine Zeitung,* March 12, 2003.

62. "Transnational coalitions of nonstate actors also pursue their interest through influence or direct participation at the supranational level, often producing greater divergence from member state concerns." See K. W. Abbott, R. Keohane, A. Moravcsik, A.-M. Slaughter, and D. Snidal: "The Concept of Legalization," p. 418.

63. The delegations worked closer with NGOs than with the US delegation in elaborating the ICC statute; the head of US Human Rights Watch is the severest critic of the Clinton and Bush administrations' uncompromising attitude toward the ICC.

64. It should be noted that "many Asian nations have explicitly rejected legalized institutions, . . . Latin American nations have been similarly cautious about pooling sovereignty in independent institutions." See Judith Goldstein, Miles Kahler, Robert O. Keohane, and Anne-Marie Slaughter, "Introduction: Legalization and World Politics." With regard to "principles, norms, rules," Asia and Latin America (the two areas with the longest experience of US policy changes) are siding with the United States, while aiming—partly in conjunction with the EU—to "domesticate" the United States through legally binding treaties, conventions, and multinational procedures.

65. John R. Bolton, "Unilateralism Is Not Isolationism," p. 74.

66. "The expansion of international law and institutions has been so rapid over the past decade that, even though the US has largely been supportive of this trend, it has been made to look relatively reluctant compared to its partners across the Atlantic (and the Pacific as well)." Edward C. Luck, "False Choices: Unilateralism, Multilateralism, and US Foreign Policy," p. 162. The irony is that US NGOs seek to influence international conferences and organizations with a view to reimporting their views and thus increasing their impact at home: "Activist groups seek international legalization to gain leverage in domestic politics, a process Margaret E. Keck and Kathryn Sikkink call the 'boomerang effect.'" K. W. Abbott and D. Snidal, "Hard and Soft Law in International Governance," p. 451; Margaret E. Keck and Kathryn Sikkink, *Activists Beyond Borders,* pp. 12–13.

67. "Police" in the dual sense of "law and order" and taking care of the subsistence of the "poor" (Armenfürsorge).

68. "Hard law restricts actors' behavior and even their sovereignty. . . . Legalization provides actors with a means to instantiate normative values." K. W. Abbott and D. Snidal, "Hard and Soft Law in International Governance," p. 422.

69. The eyes and minds are so fixed on the United States that the question of whether "civic organizations" are given any chance to make headway in Russia, China, India, or the "big" Muslim states is pushed under the rug.

70. US trade legislation (1974, 1988) referred to GATT clauses, but extended the coverage of the terms. See Gustav Schmidt, *Geschichte der USA,* pp. 222–224. The authority on this is I. M. Destler, who has a book out nearly every other year.

71. Unfortunately, politicians in Europe get away with the thesis; raising doubts leads to questions about one's "political correctness."

72. The background to this is that the share of youths under fourteen in the population plus the rate of unemployed in those over fourteen is beyond a third in Egypt or Turkey; here statistics exist and are somewhat reliable.

73. William Wallace, *The Dynamics of European Integration,* introduction, chapter 5.

74. "The Europeans are confronted with the—paradox—danger of becoming imperially overstretched without being themselves an Empire" ("Hier stehen die Europäer vor der—paradoxen—Gefahr, imperial überdehnt zu werden, ohne selbst ein Imperium zu sein"). See Herfried Münkler, *Imperien,* p. 247; Jan Zielonka, *Europe as Empire;* John McCormick, *The European Superpower.*

75. Steven McGuire and Michael Smith, *The European Union and the United States.*

76. Michael Emerson, Nathalie Tocci, Marius Vahl, and Nicholas Whyte, *The Elephant and the Bear.*

77. The dissolution of Yugoslavia is a case of Europeans working at cross-purposes. The British (tactical use of force in peacekeeping) and the French (safe havens) pursued different methods during their leadership of the UN Protection Force, whereas recently united Germany did not wish to burden itself with a constitutional conflict.

78. Russia is one of the main sources of Mafia-type destabilization domestically and abroad. The EU attempts—via treaty agreements—to commit (and assist) Russia in fighting human trafficking and corruption, but since the "Mafias" succeed in murdering public prosecutors as well as in penetrating the public administration, the record is depressing.

79. *Die Zeit,* December 8, 2002.

80. The EU's Political and Security Committee, chaired by Javier Solana, and the European Security and Defense College possess neither regulatory competence concerning the structure and employment *(Einsatz)* of the member states' armed forces and armaments planning, nor the organizational competence to manage the buildup of integrated armed forces and command structures. The political will to commit itself to collective military action is underdeveloped. See Sebastian Graf von Kielmannsegg, *Die Verteidigungspolitik der Europäischen Union;* Lutz Holländer and Peter Schmidt, "Möglichkeiten der ESVP angesichts nationaler europäischer Politik," Teil 2, pp. 19–26; Elfriede Regelsberger, "Die vertraglichen Grundlagen der Gemeinsamen Außen-und Sicherheitspolitik der EU–Angebotsvielfalt und Wachstumstrends"; and Regelsberger, "Die Gemeinsame Außen-und Sicherheitspolitik der EU. Das Regelwerk im Praxistest."

81. Rich Thomas, "Europe's Grasp for Power Shapes the Global Agenda," *International Herald Tribune,* July 3, 2001. The specific case is the EU's attempt to set the world standard on genetically modified food.

82. For details, see Gustav Schmidt, "Getting the Balance Right: NATO and the Evolution of EC/EU Integration, Security and Defense."

83. This is not the place to rehearse either the story of ESDI-CJTF-CESDP or French objections to enhancing NATO's functional agenda as an exporter of security, political stability, peace, and preventive diplomacy in the context of institutional competition between the EU, NATO, and the OSCE (formerly CSCE) and balancing obligations toward the newly independent states and Russia.

84. Colin S. Gray, "European Perspectives on US Ballistic Missile Response," p. 291.

85. Wyn Rees, "Britain's Contribution to Global Order," pp. 29–48; Jolyon

Howorth, "European Integration and Defense: The Ultimate Challenge?"; Michael Quinlan, *European Defense Cooperation;* Michael J. Brenner, "Europe's New Security Vocation,"; Jolyon Howorth and John T. S. Keeler, eds., *Defending Europe;* see also note 97.

86. For Charles de Gaulle, it was "eternal" Russia, not the "Soviet Union," when it came to foreign policy and security.

87. J. Fitchett, "An Old Feud Resurfaces: Britain and France Trade Barbs over Iraq but the Split Has Deeper Import for the EU," *International Herald Tribune,* March 18, 2003.

88. The Benelux countries and Italy were always suspicious that the so-called Franco-German engine, driving the integration process, was a Directoire in disguise.

89. Kaiser Wilhelm II (1888–1918) is known for his pompous statements and strong-arm tactics (Kraftmeierei); for example, the claim for a German place in the sun, or his "Viel Feind, viel Ehre" (the more enemies you have, the more honor you deserve).

90. Lothar Ruehl, "Der Dreibund: Alte Chimären und eine neue Balance-Politik," *Frankfurter Allgemeine Zeitung,* February 18, 2003. Ruehl has shown in his studies that France pursued NATO-compatible venues in neither its military strategy nor forces structure; see, for example, Ruehl's "Article." France does, however, contribute troops to KFOR, ISAF, and the NATO Response Force.

91. France referred to US pressure on Turkey to participate in a war against Iraq. NATO secretary-general Lord Robertson worked hard to meet the French argument that NATO must do nothing that could legitimize the US-UK war against Iraq. Since NATO requires consensus, France blocked the decision for a while. The decision was taken in the Council of Defense Ministers, where France was not a member; Germany voted for the Robertson resolution.

92. This showed as France—under Sarkozy—wields the EU presidency in the second half of 2008 and pursues its Africa, Mediterranean Union, and European Armed Forces projects. Past examples of French ventures to engage "Europe" instead of NATO missions include Operation Artemis (East Congo, 2003), the EU stabilization force in the Democratic Republic of Congo (2006), and the UN Interim Force in Lebanon (2006–). See Peter Schmidt, "Nationale Entscheidungsspielräume in der Europäischen Union und den Vereinten Nationen." In 1994, Defense Minister Volker Rühe was furious about the situation that France viewed the EUROCORPS as France's Africa Corps. French policy under Mitterrand and Chirac fluctuated between enhancing its stakes in Africa and cooperating with the United States in West Africa.

93. Roland Koch, "Im deutschen Interesse," *Frankfurter Allgemeine Zeitung,* December 7, 2002.

94. Fischer, interview with Frank Schirrmacher and Christian Schwägerl, *Frankfurter Allgemeine Zeitung,* March 18, 2003. At a French-German conference of former ministers, legislators, and academics in early July 2002, Alain Lamassoure stated: "Zwischen Deutschland und Frankreich (müsse) Einigkeit darüber herrschen, daß nicht nur die USA in internationalen Konflikten die sog. 'Drecksarbeit' machen können. Europas Engagement in Konflikten dürfte militärisches Handeln nicht mehr per se ausschließen. Vor diesem Hintergrund sei es dringend notwendig, die Diskussion über die militärischen Möglichkeiten Europas voranzutreiben. Auch eine Diskussion über nukleare Kapazitäten dürfe davon nicht ausgeschlossen bleiben" (Germany and France must be in complete agreement that not only the United States must do the dirty work in international conflicts. Europe's engagement in solving conflicts must not rule out military actions. Against this background it is imperative

and absolutely essential to press the debate about Europe's military possibilities ahead. Even a debate about nuclear capabilities should not be excluded from the agenda.). See Ulrike Guérot, "Die deutsch-französischen Beziehungen zwischen Geopolitik und GASP," p. 13, note 104.

95. Fischer shares the British view that US voters would not long support a hegemonic role, if the allies make no effort to improve their capabilities and hesitate (or refuse) to share the burdens of engagement; Brzezinski reminds his audiences of this factor.

96. Volker Heise, "Die ESVP in den Transatlantischen Beziehungen." According to Michael Clarke and Paul Cornish, some European forces have "high levels of demonstrated competence." Clarke and Cornish, "The European Defense Project and the Prague Summit." See also Julian Lindley-French, "Terms of Engagement. The Paradox of American Power and the Transatlantic Dilemma Post–11 September"; Gordon Adams and Guy Ben-Ari, "Transforming European Militaries. Coalition Operations and the Technology Gap"; Center for Strategic and International Studies: European Defense Integration: Bridging the Gap Between Strategy and Capabilities (October 2005), www.csis.org/isp/edi/index.htm; Gustav Lindstrom, "EU-US Burdensharing"; Christopher Reynolds, "All Together Now? The Governance of Military Capability Reform in the ESDP," October 2006, www.coleurope.eu.

97. Michael Clarke and Paul Cornish, "The European Defence Project and the Prague Summit," p. 784; Volker Heise, "Die ESVP in den Transatlantischen Beziehungen," pp. 12–13. The Headline Goals 2010 and the formation of thirteen national and multinational battle groups enhance the stock of interoperational armed forces, but the lack of political resolve to act together as a military "unit" and the strain on the twenty-seven member states to unite for attaining a mandate from the UNSC indicate that at best Britain and/or France would have to collect supportive actors if the EU resolved to back up preventive or coercive diplomacy with military threats or intervention capabilities.

98. France has peacekeeping or peace-enforcement missions in Côte d'Ivoire and Chad, and Germany is the second largest European contributor in Kosovo, Afghanistan, and Bosnia. Even though France balked at NATO taking upon the Lebanon mission, it had to be urged by its EU partners to face the consequences of its diplomatic intervention and contribute a more sizable contingent to the multinational UNSC-mandated mission; the German government—for political considerations (no risk of being urged to fire on Israelis) and with respect to its existing engagements—insisted on restricting its share to heading the naval control regime.

99. "Vorerst keine Verstärkung. EU-Polizeimission in Afghanistan wird nicht vergrößert," *Frankfurter Allgemeine Zeitung,* February 28, 2008; Kenneth Katzman, "Afghanistan: Post-War Governance, Security, and US Policy,"(*CRS Report for Congress,* RL 30588, September 10, 2007; Reinhardt Rummel, "Die zivile Komponente der ESVP," pp. 13–14, http://www.eu2007.de/de/Policy_Areas/General_Affairs_and_External_Relations/ESDP/ESDP-Operations.html. The EU Rule of Law Mission in Kosovo (EULEX Kosovo) commits the EU to deploy some 2,200 police and civil-administrative personnel. The Ministerial Declaration of Civilian Capabilities Commitment Conference, held in Brussels in December 2004, set out 5,763 police forces, 631 experts for law and order, 560 experts for administration and management, and 4,968 personnel for emergency services. See http://www.intermin.fi/intermin/images.nsf/files/978d06a6f2b6c22573be0044bda/$file/civiliancapabilitiesconference2004.pdf.

100. In this respect, both Barack Obama and John McCain expect Europeans to

play a big role in stabilization operations, both military and civil-administrative. McCain explicitly equates multilateralism to establishing a league of democracies and urges allies to do more at the military front while the United States does more stabilization work.

101. German military officials mention that the 60,000-strong deployment force will be fully operational by 2010. The German forces commissioned to SFOR, ISAF, and some small-scale missions have exhausted the existing potential for peace enforcement and support missions. Concerning difficult military engagements, the EU has settled on a 4,000-kilometer (2,485-mile) perimeter, centered on Brussels; for the EU Battlegroups, the projected range of missions is a 6,000-kilometer (3,728-mile) perimeter.

102. Michael Clarke and Paul Cornish, "The European Defense Project and the Prague Summit," pp. 783ff.

103. Such was the motif behind the French-German agreement, joined by Belgium, at the EU summit on March 21–22, 2003; it was prepared on the eve of the fortieth anniversary of the 1963 treaty. In late March 2008, Sarkozy and Brown, joined by Merkel, asserted their intent to cooperate more closely in enhancing the military capabilities within the EU; these assets should be at the disposal of both EU and NATO missions.

104. Barack Obama, speech on February 29, 2008, in Beaumont, Texas; on Lamassoure, see note 94.

105. A possible solution is that (1) NATO concludes an accord with the UN similar to the existing EU-UN settlement and (2) the EU pledges its civilian capabilities to serve with NATO, reciprocating the Berlin-plus contract relating to NATO military assets, to be assigned to EU-led missions. The first is done, and the second is likely to be finalized.

106. When this is denied, as in the Rome Statute, China and Russia belong to the group of outsiders; France got an exemption for a seven-year transition period; Britain—as the first lead nation of ISAF—negotiated a contract with Kabul that exempted the protective forces from the eventual application of the statute. Thus Britain got (before the July 1, 2002, deadline) what the United States asked for (after July 1, 2002) with respect to its units deployed in Bosnia.

107. The constitutional treaties, including the Lisbon Treaty, on purpose guarantee national control over external affairs.

108. Susan Strange, *States and Markets.*

109. Münkler, *Imperien.*

110. The unspoken assumption is that, given the position of the United States, the call for multilateral diplomacy—as the "better" venue to achieve sustainable world order—implies the consolidation of other poles. It is further assumed that intraregional cooperation and eventual "integration" does help the consolidation of "poles." The EU claim for multilateralism as a virtue is predicated upon the progress in constituting a new actor. The notion of multilateralism could, of course, refer to the experience with consultation groups (on Kosovo, Namibia, Near East Quartet), the activities of the G7/G8 and G24, the Basle Group, and various regime-building efforts, through which asymmetric relationships are adjusted.

111. The compromises at the Bucharest summit (April 2–4, 2008) plastered over many differences. Wanting to use its presidency in the second half of 2008 for consolidating the ESDP, the French might have been carried away by the ambition to "Europeanize" the defense effort. The differences over due consideration for Russia's security concerns and the economic backlash attributed to US responsibility for the financial crisis could easily reinforce "America-bashing" in German domestic politics and induce the government to invest in the empowerment of the EU.

112. Charles G. Cogan, *The Third Option.*

113. Volker Heise and Peter Schmidt, "NATO und EU: Auf dem Weg zu einer strategischen Partnerschaft"; Lutz Holländer and Peter Schmidt, "Möglichkeiten der ESVP angesichts nationaler europäischer Politik"; Gunter Hauser, *Sicherheit, Energie und Wirtschaft,* pp. 83–106, 116ff; Heinz Gärtner, "European Security and Transatlantic Relations After 9/11 and the Wars in Afghanistan and Iraq," pp. 134–148; Hans-Georg Ehrhart, "Abschied vom Leitbild 'Zivilmacht'? Konzepte zur EU-Sicherheitspolitik nach dem Irak-Krieg," pp. 149–163.

114. Frédéric Bozo, "France and NATO Under Sarkozy: End of the French Exception?" www.fondapol.org (March 2008).

115. Johannes Leithäuser, "Zwischen gutem Willen und Ratlosigkeit," *Frankfurter Allgemeine Zeitung,* October 10, 2006. A similar instance occurred when Steinmeier accused the Bush administration of unnecessarily offending Russia, suggesting that Moscow was not consulted about the projected antimissile deployment in Poland and in the Czech Republic, and the CDU/CSU spokesmen criticized the foreign minister for putting the United States into the wrong while ignoring mischievous developments in Russia. See "Union greift Steinmeier scharf an," *Frankfurter Allgemeine Zeitung,* February 23, 2007.

116. For similar views, see Thérèse Delpech in an interview with John Vinocur, "Tough Talk in France on Iran and the Bomb," *International Herald Tribune,* March 6, 2007.

117. Emil Kirchner and James Sperling, *Global Security Governance;* Kirsten Westphal, ed., *A Focus on EU-Russian Relations.*

118. Barry Buzan, *The United States and the Great Powers.*

119. EU-US Summit: Promoting Peace, Human Rights and Democracy Worldwide, April 30, 2007, http://www.eurunion.org/partner/summit/Summit 20070430/Pol&SecurIssues.pdf; EU Factsheet, "The Fight Against Terrorism," June 2005, http://ue.eu.int/uedocs/cmsUpload/3Counterterrorfinal170605.pdf; Wyn Rees, *Transatlantic Counter-Terrorism Cooperation.*

120. United Nations, "2005 World Summit Outcome" (September 15, 2005), final document http://www.un.org/summit2005/documents.html; Security Council Resolution 1674, April 28, 2006, protection of civilians in armed conflict.

121. On the problems of early intervention or impartial intervention, see Bruce W. Jentleson, "Coercive Prevention: Normative, Political, and Policy Dimensions" ; Richard K. Betts, "The Delusion of Imperial Intervention."

122. Strictly speaking, the principle of non-resort-to-force (Gewaltverbot) supersedes the question deriving from mandating humanitarian intervention when the UNSC is the singular authority that may permit use of military force. For a comprehensive record, see Kurt R. Spillmann, Thomas Bernauer, Jürg M. Gabriel, and Andreas Wenger, eds., *Peace Support Operations.*

123. Jane Stromseth, David Wippman, and Rosa Brooks, *Can Might Make Rights?* p. 34.

124. Francis Deng and I. William Zartman, *A Strategic Vision for Africa.*

125. J. G. Ruggie, *Constructing the World Polity,* pp. 245ff, 253ff.

126. Seth G. Jones, J. M. Wilson, Andrew Rathwell, and K. Jack Riley, *Establishing Law and Order After Conflict.*

127. Benjamin Schwarz and Christopher Layne, "A New Grand Strategy," pp. 38ff, argue in favor of offshore balancing, that is, the situation in which Washington urges the EU, Russia, China, and India to resume the responsibility of organizing "order" in their region. It is not only the French, but German, Dutch, Belgian ministers, EU Commissioners, MdEP—not to speak of the powers-that-be in Moscow and Beijing—who urge that the EU must labor to be a counterweight for "the need to be

respected," "to have nerves of steel, . . . to have to persevere." Quotes taken from Peter W. Rodman, "US Leadership and the Reform of Western Security Institutions," pp. 73–74.

128. The EU would have to take precedence over the OSCE; the OSCE would go on linking the EU, Canada and the United States, and Russia. The CSCE/OSCE, being a sort of pan-European "regional" collective security body, on paper possessed model charters (1990, 1999), but—like the UN—was not able to act "in time" or impress the aggressor with its deployment of observers. In a true Commonwealth of Independent States, Russia would have to accommodate its partners. But what about the other areas? Are (sub)continent-wide organizations the alternative to the rise of individual pole powers? The Organization of American States and the former Organization of African Unity have always postulated that their "continental" organization should decide and inform the UN but not have to wait for the UNSC or suspend action if the UNSC is ready to take over.

8

Balancing Order and Justice in a Globalized World

Farhang Rajaee

In what follows I argue that a double order, one emphasizing security and the other emphasizing justice, is both desirable and possible in the globalized world just past the new millennium. The present human condition makes it imperative to think about order as Janus, the Roman God with two faces looking in opposite directions. One face of order is security, and the other face is fairness and justice. It is time to think of them as complementary because order without justice will lead to tyranny and justice without order ends in chaos. What makes this all the more necessary is a powerful push and a strong pull. The push comes from the indiscriminate power of globalization, and the pull comes from the prevalence of two extreme positions: One is the imperial posture that sees the ways of the world as a clash, even between civilizations, and thus emphasizes security, order, control, military strength, and power.[1] The other side cries for justice, sees and feels the way to provide it is through rebellion and struggle, and considers the establishment of justice an impossibility "without shedding blood."[2] The tragedy of September 11, 2001, among others, was a wakeup call pointing to the increase in people's expectations worldwide and the fact that "the revolt of the masses," as well as the entry of ordinary citizens into the public sphere, is now a universal phenomenon.[3] Information technology has enabled these awakened masses to become a force, even if destructive, on the global scene. For example, one could make the argument that the indiscriminate power of globalization and information technology facilitated the rage of the dispossessed, self-proclaimed Muslims who committed the September 11 attacks—and who think launching terrorism against whomever they consider an enemy, Muslims and non-Muslims, is justified and acceptable. Also, the resistance of nonstate actors to and the chain of reactions against the US invasion of Iraq almost right after it began on March 20, 2003, proves that the world of nation-states where only diplomats and soldiers were the exclusive players has been weakened. In fact, the coming of the new information civilization has made evident, in Amartya Sen's words, "the empirical fact of pervasive human diversity," which requires broader thinking about not merely order but more importantly a just order, even though the immediate problems challenging orderly conduct (namely terrorism, rogue states, and radicalism) need to be addressed.[4]

I make this claim not because of my commitment to some high moral principles but because of the imperatives of our time. I agree wholeheartedly with Hans Morgenthau when he writes: "The appeal to moral principles in the international sphere has no concrete universal meaning. It is either so vague as to have no concrete meaning that could provide rational guidance for political action, or it will be nothing but the reflection of the moral perception of a particular nation and will by that same token be unable to gain the universal recognition it pretends to deserve."[5] My plea and concern for a just order stems from the kind of world that is unfolding literally by the minute before us, as well as from our responsibility for upholding it beyond the anger of post–September 11 or the continued burning of Baghdad at the time of this writing. The insightful thinker Marshall McLuhan, referred to by some as the "oracle of the electronic age," predicted that the advancement of communication would make a global village out of the humanity scattered across the continents. Regional civilizational production would merge and aggregate into one universal mode of civilization production. It seems that McLuhan's prediction has become a reality and the information revolution has ushered in a new age in human civilizational ventures, namely the birth of one civilization whose impact is global in the literal sense of the word.

At the same time, unlike the modernity project of the Western strand that insisted on one civilization/one culture, the new global civilization allows for diversity in cultural expressions. This new condition does not mean harmony and conversion, however. Indeed, almost two decades before it became fashionable and so obvious, political scientist Zbigniew Brzezinski spoke about the coming of this connected world but also reminded humanity of the destructive aspect of this world as follows: "The paradox of our time is that humanity is becoming simultaneously more unified and more fragmented."[6] I will deal with order in this unified and fragmented world by addressing the following three questions, respectively: What does the condition of one civilization/many cultures mean? How should one understand world order? And finally, what is the place of justice in that order?

One Civilization/Many Cultures

This unifying and fragmenting trend suggests that the world arena has expanded beyond political struggle and competition among sovereign states and major powers. Today, world order is no longer limited to what has replaced or may replace competition between the United States and the Soviet Union. In some ways, the destruction of the latter was a consequence of a broader phenomenon that is the coming of the information civilization. The breakup of the bipolar world was only one among many signs that marked the changes that have been occurring. Any future order has to address the classic question, how do we order our lives together in a new fashion? If the fall of the Soviet Union marks the breakdown of political realm, there are other events that point to changes in other spheres. In the cultural realm, first there emerged postcolonial critics in art, literature, painting, and architecture who have been questioning the dominant culture of modernity. But most significantly, the tragic massive deaths resulting from HIV and AIDS, negatively, and the emerging of religiously motivated activism and the acknowledgment of the "inconvenient truth" about the environment, worldwide, positively marked the end of the domination of secularism and its utilitarian view of our human condition.

In the general realm of material production in the civilizational process, the birth of the Internet has ushered in the coming of a new age in the realm of both contemplation and action. "The birth of the Internet," however, "could not have come about without the melding of communication hardware and the software of computer data-processing technologies."[7] One of the direct consequences of this latter development is the transformation of the structure of the industrial mode of industry and the world of making. Economically, the hierarchical structure of center and periphery, which divided the world into the providers of raw materials on the one side and the manufacturing regions on the other side, or bottom and top in terms of assembly line and management, has given rise to a mode of processing that operates horizontally and globally. In terms of distance, economic production has spread across the globe by way of "production sharing," but in terms of content it focuses on "niche market," that is, the consumption of distinct and specific goods. The mass market, production, society, and state have fragmented into a collection of geo-demographically targeted niche markets. In short, the combination of these developments in the political, economic, and cultural spheres has marked the dawn of a new epoch. Politically, we are living in a post–Cold War world, culturally in postmodern epistemology, and economically in the world of post-Fordism.

If our world has gone beyond the world of modernity and its rules and procedures, what has replaced it? I contend that the world of modernity was marked by one civilization based on the industrial mode of production and one worldview that is the secular humanist meganarrative of autonomous agency, both at the individual and state levels. Such a world shaped and reshaped Europe for more than a century before it became a global trend in the aftermath of World War I.[8] Only in the recent decades the centrality of sovereignty has come under question.

Now, however, the monopoly of modernity has been broken, giving rise to many cultures and ways of expression and even interpretations of the material life of the information civilization. It is a new domain marked and characterized by one civilization and many cultures. Obviously, this world has its own epistemology, its own rules, and has introduced its own players. Like all other episodes in human history, it has generated promises and presented challenges simultaneously. International relations scholar James Rosenau has suggested that what characterizes the impact of globalization on humanity could be expressed by the notion of "fragmegration," a neologism combining the two processes of fragmentation and integration. Our world has become decentralized, and global and local interests are fused. In Rosenau's words,

> [Fragmegration] juxtaposes the processes of fragmentation and integration occurring within and among organizations, communities, countries and transnational systems such that it is virtually impossible not to treat them as interactive and causally linked. . . . Viewed in this way . . . the global system is so disaggregated that it lacks overall patterns and, instead, is marked by various structures of systemic cooperation and subsystemic conflict in different regions, countries, and issue areas.[9]

What are the actual consequences of this fragmegration for contemporary world order? The process of integration and fragmentation could not have happened without a combination of conceptual and actual transformation in three areas: (1) the number of players, (2) the procedures or the rules of the game, and finally (3) the coming of a new form of identity perception for humanity. All three developments could be captured by one concept, namely, plurality. In what follows, I canvass the meaning of the term "plurality" in three areas of politics, rules for public behavior, and the issue of identity. In the realm of politics, the most obvious implication of plurality is the emergence of multiple actors and the dispersal of authority away from states. In fact, in what I call a largely "no-polar world," it seems that the most powerful player, namely the United States, is beginning to deal directly with nonstate international players, thus subverting the seventeenth-century concepts of nation-state even more. The complex reasons behind the wars aside, in both the Iraq War (launched in 2003) and the war in Afghanistan (launched in 2001), the formal claim is that war was fought against a dubious nonstate entity called Al-Qaida.

Obviously, the presence of these many actors requires that the interactions as well as the issues at hand be conducted and settled by multilateralism, not only as a way of recognizing the diversity of players but also as a way of acknowledging that any forms of order have to accommodate this diversity at all levels. One good example in this regard relates to the treaty for banning land mines that came out of a global gathering in Ottawa in

December 1997. This effort resulted from the participation not only of sovereign states but also of civil society. One of the players, then Canadian foreign minister Lloyd Axworthy, attributed the success and speed of this process to a "unique coalition of governments, civil society and international groups."[10] Even with regard to the Iraq War, both states and civil societies took part and voiced their concerns and positions about the war.

In both cases, what became obvious is that the states and their spokespersons were mainly concerned with order and security, whereas civil societies and international groups were emphasizing justice and care. I am not saying that states are only and at all times concerned with order at the expense of justice, but even when they address themselves to the concerns of justice, it is to a particular kind of justice. In other words, even their notion of justice is accentuated by order and security, whereas civil societies and social movements are more preoccupied with universal justice and are prepared to forgo order for the sake of justice. The fact that the power of nongovernmental organizations (NGOs), social movements, transnational economic enterprises, and other transnational networks has increased significantly shows a new and different mixture of players. These multiple poles in global politics could only come about as a result of the emergence of what I may term "cosmic-oriented movements" such as feminist, ecological, ecofeminist, and religious movements and groups. The contemporary world constitutes one interconnected cosmos that requires an organic approach to understanding the public sphere and establishing norms and order.

In the realm of political modus operandi, plurality manifests itself in the notion of multiple narratives for setting the rule of the game. Since the players have increased in number and most of them have demanded a presence in the global public sphere, the politics of bellowing has emerged. Traditional international relations in the past limited the game to those agents who represented sovereign states. It was assumed that international politics was the exclusive domain of either the soldier or the diplomat. Now, the global revolt of the masses dictates a different game: globalization seems to be the new paradigm, and the notion of globalization from below is the new modus operandi. Ironically, one important consequence of globalization from above through information technology and the Internet has been the expansion of technological capabilities on a global scale, which in turn has led to the de-territorialization of the very foundation of the Westphalian territorial states. As a result, a powerful trend consisting of transnational social forces, environmentalists, and human rights activists, based on the unity of diverse cultures, seek to fight natural imbalance, poverty, oppression, and humiliation.

On the surface, globalization from below appears to be a normative principle wishing for cosmopolitan democracy, but the reality is that the forces behind globalization from below have resulted from broad trends of modernization and contemporary civilization production. As the international lawyer Richard Falk observes, globalization from below represents a new politics of resistance, practiced by many civil society groups, including transnational civic initiatives, women, indigenous peoples, and human rights and environmental activists.[11] He thinks that globalization from below has an "emergent capacity to balance the influence of globalization from above through regulation of global economy and by way of accountability for those beyond the reach of regulatory operations of states."[12] In general, but particularly in its last role of promoting accountability, globalization from below is "not dogmatically opposed to globalization from above,"[13] but rather it is a balancing force; it promotes with increasing success democracy without frontiers, democracy that goes "beyond constitutional and free periodic elections."[14] The direct impact of these measures was observed in the antiwar demonstrations against the US invasion of Iraq, which took place all over the world on February 15, 2003, and in subsequent days (more than one month before the invasion). Indeed, the demonstration was so massive that one observer in the *New York Times* commented that now there were two superpowers, one the United States and the other "public opinion."[15]

On a more contemplative plane, John Rawls, who questioned contemporary insistence on liberal-based international law, proposed a more tolerant way of defining and formulating the rules of political conduct. In a sophisticated way, he is challenging the homogenizing and wholesale imposition of liberal rules, whether in the economic, political, or cultural realms. He asks for observation of a minimum standard that has to be observed, namely respect for human integrity. Beyond this, one should allow for diverse expressions. As Rawls writes, "Surely tyrannical and dictatorial regimes cannot be accepted as members in good standing in a reasonable society of peoples. But equally not all regimes can reasonably be required to be liberal; otherwise, the law of peoples itself would not express liberalism's own principle of toleration for other reasonable ways of ordering society."[16] What Rawls is inviting humanity to do is to expand its understanding of tolerance while emphasizing the fundamental principle of respect for human integrity. As long as minimum respect for human life and peoples' fundamental rights are observed, then even those regimes that have hierarchical ways of conducting public life could and should be tolerated.

Finally, in the realm of culture and identity, plurality has manifested itself as multiculturalism and diversity, which in turn is based on a new understanding of loyalty and its sources. It used to be that loyalty to the state defined one's political, social, and even personal identity for a long time. Now, loyalty to the state is being overtaken by multilayered modes of living, experiencing, and construing reality in a world where humanity's life-world is transformed almost every second. This conversion is premised on the notion that the linear paradigm of understanding categories such as time and history does not correspond to current reality. Linearity appears static, mechanical, and unambiguous, whereas reality is dynamic, organic, and cosmological. As a result, there is an increasing realization that identity can have many sources, and that it is being reshaped by a dialogical and interactive crisscrossing of human agencies with one another as well as with their life experiences. The realization that we are now citizens of the global village and, in Falk's words, "replacing the idea of 'citizen' with that of 'citizen pilgrim,' a distinctly religious understanding of essential political identity by reference to a spiritual journey that is unseen and unlikely to be completed with the span of this lifetime."[17]

Underlying this transformation is the questioning of the linear understanding of reality, as promoted by modernity. To understand this worldview, one has to note the distinction that Marshall McLuhan (1911–1980) has made between linear and acoustic thinking. He says that linear thinking is associated with contemporary, dominant, left-sphere thinking, whereas technology, and particularly the technology of communication, has made it possible to think with the right sides of our brains. The latter means "a capacity to be a conscious presence in many places at once."[18] As a result, our world is one where humanity recognizes the multiplicity of thought systems, no longer captured by the sequence of points that one has to progressively pass. The following is the prediction he made in the 1960s: "The United States by 2020 will achieve a distinct psychological shift from a dependence on visual, uniform, homogeneous thinking, of a left-hemisphere variety, to a multi-faceted configurational mentality, which we attempted to define as audile-tactile, right-hemisphere thinking. In other words, instead of being captured by accountant, most Americans will be able to tolerate many different thought systems at once, some based on antagonistic ethnic heritage."[19] The last sentence insightfully captures the essence of our contemporary human condition. We live in a world where our conceptual epistemology is made out of "different thought systems at once," and the bases of these systems are antagonistic.

Understanding Order

What does order mean in the contemporary human condition of one civilization/many cultures? Is this new order so novel that all previous thinking has become obsolete? These are pertinent questions to consider in light of the events unfolding at the beginning of the new millennium. On the surface, our condition appears very novel, but careful consideration reveals that it is not. Present concern for order resembles similar anxiety at the beginning of the twentieth century. In those days, the world of the European aristocratic international system and society had come to an end with the bullet that assassinated Archduke Francis Ferdinand on June 28, 1914, and led to World War I. Two ways of thinking about postwar order presented responses to the challenges posed then. One answer emphasized that it is possible to create a just order. The other answer was the possibility of order as dictated by a hegemonic understanding of human relationships manifesting itself in the notions of sovereignty and national interest. In practice, the international relations of subsequent decades included both trends, with the hegemonic narrative more or less as the dominant mode of thought and action.

The first trend optimistically emphasized that humanity could be organized based on "transnational social bonds that link the individual human beings," even though its members were living in various polities and were "citizens of states."[20] By empowering democratic forces, known as Wilsonianism, this position operates from a "bottom-up" view of politics, where the demands of individuals and societal groups have priority over those of the state and collectives. The concerns of the members of the society take precedence over the requirements of an abstract idea such as sovereignty. This notion gave rise to powerful and at times extreme nationalist movements and demands for justice and equity among all actors. The Wilsonian liberal position optimistically emphasizes the possibility of harmony and collaboration among peoples and nations. President Woodrow Wilson hoped for a world in which all relations were open and wherein discord, competition, and war would be redundant and futile. He stated this in the first of his "fourteen points" as follows: "Open covenants of peace, openly arrived at, after which there shall be no private international understandings of any kind but diplomacy[,] shall proceed always frankly and in the public view."[21] This trend, popular with academics and visionaries, insists on Enlightenment ideals of human dignity, rights, freedom, and justice. Soon it became a global demand, thanks to the contribution of scientific and technological innovations.

The second trend included the expansion of the Westphalian system of "anarchical order," based on the principles of self-help, sovereignty, nationalism, and the territorial state, and it gradually became the predominant paradigm for practitioners and the new emerging nationalist movements that wanted to gain access to full membership in this international system. World order and its preservation were the goals. It emphasizes that modern territorial states have formed and continue to form an international system based on anarchy, not so much as a situation to overcome but rather as a permanent human condition to deal with and manage. Power would be the brokering currency for the units composing the system. The most one could expect would be the creation of a balance, but one based on competing interests and power.

This approach is known as Hobbesian, with its strong emphasis on competition, discord, and struggle. It perceives politics as a condition of the divide between friends and enemies, the war of all against all, and zero-sum games. For the proponents of this school, the rule of the game between nations is a struggle for national interest and security, and it was called "high politics." In the aftermath of World War II and the coming of the Cold War, the predominant epistemological paradigm for understanding politics was termed "political realism," with interest defined in terms of power as its core concept. In fact, all politics was considered to be a struggle for power. For the father of modern political realism and the most elegant spokesperson of the Hobbesian view, Hans Morgenthau, politics is directly linked with power: "International politics, like all politics, is a struggle for power,"[22] that is, it amounts to "a continuing effort to maintain and to increase the power of one's own nation and to keep in check or reduce the power of other nations."[23] Nevertheless, in practice, both trends have continued side by side, each having its distinctive voice.

In the next phase, (the end of Cold War, the fall of the Berlin Wall, and the dismantlement of the Soviet Union in the late 1980s), a new era began in which the anarchic worldview has been shaken. These developments have given impetus to the thinking that some form of neo-Wilsonianism would carry the day, but globalization has inaugurated a new age in which neither idealism nor liberalism, nor even a combination of the two, would suffice. In the dawn of the globalized world in 1989, there was a lot of hope for the emergence of new thinking about order and for a new beginning. No wonder that in the early 1990s, the buzzword among policymakers and theorists became the "new world order," by which it was suggested that in the post-bipolar world the United States would foster a new world of democratization and democracy. On September 11, 1990, and in his message to a joint session of the US Congress, President George H. W. Bush described the new world order in the following words: "Out of these troubled times, our fifth objective—a new world order—can emerge: a new era, free from the threat of terror, stronger in the pursuit of justice, and more secure in the quest for peace. An era in which the nations of the world, East and West, North and South, can prosper and live in harmony."[24]

Instead, there emerged triumphalist attitudes, advocating yet again the same old hegemonic approach, merely in new forms. These positions did not help world order, and moreover they suppressed any form of creative imagination that would propose a new mixed balance.The familiar approaches of liberal and realist international relations theories reemerged in different garb. Both liberal and realist perceptions continue to describe the world in terms of "us" and "them," a place where hegemons flourish.

The new liberal internationalism, as popularized by the Hegelian scholar Francis Fukuyama and the journalist Thomas Friedman, heralded the coming of a boring world where conflict and discord have been replaced with

McWorld in its various forms. Fukuyama begins his portrait of the new order by observing that the twentieth century began with the promise of liberalism and ended with its materialization. As he puts it, "the century that began full of self-confidence in the ultimate triumph of Western liberal democracy seems at its close to be returning full circle to where it started: not to an 'end of ideology' or a convergence between capitalism and socialism, as earlier predicted, but to an unabashed victory of political liberalism."[25] And in *The Lexus and the Olive Tree,* Thomas Friedman echoed the idea that liberal and democratic states do not fight due to what he calls the "golden arch" theory, suggesting, "No two countries that both have McDonald's have ever fought a war against each other."[26] His logic is that "when a country reaches the level of economic development where it has a middle class big enough to support a McDonald's network, it becomes a McDonald's country. And people in McDonald's countries don't like to fight wars anymore, they prefer to wait in line for burgers."[27] That is the victory of McWorld.

A more pessimistic approach, voiced by Samuel Huntington and Robert Kaplan, portrayed the contemporary human condition as the "clash of civilizations" or the "coming of anarchy," respectively. For both of them, politics understood as power and the competitions of powers has not changed, only the fault lines have. In the familiar logic of the Westphalian system, the fault lines of security and loyalty coincided with state boundaries; now the fault lines fall within the parameters of identities and communal boundaries, both inside and outside states, the latter described as between civilizational borders. As Huntington writes: "The distribution of cultures in the world reflects the distribution of power. Trade may not follow the flag, but cultures almost always follow power."[28] Now that the game of politics among states is undermined, cultures face each other, based on the old strategy of self-help. "North Americans," writes Kaplan, "will take refuge in their insulated communities and cultures."[29] The new order will be shaped by alliances between cultures. Huntington predicts that in the short run, policy will promote what he call "kin politics," and in the long run the resort to power and amalgamation of power. In his own words: "In the short term it is clearly in the interest of the West to promote greater cooperation and unity within its own civilization. . . . In the longer term . . . this will require the West to maintain the economic and military power necessary to protect its interest in relation to these [non-Western] civilizations."[30] Both the optimistic and pessimistic positions are problematic. They try to impose the old logic of power onto a condition where the possibility for a more humanist logic appears to be emerging. Power is important, but it does not constitute everything. Logic of power leads to more power and more competition. At the same time, there is an epistemological problem with using culture as a unit of analysis. Edward Said summarized the problem with both views recently as follows.

> The fallacy of Fukuyama's thesis about the end of history, or of Samuel Huntington's clash of civilization theory, is that both wrongly assume that cultural history has clear boundaries, or beginnings, middles and ends, whereas the cultural-political field is a place of struggle over identity, self-definition and projection into the future. Both theorists are fundamentalist about fluid cultures in constant turbulence, and try to impose fixed boundaries and internal order where none can exist.[31]

In addition to Said's observation, there are at least two problems with both positions. One is that they overlook the reality of the globalized world. As stated before, humanity lives and functions within the parameters of one civilizational process while at the same time allowing for varieties of cultural expression and revival. Cultural diversity and the growth of identity politics run contrary to homogenizing tendency of both optimistic/liberal and pessimistic/realist positions. Second, their ways of expression project such a sense of hubris that the nuances and ambiguities of public life are lost. They claim moral clarity in all cases of politics and project the possibility of always seeing right and wrong and good and evil. As a participant observer, with a sympathetic eye for security in the United States as well as for the world, I regret that a combination of both positions has become the dominant thinking among policymakers in the United States today. The libertarian and the isolationist have formed an odd alliance. Both positions operate on the assumption that global order would materialize only through hegemonic politics.

Then the disaster of September 11, 2001, occurred. What did it mean? For now, it has served many as a scapegoat to promote policies that they could not have adopted otherwise. For some others, it gave credence to the Hobbesian world as it manifested itself in the garb of the clash of civilizations, and for others still it forced their beliefs in further Americanization and encouragement of McWorld. However, the failure of the "coalition of the willing" has helped the dissenting voices. I had hoped that the tragedy itself and subsequent events would be seen as a new opportunity to think more comprehensively about global order and possibly update the mixed balancing of the two positions of order and justice. September 11 could and should have been treated as a wakeup call, but for a while, anyway, it created further polarization and extremism. More and more, the wisdom of following the logic of power is questioned, as when major US allies such as Britain declare its decision to withdraw its forces from Iraq soon.

Justice and Order

Now, if optimistic/liberal and pessimistic/realist positions appear extreme, how can one enhance a more acceptable and fair order? Isn't it possible to combine the two positions? Just as it has been attempted before, I would propose that they could and should be combined. In the past, a third position emphasizing international law, backed by efficient functioning of international organizations in various fields, was proposed. The proponents of such a view hold that although a system of anarchy and self-help is at work, it should not be seen as a given or a natural state of being. Just as the experience of human civilization shows that war is only a part of human life and does not constitute its totality, the contemporary condition of discord should be seen as permanent. In other words, although it is true that the international system is acephalous, social life could be both orderly and fair if managed and adjudicated not by power as the arbiter, but by the rule of law based on principles of rationality and care. Politics in such an understanding is not limited to the establishment of order, but much more. Order is simply a means to a higher end, conditioned by culture and the civilizational framework. This position has been termed "Grotian" based on the views of the founder of modern international law—Hugo Grotius (1583–1645), also known as Huigh de Groot—whose most eloquent contemporary voice is Hedley Bull. For the followers of this school, international politics takes place within a framework of anarchy, accompanied by orderly life as part of the historical record of international relations. International politics is partly distributive and partly productive, with rules of prudence and expediency and imperatives of morality and law binding the game. The proponents of this position uphold and encourage the idea of international society, and politics for them relates to prudence, law, and diplomacy. What is optimistic and hopeful about the past couple of centuries is that although on the surface the Hobbesian paradigm was very dominant and priority was given to order, in reality it was the mixed trend that guided the practices of statesmanship. It is true that there was extreme competition among the superpowers, but the majority of states used both power relations and international law in their policy decisions. Today, global politics is more in need of such combination.

To repeat what I said in the previous section, a different reading of the tragedy of September 11, 2001, could lead to a different imagination of world order for the following reasons. First and foremost, 9/11 drove home the fact that the world, which "was once thought to be flat, then proved to be round, now is quite definitely web shaped." To isolate one's community from others or to impose a homogenizing order is very hard, if not impossible. Second, the indiscriminating power of globalization knows no cultural or political boundary. The politics of the masses is now something everyone has to reckon with, locally, nationally, regionally, and globally. Third, 9/11 showed that any global order requires bridging the gap of understanding between various civilizational and cultural milieus. One of the widest gaps seems to be between the Western world and Muslims. The meaning of a bumper sticker distributed in California as part of the campaign for and against Proposition 13, which read, "If you think education is expensive, try ignorance," is applicable to that relationship.

There is much "ignorance" on the part of each toward the other, but one aspect is ironic. Even though there is an enormous degree of animosity in the Muslim world toward the West and particularly the United States as the torchbearer of the Western world, even the most radical enemies seek justice and retribution from no other entity than the same United States. Note the first message of the chief culprit of September 11, Osama bin Laden, which was directed at the United States: "What America is tasting now [is] something insignificant compared to what we have tasted for scores of years. Our nation [the Muslim world] has been tasting this humiliation and this degradation for more than 80 years. Its sons are killed, its blood is shed, its sanctuaries are attacked, and no one hears and no one heeds."[32] It is interesting to note that although he refers to humiliation and degradation, he ends his statement with how Muslims have been excluded: "no one hears and no one heeds." He is appealing for inclusion and redress. One could easily conclude from this statement that Muslim terrorists are in effect crying for recognition and inclusion.

While the globalized world has paved the way for the condition of one civilization/many cultures, the challenge remains: how to create an order where the politics of inclusion would become the rule. Some insist on order; others on justice. Once again, order alone is not enough because it could easily degenerate into unfairness, while emphasizing justice alone is insufficient because it may lead to extreme conditions of disorder and chaos. One way to conceptualize this paradox is to suggest that what has been emerging in world politics since the 1990s is something akin to the notion of "double movement" outlined by the economic historian Karl Polanyi. According to him, "For a century the dynamics of modern society was governed by a double movement: the market expanded continuously but this movement was met by a countermovement checking the expansion in definite directions."[33] Applied to politics, one movement emphasized security, order, and safety; the other insisted on fairness, justice, and care: "While on the one hand markets spread all over the face of the globe and the amount of goods involved grew to unbelievable dimensions, on the other hand a network of measures and politics was integrated into powerful institutions designed to check the action of the market relative to labor, land and money. . . . Society protected itself against the perils inherent in a self-regulating market system—this was the one comprehensive feature of the history of the age."[34]

Polanyi applies the double movement thesis as a theory of social breakdown for the contemporary capitalist condition, it is possible to use it as a general theory of production and reproduction of social structures, relations, and institutions. In this sense the double movement could be employed to transcend capitalism and its dehumanizing effects and could be used as a general conception of society along the lines of other general theories. For Polanyi, if the two forces operate in balance, an economic system embedded in its respective social and cultural context would not lead to self-regulating markets but would rather create conditions for reciprocity, redistribution, and householding. Those conditions are mutual respect, social justice, and attention to communal good and obligations.

The combined and interconnected functioning of the aforementioned conditions creates an economy embedded in social relations. But in modern times, a great transformation has occurred whereby the economy has become the master, and now humanity is faced with the emergence of a powerful self-regulating market with the end result of commodification in all spheres of human life. As a result, "Instead of economy being embedded in social relations, social relations are embedded in the economic system."[35] With a little degree of imagination, however, one could apply the same argument to the power system at work in the world today. If the power system works as embedded in the new global context of many cultures and is mindful of societal forces and their broader concerns, then it would thrive and flourish.

I am not suggesting that one should forget about power. Quite the contrary, public life has always entailed power and continues to do so. What is warranted is avoiding the two extreme positions of either being seduced and subsumed by power or intimidated and threatened by it. The virtue of adopting and promoting the double movement notion is that it does not consider the international system and its global order in isolation from international society and its global concern and care. The double order position invites players to handle power and manage it with responsibility and care. There is a need for a politics of deliberation and inclusion that not only is mindful of power but also is mindful of freedom and human decency, without which even glory would die out. The civilization of Rome, wrote Edward Gibbon in his classic account of the decline and fall of the Roman Empire, "under the mild and generous influence of liberty might have remained invincible and immortal."

Combining and balancing the Wilsonian and Hobbesian views, justice and order, globalization from below and globalization from above, and finally international society and the international system, is both necessary and desirable, not only for an orderly life but also for humanity to thrive. The experience of previous civilizations reveals that such a mixture has been at work and has always been part of politics. Presently, both at the national and international levels, the experience of Canada in combining both order and justice can provide important clues. "Peace, order and good government" (Article 2 of the Canada Constitution Act, 1871) are set as the ultimate ideals of the polity, and they permeate not only all aspects of life but also include all levels of rule, local, national, regional, and international. To guarantee that these ideals are followed and implemented, there is the Charter of Rights and Freedoms, adopted in 1982, that delineates individual rights, and there are the principles of multiculturalism that guarantee communal rights and responsibilities. Another example is the foresight of the Founding Fathers of America, who argued for a combination of both idealism and realism in the public domain. For example, Jeffersonian democracy is concerned with order but warns against too much of it. Government governs best that governs least, and order is good, provided it helps promote honesty, integrity, community, and education; "Educate the people generally, and tyranny and injustice will vanish like evil spirits at the dawn of the day."[36]

To put it generally, without some degree of struggle and securing of interests, order cannot be established. At the same time, without common values, fairness, and justice, order becomes draconian and chaotic. Only those who pursue order and justice combined can establish a legitimate way of managing and conducting public life. Many times humanity forgoes one at the expense of the other. What guarantees the continuation of this balance is the art of statesmanship predicated on the understanding that we truly have become citizens of the world. What Franklin Delano Roosevelt said in his fourth inaugural address echoes the reality of our world today: "We have learned that we cannot live alone, at peace; that our own well-being is dependent on the well-being of other nations, far away. We have learned that we must live as men, and not as ostriches, nor as dogs in the manger. We have learned to be citizens of the world, members of the human community."[37] Have we really learned? We may have, but we require constant reminding. Even if we have not, the world we live in today forces us to think seriously about the notion of "the citizen of the world."

In any case, the learning process has to be complemented by a dynamic renewal of statesmanship and high-quality diplomacy if we have to approximate an orderly life at the global level. In this context, diplomacy should not be understood as defined in the classic work of Sir Harold Nicolson, that is, "the management of international relations by negotiation; the method by which these relations are adjusted and managed by ambassadors and envoys," because his definition, contrived in the 1930s, in the thick of the expansion of the Wesphalian international system, is overshadowed by a state-centric understanding of politics.[38] I concur with former Canadian diplomat Gordon Smith, who defines diplomacy as "the art of advancing national interests through the sustained exchange of information among governments, nations, and other groups. Its purpose is to change attitudes and behaviour as a way of reaching agreements and solving problems."[39] What makes this definition more accurate is that the new web of global linkages, growing outside the more traditional state system and reinforced by the Internet, is congenial to inclusive global cooperation. To achieve one's objective in this new web of global linkage, two ideas come to mind.

The first is old but bears repeating: the notion of "care." One has to take every step in public life with care, since every step has multiple and overreaching consequences. Recently the former secretary of state, George Shultz, expressed the same idea in the following words: "We need to do what I call 'gardening.' We need to tend our relationships."[40] The metaphor of gardening is significant. Gardening appears to be soft, but the gardener is no friend to weeds or pests. Just as the gardener is caring with flowers and vegetables, he is restrictive with weeds and pests. They have to be eliminated, but in a careful fashion so as not to damage or destroy the friendly plants and flowers that require tending and tending with care. Global politics is no exception. It is important and necessary to be concerned with security and order, but as much importance should be granted to justice, inclusion, and fairness.

The second principles relates to a constructive way of dealing with the "other." One important byproduct of our globalized world is that the "other" no longer means what it used to. Physical proximity and interconnectedness have brought a sense of history, personality, and reality to the abstract notion of "those people" out there. Once again, we are living in the condition of one civilization/many cultures. Borders have crumbled, or at least we can see through or over them. Also as a result of massive immigration and population movement, the "others" live next door, and even if not, because of the glass border, we know all about them. The drama of their lives is played on television in our living room daily. Here, we need what business consultant R. Roosevelt Thomas has called "managing diversity." I would like to call it the "Managing Diversity Model." It is no idealistic gesture; instead it is based on self-interest because it functions according to the premise that, in Thomas's words, "learning to manage diversity will make you more competitive."[41] He is talking about companies and entrepreneurs, and he bases his position on a purely utilitarian approach for securing interest and advantage. Still it is possible to extend it to global players, and it is also a useful reminder that even to pursue material interest, one has to accommodate the demands of the new human condition. "The other" can no longer be exploited or even taken for granted.

At the same time, I like to think that there is a more powerful appeal for the politics of care beyond mere interest, namely, human decency, which is at the heart of the old slogan of the power of love. The politics of care should be based on the ideas of common humanity and the one earth ship. This notion has been echoed in variety of ways, but I would like to invoke the frequently cited saying of the American Catholic spiritual writer, Thomas Merton (1915–1968), as follows:

> Violence rests on the assumption that the enemy and I are entirely different: the enemy is evil and I am good. The enemy must be destroyed and I must be saved. But love sees things differently. It sees that even the enemy suffers from the same sorrows and limitations that I do. That we both have the same hopes, the same needs, the same aspirations for a peaceful and harmless human life. And that death is the same for both of us. Then love may perhaps show me that my brother and sister are not really my enemy and that war is both their enemy and mine. War is our enemy. Then peace becomes possible.

Combining the idea of gardening with managing diversity leads to a different politics than that pursued by people who behave according to the assumption that power is a panacea. The latter leads to the politics of empire. The former leads to the politics of civilizational process where order and justice are "commutative," that is, formulated through a process of claim and counterclaim for what rights and duties should be recognized and how they would be applied. The politics of empire is the business of power units, whereas the politics of civilizational process deals with values and the art of governance, or in Plato's words, "tendance freely accepted by herds of free bipeds."[42] Should any prospective player in the world today, regardless of power position, act as a member of contemporary civilization or continue to act as an agent of a political powerhouse? In other words, should public players today cast themselves as politicians (concerned with the interest of their respective polity alone), or should they act as leaders (concern with broader processes of human civilization building)? History provides an answer. It has always been civilizations that outlast other human achievements, either as a form of actual sociopolitical life or as a tradition shaping future generations and future civilizational processes. States, empires, and power units only remain dynamic as long as they have the physical power to defend themselves and enforce their existence, whereas civilizations and their appeal last for eternity because of their internal values and the commitment they display to human decency and integrity. As the historian Walid Khalidi put it several years ago in a lecture at Oxford: "History shows that empires do not last forever. . . . Where are the empires of Assyria and Rome, of France, Holland, Italy, Belgium, Portugal, Germany, Russia . . . and Great Britain?"[43]

Conclusion

My argument could be summarized in a general maxim. In political life, humanity is faced with three options; tyranny, rebellion, and civility, and the boundary between them is ambiguous, fluid, very thin, and fragile. The first option is to be a conqueror, a bully, a tyrant, and an emperor, and the rule is to pursue politics of order through might and force alone. Here the logic dictates that it is better to be feared than loved, and power stems from the barrel of a gun and, of course, these days, from one's bank account. Extreme examples are those of Stalin's Russia and Hitler's Germany, but it is not limited to them; the will to tyranny exists in all societies because it resides within each member of the human race. The second option is to be a rebel, to cause chaos and to produce disorder. To limit ourselves to the twentieth century, one could name Leon Trotsky (1879–1940), Ernesto "Che" Guevara (1928–1967), and Osama bin Laden, or radical liberation/terrorist groups that think they pursue the politics of care and justice, but they do that without concern for order. Here the logic is, let order fall if there is even a slight sense of injustice.

In both conditions of disciplined order and anarchic milieu, the most precious ingredient of human collectivities, namely freedom, is the first sacrifice. The first does it through calculated policy for the pursuit of power alone, and the second through blind following of good intention alone. The irony is that an active and dynamic human life needs both, but in a magical mix, so the third choice is combining order and justice. It requires not only securing order but also managing injustice, supporting freedom, and upholding civility and culture. In short, it means striving to produce civilization, where it would be possible to enhance human integrity and ingenuity. Thus the only way is to keep the tension in the double movement of competition for power with concern for distributive justice alive. Here the logic is the recognition that pure justice belongs to an imagined heaven, or the city of saints, and is thus above the human condition, and cruelty and pure competition of forces are below the human condition. In the city of humanity, where most people want to be secure and cared for, the rule is the management of injustice and the regulation of interactions in the face of overzealous or overly fragile players. Civility thus requires vigilance and prudence that hopefully leads to a condition of a relatively just order where humanity would be able to display its highest potential. The choice is before us and will always remain so.

Notes

1. The most debated position is developed by Samuel P. Huntington, *The Clash of Civilizations and the Remaking of the World Order.*
2. Osama bin Laden, "Declaration of War Against the Americans Occupying the Land of the Two Holy Places," first published in *Al-Quds Al-Arabi,* a London-based newspaper, in August, 1996. It can be found at http://www.pbs.org/newshour/terrorism/international/fatwa_1996.html.
3. Jose Ortega y Gasset, *The Revolt of the Masses.*
4. Amartya Sen, *Inequality Reexamined,* p. xi.
5. Hans J. Mogenthau, *In Defense of National Interest,* p. 35.

6. Zbigniew Brzezinski, *Between Two Ages,* p. 3.
7. Farhang Rajaee, *Globalization on Trial,* p. 5.
8. For the globalization of the international system, see Hedley Bull and Adam Watson, eds., *The Expansion of International Society.*
9. James Roseneau, "Global Affairs in an Epochal Transformation," p. 35.
10. L. Axworthy and S. Taylor, "A Ban for all Seasons: The Landmines Convention and Its Implication for Canadian Diplomacy," p. 190.
11. See, for example, Richard A. Falk, "The Religious Foundations of Human Global Governance," on the web page of Global Education Associates, http://www.g-e-a.org/falk.pdf (March 2003).
12. Richard A. Falk, *Predatory Globalization,* p. 46.
13. Ibid., p. 139.
14. Ibid., p. 147.
15. Patrick Taylor, "A New Power in the Street," *New York Times,* February 17, 2003.
16. John Rawls, *The Law of Peoples,* p. 37.
17. Richard A. Falk, "The Religious Foundations."
18. Marshall McLuhan and Bruce R. Powers, *The Global Village,* p. 83.
19. Ibid., p. 86.
20. Hedley Bull, *The Anarchical Society,* p. 25.
21. Woodrow Wilson, speech delivered to a joint session of Congress, January 8, 1918.
22. Hans J. Morgenthau, *Politics Among Nations,* p. 29.
23. Ibid., p. 237.
24. Quoted in *Public Papers of the Presidents of the Unites States,* George Bush 1990, book two, p. 1219.
25. Francis Fukuyama, "The End of History," p. 161.
26. Thomas L. Friedman, *The Lexus and the Olive Tree,* p. 195.
27. Ibid., p. 196.
28. Samuel P. Huntington, *The Clash of Civilizations and the Remaking of World Order,* p. 90.
29. Robert Kaplan, "The Coming of Anarchy," p. 60.
30. Samuel P. Huntington, "The Clash of Civilizations," p. 21.
31. Edward Said, "The Alternative United States," *Le Monde Diplomatique* (March 2003).
32. Quoted in "There Is America, Full of Fear: Osama Bin Laden," *Ottawa Citizen,* October 8, 2001, p. A4.
33. Karl Polanyi, *The Great Transformation,* p. 136.
34. Ibid., pp. 79–80.
35. Ibid., p. 60.
36. Cited in William Alexander Robinson, *Jeffersonian Democracy in New England,* pp. 26–30.
37. Cited in Kofi Annan, "The Politics of Globalization," p. 130.
38. Harold Nicolson, *Diplomacy,* p. 15.
39. Gordon S. Smith, "Reinventing Diplomacy: A Virtual Necessity," paper presented at the International Studies Association Conference, "Virtual Diplomacy: A Revolution in Diplomatic Affairs," February 18, 1999, www.usip.org/oc/vd/vdr/gsmithISA99.html [08/20/00].
40. Cited in Doyle McManus, "What Happened to 'Humble'?" *Ottawa Citizen,* March 9, 2003, p. A13.
41. R. Roosevelt Thomas, *Building a House for Diversity.*
42. *Plato's Statesman,* p. 276e.
43. Walid Khalidi, "The Prospect of Peace in the Middle East," p. 62.

9

Resource Competition in the New International Order

Michael T. Klare and Peter Pavilionis

As in previous epochs, the world of the twenty-first century faces a variety of political, economic, social, and ecological pressures that threaten stability in many areas and embody a potential for violent conflict. Many of these pressures are akin to those that have imperiled regional and international stability in the past: ethnic and religious antagonisms, the struggle for dominance between aspiring and established powers, territorial disputes, economic competition, and so on. It is likely, however, that additional sources of friction and instability will arise in this century, emerging from the distinctive features of the current era. Of these, one of the most significant will be global competition for access to scarce supplies of critical resources: arable land, raw materials and certain gems and minerals, old-growth timber, and the increasingly "vital" resources of water and oil.[1]

The significant role played by resource competition in sparking conflict is evident in many of the recent instances of armed violence, such as those in Aceh, Angola, Borneo, Chechnya, Chiapas, Colombia, Democratic Republic of Congo (DRC), Congo-Brazzaville, Liberia, Sierra Leone, Somalia, Sudan, Zimbabwe, and the 2003 war in Iraq. Like all human conflicts, these upheavals have more than one cause; all, however, are driven to a considerable extent by competition over vital or valuable resources: diamonds in the case of Angola, Liberia, and Sierra Leone; oil in the case of Aceh, Chechnya, Colombia, Congo-Brazzaville, Sudan, and the war in Iraq; timber and minerals in the DRC; arable land in Chiapas and Zimbabwe; timber in Borneo, and so on.

It is true, of course, that competition over scarce and vital materials has long been a source of conflict. Indeed, many of the earliest recorded wars—notably those occurring in ancient Mesopotamia, Egypt, and the Jordan River valley—were driven by struggles over the control of critical water sources and arable land. Similarly, many of the wars of the sixteenth, seventeenth, eighteenth, and nineteenth centuries were sparked by competition between the major European powers for control over resource-rich colonies in Africa, Asia, the East Indies, and the New World—struggles that culminated in World War I. The rise of Nazism and the US-Soviet rivalry of the Cold War era tended to overshadow (but not eliminate) the importance of resource competition in the mid-twentieth century, but the end of the Cold War brought this factor once again to the fore, as evinced by the conflicts identified above.

One can argue, then, that the reemergence of resource conflict in the current period is nothing more than a return to the status quo ante, to the long stretch of time in which resource competition was a dominant force in world affairs. But it is the contention of this chapter that the situation we face today is not just more of the same: it is, instead, a qualitatively different situation in which resource competition has assumed a more decisive and central role in armed conflict than has been the case in the past. Further, the distribution of vital resources across geopolitical boundaries—or simply across the borders of contending nation-states—compounds resource scarcity, raising competition to the level of "securitization," with its attendant multilateral institutional apparatus. To appreciate this, it is necessary to consider both the importance of key resources to contemporary human endeavors and the unique pressures on the world's resource base at the onset of the twenty-first century.

Some resources are, of course, essential for human survival. All humans need a certain amount of food and water, plus access to shelter, clothes, and (in northern climates) heat. At a very primitive level of existence, human societies can function on relatively modest quantities of these materials, so long as their numbers remain few. But modern societies, with large numbers of people living in crowded urban settings, require vast supplies of these commodities along with a wide range of others: timber and metals for construction, fuel for transportation and industrial production, minerals and chemicals for industry, and so on. The more developed, urbanized, and prosperous a society, the greater its requirement for resources of all types.

The dilemma that confronts us at the dawn of the twenty-first century is the fact that human consumption of almost all types of materials is growing at an ever-increasing rate, imposing growing and possibly intolerable pressures on the world's existing stockpile of natural resources. Until now, humans have been able to mitigate these pressures by developing new sources of supply—for example, by digging deeper into the earth for metals and oil—and by inventing alternative materials and fuels. No doubt human ingenuity and the power of the market will continue to generate solutions of this sort. At some point, however, the demand for certain vital resources will simply overwhelm the available supply, producing widespread shortages and driving up the price of what remains; in some cases, moreover, it may prove impossible to develop viable substitutes. (There is no substitute, for example, for water.) As resource stocks dwindle and prices rise, the divide between those with access to adequate supplies and those without will widen, straining the social fabric and in some cases leading to violent conflict.

Even if disputes over the distribution of resources do not result in violence, the ecological stresses engendered by resource pressures will affect human society in many ways. For many countries, the tempo of economic growth will decline as domestic supplies of vital materials contract and the price of imports rises. For those states still in possession of valuable resources, the impulse to extract and sell as much as possible while prices are high could lead to severe and costly environmental damage. And the entire planet will suffer from the byproducts of unrestrained resource consumption—among them, increased greenhouse gas emissions, the buildup of toxic wastes, fisheries collapse, biodiversity loss, and severe soil degradation.

Sources of Pressure

It is apparent, then, that resource competition will play an increasingly significant role in world affairs as time proceeds. Just *how* substantial its impact will be depends, to a considerable extent, on the evolution of human consumptive patterns. The greater the pressure we bring to bear on the world's existing resource base, the higher the risk of major social and environmental trauma. It is essential, then, that we consider the implication of four key trends in contemporary human behavior: globalization, population growth, urbanization, and resource depletion.

Globalization

The growing internationalization of finance, manufacturing, and trade is having a powerful effect on many aspects of human life, including the demand for and consumption of basic resources. Globalization increases the demand for resources in several ways. Most significant is the spread of industrialization to more and more areas of the world, producing a dramatic increase in the demand for energy, minerals, and other basic commodities. The spurt in demand for energy is especially evident in the newly industrialized countries of Asia, which are expected to continue growing at a rapid pace in the coming decades. According to the US Department of Energy, energy consumption in developing Asia (including China, India, South Korea, and Taiwan) will grow by an estimated 3.2 percent per year during the first three decades of the twenty-first century, producing a net increase in demand of 160 percent over this period. The growth in demand for petroleum will be particularly pronounced, with total consumption in developing Asia jumping from 28 million barrels per day in 2003 to a projected 62 million barrels in 2030. A similar pattern is evident with respect to consumption of natural gas and coal—both of which are projected to experience a substantial increase in demand in this region in the coming decades.[2] The rising consumption of energy, along with other materials needed to sustain economic growth in the newly industrialized countries, will significantly increase the pressures already being placed on the global resource base.

Globalization is further adding to the pressure on resources by contributing to the emergence of a new middle class in many parts of the world. As families acquire additional income, they tend to acquire more goods and appliances, eat higher-end foods (such as beef and pork), and move into larger living quarters—all of which generate a steep increase in the consumption of basic materials. Most significant in this regard is the growing international demand for private vehicles, a process known as the "motorization" of society. The motorization rate (usually measured in number of vehicles per thousand population) is skyrocketing in many developing countries as economic growth accelerates and personal income rises. "In many urban centers, such as Bangkok, Manila, Jakarta, Shanghai, and Mumbai, car ownership is among the first symbols of emerging prosperity."[3] By 2020, the global population of motor vehicles will grow to an estimated 1.1 billion units—425 million above the level for 1996.[4] Just to produce all those vehicles will entail the consumption of vast amounts of iron, aluminum, and other minerals; once in operation, they will consume millions of gallons of oil per day, year after year.

Finally, globalization affects the global resource equation by extending the worldwide reach of multinational companies (MNCs), generating significant economic benefits for many poor and isolated countries but also providing incentives for cash-starved governments to permit the extraction of raw materials beyond sustainable levels or the destruction of forests to make way for export-oriented ranching and agriculture. The ever-expanding reach of MNCs also facilitates the entry of warlords, insurgent groups, and corrupt military factions into resource-related enterprises. In many cases, these actors have used their ties to such firms to finance the illicit acquisition of arms and other military items. In Liberia, for example, the rebel force once led by Charles Taylor traded timber and mineral rights for the cash needed to purchase arms and ammunition; in Sierra Leone and Angola, the rebels traded diamonds for guns.[5] These transactions have increased the duration and severity of a number of internal conflicts, producing vast human suffering and placing a mammoth burden on the world's humanitarian aid organizations.

Population Growth

The exponential increase of more people on the planet is further adding to the pressures on the world's resource base. According to the World

Resources Institute (WRI), total world population will reach approximately 8 billion people in 2025, or 2 billion more than the number in 2000. These 2 billion additional people will need to be fed, housed, clothed, and otherwise provided with basic necessities—producing a corresponding requirement for food, water, wood, metals, fibers, and other materials. Although the earth can supply these materials, at least in the amounts needed for a relatively modest standard of living, it cannot continue to sustain an ever-growing human population *and* satisfy the rising expectations of the world's middle and upper classes. At some point, significant shortages will occur, intensifying the competition for access to remaining supplies and producing severe hardship for those without the means to pay the higher prices thereby incurred.

Of all basic necessities, the one that is most likely to be affected by population growth is fresh water. Humans must have access to a certain amount of water every day, for drinking, personal hygiene, and food production. Fortunately, the world possesses sufficient renewable supplies of fresh water to satisfy current requirements and to sustain some increase in the human population. But the pressure on many key sources of supply is growing, suggesting that severe shortages will develop in some water-scarce areas over the next few decades. This is especially true in the Middle East and North Africa, where fresh water is already in short supply and population growth rates are among the highest in the world. For example, the number of people who will be relying on the Nile River, the Jordan River, and the Tigris-Euphrates system for all or most of their water supply will grow from approximately 325 million in 2000 to 740 million in 2050—without any appreciable increase in the net supply of water in the region. Unless the existing sources of supply are used more efficiently, or the desalination of seawater proves more affordable, competition over access to water will become more intense in these areas and could lead to war.[6]

Population growth is also likely to place growing pressure on the world's supply of arable land. This is especially true in developing areas, where many people still rely on agriculture for their basic survival or for family income. As population expands, farmers tend to crop their existing plots more intensively or to bring marginal lands into cultivation, thereby depleting the soil of essential nutrients and risking the onset of erosion. The ever-growing demand for cropland also leads to the accelerated clearing of virgin forests, eradicating the habitats of many unique plant and animal species. Global climate change is likely to make these problems even more intractable, as many once-fertile areas become too parched to support agriculture.

Urbanization

Closely related to population growth but adding distinctive pressures of its own is the growing concentration of humans in large towns and cities.

Throughout the world—but especially in the developing world—people are moving from rural to urban areas and from small to large cities. According to WRI, the world's urban population surged from 1.5 billion people in 1975 to 2.6 billion in 1995 and is expected to jump again to 5.1 billion by the year 2025.[7] In many cases, moreover, people are moving to very large cities: by 2015, an estimated 1.7 billion people (nearly one-fourth of the world's total population) will be living in cities of over 1 million people.[8] This migration has enormous implications for global resource stocks, because urban communities tend to consume more energy, water, and building materials and to generate far more waste products than rural areas. The outward expansion of cities and suburbs is also usurping areas previously used for agriculture, thereby adding to the pressure on the world's remaining supply of arable land.[9]

From a resource perspective, the impact of urbanization cannot always be distinguished from that of globalization and population growth. All these phenomena are adding to the worldwide demand for water, energy, and other basic commodities. But the concentration of more and more people in large cities does have a particularly pronounced impact on global water supplies, because urban areas require vast quantities of water for sanitation and personal use and also because cities produce copious waste products that are often poured into rivers and lakes—thereby diminishing the amount of clean water available to other users. Providing adequate supplies of water to large urban centers and neighboring areas, therefore, will prove to be one of the most demanding tasks facing local and national leaders in the twenty-first century.

Resource Depletion

The irreversible depletion of some nonrenewable resources is the combined result of the three factors described above—globalization, population growth, and urbanization. Although the earth contains large amounts of many vital materials, these supplies are not unlimited and can be exhausted through excessive extraction or utilization. And, in the case of some vital resources, humans have reached this point or are likely to do so in the early decades of the twenty-first century. For example, humans have harvested some species of fish (such as the once-prolific cod) so intensively that they have virtually disappeared from the world's oceans and are not expected to recover. Similarly, some valuable types of hardwood have largely disappeared from the world's forests.

Of the resources that are facing depletion in the decades ahead, none is more important to human life and society than natural petroleum. Oil supplies about two-fifths of the world's basic energy supply—more than any other source—and provides about 97 percent of the energy used for transportation. It is an essential resource for many valuable products, including plastics, fertilizers, pesticides, asphalt, and certain pharmaceuticals. Petroleum is also a nonrenewable resource: once we consume the existing world supply (produced by geological processes many eons ago), there will be none left for future generations. So far, humans have consumed approximately 45 percent of the earth's original petroleum inheritance (1.0 trillion barrels out of the 2.2 trillion barrels that are thought to have existed in 1860, when commercial extraction began), but we are extracting oil at such an intensive rate that much of the remaining supply could disappear in the next thirty to forty years. The introduction of new technologies and fuel sources—such as hydrogen-powered fuel cells and cellulosic ethanol—could slow the rate of oil depletion in the years ahead, but at present we are continuing to increase our total consumption every year.

Fresh water is a renewable resource and so will never disappear, but it can be viewed as nonrenewable because the earth's habitable areas receive only a certain amount each year in the form of precipitation. Of this amount—approximately 110,000 cubic kilometers—a large share is lost to evaporation, discharge into the oceans, and absorption by plants and the soil, leaving only 12,500 cubic kilometers for use by humans. At present, the human population is using approximately half this supply and is increasing its utilization at such a high rate (because of population growth, urbanization, industrialization, and irrigated agriculture) that it will begin to approach full utilization by the middle of the century. In fact, many millions of people already suffer from water scarcity, because the world's water is not evenly distributed: some areas of the world enjoy an abundance of supply, while others (especially in equatorial regions) lack adequate supplies. As global consumption rises, the number who suffer from scarcity will increase dramatically.

The Potential for Conflict

Together, these factors are producing increasing pressure on the world's resource base—pressure that can only increase as we proceed deeper into the twenty-first century. The resulting shortages are likely to produce or magnify antagonisms between and within societies as governments and factions compete for access to or control over major sources of vital materials. In the extreme case, such antagonisms can lead to the outbreak of armed violence.

In general, violent struggle over resources can take one of four forms: (1) *territorial disputes* between competing states over the ownership of contested border zones or offshore areas harboring valuable supplies of critical materials; (2) *allocation disputes* arising from disagreements over the distribution of supplies from a shared resource (such as an interstate river system); (3) *access conflicts* arising from efforts by an outside power to gain or preserve access to a foreign source of critical materials; and (4) internal *asset struggles* involving competition between contending factions for control over the revenues generated by a valuable resource site, such as a diamond field or copper mine. Most of the conflicts of the post–Cold War era embody aspects of one or another of these conflict types.

Territorial Disputes

Arising from disputed claims to contested border areas and offshore economic zones, territorial disputes have long been a source of international friction and conflict. Conflicts over contested land areas still occasionally provoke armed violence—the Eritrean-Ethiopian War of 1998–2000 is a conspicuous example—but have become less frequent in recent years as states have slowly but surely resolved outstanding boundary disputes. Conflicts over *offshore* territories, however, appear to be becoming more frequent as governments fight over contested maritime exclusive economic zones (EEZs) with valuable fisheries and undersea resources, such as oil and natural gas. For example, China has fought with Vietnam and the Philippines over ownership of the Spratly Islands in the South China Sea, a potential source of energy; likewise, Iran and Azerbaijan have clashed over disputed offshore territories in the Caspian Sea.[10] So long as states see a vital national interest in controlling such areas, disputes over contested EEZs will be a recurring factor in international affairs.

Allocation Disputes

These arise when neighboring states jointly occupy or rely on a shared resource—a river system, an underground aquifer, or an oil field. In such cases, conflict can erupt from disagreements over the distribution of materials taken from the shared resource. For example, Iraq, Syria, and Turkey have been fighting over the allocation of water from the Tigris-Euphrates River system, which originates in Turkey but travels for much of its length through Iraq and Syria. The Jordan and Nile Rivers have also provoked allocation disputes of this sort, both in ancient times and in the present. The extraction of petroleum from a shared underground reservoir can also be a source of conflict, as demonstrated by Iraq's dispute with Kuwait over the prolific Rumaila field.

Access Conflicts

Conflicts over access arise from efforts by an importing nation to gain or preserve control over an overseas source of vital materials, such as an oil or natural gas field, or to ensure the uninterrupted flow of materials from that source to its own territory. Many of the colonial wars of past centuries were sparked by such efforts, as was Germany's 1941 invasion of the Soviet

Union (intended in part to seize control of the oil fields of the Caucasus region) and Japan's subsequent invasion of the Dutch East Indies (also sparked by the pursuit of oil). More recently, US intervention in the Gulf War (1990–1991) was spurred to a considerable degree by concern over continued Western access to Persian Gulf oil.

Asset Struggles

These usually occur in failed or failing states where the national government has lost control of much or part of its territory and where competing factions—warlords, ethnic or tribal militias, separatist groups, and the like—are fighting for control of a mine or diamond field or some other resource that represents a significant source of revenue. Such struggles can prove particularly intense, as the outcome will often determine which faction will secure the revenues it needs to procure arms and ammunition, pay its soldiers, and otherwise ensure its survival; such revenues can also become a major source of personal wealth for the key figures involved. Hence the tenacity with which groups like the National Union for the Total Independence of Angola (UNITA) and the Revolutionary United Front (RUF) of Sierra Leone fought for control over their nation's diamond fields and resisted all attempts at a negotiated settlement. Conflicts over the possession of valuable resources sites can also figure in efforts by minority groups living in areas adjacent to such assets to establish a separate ethnic enclave and the corresponding efforts by the dominant state to retain possession of the region—a pattern seen in Indonesia's struggle to retain control of oil-rich Aceh and copper-rich Irian Jaya (West Papua).

Violence is not, of course, the only possible response to resource competition. As will be argued later, there are many other plausible responses to scarcity. But the risk of violence is always latent when states perceive the possession of certain materials as a *national security* matter—that is, as something so vital to the survival and well-being of a nation that it is prepared to employ military force when deemed necessary to ensure access to that resource, even if this means that other countries will be forced to make do with less. Indeed, the exigencies of national security have been cited by government officials to justify the onset or continuation of combat in many of the conflicts mentioned above.

Vital Resources

For some countries—notably those with very limited supplies—*water* has been portrayed as a national security matter. For example, Israel has declared that access to the waters of the Jordan River is vital to its survival. "Water for Israel is not a luxury," former Prime Minister Moshe Sharett once declared. "It is not just a desirable and helpful addition to our natural resources. Water is life itself." Israel's determination to retain control over the Jordan's headwaters was one of the causes of the 1967 Arab-Israeli war and helps explain its reluctance to surrender control over the Golan Heights. A similar outlook has long governed Egypt's stance with respect to the Nile River. "The next war in our region will be over the waters of the Nile, not politics," then minister of state for foreign affairs Boutros Boutros-Ghali (later Secretary-General of the United Nations) declared in 1988.

Other nations, especially the United States and China, have viewed energy—principally oil and natural gas—viewed in this manner. What might be termed the "securitization" of imported petroleum was first given formal expression in the Carter Doctrine speech of January 23, 1980: any effort by a hostile power to disrupt the flow of Persian Gulf oil "will be regarded as an assault on the vital interests of the United States of America," then president Jimmy Carter told Congress, and such an assault "will be repelled by any means necessary, including military force." This precept was later cited by President Ronald Reagan to justify both the "reflagging" (with American flags) of Kuwaiti oil tankers and their protection by US warships during the Iran-Iraq War (1980–1988) and by President George H. W. Bush to justify the use of US troops to defend Saudi Arabia following Iraq's August 1990 invasion of Kuwait.

So long as vital resources are viewed through the lens of national security, governments will often respond with military force when possession of or access to critical sources of supply is deemed to be at risk. Violence is also likely when internal factions in divided states believe that control over a valuable resource site is essential to their survival. Only by posing an alternative perspective—one that posits the advantages of cooperative, nonviolent outcomes to such disputes—will it be possible to avert recurring conflict over scarce and valuable resources. Devising such outcomes and promoting their benefits is, therefore, an essential precondition for lasting peace and stability in the twenty-first century.

Energy Security and "Securitization"

That vital resources are unevenly distributed between principal consuming nations and principal supplier nations far away is a verity of history, global development, and industrialization. The world's colonial powers of the eighteenth and nineteenth centuries now operate under the guise of neo-imperialism, with their quest for new riches and territorial dominion over oil- and gas-rich nation-states in the global hinterland. Needless to say, such a new structure of global interaction brings with it new sources of conflict, and the question then becomes, do the paradigms used to understand and resolve traditional security problems apply to the new instances of conflict over vital resources?

Energy resources take on their own distinct securitization qualities as vital resources among advanced industrial countries. Energy demand among these countries may be more elastic, but the infrastructure built around oil and natural gas (and their delivery), as well as the global geographical distribution and economic power among both major consuming and supplying states (and seemingly corresponding realist responses to the threat of cut-offs), infuse energy resources with a high degree of securitization.

Regional Hegemony and Energy Securitization: The Cases of Russia and China

A more recent manifestation of energy resource securitization is the European response to the Russia-Ukraine "gas crisis" in the winter of 2005–2006. As with the crisis imposed by the Organization of the Petroleum Exporting Countries (OPEC) in the early 1970s, this dispute over Russian shipments of natural gas to Ukraine and transshipments to European countries has political undertones—less overt than the Arab countries' embargo against Western oil-consuming countries' support for Israel, but clearly evident in the foreign policy pronouncements of Russian president (now premier) Vladimir Putin.

As a cold winter settled over the European continent, Russia's state-owned energy firm Gazprom announced a threefold increase in the price of natural gas shipments to Ukraine. Although the pricing decision was explained as an effort to end the subsidized price to its traditional Ukrainian customer, the harshness and suddenness of the Russian state-owned energy firm's decision strongly suggested Putin's use of the old Soviet energy supply "whip" in a demonstration of Russia's disfavor with pro-Western Ukrainian president Viktor Yushchenko, whose triumph in the recent election battle with pro-Russian presidential candidate Viktor Yanukovich heralded Ukraine's eventual membership in Western regional security and economic organizations, such as the North Atlantic Treaty Organization (NATO) and the European Union (EU). On New Year's Day, 2006, Russia cut off the Ukrainian portion of natural gas shipped from its pipeline that traverses Ukraine and continues on to European consumers. Ukraine responded by siphoning off its contracted portion, thereby reducing the amount of gas legitimately bound to European countries.

In the case of the People's Republic of China, the securitization of energy competition stems from its relentless quest for exclusive rights to oil and gas reserves, mostly in Central Asia and Africa. Proximally, China has become involved in disputes with US ally Japan in the East China Sea over oil and gas deposits in uncertain delimitations of both countries' EEZs. But the challenges to the West's foreign policy goals in China's energy geopolitics revolve around two big suppliers—Iran and Saudi Arabia.

Both of these suppliers are key states in US and EU foreign policy concerns, and China's relatively recent forays into the Middle East's energy export market add a security dimension to trade relations between China on the one hand and Iran and Saudi Arabia on the other. In the case of Iran, China's Sinopec signed a $100-billion, twenty-five-year deal for the joint production and export of liquefied natural gas (LNG), in the most ambitious among prospective contracts, joining with firms from France, Italy, Norway, Turkey, Japan, and India to help develop offshore gas fields in the Persian Gulf and construct new pipelines to Europe and Asia. Many such deals involve partner firms from third countries because China's "upstream" exploration and extraction technology remains undeveloped. As such, China's deals in Iran's energy sector have a "distinctly strategic quality to them; they seem intended to ensure access to an important export market and bolster a developing political relationship rather than to bring about the transfer of civilian technologies or infusions of capital."[11] Needless to say, such a Sino-Iranian strategic partnership complicates efforts by the United States and the European Union–3 (the United Kingdom, France, and Germany) to pressure Iran to halt its nuclear program. China, of course, wields a veto in the UN Security Council.

Similarly, China has also been pursuing a strategic energy partnership with longtime US ally Saudi Arabia, which benefits by concentrating its light sweet crude oil exports to less sophisticated Chinese refineries, which are also receiving Saudi investments to upgrade. Both countries also benefit from Chinese participation in the development of Saudi Arabia's "nonassociated" natural gas deposits.

Beyond the securing of energy supplies, however, the Sino-Saudi partnership again adds a worrisome dimension in the US supervision of Middle Eastern and Asian regional security. After September 11 and the US backlash against Saudi Arabia, the kingdom has been seeking a counterbalance to the US strategic partnership, and China offers not only a reliable customer for the kingdom's energy exports but also a secure venue for recycling its petroleum revenue. More significant, though, King Abdullah is able to use his partnership with China as leverage against US policies in Iraq and the Middle East as a whole. China also relies on the Sino-Saudi partnership as protection against US alliances in the East Asian region, particularly with respect to Taiwan. China has used such energy influence to Japan's disadvantage, particularly with regard to influencing the course of a Russian gas pipeline stretching from Siberia eastward, and to gain military predominance on the high seas above the Sino-Japanese confluence of their respective EEZs, below which, in the deep seabed, lie abundant reserves of hydrocarbons.

OPEC and the Origins of Western Energy Security Policies

To be sure, energy security first entered the lexicon of Western national security officials during the 1973–1974 oil crisis resulting from OPEC's embargoes against the United States, Western Europe, and Japan. OPEC's Arab members used the supply cuts to protest the West's support for Israel during the 1973 October War between Israel and Egypt and Syria. At the heart of the dispute, though, was an underlying attempt to raise the historically undervalued price of oil to Western consuming nations, a fact reflected in OPEC's price hikes preceding the October War.

During the crisis, energy security elicited a crisis response among the nation-states of the West and Japan, a US ally in the East Asian region. Yet the crisis response could be differentiated according to the degree of vulnerability of each country to the oil supply disruption. In the United States, which imported 12 percent of its oil from OPEC's Arab members, energy security meant reducing vulnerability to OPEC, including immediate rationing and medium- to long-term conservation policies, and the creation of the Strategic Petroleum Reserve, whose planned capacity would make up for supply disruptions for approximately three months.

For Western Europe, which relied on OPEC for more than three-fourths of its oil imports, security meant accommodating to OPEC's political demands: the United Kingdom and France moderated their support for Israel, which averted the Arab embargo, yet all of Western Europe went through a painful adjustment to the price hikes.

From the US perspective, energy security meant energy "independence" —reducing its potential vulnerability to the economic and political vagaries of foreign suppliers. And it could do so because at the time, OPEC's Middle Eastern suppliers accounted for a relatively small portion of oil imports; therefore US sensitivity to OPEC price hikes, and its vulnerability to political goals associated with the embargo, were decidedly low. Interdependence, according to Kenneth Waltz, was of negligible political relevance:

> The game is ultimately given away by those who refer to psychological and political interdependence and thereby suggest that the United States is entangled, and thus constrained, because it cares about the well-being of many other nations and chooses to act to influence what happens to them. . . . We cannot practice the economics of interdependence, as we are often advised to do, because unlike many other states we are not caught in the web. Nor can we adopt policies of interdependence since interdependence is a condition, not a policy. Dependent parties conform their behavior to the preferences of those they depend on. We, instead, make use of a favorable economic position to support national political ends.[12]

In other words, Waltz's neorealist focus on the structure of the international system denied OPEC's Arab members a significant degree of power, if power is measured as constraints on the foreign policies of the strongest unit in the international system. Hence, the United States could continue its support for Israel—unlike the more dependent European oil-consuming nations, which tended to "bandwagon" with OPEC's relatively more powerful Arab members. Indeed, despite Secretary of State Henry Kissinger's nod to interdependence, the US "solution" to the energy crisis came in the form of "Project Independence."

Yet just several years later, President Jimmy Carter had a radically different assessment of US vulnerability to oil-exporting countries: "Imports have doubled in the last five years. Our nation's independence of economic and political action is becoming increasingly constrained."[13] The vulnerability of the international system's most economically and politically powerful actor had apparently reached a quantitative, if not a qualitative, threshold. Despite Project Independence and assorted energy-saving efforts advanced under Presidents Richard Nixon and Gerald Ford, Americans had to be even more vigilant about reducing their demand for oil and its refined products. President Carter got to the crux of the ensuing threat: "We must reduce our vulnerability to potentially devastating embargoes. We can protect ourselves from uncertain supplies by reducing our demand for oil, making the most of our abundant resources, such as coal, and developing a strategic petroleum reserve."[14]

It was not until the end of the Carter presidency that energy security squarely entered the realist paradigm with the Soviet invasion of Afghanistan and the formulation of the Carter Doctrine (Presidential Directive NSC-63), which defined energy security as *protecting access* to Middle Eastern oil reserves: "An attempt by any outside force to gain control of the Persian Gulf region will be regarded as an assault on the vital interests of the United States. It will be repelled by the use of any means necessary, including military force."[15]

The Carter Doctrine came five days before Ronald Reagan assumed office and essentially ended the Iranian hostage crises, which had dogged Carter's presidency. The sanctions imposed by the United States on Iran following that country's Islamic revolution, which brought to power Ayatollah Ruhollah Khomeini after the ouster of the loyal Reza Shah Pahlavi, roiled global oil markets even further. The fall of the shah and the rise of Khomeini forced a thorough reassessment of US strategy in the Gulf. Concluding that Washington could no longer rely on "surrogates" like Iran or Saudi Arabia to protect vital US interests, President Carter and his advisers determined that henceforth the United States would have to assume *direct* responsibility for stability in the Gulf. It is against this backdrop that Carter issued his famous statement of January 23, 1980, in which he described the free flow of Persian Gulf oil as a "vital interest" of the United States.

To invest this pronouncement with credibility, Carter established the

Rapid Deployment Joint Task Force (RDJTF)—a group of combat units based in the United States but available for use in the Gulf when the need arose. (In 1983, President Reagan used the RDJTF as the nucleus for US Central Command.) Carter also initiated the acquisition of new basing facilities in the region, upgraded existing bases, and authorized an expanded US naval presence in Middle Eastern waters. That included the deployment of a permanent US naval force in the Gulf, with its headquarters in Bahrain. These moves were widely derided at the time, but they laid the foundation for the much expanded US military capability now deployed throughout the region.

Although Western and Asian oil supplies were at stake with potential Soviet and actual Iraqi incursions into the Gulf from the 1980s on, the Carter Doctrine and Operation Desert Storm (1990–1991) did not envision transatlantic burden sharing. NATO's military assets were to remain for collective defense purposes in the European theater; Carter was explicit in Presidential Directive NSC-63's military component: "*Getting Our Allies to Carry More of the Burden* of coalition deterrence/defense in Europe and Northeast Asia, as part of a rational division of labor, to offset greater allocation of US resources to the security of the Persian Gulf."[16] What appeared to be a typical power projection—the Soviet Union's advance toward the Gulf and its oil fields—was unilaterally balanced by the United States, the only member of the transatlantic alliance militarily and economically strong enough to counter the Soviets' extraregional move.

NATO and Collective Energy Security Policies

The West's reliance on NATO in the energy security realm came a couple of decades later with the Russia-Ukraine gas crisis of 2005–2006. This time, the threat was decidedly within the European theater and came from the same source (in a *post*-Soviet guise). The month after the resolution of the gas crisis, officials and experts from thirty-two countries convened at the NATO Forum on Energy and Security Technology in Prague. The three-day conference in late February 2006 underscored the strategic nature of the gas crisis, for, after all, practically every participating country had overlapping membership in the regional body devoted to political-economic issues—the European Union—except for, of course, the United States.

NATO was—and is—not alone in addressing European energy security; the issue has crept to the top of the agendas of the European Union and Group of Eight (G8) summits. Yet coming so soon after the Russia-Ukraine gas crisis and consequent shortages among several European consuming nations, NATO's energy security forum seemed to signal a particular resolve on the continent to strike a defensive posture against any future such interdictions. NATO began to address energy security in its 1999 Strategic Concept and reemphasized the issue at its November 2006 summit in Riga. But the organization's visible involvement in the energy security issue so soon after the Russia-Ukraine debacle sought to underscore the dual nature of the regional security body—that is, its collective defense purpose and its relatively recent repertoire of collective security functions.

In the collective security realm, NATO's emphasis is on conflict prevention, and much like any other collective security design, prevention is aided by inclusiveness—erasing the dividing line between core members of the alliance and former adversaries. NATO has not only encompassed the East-Central European members of the former Soviet bloc, but it has also included in its Partnership for Peace former Soviet republics. It has established separate councils for Russia and Ukraine. Many of these countries—energy producers and consumers—participated in the NATO Forum on Energy Security Technology, which went beyond the Russia-Ukraine dispute to emphasize the range of possible supply disruptions—and possible responses—across the entire former Soviet political space and beyond. Underscoring the tightness of energy markets and distribution systems across the volatile area of the conference's focus were the deliberations over a proposal advanced by Poland "to create a new alliance committing NATO and EU members to act in concert 'in the face of any energy threat provoked by either a cut or a diminution of supply sources that may occur because of natural disasters, disruption of wide distribution and supply systems, or political decisions by suppliers.'"[17]

The means of responding to such threats range from an EU-wide strategic energy reserve network to the protection of production, delivery, and refining infrastructure. At first glance, the energy-reserve response falls neatly into a collective security framework, based on hedging against regional interdependence of energy suppliers and consumers—that is, reducing vulnerability among European consuming nations. Yet such a response falls short of a genuine collective security design because, as drafted by Polish national security officials (most of whom still remember the era of Soviet domination), the energy treaty proposal reinforces the regional distinction between NATO/EU consumers and non-NATO Eurasian energy producers (i.e., Russia and other former Soviet republics in the Caspian Sea region). In other words, the Polish proposal draws lines and precludes interdependence altogether—an outcome that could become a contentious source of German bandwagoning, given the West German Ostpolitik policies during the Soviet period and the more recent initiatives under the Schroeder government to fund the planned Northern European Pipeline, slated to ship natural gas from Russia to Germany across the Baltic Sea and thus increase Russian-European energy interdependence. The United States and most other European security officials disagree with Germany's assumptions about the extent and degree of such regional energy interdependence.[18] Indeed, the political dividing line among EU/NATO countries is still informed by the transatlantic alliance's traditional nemesis:

Russia in its post-Soviet role as primus inter pares among the former Soviet republics. This time, however, the security interdependencies of geostrategic military threats are overlaid with those of predictable energy flows and European investments in Russia's energy infrastructure.

The second response is problematic, for it entails not only the deployment of NATO's joint military assets (including US assets), but also the issue of diversifying European energy sources beyond the Russian pipeline network. One obvious proximal venue of energy resources is the Caspian Sea subregion, bordered by Iran and the former Soviet republics of Russia, Azerbaijan, Kazakhstan, and Turkmenistan. The NATO energy security forum featured an update on the US installation of radars in Azerbaijan and Kazakhstan to monitor Iranian naval activity in a disputatiously delimited sea, whose uncertain legal regime has led to military confrontations in the attempt to demarcate the extent of EEZs for the purposes of offshore drilling for oil and gas wells.[19] Azerbaijan's state-owned oil firm is a member of an international consortium, including British Petroleum, that operates an oil pipeline from Baku to the Turkish terminal at Ceyhan. In the early phases of planning the pipeline, Kazakhstan was slated to join the pipeline with a connection running under the Caspian; both Azerbaijan and Kazakhstan are members of NATO's Partnership for Peace. However, both Russia and Iran have stymied the trans-Caspian pipeline because of the uncertain legal regime surrounding delimitation of the seabed. As a charter member of the Bush administration's "axis of evil" for its defiance of International Atomic Energy Agency and UN Security Council resolutions to curb its nuclear program, and as an accused state sponsor of terrorism and target of earlier US sanctions, Iran both complicates and highlights the potential of the Caspian region for the global energy market.[20]

To be sure, terrorism was a central topic at the NATO forum, but the organization's regional focus in terms of energy security goes beyond the Caspian's littoral states. NATO member states participated in Operation Earnest Will to protect oil tankers in the Persian Gulf during the Iran-Iraq War (1980–1988), and NATO as a whole launched Operation Active Endeavor as a counterterrorism program to enhance maritime security in the Mediterranean Sea after 9/11. Yet an even broader scope of infrastructure protection was outlined for the organization by NATO director of policy planning Jamie Shea in the pages of *NATO Review*. That meant new sources of energy—specifically, natural gas—and new corresponding venues of such protection:

> We need in particular to develop a transport system that is not so massively dependent on oil by developing commercially alternative sources. We must also diversify our network of liquefied petroleum gas (LPG) terminals and pipelines. In order to minimize the effects of a potential disruption in supply and increase energy security strong links should be formed

> with other energy producing countries. These good relations would reduce the current dependence of many consumer states on just one or two producers of oil or gas. In view of the criticality of the Middle East, working toward a viable and durable peace in that region has become not just a political priority but a priority for energy security. . . .
>
> Many of our Partnership countries are either important suppliers of oil and gas or leading transit countries which are closely involved in the current discussions about existing pipeline routes and new pipeline projects. Energy security is thus an obvious topic for enhanced Euro-Atlantic Partnership Council consultations (consultations involving all twenty-six NATO members and twenty Partnership for Peace countries). Some of our Mediterranean Dialogue and Istanbul Cooperation Initiative partners are also among the world's leading suppliers of oil and natural gas. It would therefore make obvious sense to also consult with them over the energy security issue. Special seminars such as those we have held at the NATO Defense College in Rome, could also be devoted to an analysis of energy security trends and challenges to gain further expertise of the subject matter and in order to prepare for future challenges.[21]

If NATO's collective security mission in the energy security issue area is defined by the diversification of energy sources (by type and by venue), and by the expansion of the organization's members and partners far beyond its core transatlantic membership, the organization's collective defense mission in energy security becomes simultaneously more diffuse and yet more apposite. New energy interdependencies (of type and venue) replace old, as do threats. NATO Europe reduces its vulnerability to future Russia-Ukraine political squabbles over natural gas by turning such squabbles into bilateral contretemps and thus depoliticizes the issue per the alliance. The new threats are somewhat less visible but somehow more actionable: Military assets deployed in a preventive, protective mode—such as establishing a secured perimeter around a Gulf state's LNG terminal, or gunships ordered to accompany a supertanker on its way to a Western receiving terminal—face small yet determined terrorist cells trained to carry out surgical strikes against such strategic infrastructure, not large nation-states that are bent on politically demarcating spheres of influence on the European continent.

Yet if the dividing lines are to remain in a NATO Europe that operates in a new energy security framework, they will be attributable largely to Russia's various foreign policy initiatives that seek to advance it as the *Eurasian* hegemon, not merely a *European* "petro-state." Russia's refusal so far to sign the EU Energy Charter and its "strategic partnership" with China (a relatively large customer of Russian oil and natural gas, despite insufficient delivery infrastructure) are significant indicators of Russia's geopolitical intentions. Yet Europe remains the premium customer for Russian energy: production and exports are geared toward the European market, and the vulnerabilities inherent in Russian-European energy interdependence tilt heavily westward. In terms of NATO's collective defense mission, the question of the organization's Article V commitment then becomes, "How far westward?"

In one significant sense, the transatlantic energy security relationship has come full circle: Once again, the West is subject to the political goals of a major energy-supplying country, but Europe is much more vulnerable, given its significantly higher dependence on Russia's natural gas. In the early 1970s, NATO's mission was entirely collective defense against a Soviet threat, and the US could "solve" the OPEC oil crisis by pursuing energy independence: With less global demand (and with Saudi Arabia's help), the oil price hikes would be difficult for the cartel to sustain. Yet the political goals of OPEC's Arab member states were equally difficult for Europe to avoid—it had few alternate, relatively inexpensive suppliers.

The same "structural" conditions obtain in the Russian-Ukraine dispute and its ramifications for energy security in Europe. And even though the United States can avoid the westward energy threat and its implicit political agenda emanating from Russia, the transatlantic partnership seems to require more unity in its collective security motif of expansion (or enlargement) into the former Soviet republics—especially, in this case, to sustain the belief among Ukraine's democratic forces that the country can indeed enjoy the benefits of membership in the European project without having to fear Russia's retaliation.

"We are used to thinking in terms of conventional warfare between nations, but energy is becoming the weapon of choice for those who possess it," declared then chairman of the US Senate Foreign Relations Committee Senator Richard Lugar (R-IN) at a Brookings Institution policy address in early spring 2006. "It may seem to be a less lethal weapon than military forces, but a natural gas shutdown to Ukraine in the middle of winter could cause death and economic loss on the scale of a military attack. Moreover, in such circumstances, nations would become desperate, increasing the chances of armed conflict and terrorism. The use of energy as a weapon might require NATO to review what alliance obligations would be in such cases."[22]

Indeed, should the United States be expected to enlist its substantial commitment of NATO military assets in the cause of a collective defense response to such energy interdictions affecting the European continent? The US policy response during the 1973 OPEC embargo, and that of the Carter Doctrine several years later, provide some important lessons in that regard.

Energy independence and domestic energy-saving initiatives in the United States during the 1970s insulated the country from the pressure of OPEC's oil embargo; Europe's higher dependence on OPEC oil made the continent's most economically powerful countries succumb to the political agenda of OPEC's Arab members. Now, the interdependent relationships in the transatlantic energy sector remain, but with a new actor setting the implicit political agenda. The model US policy response, then, also remains: Senator Lugar's policy recommendations make an even more concerted appeal for a national energy-saving program, including more stringent industrial standards and legislation promoting the domestic pursuit of alternative fuels production. Then again, the United States is not as dependent on natural gas as the Europeans, and even though Washington has officially supported Ukraine's bid for EU and NATO membership, Ukrainian integration into the European project is a European initiative and redounds mostly to the benefit of the European Union (but as a geostrategic asset for NATO). Washington has also supported Georgia's quest for NATO membership, as Georgia serves as another important geostrategic asset for the transatlantic alliance. Yet Russia's August 2008 incursion into the former Soviet republic (not incidentally through which a segment of the Baku-Ceyhan oil pipeline courses) highlighted again the political divide among EU/NATO countries, with most East European member states calling for a strong, concerted NATO response to Russia's military actions and Western Europe advocating a more conciliatory posture.

A European strategic initiative to diversify energy suppliers leads the continent farther afield and into murkier waters—specifically, the Caspian Sea, the Mediterranean, and the Persian Gulf. In the first venue, Russia and Iran strategically complicate the advance of "Western" natural gas pipelines from Kazakhstan and Turkmenistan; so does China, as a source of competition for new, proximal sources of energy. NATO already has a counterterrorism operation in the Mediterranean, and that initiative could be refocused to protect infrastructure, such as LNG terminals in and shipping from increasingly important suppliers—Algeria and Libya. The Gulf States are also subject to NATO's protection of infrastructure and shipping against terrorist attacks, but such a presence may run the risk of conflating NATO activities with an overarching US purpose.[23] In these venues, the Carter Doctrine's new target is terrorism, and this time, the burden is shared among select NATO countries.

Bilateral Partnerships and Energy Security: The United States and the People's Republic of China

This leaves us with major competitors for "equity" oil and gas reserves—specifically, China—and it is here that the United States has the burden of work to convince the People's Republic of the benefits of global energy markets, rather than the premiums paid for the exclusive development and exploitation of reserves. In the United States, congressional threats against China's bid for US-based Unocal certainly didn't help matters, but Washington can make up for the rebuff in a significant way by making the argument that the more Western firms—including US firms—participate in Chinese energy deals, particularly in upstream production, the quicker the oil or gas will get out of the ground (or seabed) and into the pipeline (or tanker). More important, the People's Republic of China gets a security premium with the addition of Western firms' participation. As suggested by Flynt Leverett and Jeffrey Bader, "Pursuing joint ventures with Chinese companies appears to be an important element of several European oil companies' upstream strategies, but Washington's current policy is at best ambivalent toward US companies' participation. Encouraging such participation would give China a sense of partnership with the United States in its search for energy security."[24] Such a "sense" of partnership could go a long way in countering China's strategic partnership with Russia and however that condominium manifests itself in the quest for new energy deals in the Middle East.[25]

Averting Conflict over Scarce Resources

Whatever the resource in dispute, nation-states can avoid conflict through autarkic or collaborative responses. Neither choice is easy, given the political economies and structural dependencies involved—domestically and internationally. Nevertheless, assuming that the necessary political will can be generated, friction arising from resource scarcity can be channeled into constructive, nonviolent outcomes through three types of initiatives: technological innovation; adjudication, mediation, and cooperation; and conservation.

Technological Innovation

This can go a long way to reducing the threat of conflict over scarce resources by providing alternative materials and less resource-depleting processes. For example, improvements in desalination technology would make it possible to convert seawater into fresh water at an affordable cost (existing methods consume large amounts of energy and are very costly.) Similarly, the consumption of petroleum in transportation could be substantially reduced through the widespread use of cellulosic ethanol, hybrid (gas/electric) vehicles, and fuel-efficient diesel engines. Eventually, the use of petroleum products for ground transportation could be eliminated altogether through the introduction of hydrogen-powered fuel cells. Improved methods of harnessing solar and wind energy would also reduce the need for petroleum. Technological innovation can help eliminate or minimize a wide variety of other resource constraints, greatly reducing the risk of conflict.

Adjudication, Mediation, and Cooperation

Given the risky and costly nature of war, states and other parties often conclude that it is preferable to resolve resource disputes through mediation and adjudication or through schemes for the joint exploitation of a shared or contested resource site. Boundary disputes are particularly well-suited to international mediation and adjudication: a number of such disagreements have been resolved in recent years when the parties involved agreed to seek a determination from the International Court of Justice (ICJ) in The Hague. For example, the ICJ has taken up the disputes between Bahrain and Qatar over Hawar Island and between Cameroon and Nigeria over the Bakassi Peninsula. (Both areas are thought to sit above significant reserves of oil or natural gas.) Mediation by the World Bank also led to the adoption of the Indus Waters Treaty in 1960, thus averting war between India and Pakistan over the distribution of water from the shared Indus River system. Joint development of contested resources is another approach that is gaining favor in some areas: China and the countries in the Association of Southeast Asian Nations have discussed the joint development of oil and gas in the South China Sea, and Egypt and its upstream neighbors have met to consider plans for the joint development of the Nile River system.

Conservation

Technology and adjudication can help address some resource problems, but ultimately the best way to avert significant shortages of scarce or limited supplies is to consume less of what we do possess of these materials. Indeed, conservation is often the least costly and most practical method of expanding the long-term supply of a resource. For example, the imposition of tougher fuel-efficiency standards on US automobiles and trucks would reduce US petroleum consumption by millions of barrels per day. Likewise, the widespread use of drip irrigation would greatly reduce the wastage of water through existing irrigation techniques. The systematic recycling of materials also helps to reduce the depletion of scarce resources.

Such techniques can be employed to slow the consumption of vital resources and to channel conflict into productive, nonviolent outcomes. Many scientists, economists, environmentalists, and government leaders perceive the urgent need for such efforts and have advocated them in every available setting. As a result, progress *is* being made in many critical areas. But strong resistance to such efforts has been mounted by some companies that benefit from existing modes of consumption and from politicians who view vital resources from a traditional national security perspective, with its zero-sum, all-for-us-and-nothing-for-them outlook. For example, the major US auto companies have fought against any increase in minimum fuel-efficiency standards, and some conservatives in the United States have advocated efforts to constrain China's access to the petroleum supplies of the Persian Gulf. Many consumers, especially in the wealthier countries, are also reluctant to reduce their consumption of water, petroleum, rare timber (like teak and mahogany), and other scarce or limited materials.

It is evident, therefore, that efforts to reduce the depletion of vital resources and to avert conflict over critical sources of supply will require a substantial change in attitude toward the utilization of these precious materials. Only by recognizing a shared human obligation to serve as stewards of the earth's precious bounty and to work in concert to preserve vital materials for future generations will we be able to take the necessary steps to avert severe shortages and the very real risk of rising bloodshed over diminishing resources.

Notes

1. This argument was first articulated by Michael T. Klare in *Resource Wars.*

2. US Department of Energy, Energy Information Administration, *International Energy Outlook 2003,* tables A1, A2.

3. US Department of Energy, Energy Information Administration, *International Energy Outlook 1999,* p. 133.

4. Ibid., p. 117.

5. On Liberia, see William Reno, "Reinvention of an African Patrimonial State: Charles Taylor's Liberia." On Sierra Leone, see Douglas Farah, "Diamonds Are a Rebel's Best Friend," *Washington Post,* April 17, 2000.

6. For background and data, see Peter H. Gleick, ed., *Water in Crisis;* Sandra Postel, *Last Oasis.*

7. World Resources Institute, *World Resources 1996–97,* p. 150.

8. Ibid., p. 9.

9. For discussion, see ibid., pp. 57–80.

10. For background on the disputes in the South China Sea and the Caspian, see Michael T. Klare, *Resource Wars,* pp. 81–137.

11. Flynt Leverett and Jeffrey Bader, "Managing China-US Energy Competition in the Middle East," p. 194.

12. Kenneth N. Waltz, *Theory of International Politics,* p. 157.

13. Jimmy Carter, "The President's Proposed Energy Policy," April 18, 1977, *Vital Speeches of the Day* 43, no. 14 (May 1, 1977): 418–420.

14. Ibid.

15. White House, Presidential Directive NSC-63, Washington, DC, January 15, 1981, http://www.fas.org/irp/offdocs/pd/pd63.pdf.

16. Ibid., original emphasis.

17. Polish deputy minister of economy Piotr Naimski, quoted in Radio Free Europe/Radio Liberty, "Energy: NATO Considers Role in Increasing Energy Security," February 24, 2006, www.rferl.org/featuresarticle/2006/02/882ba72f-a716-4016-8192-c567c3aea06d.html.

18. "These officials believe Germany may become too reliant on Russian energy supplies and move away from its EU partners and the United States. East European states in particular, once in Moscow's sphere, believe that they could find themselves unable to ensure reliable and affordable energy supplies from Gazprom, the powerful state-controlled Russian energy company. They point to the former Schroeder government's deal with Gazprom to involve German companies in the development of a Russian-German gas pipeline under the Baltic Sea as a special arrangement that appears to promise a supply to Germany that other states might not enjoy." See Paul Gillis, *NATO and Energy Security,* p. 3. See also Fiona Hill, *Beyond Co-Dependency.*

19. See Radio Free Europe/Radio Liberty, "Energy: NATO Considers Role in

Increasing Energy Security," February 24, 2006, www.rferl.org/featuresarticle/ 2006/02/882ba72f-a716-4016-8192-c567c3aea06d.html.

20. Iran's full membership in the Shanghai Cooperation Organization (SCO) in mid-2006 raises not only the nettlesome problem of overlapping membership in regional security organizations (Kazakhstan is both a NATO partner and an SCO member) but is also a sign of Vladimir Putin's determination to forge a Russia-China strategic partnership with "cooperative security" as a pillar of the partnership; see M. K. Bhadrakumar, "China, Russia Welcome Iran into the Fold," *Asia Times Online,* April 18, 2006, www.atimes.com/atimes/China/ HD18Ad02.html.

21. Jamie Shea, "Energy Security: NATO's Potential Role." NATO's Mediterranean Dialogue is the security adjunct to the EU's Barcelona Process, which seeks to include fifteen EU member states and twelve nonmember Mediterranean countries (Algeria, Cyprus, Egypt, Israel, Jordan, Lebanon, Malta, Morocco, Syria, Tunisia, Turkey, and the Palestinian Authority) in a complete free trade area by 2010; the Istanbul Cooperation Initiative, launched at NATO's 2004 Istanbul Summit, offers specific partnerships with the Mediterranean Dialogue countries in the areas of security sector reform, interoperability, antiterrorism programs (including information sharing and maritime cooperation), weapons of mass destruction nonproliferation programs, border security, and civil emergency planning. An early overview of NATO's contributions to the region can be found in Philip Gordon's survey, *NATO's Growing Role in the Greater Middle East.* For a critical view of such "out of area" missions in the Caucasus, and in the Gulf states under the Istanbul Cooperation Initiative, see, respectively, Richard Sokolsky and Tanya Charlick-Paley, *NATO and Caspian Security;* and Matteo Legrenzi, "NATO in the Gulf: Who Is Doing Whom a Favor?"

22. Senator Richard Lugar, "US Energy Security: A New Realism," address to the Brookings Institution, Washington, DC, March 13, 2006, www.brookings.edu/comm/events/20060313lugar.pdf.

23. See Matteo Legrenzi, "NATO in the Gulf."

24. Flynt Leverett and Jeffrey Bader, "Managing China-US Energy Competition in the Middle East," p. 198.

25. Or whether the strategic partnership extends into the Gulf at all. In early 2007, Russian president Vladimir Putin and Qatari emir Sheik Hamad bin Khalifa Al Thani announced plans to discuss the formation of a cartel among natural gas–producing countries. US ally Qatar possesses one of the largest gas fields in the world. Iran's supreme leader Ayatollah Ali Khamenei has supported the idea of a joint Russian-Iranian natural gas cartel. See Associated Press, "Russia, Qatar to Mull Natural Gas Cartel," February 12, 2007.

10

Challenges to World Order After September 11

Francis Fukuyama

The period following the September 11 terrorist attacks has seen the emergence of a number of serious challenges to world order that have in many ways gone beyond the parameters of the security framework established during the Cold War. The prospect of terrorism by radical Islamists making use of weapons of mass destruction (WMD) suddenly became a live issue for the world's sole superpower, the United States. In response, the latter's huge margin of military dominance was used to pursue a war on terrorism and to unseat two regimes in the Middle East, in Afghanistan and Iraq. The unilateral manner in which the latter intervention was undertaken, however, set off a huge backlash, particularly in the Middle East and among European allies of the United States. Some contested the legitimacy of the US action, others the judgment of US officials. The Bush administration had hoped that the rest of the world would at least retrospectively approve its exercise of leadership in supplying a global public good (i.e., security against terrorism). As the United States after more than five years of occupation contemplates how to extricate itself from Iraq, the prevalent non-US opinion is that the United States used its enormous margin of power for self-interested purposes.

It is clear that neither the existing structure of international institutions nor the unilateral exercise of US power will be adequate to deal effectively and legitimately with the kinds of security threats that now exist. Global order requires a different approach to the exercise of US power, as well as new institutions—indeed, probably a whole set of them. But the architecture of these institutions will be complex and their possibility dependent on active sponsorship by the existing large players in the international system.

The development of world politics since the end of the Cold War is an interesting test of different theories of international relations. Structural realist theory would predict that the current large imbalance in the distribution of power, in which the United States spends as much as virtually the whole rest of the world combined, would produce a balancing reaction with countries opposed to the United States cooperating with one another. Liberal internationalism, by contrast, would predict that the liberal democratic ideology shared by North Atlantic Treaty Organization (NATO) allies would override these considerations of power alone. One could argue that the fracturing of the Cold War alliance over the Iraq War is a step toward the emergence of a coalition designed to contain US power, and thus a confirmation of realist theory. This is indeed how certain French leaders understand their actions. Moreover, the shared values and institutions that were thought to bind the Western world were evidently not powerful enough to prevent the emergence of serious differences on the question of the sources of international legitimacy.

Nevertheless, there remain very powerful shared interests between the world's large liberal democracies: however much France and Germany opposed the war in Iraq, they are hardly about to make common cause with radical Islamism and indeed face substantial domestic unrest exacerbated by Muslim populations. Indeed, the succession of Jacques Chirac and Gerhard Schroeder by Nicolas Sarkozy and Angela Merkel has led to a distinct improvement in relations. The United States could easily have pursued a very different strategy in meeting the threat from al-Qaida that would have minimized the degree of opposition from other large powers. Differences among the Western democracies on the question of international legitimacy and the use of power remain, though even here different prudential judgments on the proper application of US power could have substantially reduced the degree of discord that eventually emerged. It is thus too early to say whether the post–September 11 world confirms or disconfirms realist theory.

The Twin Challenges

Following the destruction of the World Trade Center towers in New York City, twin challenges emerged in world politics: first, how to deal with Islamist terrorism, and second, how to deal with US power, newly mobilized by this event.

The first of these challenges, Islamist terrorism, injects into world politics the prospect of something genuinely new, what Tom Friedman calls the "superempowerment" of otherwise weak and marginal nonstate actors to the point at which they can threaten large nation-states.[1]

Neither terrorism, radical Islamism, nor weapons of mass destruction are new phenomena; all had existed as significant international issues from well before the end of the Cold War. What was new after September 11 was the perception, particularly in the United States, that all three were likely to be combined into a single deadly package that could inflict massive damage on otherwise powerful and wealthy nation-states that had previously been immune from large-scale homeland attack. This perception emerged despite the fact that the September 11 attacks were actually carried out not with WMD but by airliners and low-tech devices like box cutters. Though the possibility of terrorism using WMD had been much speculated on by security specialists, most criminal and terrorist organizations of prior decades would not have had the motivation to use WMD to inflict mass casualties in the nihilistic manner of the World Trade Center attacks. This perception changed dramatically after September 11. The fact that Islamist suicide bombers could deliberately kill nearly 3,000 Americans and bring down a major landmark convinced many people, not unreasonably, that if these groups had access to biological or nuclear weapons, they would not have hesitated to use them.

The possibility that a relatively small and weak nonstate organization could inflict catastrophic damage is something genuinely new in international relations and poses an unprecedented security challenge. In all prior historical periods, the ability to inflict serious damage to a society lay only within the purview of states.[2] The entire edifice of international relations theory is built around the presumption that nation-states are the only significant players in world politics. Although some effort has been made in recent years to broaden the theory to include nonstate actors like multinational corporations, nongovernmental organizations (NGOs), and crime syndicates, these types of organizations operated in the economic or social realms and were not perceived as having major security implications.

If catastrophic destruction can be inflicted by nonstate actors, then many of the concepts that informed security policy over the past two centuries—balance of power, deterrence, containment, and the like—lose their relevance. Deterrence theory in particular depends on the deployer of any form of WMD having a return address, and with it equities that could be threatened in retaliation.

The degree to which the world in fact faces a real and ongoing threat of Islamist terrorists using WMD is subject to debate. Indeed, following the 2001 attacks, a large gulf in perceptions between Americans and Europeans arose over this issue. Many Americans were convinced that such catastrophic terrorism was both imminent and likely, and that September 11 marked just the beginning of an upward trend in violence. Europeans more often tended to assimilate the September 11 attacks to their own experience with terrorism from groups like the Irish Republican Army or the Basque ETA, regarding it as a lucky, one-off event, an outlier in a phenomenon more commonly marked by car bombs or assassinations.

As more and more time passes without major attacks on US soil, the probability that the less alarmist view is correct has gone up. The global supply of suicide bombers willing to inflict mass casualties is finite, and it seems that the problem has been effectively contained now that a worldwide network of police and intelligence agencies is single-mindedly trained on this problem. A single lapse in that security shield, however—a car bomb in Times Square, for example—could have enormous political consequences, even if the damage done was trivial. Threat and response are interactive: because it assumed that there was a significant likelihood of catastrophic attack from Iraqi weapons, the United States engaged in activities like preemptive invasion and prisoner abuse that made the threat a self-fulfilling prophecy.

The unknowability of the magnitude of the security threat is one of the underlying causes of global discord in the post–September 11 world, because it undercuts the possibility of consensus as to what constitutes a proportionate response to the terrorist threat. If a country faced an imminent threat of a nuclear weapon being detonated in its capital city, then most people would accept the legitimacy of it taking a host of extreme measures to prevent that from happening. But what if the probability that such an event might occur in the next year drops from, say, 1 in 2 to 1 in 100, or 1 in 1,000?[3] Suppose that the weapon in question is not an explosive nuclear device but a chemical, biological, or radiological weapon that might kill hundreds and inflict billions of dollars in economic damage. What, then, constitutes an appropriately proportional response? What constitutes a prudent response, in light of the (also unknowable) costs that an active response will inevitably entail? The difficulty in coming up with clear answers to these questions suggests why there has been such discord among otherwise like-minded countries as to how to deal with this new security environment.

The National Security Strategy of the United States

The United States responded to this new security environment through a doctrinal adjustment that was then implemented in its invasion of Saddam Hussein's Iraq. The doctrine was laid out in *The National Security Strategy of the United States,* promulgated in September 2002.[4] All administrations are required to produce doctrinal statements of this sort; most are routine, tedious, and pass into history largely unnoticed. The same was not the case of the Bush administration's text.[5]

The National Security Strategy document is, on the surface, unexceptional. It repeats many of the standard goals of US foreign policy, such as the promotion of free democratic governments around the world and a global system of free trade. Its most notable innovation was to take note of the simple fact outlined above, namely, that nonstate terrorists armed with weapons of mass destruction could not be dealt with through the usual tools of containment and deterrence. The strategy asserts, quite correctly, that in the face of this kind of threat, it will be at times necessary to act preemptively to break up an attack before it is launched. It went on to say that the United States preferred to work with allies and international institutions to meet these kinds of challenges, but that at times it would find it necessary to resort to "coalitions of the willing" to deal with certain threats.

As a theory, there is absolutely nothing objectionable to anything stated in the new document. *If* a country is faced with a catastrophic threat from a nonstate actor, and *if* it is unable to get help from existing international institutions to meet that threat, it is hard to challenge the view that it can legitimately take matters into its own hands and move preemptively to break up that threat. Preemption has always been an option available not just to the United States but to all countries; it was in effect the justification for the overturning of the Taliban regime in Afghanistan, to which few in the international community objected.

Publication of the strategy document created an enormous uproar outside the United States, however, and did much to cement the view in many quarters that it was not Islamist terrorists but the United States that was the chief source of global instability. There were a number of reasons.

The first problem with the doctrine concerned not so much what it said so much as what it failed to say and how it was thus interpreted. It did not lay out any criteria or suggest that there were any limits to the US use of preemptive/preventive military force. Indeed, the doctrine was promulgated in the context of President George W. Bush's "axis of evil" line in his January 2002 State of the Union address, which naturally led many people to think that the United States was planning preventive wars not just against Iraq but against North Korea and Iran as well. Even though there may have been individual members of the Bush administration who foresaw repeated application of the new doctrine against rogue states, it is doubtful that there was anything like a consensus on this score. The United States had realistic plans to engage in only one such intervention, in Iraq. But the administration made no effort to clarify its intentions on this score, so it is not surprising that many people simply assumed Iraq was only the beginning of a US effort to use military power to remake the world in its own interests.

The second problem with the doctrine was its broad endorsement of both preemptive and preventive war. A doctrine of preemption against imminent attack is relatively uncontroversial, even if most countries choose not to place a strong rhetorical emphasis on it. A doctrine of preventive war against a threat that may emerge several years down the road is much less so. There are both normative and pragmatic reasons for this. Normatively, virtually any just war theory holds that war is a last option to which a country resorts only after all possible alternative nonmilitary approaches have been exhausted. In most cases of preventive (as opposed to preemptive) war, it is very hard to show that such threats have been exhausted against long-term threats. Prudentially, the record of states waging preventive wars—what Bismarck called committing suicide for fear of death—is not a happy one.[6] States can seldom make accurate judgments about the consequences of political events that lie several years in the future.

A third problem with the new strategy was its implicit delegation of the right to intervene and on occasion to wage preventive war to the United States and not to other countries. The United States was arguing, in effect, that as the world's sole global superpower, it had not just the right but the duty to provide global public goods like security against terrorists and rogue states. The United States was not arguing that this duty devolved on any country that happened to have this dominance in power; had Russia, China, or India been in such a position or promulgated a similar doctrine of preventive war as a means of dealing with their respective terrorist problems, one imagines that the Bush administration—indeed, any US administration—would have objected vociferously. The preventive war doctrine was not one that could be safely generalized throughout the international system. There was thus an implicit assertion of American exceptionalism in the strategy document: by virtue of the constitutional and democratic nature of US values and institutions, such responsibility for providing global public goods could be safely delegated to the United States.[7]

It is not hard to see why other countries, including other liberal democracies, objected to the implicit delegation of responsibility in the new strategy. Some, of course, objected as a matter of principle that any country could arrogate this right to itself and bypass international institutions. This argument, as we will see below, is not a strong one in view of the weaknesses of existing international institutions in providing security. But others objected on purely prudential grounds: they did not trust US judgment in using this power wisely and did not believe the particular case that the Bush administration was making in favor of immediate war with Iraq.

The final gap in the doctrine concerned the US approach toward its allies. The strategy documents asserted the need to work with allies and traditional alliances, but also talked about the need to periodically resort to "coalitions of the willing." The latter phrase is basically a euphemism for US unilateralism. That is, a coalition of the willing arises when it is impossible to get agreement from an existing, well-institutionalized multilateral organization like the UN Security Council or NATO to support US purposes.[8]

Again, as in the case of preemption, there can be no principled objection to a nation acting unilaterally in defense of its own security. Given the weaknesses of existing multilateral security organizations (about which more below) a country would be foolish to trust in the Security Council, NATO, the Association of Southeast Asian Nations (ASEAN), the European Union (EU), or any other regional organization if it came under severe threat.

What well-institutionalized multilateral organizations provide, however, is international legitimacy, which then permits broader international support.

This support was not necessary for the high-intensity combat operations in Iraq, but it certainly became important during the nation-building phase of operations. Less than a year into the US occupation of Iraq, Washington found itself completely dependent on the United Nations to help negotiate the transfer of sovereignty to an Iraqi provisional government and to hold democratic elections. Hence the real question for US strategy that the document failed to address was how much emphasis the United States would place on the attempt to seek the sanction of multilateral institutions, and whether it would be willing to modify its own goals in any serious way in deference to the views of close allies. The Bush administration did go to the UN Security Council and received unanimous backing for Resolution 1441 authorizing the return of weapons inspectors to Iraq. But it also made clear that it would go to war regardless of world opinion and in fact did so when it failed to garner support for a second resolution authorizing military force. It is fair, then, to interpret the strategy document as saying that the US will work through existing alliances when they are supportive of US purposes, but will otherwise show limited deference to allied views.

The National Security Strategy document could be seen as authorizing two types of actions under its preemption rubric. The first included small operations to actively target terrorists and break up their plans before they could be put into action, such as the rocket attacks on al-Qaida personnel in Yemen and Pakistan. The second involved major wars to unseat regimes. The first type of action is relatively uncontroversial and has been going on more or less continuously since September 11. The latter, however, had a single instantiation after the enunciation of the doctrine, the invasion of Iraq.

The war and subsequent occupation have demonstrated both the strengths and limitations of the new posture. The United States broke the stasis that had characterized policy by the international community toward Iraq over the previous twelve years and decisively enforced a series of prior UN Security Council resolutions mandating Iraqi compliance with the international inspections regime. By ending the sanctions regime, it eliminated the latter's substantial costs both to the Iraqi people and to the US position in the region (e.g., by permitting the United States to withdraw from air bases in Saudi Arabia that were established to enforce sanctions).

However, the United States went into Iraq with a much smaller coalition than it had in 1991; there were no Arab or European partners providing combat forces (apart from Britain) and no follow-on police or constabulary forces to help with the postwar stabilization of the country. Although President Bush claimed that his coalition was larger than his father's, this was true only if one abstracts from the quality of the help given the United States in terms of combat forces at risk or resources. Allies pledged more than $70 billion toward the 1991 war and less than $13 billion toward the reconstruction of Iraq in 2003, a reflection on the limitations of coalitions of the willing.

The failure to find any weapons of mass destruction in Iraq after the war underlined the problem that many US allies had with the new strategic doctrine. Many of them resisted delegation of responsibility for deciding where and when to launch preemptive wars to the United States not so much because they were opposed in principle to US leadership or hostile ideologically to the United States, but rather because they did not trust the Bush administration's judgment as to relative risks. Even though they agreed that Iraqi WMD posed a long-term threat, they did not believe it was an imminent one, or one that could not have been dealt with in other ways. The Bush administration, however, did not merely argue that the Iraqis had bad intentions and potential long-term WMD capabilities, but rather that they had actual large stockpiles of chemical and biological weapons and an active nuclear weapons program.[9]

In the wake of the failure to find actual weapons, President Bush remarked that it didn't matter whether they had weapons or merely intentions to acquire weapons. But in fact, when a country is making a case for a voluntary preventive war, it makes a great deal of difference whether the threat actually exists today or whether it could exist some years down the road. Weapons inspector David Kaye, after resigning from the Iraq Survey Group, stated that the Iraqi nuclear program was dormant and that the country was not a year or two from acquiring a nuclear weapon but probably more like seven to eight years away from this capability. The fact that the Bush administration got this wrong has done enormous damage to US credibility and does not increase other countries' confidence that they can safely delegate judgment in these matters to Washington.

The Limitations of Existing Institutions

A coalition of the willing is seen, for better or worse, by many countries around the world as a euphemism for US unilateralism, and as such it fails to attract much enthusiasm as a long-term basis for world order. The alternative approach to dealing with serious security issues through international institutions like the United Nations, which many European countries claim to favor, also has a number of serious weaknesses. The UN is deficient both with regard to legitimacy and effectiveness, and it is unlikely that any politically possible reform will fully fix either of these problems.

The concept of legitimacy is related to the concept of justice but not equivalent to it. People believe that a certain set of institutional arrangements are legitimate because they are just, but legitimacy exists only in the eyes of the beholder. That is, an institution may be considered unjust by some philosophical or absolute principle of justice and yet still be regarded as legitimate by a given group of people. What matters from the standpoint of an institution's long-term survival and effectiveness is not how it measures up to an absolute standard of justice, but whether the people affected by it regard it as legitimate.

The UN's problem with legitimacy, at least from a typically American point of view, has to do with the fact that membership in the organization is based on formal sovereignty rather than any substantive definition of legitimacy —in particular, it makes no demands on its members to be democratic.[10] This accommodation to the reality of world politics as it existed at the time of the UN's founding has in many ways tainted the subsequent activities of that body.

Both the United Nations and its predecessor, the League of Nations, trace their intellectual ancestry back to Immanuel Kant's essay *Perpetual Peace,* in which he called for a league of nations to overcome the conflicts of the state system. But Kant made clear that members of the league would have to share a republican form of government, since only that would permit consensus on the rules of justice that the international system would seek to enforce.

Since membership in the United Nations is based only on the de jure possession of sovereignty, the organization from the beginning has been populated by states of dubious legitimacy. One does not have to believe that liberal democracy is the only form of legitimacy to see why this is a problem: although there may be other potential grounds for legitimacy than a democratic government, there are clearly regimes that are illegitimate by any standard because of their gross violations of the most basic rights of their citizens.

The ideological conflicts of the Cold War were, in the end, divisions over basic principles of legitimacy, so it is no surprise that the organization was frequently deadlocked and impotent in dealing with security problems. The end of the Cold War aroused hopes that the organization would gain new effectiveness because there would henceforth be greater consensus about broad principles of human rights and democracy. But even though most UN members gave lip service to these principles, many of them did not remotely live up to them and yet continued to be treated as members in good standing. Thus the US could be displaced by Syria on the UN Human Rights Commission in 2001 and Libya could become its chair in 2003.

Americans are much more likely to point to the UN's deficit of democratic legitimacy than are Europeans, which explains their substantially higher degree of distrust for the institution and reluctance to abide by its many pronouncements. Part of this distrust has to do with differences between the United States and Europeans over the meaning of democratic sovereignty. The United States, which has seen only one democratic regime in the course of its existence as a nation-state, has an abiding belief in constitutional democracy as the source of all legitimacy, and in the legitimacy of its own democratic institutions. Indeed, there is a strong tradition in the United States of seeing its own institutions as models for the rest of the world. Most European countries, as well as newer democracies like Japan, by contrast, have seen a variety of regimes come and go in their national histories. Although most believe in democratic legitimacy as a general principle, few believe that their actual government is uniquely legitimate or universally worthy of emulation, even if it embodies those principles fully. Indeed, many Europeans have a distrust of sovereignty per se as a source of conflict and war, based on their experiences during two world wars in the first half of the twentieth century. The fact that the sovereign entities in Europe are constitutional democracies has not been sufficient reassurance; most have sought to encase those sovereignties in a series of overlapping institutions, including both the United Nations and the European Union. It is unsurprising, then, that Europeans on the whole regard the UN as more legitimate than do Americans.

A second source of US distrust of the United Nations is its special relationship with Israel and its experience of how the UN has dealt with the Arab-Israeli dispute over the years. The General Assembly has passed any number of resolutions regarded by both Israel and the United States as unbalanced or lopsidedly pro-Arab, the most infamous of which was the 1975 "Zionism is racism" resolution. The then US ambassador to the United Nations Daniel Patrick Moynihan pointed out that Zionism was no more racist than many of the nationalisms represented in the United Nations, and noted the undemocratic character of many of the states presuming to pass judgment on Israel. His stance launched him into a career in the US Senate and did much to cement the US view that the UN was an undemocratic and illegitimate institution. Similar arguments had much less resonance in Europe for a variety of complex reasons. In subsequent years the US has found itself frequently vetoing Security Council resolutions regarded as biased against Israel, thus habituating itself to standing against majority opinion in that organization.

The view of many Americans that the United Nations is illegitimate nonetheless leads to a certain blindness about the role that the UN plays today in international politics. Fareed Zakaria quotes an anonymous Bush administration official as asserting that the United States was far more legitimate than the UN as an occupying power in Iraq.[11] That is, such Americans think that because *they* do not believe that the UN is legitimate, no one else does either, and that those who argue for a greater UN role in sanctioning international action are being dishonest or self-interested. Dishonesty and self-interest certainly exist in international life, but the perceived legitimacy of the United Nations is a fact of life of which the most hard-nosed realists need to take account.

The value of the kind of legitimacy possessed by the UN but not by the

United States can be seen in the politics of postinvasion Iraq. The United States became dependent on the United Nations and its representative in Iraq, Lakhdar Brahimi, to act as an intermediary between the Coalition Provisional Authority (CPA) and Ayatollah Ali Sistani, de facto leader of the Shiite community in southern Iraq. Sistani was willing to meet with Brahimi but not with H. Paul Bremer, head of the CPA; he would accept a UN judgment about the need to delay a direct election but not that of the US occupation authorities. Occupations by the international community under UN auspices like those in the Balkans or East Timor can go on indefinitely, allowing for the slow building of institutions over time; those under sole US control exist in a time period too short to prepare the country in question for democratic self-government.

The third problem with the UN has to do with its efficacy as an institution meant to deal with serious security threats. Article 51 authorizations for the use of force must go through the Security Council. But the Security Council, whose membership reflects the winning coalition in World War II, was deliberately designed to be a weak institution: by giving a veto to the five permanent members, it guaranteed that the Security Council would never act contrary to their interests. The wartime coalition fell apart, of course, in the Cold War, and the Security Council was thereafter never able to agree on responses to serious security threats requiring the use of force, with the exception of Korea, when the Soviet Union mistakenly walked out of the Security Council. With the Cold War's end, the Security Council came together in authorizing UN action against Iraq after the latter's 1990 invasion of Kuwait. But the organization failed to follow through in enforcing its own disarmament resolutions on Baghdad in the decade following, laying the ground for the US intervention in 2003.

Deficiencies in the UN's ability to authorize force to deal with major security threats does not mean that the organization cannot play an important role in postconflict reconstruction and other nation-building activities. This has indeed happened in Cambodia, Somalia, Bosnia, Kosovo, and many other places.[12] But although the UN provides legitimacy and a useful umbrella for organizing international peacekeeping and stabilization operations, even here its limitations are evident. The United Nations is not a hierarchical organization that is capable of taking decisive action. It necessarily moves by consensus and is particularly dependent on its major donors—which in practice means the United States, the Europeans, and Japan—for money, troops, and technical assistance.

Over the years, there have been any number of proposals to alter the membership of the Security Council to reflect changes in the distribution of power around the world and to thereby improve the council's perceived legitimacy—by adding Japan, large developing countries like India or Brazil, or replacing the British and French seats with a single EU one. It is very doubtful that any of these reform schemes will work, short of a major crisis. Existing members will veto any proposal that will deprive them of their current influence, and new members will inevitably be opposed by other countries that believe themselves equally deserving of a seat.

Even if the membership of the council could be expanded or changed, the collective action problem will remain. A larger council with veto-bearing members will suffer from even greater paralysis than at present. But to change the voting rules from consensus to some form of majority rule risks making the council more active than any of its members would like. The United States in particular, which has found itself isolated in many Security Council votes, is not realistically ever going to approve a change from the unanimity rule. There is a real question, indeed, whether the world would benefit from a supercharged United Nations that could authorize a major use of force under conditions where its constituent members were sharply divided on its wisdom or legitimacy.

Realistic Institutions for World Order

It is thus doubtful that the United Nations can ever be successfully reformed and turned into an institution that can meet the kinds of security challenges that have arisen in the period since September 11. Self-help will remain the last resort for nations facing serious security threats. This will be true not just of the United States, but of those countries that criticized it for not obtaining the blessing of the United Nations prior to its invasion of Iraq.

Even if one retains a realist perspective on international relations and believes in the ultimate necessity of self-help, the legitimacy afforded by the UN and other international institutions can be extremely valuable in achieving national purposes. Unilateralism in the form of coalitions of the willing may be justified and necessary at times but can also be self-defeating if it alienates important potential allies. The Bush administration was shortsighted in not recognizing that it would need a broader range of partners in the reconstruction of Iraq, despite the fact that it could undertake the war itself largely on its own. Even if some Americans don't accept the legitimacy of the United Nations, others do, which makes the UN imprimatur the sine qua non of action for them.

Realistic institutions for world order in the post–September 11 period require two things that are often mutually inconsistent, power and legitimacy. Power is needed to deal with threats not just from rogue states but from the new nonstate actors that may in the future employ weapons of mass destruction. It must be capable of being deployed quickly and decisively; its use will in some cases require the violation of national sovereignty and may in some cases require preemption.

International legitimacy, however, requires working through international institutions that are inherently slow-moving, rigid, and hobbled by cumbersome procedures and methods. Legitimacy is ultimately based on consent, which is in turn a byproduct of a slow process of diplomacy and persuasion. International institutions exist in part to reduce the transaction costs of achieving consent, but under the best of circumstances they necessarily move less quickly than security requires.

The power side of the equation will have to be supplied for the foreseeable future largely by the United States and other developed nations The US in particular has forces with a reach and technological sophistication that will not be challenged for the foreseeable future. The Europeans, Russians, and Chinese could in principle sharply upgrade their capabilities and spending, but they show little inclination in the near term. The Europeans are correct when they say that there are other forms of soft power, like the ability to manage nation-building projects, that they can deploy more readily than the United States. But, ultimately, hard power is necessary to meet an important range of security challenges in the current environment.

The real issue for the future is how best to prudently apply US power. The Bush administration's approach to Iraq was wrong less in principle than in the way that it was applied to this specific case. The administration argued that by disarming Iraq it was performing, in effect, an international public service, enforcing a series of UN Security Council resolutions in a situation where the global community was too timid and divided to act. It was expending its own blood and treasure not just to eliminate a serious security threat but to bring down a tyranny and build a new, democratic society in its place.

There are indeed times when only a hegemonic power can cut through the collective action problems of international institutions and unilaterally supply certain kinds of global public goods. Thus Britain is often credited with having used its navy to enforce a free trade regime in the nineteenth century, as did the United States with a broad variety of power instruments in the post–World War II period. As Mancur Olson suggests in *The Logic of Collective Action,* actors that are much larger than the rest often end up providing a needed public good as a byproduct of their pursuit of their own self-interest, on which other players can free ride. Unilateralism is a pejorative term for what is called *leadership* if the goals are seen in retrospect as legitimate and serving a broad international interest.

There have been other cases in the past in which existing international institutions clearly failed and strong US leadership was needed to break the logjam. A case in point was the Balkans during the 1990s. Through successive conflicts in Croatia, Bosnia, and Kosovo, the Europeans were largely in agreement on the nature and source of the problem (i.e., Serbia) and the need to end a conflict that was occurring on their doorstep. Yet they were totally ineffective in deploying the power necessary to solve the problem: their even-handed arms embargo helped the Serbs, and their peacekeepers failed to prevent genocide from taking place and were themselves taken hostage. It took US airpower in conjunction with a Croatian ground offensive to bring about the Dayton Accords, and a US general leading a US-dominated NATO force to expel the Serbs from Kosovo and ultimately topple the Milosevic regime. The Europeans were paralyzed by collective action problems and a deep-seated reluctance to use power for moral purposes; their problem had to be solved in Washington.

There was a large difference in the perceived legitimacy of US leadership in the Balkans and in the Iraq war. It had less to do with the nature of the moral wrong at the heart of the conflict, the fact of US leadership, or the use of power per se. The lack of legitimacy lay in other factors, like the US haste to prosecute the war, its perceived lack of interest in and support for international institutions, and ultimately its willingness to ignore or bypass the UN when the latter proved not to be supportive of the second resolution authorizing military action. Retrospective approval did not materialize because the threat from Iraq was quite evidently not as great as the administration claimed, and the aftermath was far messier than it expected.[13]

I do not mean that the US should shy away from using power, exercising leadership, and at times acting without broad international support. I do mean that Washington needs to be much more careful in its exercise of that power. Given the fact of US military dominance, it is almost inevitable that the use of force by the United States will provoke a backlash. US policy should devise a strategy to minimize that backlash and avoid the emergence of hostile coalitions. On numerous occasions, the administration has seemingly gone out of its way to alienate friends and potential allies in ways that were gratuitous and counterproductive.[14] What it should have been doing instead was to speak much more softly and deferentially, disguising the steel underneath its policy. The United States should have sought to make more use of international institutions (where it usually has enormous leverage), even at some cost to its own freedom of action, and spent much more time explaining, cajoling, bargaining, and negotiating.

The Bush administration itself learned this lesson, or was forced to do so, in its second term. It has been far more willing to work multilaterally in dealing with the proliferation problems posed by North Korea and Iran, using the Six-Party Talks and the European contact group respectively. The old instinct to use power unilaterally to achieve transformative change has not disappeared, however, as evidenced by the administration's effort to delay a cease-fire in the July 2007 war between Israel and Hizbollah in Lebanon.

Besides the more prudent application of US power, there is the question of international institutions. If the United Nations is not ultimately reformable, what can take its place? The answer is likely to be not a single global institution but rather a multiplicity of international organizations that can provide both power and legitimacy for different types of challenges to world order. A multiplicity of geographically and functionally overlapping institutions will permit the United States and other powers to "forum shop" for an appropriate instrument to facilitate international cooperation. This happened during the Kosovo conflict: when a Russian veto in the Security Council made it impossible for the UN to act, the United States and its European allies shifted the venue to NATO, where the Russians weren't members. The NATO alliance, while operationally cumbersome, provided legitimacy for the military intervention in a way that the UN could not.

The problem with the multi-institution approach is that there is a dearth of suitable international organizations that can perform this type of legitimating and mobilizing function. There is, for example, no organization comparable to NATO in East Asia under whose auspices the United States could organize opposition to the North Korean nuclear program. But this is where some creativity and institution building could be useful. The Community of Democracies, for example, was founded in 2000 with strong support from Madeleine Albright and the Clinton administration, as a club of like-minded democracies that would not suffer from the kinds of legitimacy problems that plague the UN. This organization does not have a security function at present—in fact, few people are even aware of its existence—but with strong backing from the United States, it could in time grow into a much more widely accepted international player and take on a security role. The Six-Party framework that has been used to deal with the North Korean nuclear problem could be made permanent beyond the current crisis as a northeast Asian forum for handing regional security issues. Similarly, ASEAN and the burgeoning proposals for Southeast Asian free trade zones could one day be the seeds for more political sorts of organizations.

In the past, the United States has taken very seriously the task of promoting new international organizations. It played a crucial role in founding the League of Nations, the Bretton Woods organizations, the UN, and most recently the World Trade Organization. But it has become much more wary of participating in new organizations like the International Criminal Court, partly out of disappointment with its experiences with earlier international organizations, and partly as a result of fears that such participation would dilute US sovereignty.

There are, of course, reasons to be wary of the endless multiplication of international institutions. Many would argue that we should concentrate on closing down those like NATO that have outlived their original rationale. International organizations are bloated, bureaucratic, self-serving, costly, and can constrain US freedom of action. But there is also something to be said for organizational competition: if organizations must actually prove their usefulness for solving problems of international cooperation, they may develop incentives to reform. Certainly an organization like the Community of Democracies that is established on a clear set of political principles will serve as a useful counterweight to organizations (like the UN) that are not built around a core of common values.

The more prudent use of US power can be coupled directly to a new institutional framework for dealing with security problems. The US does not have to commit itself to multilateralism on principle; international organizations are simply useful tools for legitimizing cooperative action and serving national objectives. The fear that participation in such organizations will dilute the principle of sovereignty and a world order based on nation-states would seem to be overdrawn, since nation-states remain the only entities capable of deploying hard power for the foreseeable future.

Structurally, the distribution of power within the international system is not likely to change anytime soon. US power is not about to collapse (though there may be greater reluctance to intervene on the part of the American public following the Iraq War), nor is it likely that peer competitors will emerge in either Europe or Asia in the next decade. The major security challenges will continue to come not from great powers but from failed states or from technologically empowered nonstate actors. The United States will inevitably play a central role in providing world order, and world politics will center around how other powers relate to this global hegemon.

It seems reasonably clear that neither reliance on existing international institutions nor US unilateralism will be adequate to meet the nexus of problems involving terrorism, weapons of mass destruction, failed states, and weak governance in unstable parts of the world. None of the suggestions laid out here will solve these problems either, but they will in at least some subset of cases provide a better mix of usable power and international legitimacy than we have seen to date.

Notes

1. Thomas L. Friedman, *The Lexus and the Olive Tree*.

2. There may be some minor exceptions to this generalization, such as the deliberate infecting of populations with plague or smallpox agents.

3. In the wake of September 11, many Americans would have answered that even a miniscule probability of this happening would justify an extreme response (like invading another country), given the magnitude of the stakes. During the Cold War, there was always some non-zero probability that the Soviet Union or China would not behave like a rational actor and would undertake first use of nuclear weapons. Yet the United States did not base its security policy on this possibility, opting instead for a containment/deterrence strategy that forced it to accept the (small) risk that it was wrong in its assumptions about the rationality of its opponents.

4. White House, *The National Security Strategy of the United States of America.*

5. See John Lewis Gaddis, *Surprise, Security, and the American Experience.*

6. Richard K. Betts, "Suicide from Fear of Death?"

7. Pierre Hassner points out that the US constitutional system of checks and balances is designed to limit the delegation of authority to the government, even when that government is democratically elected, and that it is strange that Americans accept the need for checks in their domestic political life but not internationally. See Pierre Hassner, "Definitions, Doctrines, and Divergences."

8. President Bush and other members of his administration asserted on a number of occasions that the coalition assembled for the 2003 Iraq War was as large as or even larger than the one assembled for his father's 1991 Gulf War. That statement completely ignores the quality of the support for intervention in the Gulf War. The real test of an alliance is the willingness to put forces at risk in support of military operations, and in that respect, only Britain and to a lesser extent Australia were willing to do so in 2003, compared to the significantly larger military coalition in 1991.

9. Secretary of State Colin Powell's speech to the UN Security Council on February 5, 2003, refers to, among other things, Iraq's possession of 35,000 liters of anthrax and 500 tons of chemical and biological weapons.

10. For a comprehensive discussion of the legitimacy of UN action, see the new foreword to the paperback edition of Robert Kagan, *Of Paradise and Power;* and Robert Kagan, "America's Crisis of Legitimacy."

11. Fareed Zakaria, "Suicide Bombers Can Be Stopped," *Newsweek,* August 25, 2003.

12. See James Dobbins and Seth Jones, *The UN's Role in Nation-Building.*

13. The ultimate legitimacy of an action can emerge only in the fullness of time; depending on how events develop in Iraq, broader approval for the US action may yet materialize.

14. Two prominent examples of this were the administration's withdrawal from the Kyoto Protocol on global warming, and the National Security Strategy noted earlier. There was no need for President Bush to publicly reject the treaty and to do so in the rather casual way he did; he could have drawn a page from Clinton's playbook and simply never have sent the treaty to the Senate. The part of the National Security Strategy on preemption should never have been published, or else there should have been a clear statement of the policy's limits.

Part 3

Conclusion

11

The Shape of a Shapeless World

I. William Zartman

There is no doubt, after reading the preceding chapters, that the current system of world order is one of uncertainty, replacing the neat balancing of its bipolar predecessor or the hierarchical colonial predecessor before that. Is it unipolar? Is it multipolar? Is it undifferentiatedly globalized? The answer to those troubling questions is a clear and resounding *Yes* and *No*. Of course, all contributors agree that there is a single hegemon but also that it cannot get its way by itself. Similarly, all agree that the theoretically predicted balance of power is ineffective, but that it does operate in unpredicted ways. Each in its way emphasizes that the hegemon should endeavor to exhibit leadership, not domination, but that it will be condemned for its predominant position anyway. And each identifies the ideational element to complement the structure, found in a number of crucial values from justice to welfare that present a challenging worldwide agenda for an amorphous anarchic system.

The Hegemon in Polyarchy

All analyses of world structure in the current era begin by recognizing the predominant power position of the United States. In gross national power (GNP), using the term introduced by Seyom Brown, comprising measures of military forces levels, economic production, and international trade, the US dominates. But almost as soon as that fact is stated, the disagreement begins over its meaning and implications. What does it mean to hold the predominant power position? What role(s) can be ascribed to such status? What capabilities are inherent in GNP? Gross national power, of course, is not the ability to move another state in an intended direction, any more than gross national product translates directly into purchasing power. But therein lies the beginning of the debate, whether power is seen in a relation of cooperation or domination, as Robert Jervis and Paul Schroeder discuss, or over time as long-term cycles, as Charles Doran proposes. A debate on the shape of the world reopens the search for a clear concept of the nature of power.

The debate turns to the ascribed role of the predominant actor and, in turn, to the definition of that role. Is it one of primacy, leadership, hegemony, or empire, and do these terms overlap or embody clear distinctions? If one tries to put the roles into containers, "empire" traditionally means absorption of other states under an overarching sovereignty, whether British or Napoleonic or Roman as the reference, but that does not seem to be the appropriate image for the twenty-first century. Empire to most observers implies imposing decisions on other states (although to Paul Schroeder it is close to hegemony), yet there is still no indication whether imposing decisions on others means unilateralism, that is, acting alone and letting others suffer the consequences, or *unanimism,* forcing others to make the same decisions. In this empire, the fear is not of what the imperial state will do to others, but what it will do without them.

Most of the other contributions to the debate agree that the US holds a position not only of primacy but of hegemony. But hegemon—which to the Greeks meant "guide" or "leader"—has a broad range of implications and, in the end, is in definitional contradiction with an anarchical (i.e., leaderless) society. Like the standard definitions of power, hegemony has a resource and a consequentialist basis. It refers to the raw ingredients underlying the ability to move another in an intended direction, but it also refers to the outcomes of such attempts and so is ultimately in the hands of the follower rather than the leader. Gross national power does not guarantee compliance, and compliance does not flow from GNP (alone). Furthermore, the announced willingness to go it alone is an important ingredient in the ability to draw others to cooperate, and like other threats, it depends on its credibility, shown by a willingness to carry through with the threat. How the hegemon uses this primacy is then a question of policy, not of structure, and the chapters from Robert Jervis to Francis Fukuyama tend to come back to a general consensus on the need to turn primacy into directed multilateralism, without, however, resolving the consequentialist condition.

But beyond the structural imbalance of roles, there is an inherency in the hegemonic status that is beyond the control of policy decisions. A number of contributors, notably Francis Fukuyama in Chapter 10 and Gustav Schmidt in Chapter 7, recognize Walter Lippman's observation that the ends and means of a state are always (by the medium run) in balance, which played to the level of the hegemon means that the disproportionate power of the US position will inevitably lead to aims and therefore envies of the next tier, as Robert Jervis and Kenneth Waltz note in Chapters 3 and 2, respectively. There is a human tendency to distrust the superlative: we are envious of strength, cynical about piety, and jealous of beauty, and so the hegemon inevitably suffers from what could be called a Venus Envy Complex. But to understand its implications, the analysis must turn to the rest of the world beyond the hegemon.

There is a consensus that the world of the new millennium contains a new international system, new both in comparison to that of the Cold War and also to that of earlier periods. The striking characteristic of the current system of world order is polyarchy, following Seyom Brown's application of Robert Dahl's terms in Chapter 6—not a multilateral system implying equal (or at least equivalent) leading parties but a system of many parties of varying capabilities, "highly inclusive and extensively open to public contestation," clustered around the hegemon in a dynamic and uneasy relationship.[1] Working out from the hegemon are, first, the member states of the European Union (EU) and surrounding unaffiliated states, fellow components with the United States and Canada of the North Atlantic security community. The existence of a community where war is not a conceivable option at the center of the international system is a unique experience, as Robert Jervis and Gustav Schmidt analyze, not only because it is historically unprecedented but also because other subordinate state systems in various regions have not yet abolished war in their midst. This means that for the Atlantic subsystem—and indeed more globally, as Farhang Rajaee shows in Chapter 8—the primary issue is welfare, not security, as liberal interpreters insist against the realists. But almost as soon as that fact is stated, the disagreement begins again over its meaning and implications, much of it normative rather than directly policy related.

The Balance of Power

Part of the variance in interpretation concerns the interplay of the hegemonic and polyarchic aspects of the system's structure. A different dynamic that classically characterizes such relations is the balance of power (not to be confused with the static concept of the distribution of power), a mechanism—variously considered either automatic or policy-driven—in which states coalesce to ensure their security by constraining a rising hegemon. The opposite security policy is bandwagoning, to which Seyom Brown has added a third option, that of balking. The current situation has all the ingredients that would predict the operation of the mechanism—the sole remaining superpower throwing its weight around and other states with serious capabilities looking on somewhat askance. The contributors to this book differ as to whether there is or indeed can be a balance of power in the current context. Kenneth Waltz shows that no state or group of states has the capability to balance the gross national power of the hegemon, or that military and/or economic interdependency prevents the mechanism from operating, or that the potential balancers are too deeply tied to the hegemon by common values and/or institutions, or that there is enough bandwagoning to undermine the mechanism, or that welfare as the predominant goal does not lend itself to power balancing as security does. Others such as Robert Jervis, Gustav Schmidt, and Francis Fukuyama argue that, with allowances made for a necessary lag time, the balance of power is beginning to operate, notably in the reaction of the European core provoked by US policies in the beginning of the millennium. Furthermore, the reaction of "second-tier" members of the EU like Spain and Poland—and all the more so the new eastern members—to the prospective dominant role of countries like France and Germany is indeed an example of the balance of power operating in a regional context.

Yet the contributors agree in various ways that despite reactions of affective petulance, the effective operation of a balance of power is weakened by the incoherence of European politics, with member states aiming farther than their guns' range and hanging onto their sovereignty for dear life to undermine the very assertion of collective sovereignty to which their union aspires, as Gustav Schmidt and Charles Doran emphasize. Of course, it is only a passing phase, a growing pain of the most adventuresome and far-reaching integration effort of already sovereign states that world history has ever seen. Yet for that very reason the passing phase is likely to be a long one, to the point at which none of the contributors contemplates a single coherent European actor within the range of these chapters' vision. If and when true unification occurs, the game will change mightily, but most analysis foresees a Chinese entry into a major power position before a European entry.

Some of the analyses, such as those by Gustav Schmidt in Chapter 7 and Charles Doran in Chapter 5, pay more than passing attention to other rising powers and regional constellations, none of which is likely to disturb the dominant nature of the polyarchic system or its hegemonic center. Like Europe, China, India, and other rising powers are engrossed in domestic economic and political development for the foreseeable future, building the ingredients of a later power role but for the time being turned inward. This domestic preoccupation reinforces the importance of welfare as a goal value for the international system itself but does not reduce the importance of security for their regional and hence global relations, as the cases of China (regarding Taiwan and Tibet) and India (regarding Pakistan) and the two together (China regarding India) emphasize. Regional constellations can be expected to play an increasingly important role in managing their own conflicts and coordinating their own economies and polities. The more such self-help develops, the more the burden of security is lifted from the global system, without, however, creating a system of political autarkies, and the intensification of economic and cultural globalization exerts a powerful force to counteract centrifugal tendencies. None of the contributors takes seriously the Kulturkampf foreseen in the visions of a clash of civilization (Samuel Huntington), making an implicit distinction between Islamic (or other fundamentalist) extremists and their Muslim (or other) context, as emphasized in Farhang Rajaee's emphasis on one civilization/many cultures.

Another form of the balance of power more appropriate to the current age is also noted, by Robert Jervis and Francis Fukuyama among others. The anti-Western reaction incarnated by Al-Qaida and its terrorism can be seen as a manifestation of the balance of power adapted to the era of globalization. After all, Al-Qaida is a transnational corporation composed of many nationalities, a corporate culture, international funding, and agents, bases, and operations around the globe, reacting against the cultural penetration of the West, the United States in the lead, into its traditional heartland. In the new millennium, the balance of power cannot be confined to state reactions using conventional military sources of power but needs to be extended to fit the evolving nature of international relations that go beyond a merely state system. This understanding of the terrorist reaction helps place it into a familiar conceptual context, but it does not remove the new fact that for the first time terrorism, eschatological motivation, and weapons of mass destruction combine to constitute a security threat that is viewed differently among the threatened populations, as Francis Fukuyama signals.

Normative change in the system is seen above all by Europeans as growing out of the continental subsystem characterized by welfare over security or security without defense, both in regard to their internal relations and their relation to the hegemon (see Farhang Rajaee in Chapter 8 and Gustav Schmidt in Chapter 7). On the one hand, in a return to Wilsonian idealism, some on the European side of the Atlantic security community expect their own relations to be mirrored in a world security community run by the UN Security Council, confusing a normative and an analytical perspective. On the other hand, some see the international system functioning according to norms prevalent in a domestic system, run by rules of democracy with participation by government and nongovernmental organizations (NGOs). On still another hand, the complex interdependence codified in international regimes, establishing rules, regulations, norms, principles, and expectations in international issue areas, provides a lawlike network, an agenda for activity, and opportunities and constraints for policy, noted by Michael Klare and Peter Pavilionis in Chapter 9.

The ever-enmeshing network of international regimes that ties together the international system may help explain the weakness of a balance of power reaction but is also less discussed. Soft legislation established by various multilateral negotiation forums, from formal UN conferences to regional state agreements or even NGO meetings, provides constraining if not binding norms for territorial waters, nuclear proliferation, greenhouse gas emissions, landmine use, endangered species treatment, fishing intake, postal dimensions, and stop sign shapes, among many others. New sources of conflict arise as increasing population and product demands impose Malthusian pressures and regulation requirements for current resources, and further sources of conflict arise as regimes run into each other and impose conflicting codes of conduct, as Michael Klare and Peter Pavilionis emphasize. Such rules, regulations, norms, principles, and expectations reach past states' borders into the lives of their citizens, creating new upwelling pressures for further problem-solving efforts in recursive regime negotiations. If the chimera of "black helicopters" and "UN legislation" was once waved in US electoral campaigns, the reality of expanding norms to provide order for transactional problems is an increasing necessity in the international system.

Yet nothing in this extension is incompatible with the persistence of the state as the principal actor, almost all the contributors agree. The state remains the basic component of the international system, even if it now has new company from nonstate actors, new depth in the contribution of domestic sociopolitics, and new texture from extended types of interaction. The constructivist enrichment to the realist analysis reveals a more complicated structure to the polyarchic system. But nonstate actors continue to work through, against, beneath, and alongside the state, not instead of it. Though the state may become more permeated and permeable, overburdened with new tasks and charged with controlling the growing forces that circumvent it, it remains the supreme agent of identity, allegiance, regulation, legitimization, and security; the subject of power cycles; and the object of normative constraints.

Nor is anything in the complex picture incompatible with a concert system of international politics, institutionalized in not only the UN Security Council (UNSC) but also in the G8 meetings, regional summits, and conferences of the parties in recursive regime negotiations—Francis Fukuyama's "multiplicity of international organizations." Balancing, bandwagoning, and balking serve as the basis for fluid minority-, majority-, and neutral-state coalitions within the UNSC and other forums. But the UNSC remains only a place, not a thing, a concert hall of sovereign states engaged in policy coordination and legitimization and not a corporate actor with a will of its own. Nor is this characteristic open to probable change, as emphasized by Francis Fukuyama; what is required for the system to work effectively is not an unlikely reform of the UN but a reform of the members to assume their responsibilities within the system. It therefore seems ahead of the foreseeable times to confuse momentary policy decisions with international law, just as it is premature to confuse the evolving rules and regulations of international regimes with global legislation. Even the contributors who recognize the importance of the UNSC as a forum for policy and the network of regimes as a constraint on both globalization and domestic activities, such as Robert Jervis, Seyom Brown, Gustav Schmidt, and Farhang Rajaee, do not see these institutions as imposing a tightened international legal framework on the current international system.

Systems of World Order

Can a system so constituted provide world order in the coming half-century, as the Cold War did in its time, at a high cost in resources, lives, and tension? Order in the first half of the twenty-first century means many more things than just "security and let sovereign states handle their own affairs." It means conventional security in some places, security without defense in others, and welfare along with security throughout. It means that the dangerous doctrine of sovereignty as protection, where states have the right to do what they want to their populations without fear of interference, becomes increasingly challenged by the equally dangerous doctrine of sovereignty as responsibility, where states are held responsible for the welfare of the people and other states are responsible for helping their populations when necessary. Neither the meeting place nor the limits of these two doctrines has yet been worked out, a process that will occupy the international system both in case and in concept.

A number of foreseeable challenges face this system over the coming period, in addition to those still unforeseen. One is the threat of terror, fanaticism, and weapons of mass destruction laid out by Francis Fukuyama. A second is the conventional conflict of rank and relation in some regions, exacerbated by the growing pains of regional hegemons, as adumbrated in Charles Doran's analysis. A third concerns the welfare relations within the Atlantic core area, a source of serious even if not violent conflict, as Robert Jervis mentions. A fourth is the balance of power in either of its configurations—a traditional reaction of others against a freewheeling hegemon or a globalist reaction, terrorist or not, against cultural-economic impingement, as Kenneth Waltz, Paul Schroeder, Gustav Schmidt, and Seyom Brown discuss. A fifth involves raw material conflicts of possession, allocation, access, and domestic politics, as presented by Michael Klare and Peter Pavilionis. The sixth is the anarchic, often ethnic violence born of underdevelopment that exacerbates its own cause and shocks, dulls, and invites external intervention. And seventh is the struggle to define and to capture legitimacy, discussed by Farhang Rajaee, Francis Fukuyama, and Robert Jervis.

Some of these are conventional challenges, but also in new forms befitting the current millennium—balance of power both traditional and global, regional rank and relations with growing pains, resource redistribution under population pressures, and the recurrent struggle for legitimization. The balance of power reaction against US-led globalization, as expressed by Al-Qaida and the wellspring of resentment it represents, is a Luddite reflex but one combined with religious fanaticism and modern technology, a complex and difficult combination to manage. The growing pains that exacerbate the usual struggles for rank and relation in a region have a double-edged impact: in Europe, for example, success in uniting gives both the ends and the means for a stronger antihegemonic reaction, whereas failure in uniting fuels the same reaction out of spite and resentment; another special challenge within the core nation-states is the pressure of ethnic assertion on both national identity and territorial cohesion. The modern twist on resource-based conflicts is their global scope and the depth of their coverage into the control and distribution of new substances both positive and negative, such as water and carbon dioxide. Each era has its fundamental contest to control and enjoy the sources of legitimization that lie at the basis of any system of world order; in this case, the key is the meaning of democracy as the domestic source of responsibility and participation versus democracy as the international decision rule for authorizing action, or the clash between sovereignty as responsibility and as protection.

Other challenges are patently new—the triple threat of armed neo-atavism and the shift from security to welfare as the goal value or the conflict source in the international system. The terrorist threat as a security issue is impervious to conventional measures and, in addition to its array of unconventional weapons, has the ability to wield fear as a powerful armament against its opponents. Even more seriously, it joins and benefits from the spread of global crime, drugs, and racketeering. At the same time, the growing emphasis on welfare as the coin of relations among the members of the Atlantic core makes them less attuned to a security threat they do not understand but more vulnerable to emotional and material engagement in economic and social conflict. Both the above challenges and the subsequent responses assume continuation of the system as a nation-state system, yet the fissiparous tendencies produced by ethnic nationalism are the potentially strongest forces that can weaken the state as a coherent actor, whether they produce many smaller ethnostates or internal strains on current states trying to maintain their integrity. Again, paradoxically, both the weakening and the persistence of sovereignty, as well as the ascendancy of welfare over security as a goal value, can work to enhance these tendencies. Similarly in the poorer parts of the world, in socially and economically divided states, the collapse of domestic order allows political entrepreneurs to seize on ethnic appeals or economic opportunities to take their "time at the trough," destroying their society and spreading their rot throughout the region, and creating virulent decay that the international system, for both political and humanitarian reasons, cannot ignore.

What are the tools and mechanisms with which the current international system is endowed to meet these challenges and provide world order? The institutional structure is multiplicitous, soft, and tentative, so its own growing pains become at the same time part of the problem and part of the response. At the tenuous top of the hierarchy remains the UN Security Council, the summit of the concert system, in informal partnership with G8 meetings. At present, the UNSC is only the reflection of the informal polyarchy in the system; it can either muddle this status or evolve into a more formal clearinghouse for legitimate international action. Alongside the tensions in this evolution lie the networks of regimes, regional organizations, and other international congregations that give a disorderly order to the fabric of international and transnational relations. The dynamics within this area of institutional structure will be between continued adhockery, and pressures for increasing formalization, extension of regulation, and resolution of competing competences. These pressures are inevitable, and even if the sovereign states of the system decide to continue muddling through, their muddling has a direction. Regulations and decisions continue to remain policy rather than law, even as the pressure for more formal mechanisms of compliance and accountability continue. External shocks—violent conflagrations, anthropogenic accidents, scientific discoveries—can accelerate the pace of regulation and institutionalization of constraints, as they tend to do; they are unlikely to set it back.

The other element in the system's structure is the hegemon, whose primacy may be slipping against competition but who is unlikely to lose its predominance over the coming half-century. Those two elements provide a dynamic texture (the same kind of dynamic that underlies the balance of power), as competition gives rise to conflict, coalition, balancing, and simply balking, whereas slippage gives rise to efforts to hold on. If the hegemon holds its own along the security dimension, expressed in gross national power, it will still face conflict and challenges along the welfare dimension. In Chapter 4, Paul Schroeder has limned the policy challenges as stark alternatives, echoed by the other contributors to this volume. However, in reality the policy alternatives lie along a dynamic spectrum in depth, even though they are best portrayed as polar opposites, much as the tensions within the polyarchy between informality and formalization slip along an array rather than confronting each other as opposites. The hegemon is called on for leadership and direction, which inevitably attracts opposition as well as support. These natural tendencies evoke their own reaction on the part of the hegemon. As in other things, reality probably lies in between the stark choices, at least over time, but the alternatives are nonetheless clear.

The policy choice rests on this underlying dynamic. The hegemon can turn imperial, following republican Rome, democratic Athens, and revolutionary France. The chances of actual territorial incorporation in this day and age are small, but the temptations of installing friendly governments in countries that do not need to be actually occupied are greater. Going it alone when collective behavior cannot be coerced or dictated is more likely, and the pressures to do so are inherent in the hegemonic position, if not its role. Assertiveness may be thrust upon the hegemon by the reactions of resistant followers, as noted, and may be the only alternative to indifference and inactivity, leaving little room for benign leadership in between.

But in principle at least, the hegemon can also exercise leadership of its fellow states, convincing them of the rightness of a common path. Although there will always be pressures on the United States to try to climb off the world and exercise the third choice of indifference and inactivity, that is less and less possible; leadership, therefore, will always be a matter of moving the others in an intended direction. As in all negotiation, that implies giving something—not giving in—to allies, wielding carrots more than sticks, accepting constraints of participation and accountability applicable to all, and finding one's interest within positive-sum public-good benefits rather than narrowly defined self-interest applicable only to the special conditions of being a hegemon.

Charles-Maurice de Talleyrand, several times French foreign minister under a variety of regimes and a man who put principles above regimes, has good words to say about hegemonic behavior in changing systems of world order, in which he had some experience: "True greatness is that which is limited to itself, true force is that which moderates itself, true glory is that which surrounds itself with national recognition" (1796). "No domination, no monopoly, always the force that protects, never the force that takes over" (1797). "Allies are kept only with care, concern, and reciprocal advantages. . . . Powerful though the Republic may be, it imposes less confidence than respect. To obtain true and useful allies, it must obtain [their] confidence" (1798).[2] But it takes two to cooperate. Therein lie the tension and the dynamics of the new world order of the twenty-first century.

Notes

1. Robert Dahl, *Polyarchy,* p. 7.
2. Quotations from Jean Orieux, *Talleyrand ou le Sphinx Incompris,* pp. 290 (1796), 249 (1797), 295 (1798).

Bibliography

Abbott, K. W., R. Keohane, A. Moravcsik, A.-M. Slaughter, and D. Snidal. "The Concept of Legalization." *International Organization* 54, no. 3 (2000): 418.

Abbott, K. W., and D. Snidal. "Hard and Soft Law in International Governance." *International Organization* 54, no. 3 (2000): 421–456.

Adams, Gordon, and Guy Ben-Ari. *Transforming European Militaries: Coalition Operations and the Technology Gap*. London: Routledge, 2006.

Adler, Emanuel. "Europe's New Security Order." In Beverly Crawford, ed., *The Future of European Security*, 287–326. Berkeley: University of California Institute for International and Area Studies, 1992.

Adler, Emanuel, and Michael Barnett, eds. *Security Communities*. New York: Cambridge University Press, 1998.

Annan, Kofi. "The Politics of Globalization." In Patrick O'Meara, Howard D. Mehlinger, and Matthew Krain, eds., *Globalization and the Challenges of a New Century: A Reader*. Bloomington: Indiana University Press, 2000.

Apter, David E. *Choice and the Politics of Allocation*. New Haven, CT: Yale University Press, 1971.

Aron, Raymond. "The Anarchical Order of Power." In Stanley Hoffmann, ed., *Conditions of World Order*, 44–45. Boston: Houghton Mifflin, 1968.

Aron, Raymond. *Peace and War: A Theory of International Relations*. Garden City, NY: Doubleday, 1966.

Art, Robert J. "American Foreign Policy and the Fungibility of Force." *Security Studies* 5 (Summer 1996): 7–42.

Art, Robert J. "Force and Fungibility Reconsidered." *Security Studies* 8 (Summer 1999): 183–189.

Art, Robert J. *A Grand Strategy for America*. Ithaca, NY: Cornell University Press, 2003.

Art, Robert J. "Why Western Europe Needs the United States and NATO." *Political Science Quarterly* 111, no. 1 (Spring 1996): 1–39.

Art, Robert J., Stephen Brooks, William Wohlforth, Kier Lieber, and Gerard Alexander. "Correspondence: Striking the Balance." *International Security* 30, no. 3 (Winter 2005–2006): 177–196.

Augustine. *The Political Writings of St. Augustine*. Henry Paolucci, ed. Washington, DC: Regnery, 1962.

Axelrod, Robert. *Conflict of Interest*. Chicago, IL: Markham, 1970.

Axelrod, Robert. *The Evolution of Cooperation*. New York: Basic Books, 1984.

Axworthy, L., and S. Taylor. "A Ban for All Seasons: The Landmines Convention and Its Implication for Canadian Diplomacy." *International Journal* 53, no. 2 (1998): 189–203.

Baldwin, David A. "Force, Fungibility, and Influence." *Security Studies* 8 (Summer 1999): 173–182.

Banzhaf, J. F. "Weighted Voting Doesn't Work." *Rutgers Law Review* 19, no. 2 (1965): 317–343.

Bates, Robert, ed. *Toward a Political Economy of Development: A Rational Choice Perspective.* Berkeley: University of California Press, 1988.

Barry, Brian. *Theories of Justice*. Berkeley: University of California Press, 1989.

Barzun, Jacques. "Bagehot or the Human Comedy." In Jacques Barzun, *The Energies of Art.* New York: Harper, 1956.

Beetham, D. *The Legitimation of Power.* London: Macmillan, 1991.

Beloff, M. *Imperial Sunset.* Vol. 1, *Britain's Liberal Empire, 1897–1921.* New York: Knopf, 1970.

Bercovitch, Jacob, I. William Zartman, and Victor Kremenyuk, eds. *Handbook of Conflict Resolution.* London: Sage, 2008.

Betts, Richard. "The Delusion of Imperial Intervention." *Foreign Affairs* (November–December 1994): 30–31.

Betts, Richard. "The Soft Underbelly of American Primacy: Tactical Advantages of Terror." *Political Science Quarterly* 117 (Spring 2002): 19–36.

Betts, Richard. "Suicide from Fear of Death?" *Foreign Affairs* 82, no. 1 (2003): 34–43.

Betts, Richard. "What Will It Take to Deter the United States?" *Parameters* 25 (Winter 1995–1996): 70–79.

Bireley, R. *Religion and Politics in the Age of the Counterreformation.* Chapel Hill, NC: University of North Carolina Press, 1981.

Black, J. *British Foreign Policy in the Age of Walpole.* Edinburgh: John Donald, 1985.

Black, J. *Natural and Necessary Enemies: Anglo-French Relations in the Eighteenth Century.* London: Duckworth, 1986.

Bobbitt, P. *The Shield of Achilles: War, Peace, and the Course of History.* New York: Knopf, 2002.

Bolton, John R. "Unilateralism Is Not Isolationism." In Gwyn Prins, ed., *Understanding Unilateralism in American Foreign Relations,* 74. London: Royal Institute of International Affairs, 2000.

Bosbach, F. *Monarchia Universalis: Ein politischer Leitbegriff der frühen Neuzeit.* Göttingen: Vandenhoeck and Ruprecht, 1988.

Boutros-Ghali, Boutros. *An Agenda for Peace,* 2nd ed. New York: United Nations, 1995.

Bouwsma, William J. *John Calvin: A Sixteenth-Century Portrait.* Oxford: Oxford University Press, 1987.

Brams, Steven J., and P. J. Affuso. "Power and Size: A New Paradox." *Theory and Decision* 7, no. 1–2 (1976): 29–56.

Brenner, Michael J. "Europe's New Security Vocation." McNair Paper 66. Washington, DC: National Defense University, Institute for National Strategic Studies, 2002.

Brodie, Bernard. "The Development of Nuclear Strategy." *International Security* 2 (Spring 1978): 83.

Brooks, Stephen G., and William C. Wohlforth. "American Primacy in Perspective." *Foreign Affairs* 81, no. 4 (July–August 2002): 20–33.

Brooks, Stephen G., and William C. Wohlforth. "Hard Times for Soft Balancing." *International Security* 30, no. 1 (Summer 2005): 72–108.

Brooks, Stephen G., and William C. Wohlforth. *World Out of Balance: International Relations and the Challenge of American Primacy.* Princeton, NJ: Princeton University Press, 2008.

Brown, Seyom. *The Faces of Power: Constancy and Change in United States Foreign Policy from Truman to Clinton.* New York: Columbia University Press, 1994.

Brown, Seyom. *The Illusion of Control: Force and Foreign Policy in the Twenty-First Century.* Washington, DC: Brookings Institution Press, 2003.

Brown, Seyom. *New Forces in World Politics.* Washington, DC: Brookings Institution Press, 1974.

Brown, Seyom. *New Forces, Old Forces, and the Future of World Politics.* New York: HarperCollins, 1995.

Brunner, O., W. Conze, and R. Koselleck, eds. *Geschichtliche Grundbegriffe,* vol. 2. Stuttgart: Klett, 1975.

Brzezinski, Zbigniew. *Between Two Ages: America's Role in the Technetronic Era.* New York: Viking, 1970.

Bull, Hedley. *The Anarchical Society: A Study of Order in World Politics.* New York: Columbia University Press, 1977.

Bull, Hedley, and Adam Watson, eds. *The Expansion of International Society.* Oxford: Oxford University Press, 1984.

Bunce, Valerie. *Do New Leaders Make a Difference? Executive Succession and Public Policy Under Capitalism and Socialism.* Princeton, NJ: Princeton University Press, 1981.

Burkhardt, J. *Der Dreissig-Jährige Krieg.* Frankfurt am Main: Suhrkamp, 1992.

Busch, Marc L. *Trade Warriors: States, Firms, and Strategic-Trade Policy in High-Technology Competition.* New York: Cambridge University Press, 1999.

Butterfield, Herbert. "The Balance of Power." In Herbert Butterfield and Martin Wight, eds., *Diplomatic Investigations.* London: George Allen and Unwin, 1966.

Buzan, Barry. *The United States and the Great Powers: World Politics in the Twenty-First Century.* Cambridge: Polity, 2004.

Calder, Kent E. "China and Japan's Simmering Rivalry." *Foreign Affairs* 85, no. 2 (March–April 2006): 129–139.

Calder, Kent E. *Embattled Garrisons: Comparative Base Politics and American Globalism.* Princeton, NJ: Princeton University Press, 2007.

Callaghy, Thomas. *The State-Society Struggle: Zaire in Comparative Perspective.* New York: Columbia University Press, 1984.

Carr, E. H. *The Twenty Years' Crisis, 1919–1939: An Introduction to the Study of International Relations.* London: Macmillan, 1939.

Casper, G., and M. M. Taylor. *Negotiated Democracy: Transitions from Authoritarian Rule.* Pittsburgh: University of Pittsburgh Press, 1996.

Chace, James. "Imperial America and the Common Interest." *World Policy Journal* (Spring 2002): 1–9.

Christensen, Thomas J. "Posing Problems Without Catching Up: China's Rise and Challenges for US Security Policy." *International Security* 25, no. 4 (Spring 2001): 5–40.

Clarke, Michael, and Paul Cornish. "The European Defense Project and the Prague Summit." *International Affairs* 78, no. 4 (2002): 777–788.

Cogan, Charles G. *The Third Option: The Emancipation of European Defense, 1989–2000*. Westport, CT: Praeger, 2001.

Copeland, Dale. "The Constructivist Challenge to Structural Realism." *International Security* 25, no. 2 (Fall 2000): 187–212.

Copeland, Dale. *The Origins of Major War*. Ithaca, NY: Cornell University Press, 2000.

Croft, Stuart, Andrew Dorman, Wyn Rees, and Matthew Uttley. *Britain and Defence, 1945–2000: A Policy of Re-evaluation*. London: Pearson/Longman, 2001.

Cusimano, Maryann, ed. *Beyond Sovereignty: Issues for a Global Agenda*. Boston: Bedford/St. Martin's, 2006.

Daalder, Ivo. "Are the United States and Europe Heading for Divorce?" *International Affairs* 77, no. 3 (2001).

Daalder, Ivo, and J. M. Lindsay. "Scheidung oder Neubeginn?" *Internationale Politik*, no. 5 (2003): 14–15.

Dahl, Robert. "The Concept of Power." *Behavioral Science* 2, no. 3 (1957): 201–215.

Dahl, Robert. "Hierarchy, Democracy, and Bargaining in Politics and Economics." In Stephen K. Bailey et al., ed., *Research Frontiers in Politics and Government*. Washington, DC: Brookings Institution, 1955.

Dahl, Robert. *Polyarchy: Participation and Opposition*. New Haven, CT: Yale University Press, 1971.

Dallin, Alexander. "Causes of Collapse of the USSR." *Post-Soviet Affairs* 8, no. 4 (1992): 279–302.

Davis, Darren, and Brian Silver. "Civil Liberties vs. Security: Public Opinion in the Context of the Terrorist Attacks on America." *American Journal of Political Science* 48 (January 2004): 28–46.

Dehio, Ludwig. *The Precarious Balance: Four Centuries of the European Power Struggle*. New York: Knopf, 1962.

de Madariaga, Isabel. *Russia in the Age of Catherine the Great*. New Haven, CT: Yale University Press, 1982.

Deng, Francis, Sadikiel Kimaro, Terrence Lyons, Donald Rothchild, and I. William Zartman. *Sovereignty as Responsibility*. Washington, DC: Brookings Institution Press, 1996.

Deng, Francis, and I. William Zartman. *A Strategic Vision for Africa*. Washington: Brookings Institution Press, 2003.

Deudney, Daniel, and John Ikenberry. "Soviet Reform and the End of the Cold War: Explaining Large-Scale Historical Change." *Review of International Studies* 17, no. 2 (1991): 225–250.

Deutsch, Karl W., and J. David Singer. "Multipolar Power Systems and International Stability." *World Politics* 16, no. 3 (1964): 390–406.

Deutsch, Karl W., et al. *Political Community and the North Atlantic Area: International Organizations in the Light of Historical Experience*. Princeton, NJ: Princeton University Press, 1957.

Dobbins, James, and Seth Jones. *The UN's Role in Nation-Building: From the Congo to Iraq*. Santa Monica, CA: Rand Corporation, 2005.

Doran, Charles F. *Politics of Assimilation: Hegemony and Its Aftermath*. Baltimore: Johns Hopkins University Press, 1971.

Doran, Charles F. "Power Cycle Theory and Global Politics." *International Political Science Review* 24, no. 1 (January 2003).

Doran, Charles F. *Systems in Crisis: New Imperatives of High Politics at Century's End*. Cambridge: Cambridge University Press, 1991.

Dreyer, June T. *China's Political System: Modernization and Tradition*. New York: Longman, 1999.

Duchhardt, H. *Altes Reich und Europäische Staatenwelt, 1648–1806*. Munich: Oldenbourg, 1988.

Duffield, John S. "Transatlantic Relations After the Cold War: Theory, Evidence, and the Future." *International Studies Perspectives* 2 (February 2001): 93–115.

Easton, David. *A Systems Analysis of Political Life*. New York: John Wiley and Sons, 1965.

Ehrhart, Hans-Georg. "Abschied vom Leitbild 'Zivilmacht'? Konzepte zur EU-Sicherheitspolitik nach dem Irak-Krieg." In Johannes Varwick and Wilhelm Knelangen, eds., *Neues Europa—alte EU?* 149–163. Opladen: Leske and Budrich, 2004.

Ehrhart, Hans-Georg. "Die EU als zivil-militärischer Krisenmanager. Zwischen Anspruch und Wirklichkeit." *Integration* 27, no. 2 (2005): 217–232.

Eisenstadt, Shmuel N. *Modernization: Protest and Change*. Englewood Cliffs, NJ: Prentice Hall, 1966.

Eisenstadt, Shmuel N. "Empires." In D. L. Sills, ed., *International Encyclopedia of the Social Sciences,* vol. 5. New York: Macmillan, 1968.

Eland, Ivan. *The Empire Has No Clothes: US Foreign Policy Exposed*. Oakland, CA: Independent Institute, 2004.

Elster, John. *Local Justice*. New York: Russell Sage, 1992.

Emerson, Michael, Nathalie Tocci, Marius Vahl, and Nicholas Whyte. *The Elephant and the Bear: The European Union, Russia and Their Near Abroads*. Brussels: CEPS, Brussels, October 2001.

Evans, Gareth, and Mohamed Sahnoun, eds. *The Responsibility to Protect: Report of the International Commission on Intervention and State Sovereignty*. Ottawa: International Development Research Centre, 2001.

Falk, Richard A. *On Humane Governance: Toward a New Global Politics*. Cambridge: Polity Press, 1995.

Falk, Richard A. *Predatory Globalization: A Critique*. Cambridge: Polity, 1999.

Farber, Henry S., and Joanne Gowa. "Polities and Peace." *International Security* 20, no. 2 (1995): 123–146.

Faure, Guy Olivier. "Negotiating Joint Ventures in China." In Gunnar Sjöstedt and Victor Kremenyuk, eds., *International Economic Negotiations: Models vs. Reality*. Cheltenham: Edward Elgar, 2000.

Fehl, Caroline, and Johannes Thimm. "Weltmacht und Weltordnung: Multilateralismus im Transatlantischen Spannungsfeld." *SWP-Studie,* S 6, March 2008, Berlin.

Feinstein, Lee, and Anne-Marie Slaughter. "A Duty to Prevent." *Foreign Affairs* 83, no. 1 (January–February 2004).

Ferguson, Niall. *Empire: The Rise and Demise of the British World Order and the Lessons for Global Power*. New York: Basic Books, 2003.

Ferguson, Niall. "Hegemony or Empire?" *Foreign Affairs* 82, no. 5 (2003): 154–161.

Freedman, Lawrence. *The Revolution in Strategic Affairs*. Adelphi Paper 318. Oxford: Oxford University Press for the International Institute for Strategic Studies, 1998.

Friedman, Thomas L. *The Lexus and the Olive Tree*. New York: Farrar, Straus and Giroux, 1999.

Fukuyama, Francis. "The End of History." In Patrick O'Meara, Howard D. Mehlinger, and Matthew Krain, *Globalization and the Challenges of a New Century: A Reader,* 161–181. Bloomington: Indiana University Press, 2000.

Gaddis, John Lewis. "A Grand Strategy of Transformation." *Foreign Policy* 133 (November–December 2002): 50–57.
Gaddis, John Lewis. "International Relations Theory and the End of the Cold War." *International Security* 17, no. 1 (1992): 5–58.
Gaddis, John Lewis. *Strategies of Containment: A Critical Appraisal of American National Security Policy During the Cold War,* rev. ed. New York: Oxford University Press, 2005.
Gaddis, John Lewis. *Surprise, Security, and the American Experience.* Cambridge, MA: Harvard University Press, 2004.
Galbraith, John S. *Reluctant Empire: British Policy on the South African Frontier, 1834–1854.* Berkeley: University of California Press, 1963.
Galbraith, John S. "The 'Turbulent Frontier' as a Factor in British Expansion." *Comparative Studies in Society and History* 2 (January 1960): 34–48.
Gärtner, Heinz. "European Security and Transatlantic Relations After 9/11 and the Wars in Afghanistan and Iraq." In Gärtner and Ian M. Cuthbertson, eds., *European Security and Transatlantic Relations After 9/11 and the Iraq War.* Basingstoke: Palgrave, 2005.
Gärtner, Heinz, and Ian M. Cuthbertson, eds. *European Security and Transatlantic Relations After 9/11 and the Iraq War.* Basingstoke: Palgrave, 2005.
Gause, F. Gregory III. "Can Democracy Stop Terrorism?" *Foreign Affairs* 84, no. 5 (September–October 2005): 62–76.
Geller, Daniel S. "Material Capabilities: Power and International Conflict." In John A. Vasquez, ed., *What Do We Know About War?* 259–280. Lanham, MD: Rowman and Littlefield, 2000.
Gholz, Eugene, Daryl G. Press, and Harvey M. Sapolsky. "Come Home, America: The Strategy of Restraint in the Face of Temptation." *International Security* 21, no. 4 (Spring 1997): 4–49.
Gilbert, Martin. *Winston S. Churchill.* Vol. 6, *Finest Hour: 1939–1941.* London: Heinemann, 1983.
Gillis, Paul. *NATO and Energy Security.* CRS Report for Congress, no. RS22409. Washington, DC: Congressional Research Service, December 21, 2006.
Gilpin, Robert. *The Political Economy of International Relations.* Princeton, NJ: Princeton University Press, 1987.
Gilpin, Robert. *War and Change in World Politics.* Cambridge: Cambridge University Press, 1981.
Gleick, Peter H., ed. *Water in Crisis: A Guide to the World's Fresh Water Resources.* New York: Oxford University Press, 1993.
Goldgeier, James M., and Michael McFaul. "A Tale of Two Worlds: Core and Periphery in the Post–Cold War Era." *International Organization* 46 (Spring 1992): 467–491.
Goldstein, Joshua. *International Relations.* New York: Longman, 2003.
Goldstein, Judith, Miles Kahler, Robert O. Keohane, and Anne-Marie Slaughter. "Introduction: Legalization and World Politics." *International Organization* 54, no. 3 (2000): 386.
Goodin, Robert. "Structures of Political Order." In Ian Shapiro and Russell Hardin, eds., *Political Order: Nomos* 39. New York: New York University Press, 1993.
Gordon, Philip. "Bush's Middle East Vision." *Survival* 45 (Spring 2003): 155–165.
Gordon, Philip. *NATO's Growing Role in the Greater Middle East.* Emirates Lecture Series 63. Abu Dhabi: Emirates Center for Strategic Studies and Research, 2006.
Gordon, Philip H., and Jeremy Shapiro. *Allies at War: America, Europe, and the Crisis over Iraq.* New York: McGraw-Hill, 2004.

Gordon, Stuart. "Exploring the Civil-Military Interface and Its Impact on European Strategic and Operational Personalities: 'Civilianisation' and Limiting Military Roles in Stabilisation Operations?" *European Security* 15, no. 3 (2006): 339–361.

Goubert, P. *Mazarin*. Paris: Fayard, 1990.

Graham, Thomas E., Jr. "US Leadership and Domestic Factors in Dealing with Russia During the Clinton Administration." In Bernhard May and Michaela Hönicke Moore, eds., *The Uncertain Superpower: Domestic Dimensions of US Foreign Policy After the Cold War,* 134. Opladen: Leske and Budrich, 2003.

Grant, Ruth W., and Robert O. Keohane. "Accountability and the Abuses of Power in World Politics." *American Political Science Review* 99, no. 1 (February 2005): 29–43.

Gray, Colin S. "European Perspectives on US Ballistic Missile Response." *Comparative Strategy* 21, no. 4 (2002): 279–310.

Green, Donald, and Ian Shapiro. *The Pathologies of Rational Choice.* New Haven, CT: Yale University Press, 1994.

Green, Michael J. "Japan Is Back: Why Tokyo's New Assertiveness Is Good for Washington." A review essay of *Japan Rising: The Resurgence of Japanese Power and Purpose* by Kenneth Pyle (Public Affairs, 2007), in *Foreign Affairs* 86, no. 2 (March–April, 2007): 142–147.

Guérot, Ulrike. "Die deutsch-französischen Beziehungen zwischen Geopolitik und GASP: Bericht über die deutsch-französische Konferenz der Association Jean-Monnet in Houjarray 5–7 July 2002." *Dokumente* 58, no. 3 (2002): 13.

Guinier, Lani. *The Tyranny of the Majority: Fundamental Fairness and Representative Democracy.* New York: Free Press, 1994.

Gulick, Edward V. *Europe's Classical Balance of Power*. Ithaca, NY: Cornell University Press, 1955.

Gulliver, P. H. *Disputes and Negotiations: A Cross-Cultural Perspective*. London: Academic Press, 1979.

Haass, Richard N. "The Age of Nonpolarity: What Will Follow US Dominance?" *Foreign Affairs* 87, no. 87 (May–June 2008): 44–56.

Haass, Richard N. *The Opportunity: America's Moment to Alter History's Course.* New York: Public Affairs, 2005.

Haass, Richard N. "US Foreign Policy in a Nonpolar World." *Foreign Affairs* 87, no. 87 (May–June 2008): 44–56.

Haass, Richard N. "What to Do with American Primacy?" *Foreign Affairs* 78, no. 5 (1999): 37–49.

Habeck, Mary R. *Knowing the Enemy: Jihadist Ideology and the War on Terror.* New Haven, CT: Yale University Press, 2006.

Hampson, Fen Osler. *Multilateral Negotiations*. Baltimore: Johns Hopkins University Press, 1995.

Hartmann, Frederick. *The Conservation of Enemies: A Study in Enmity.* Westport, CT: Greenwood Press, 1982.

Hasenclever, Andreas, Peter Mayer, and Volker Rittberger. *Theories of International Regimes.* Cambridge: Cambridge University Press, 1997.

Hassner, Pierre. "Definitions, Doctrines, and Divergences." *National Interest,* no. 69 (2002): 30–34.

Hauser, Gunter. *Sicherheit, Energie, und Wirtschaft: Europa als globaler Akteur.* Wien: Schriftenreihe der Landesverteidigungsakademie, 2006.

Hayek, Friedrich von. *Rules and Order.* Chicago: University of Chicago Press, 1973.

Heise, Volker. "Die ESVP in den Transatlantischen Beziehungen." *SWP-Studie,* S 23, August 2007, Berlin.

Heise, Volker, and Peter Schmidt. "NATO und EU: Auf dem Weg zu einer strategischen Partnerschaft." In Thomas Jäger and Kai Oppermann, eds., *Transatlantische Beziehungen. Sicherheit—Wirtschaft—Öffentlichkeit.* Baden-Baden: Nomos, 2005.

Helms, Jesse. "American Sovereignty and the UN." *National Interest* (Winter 2000–2001): 31–34.

Hildebrand, K. *Das vergangene Reich: Deutsche Aussenpolitik von Bismarck bis Hitler.* Stuttgart: Deutsche Verlags-Anstalt, 1995.

Hill, Fiona. *Beyond Co-Dependency: European Reliance on Russian Energy.* US-Europe Analysis Series. Washington, DC: Brookings Institution, July 2005.

Hillgruber, Andreas. *Bismarcks Ausenpolitik.* Freiburg: Rombach, 1972.

Hoffmann, Stanley, ed. *Conditions of World Order.* Boston: Houghton Mifflin, 1968.

Holländer, Lutz, and Peter Schmidt. "Möglichkeiten der ESVP angesichts nationaler europäischer Politik." In Erich Reiter, ed., *Beiträge zur Entwicklung der ESVP,* Teil 2, 19–26. Wien: Schriftenreihe der Landesverteidigungsakademie, 2005.

Holtrup, Petra. "The Lack of US Leadership in Climate Change Diplomacy." In Bernhard May and Michaela Hönicke Moore, eds., *Uncertain Superpower: Domestic Dimensions of US Foreign Policy After the Cold War.* Opladen: Leske and Budrich, 2003.

Hopmann, P. Terrence. *The Negotiation Process and the Resolution of International Conflicts.* Columbia: University of South Carolina Press, 1996.

Horowitz, Donald. *Democratic South Africa? Constitutional Engineering in a Divided Society.* Berkeley: University of California Press, 1991.

Horowitz, Donald. *Ethnic Groups in Conflict.* Berkeley: University of California Press, 1985.

Howorth, Jolyon. "European Integration and Defence: The Ultimate Challenge?" Chaillot Paper No. 43, Institute for Security Studies, Paris, France, November 2000.

Howorth, Jolyon, and John T. S. Keeler, eds. *Defending Europe: The EU, NATO and the Quest for European Autonomy.* Basingstoke: Palgrave, 2003.

Huddy, Leonie, Stanley Feldman, Theresa Capelos, and Colin Provost. "The Consequences of Terrorism: Disentangling the Effects of Personal and National Threat." *Political Psychology* 23 (September 2002): 485–510.

Huddy, Leonie, Stanley Feldman, Charles Taber, and Gallya Lahav. "The Politics of Threat: Cognitive and Affective Reactions to 9/11." Paper presented at the annual meeting of the American Political Science Association, Boston, August 28, 2002.

Huntington, Samuel P. "The Clash of Civilizations." In Patrick O'Meara, Howard D. Mehlinger, and Matthew Krain, eds., *Globalization and the Challenges of a New Century: A Reader,* 3–22. Bloomington: Indiana University Press, 2000.

Huntington, Samuel P. *The Clash of Civilizations and the Remaking of the World Order.* New York: Simon and Schuster, 1996.

Huntington, Samuel P. "The Lonely Superpower." *Foreign Affairs* 78, no. 2 (March–April 1999): 42.

Huntington, Samuel P. *Political Order in Changing Societies.* Ithaca, NY: Cornell University Press, 2006.

Huntington, Samuel P. *The Third Wave: Democratization in the Late Twentieth Century.* Norman: University of Oklahoma, 1991.

Huntington, Samuel P. *Who Are We? The Challenges to American National Identity.* New York: Simon and Schuster, 2004.

Hyam, Ronald. *Britain's Imperial Century, 1815–1914.* New York: Harper and Row, 1976.

Ikenberry, G. John. "After September 11: America's Grand Strategy and International Order in the Age of Terror." *Survival* 43 (Winter 2001–2002): 19–34.

Ikenberry, G. John. *After Victory: Institutions, Strategic Restraint, and the Rebuilding of Order After Major Wars.* Princeton, NJ: Princeton University Press, 2001.

Ikle, Fred Charles. *How Nations Negotiate.* New York: Harper and Row, 1964.

Jentleson, Bruce. "Coercive Prevention: Normative, Political, and Policy Dimensions." *Peaceworks,* no. 35 (October 2000), United States Institute of Peace.

Jervis, Robert. *American Foreign Policy in a New Era.* New York: Routledge, 2005.

Jervis, Robert. "The Future of World Politics: Will It Resemble the Past?" *International Security* 16 (Winter 1991–1992): 39–73.

Jervis, Robert. "International Primacy: Is the Game Worth the Candle?" *International Security* 17 (Spring 1993): 52–67.

Jervis, Robert. "Kargil, Deterrence, and IR Theory." In Peter R. Lavoy, ed., *Asymmetric Warfare in South Asia: The Causes and Consequences of the Kargil Conflict.* Monterey, CA: Naval Postgraduate School, Center for Contemporary Conflict, 2006.

Jervis, Robert. *Perception and Misperception in World Politics.* Princeton, NJ: Princeton University Press, 1976.

Jervis, Robert. "The Remaking of a Unipolar World." *Washington Quarterly* 29 (Summer 2006): 7–19.

Jervis, Robert. "Was the Cold War a Security Dilemma?" *Journal of Cold War History* 3 (Winter 2001): 36–60.

Joffe, Josef. "The Secret of Genscher's Staying Power: Memoirs of a 'Slippery Man.'" *Foreign Affairs* (January/February 1998).

Johnson, A. G., ed. *The Blackwell Dictionary of Sociology,* 2nd ed. Oxford: Blackwell, 2000.

Johnson, Chalmers. *The Sorrows of Empire: Militarism, Secrecy, and the End of the Republic.* New York: Metropolitan Books, 2004.

Johnston, Alastair Iain. "Cultural Realism and Strategy in Maoist China." In Peter Katzenstein, ed., *The Culture of National Security: Norms and Identity in World Politics.* New York: Columbia University Press, 1996.

Jones, E. L. *The European Miracle: Environments, Economies, and Geopolitics in the History of Europe and Asia,* 2nd ed. Cambridge: Cambridge University Press, 1987.

Jones, Seth G., J. M. Wilson, Andrew Rathwell, and K. Jack Riley. *Establishing Law and Order After Conflict.* Santa Monica, CA: Rand Corporation, 2005.

Jusis, John B. *The Folly of Empire: What George W. Bush Could Learn from Theodore Roosevelt and Woodrow Wilson.* New York: Scribner, 2004.

Kagan, Robert. "America's Crisis of Legitimacy." *Foreign Affairs* 83, no. 2 (2004): 65–87.

Kagan, Robert. *Of Paradise and Power: America vs. Europe in the New World Order.* New York: Knopf, 2004.

Kagan, Robert. "Power and Weakness." *Policy Review* (June 2002).

Kahneman, Daniel, and Amos Tversky, eds. *Choices, Values, and Frames.* New York: Cambridge University Press, 2000.

Kanet, Roger, and Edward Kolodziej, eds. *The Cold War as Cooperation.* London: Macmillan 1991.

Kant, Immanuel. "Perpetual Peace." In M. I. Forsythe, ed., *The Theory of International Relations.* New York: Atherton, 1970.

Kaplan, Morton. *New Approaches to International Relations.* New York: St. Martin's, 1968.

Kaplan, Robert. "The Coming of Anarchy." In Patrick O'Meara, Howard D. Mehlinger, and Matthew Krain, eds., *Globalization and the Challenges of a New Century: A Reader,* 34–60. Bloomington: Indiana University Press, 2000.

Katzenstein, Peter J., and Takashi Shiraishi, eds. *A World of Regions: Asia and Europe in the American Imperium.* Ithaca, NY: Cornell University Press, 2005.

Katzman, Kenneth. "Afghanistan: Post-War Governance, Security, and US Policy." *CRS Report for Congress,* RL 30588, September 10, 2007.

Kaul, H. P. "Internationaler Strafgerichtshof: Ein bedeutender Anfang in Rom." In G. Baum, E. Riedel, and M. Schäfer, eds., *Menschenrechte in der Praxis der Vereinten Nationen,* 273–278. Baden-Baden: Nomos, 1998.

Kaul, H. P., and C. Kress. "Jurisdiction and Cooperation in the Statute of the International Criminal Court: Principles and Compromises." *Yearbook of International Humanitarian Law* 2 (1999): 143–173.

Kazemzadeh, F. *Russia and Britain in Persia, 1864–1914: A Study in Imperialism.* New Haven, CT: Yale University Press, 1964.

Keck, Margaret E., and Kathryn Sikkink. *Activists Beyond Borders: Advocacy Networks in International Politics.* Ithaca, NY: Cornell University Press, 1998.

Kennan, G. F. *The Decline of Bismarck's European Order: Franco-Russian Relations, 1875–1890.* Princeton, NJ: Princeton University Press, 1979.

Kennedy, Paul. *The Rise and Fall of the Great Powers: Economic Change and Military Conflict from 1500 to 2000.* New York: Random House, 1987.

Keohane, Robert, and Lisa L. Martin. "The Promise of Institutional Theory," *International Security* 20, no. 1 (Summer 1995): 39–51.

Keohane, Robert, and Joseph Nye. *Power and Interdependence,* 2nd ed. Glenview, IL: Scott, Foresman, 1989.

Keohane, Robert, and Joseph Nye. *Power and Interdependence: World Politics in Transition.* Boston: Little Brown, 1977.

Khalidi, Walid. "The Prospect of Peace in the Middle East." *Journal of Palestine Studies* 32, no. 2 (Winter 2003): 50–62.

Kielmannsegg, Sebastian Graf von. *Die Verteidigungspolitik der Europäischen Union.* Stuttgart: Richard Boorberg Verlag, 2006.

Kindleberger, Charles. *The World in Depression, 1929–1939,* rev. ed. Berkeley: University of California Press, 1986. Originally published in 1973.

Kirchner, Emil J. "Genscher and What Lies Behind 'Genscherism.'" *West European Politics* 13, no. 2 (April 1990): 159–177.

Kirchner, Emil, and James Sperling. *Global Security Governance.* London: Routledge, 2006.

Kissinger, Henry. *Diplomacy.* New York: Simon and Schuster, 1994.

Klare, Michael T. *Resource Wars: The New Landscape of Global Conflict.* New York: Metropolitan Books, 2001.

Knutsen, Torbjørn L. *A History of International Relations Theory,* 2nd ed. Manchester: Manchester University Press, 1997.

Kohler, A. *Karl V: 1500–1558: Eine Biographie.* Munich: C. H. Beck, 1999.

Kohler, A. *Das Reich im Kampf um die Hegemonie in Europa, 1521–1648.* Munich: Oldenbourg, 1990.

Kolodziej, Edward. "The Pursuit of Order, Welfare and Legitimacy: Explaining the End of the Soviet Union and the Cold War." *International Politics* 34, no. 2 (June 1997): 111–151.

Korb, Lawrence J. *A New National Security Strategy in an Age of Terrorists,*

Tyrants, and Weapons of Mass Destruction. New York: Council on Foreign Relations, 2003.

Krasner, Stephen, ed. *International Regimes*. Ithaca, NY: Cornell University Press, 1983.

Krasner, Stephen. "State Power and the Structure of International Trade." *World Politics* 28, no. 3 (April 1976): 317–347.

Kratochwil, Friederich. "The Embarrassment of Changes: Neo-Realism as the Science of *Realpolitik* Without Politics." *Review of International Studies* 19, no. 1 (1993): 63–80.

Krauthammer, Charles. "The Unipolar Moment." *Foreign Affairs* 70, no. 1 (1990–1991): 23–33.

Krauthammer, Charles. "The Unipolar Moment Revisited." *National Interest*, no. 70 (Winter 2002–2003): 5–20.

Kreß, Claus. "Der Internationale Strafgerichtshof und die USA. Hintergründe der Sicherheitsresolution 1422." *Blätter für Deutsche und Internationale Politik*, no. 9 (2002): 1088–1100.

Kristol, William, and Robert Kagan. "Toward a Neo-Reaganite Foreign Policy." *Foreign Affairs* 75, no. 4 (July–August 1996): 18–32.

Kristol, William, and L. F. Kaplan. *The War over Iraq: Saddam's Tyranny and America's Mission*. New York: Encounter, 2003.

Krugman, Paul. *Rethinking International Trade*. Cambridge, MA: MIT Press, 1991.

Kudrle, Robert. "Hegemony Strikes Out: The US Global Role in Anti-Trust, Tax Evasion, and Illegal Immigration." *International Studies Perspectives* 4 (February 2003): 52–71.

Kugler, Jacek, and Douglas Lemke. *Parity and War: Evaluations and Extensions of the War Ledger*. Ann Arbor: University of Michigan Press, 1996.

Kuhn, T. S. *The Structure of Scientific Revolutions*. Chicago: University of Chicago Press, 1962.

Kumar, Krishna, ed. *Post-Conflict Elections, Democratization, and International Assistance*. Boulder, CO: Lynne Rienner, 1998.

Kupchan, Charles A., and Clifford A. Kupchan. "The Promise of Collective Security." *International Security* 20, no. 1 (Summer 1995): 52–61.

Laatikainen, Katie Verlin, and Karen E. Smith, eds. *The European Union at the United Nations: Intersecting Multilateralism*. London: Routledge, 2006.

Lasswell, Harold, and Abraham Kaplan. *Power and Society*. New Haven, CT: Yale University Press, 1950.

Layne, Christopher. "Casualties of War: Transatlantic Relations and the Future of NATO in the Wake of the Second Gulf War." *Policy Analysis* (August 13, 2003): 1–18.

Lebow, Richard Ned. "The Long Peace, the End of the Cold War, and the Failure of Realism." *International Organization* 48, no. 2 (1994): 249–278.

Legrenzi, Matteo. "NATO in the Gulf: Who Is Doing Whom a Favor?" *Middle East Policy* 14, no. 1 (Spring 2007): 69–75.

Leverett, Flynt, and Jeffrey Bader. "Managing China-US Energy Competition in the Middle East." *Washington Quarterly* 29, no. 1 (Winter 2005–2006): 187–201.

Levy, Jack. "Declining Power and the Preventive Motivation for War." *World Politics* 40 (October 1987): 82–107.

Levy, Jack. "What Do Great Powers Balance Against and When?" In T. V. Paul, James J. Wirtz, and Michel Fortmann, eds., *Balance of Power: Theory and Practice in the Twenty-First Century*. Stanford, CA: Stanford University Press, 2004.

Levy, Jack, and Joseph Gochal. "Democracy and Preventive War: Israel and the 1956 Sinai Campaign." *Security Studies* 11 (Winter 2001–2002): 1–49.

Lewin, Kurt, Ronald Lippitt, and Ralph K. White. "Patterns of Aggressive Behavior in Experimentally Created 'Social Climates.'" *Journal of Social Psychology* 10, no. 3 (1939): 43–195.

Lieber, Keir, and Gerard Alexander. "Waiting for Balancing: Why the World Is Not Pushing Back." *International Security* 30, no. 1 (Summer 2005): 121–122.

Lieber, Robert J. *The American Era: Power and Strategy for the Twenty-First Century*. Cambridge: Cambridge University Press, 2006.

Lieberthal, Kenneth. *Governing China: From Revolution to Reform.* London: Norton, 1995.

Lijphart, Arend. *Democracy in Plural Societies.* New Haven, CT: Yale University Press, 1977.

Lindley-French, Julian. "Terms of Engagement: The Paradox of American Power and the Transatlantic Dilemma Post–11 September." Chaillot Paper No. 52, Institute for Security Studies, Paris, France, May 2002.

Lindstrom, Gustav. "EU-US Burdensharing: Who Does What?" EUISS–Chaillot Paper No. 82, Institute for Security Studies, Paris, France, 2005.

Linz, Juan. "Totalitarian and Authoritarian Regimes." In Fred I. Greenstein and Nelson Polsby, eds., *Handbook of Political Science,* vol. 3. Reading, MA: Addison-Wesley, 1975.

Linz, Juan, and Alfred Stepan. *Problems of Democratic Transition and Consolidation: Southern Europe, South America, and Post-Communist Europe.* Baltimore: Johns Hopkins University Press, 1996.

Lippman, Walter. *US Foreign Policy: Shield of the Republic.* Boston: Little, Brown, 1943.

Lipset, Seymour Martin. *Political Man.* New York: Doubleday, 1960.

Lipset, Seymour Martin. "Some Requisites of Democracy: Economic Development and Political Legitimacy." *American Political Science Review* 53, no. 1 (March 1959): 69–105.

Lobell, Stephen E. *The Challenge of Hegemony: Grand Strategy, Trade, and Domestic Politics.* Ann Arbor: University of Michigan Press, 2003.

Lossky, A. *Louis XIV and the French Monarchy.* New Brunswick, NJ: Rutgers University Press, 1994.

Louis, W. R., ed. *The Oxford History of the British Empire.* 5 vols. Oxford: Oxford University Press, 1998–1999.

Louis, W. R., ed. *The Robinson and Gallagher Controversy.* New York: New Viewpoints, 1976.

Luard, Evan. *War in International Society: A Study in International Sociology.* London: I. B. Tauris, 1986.

Luck, Edward C. "False Choices: Unilateralism, Multilateralism, and US Foreign Policy." In Berhard May and Michaela Hönicke Moore, eds., *The Uncertain Superpower,* 161–184. Opladen: Leske and Budrich, 2003.

Lyons, Gene, and Michael Mastanduno, eds. *Beyond Westphalia: State Sovereignty and International Intervention.* Baltimore: Johns Hopkins University Press, 1995.

Maddison, Angus. "The Nature of US Economic Leadership: A Historical and Comparative View." In Patrick Karl O'Brien and Armand Clesse, ed., *Two Hegemonies: Britain 1846–1914 and the United States 1941–2001,* pp. 183–198. Aldershot: Ashgate, 2002.

Malettke, K. *Frankreich, Deutschland, und Europa im 17 und 18 Jahrhundert.* Marburg: Hitzeroth, 1994.

Mandelbaum, Michael. "Is Major War Obsolete?" *Survival* 40 (Winter 1998–1999): 20–38.

Mansfield, Edward D., and Jack Snyder. "Democratization and the Danger of War." *International Security* 20, no. 1 (1995): 5–38.

Marks, S. *Illusion of Peace: International Relations in Europe, 1918–1933*. London: Macmillan, 1976.

Mastanduno, Michael. "Preserving the Unipolar Moment: Realist Theories and US Grand Strategy After the Cold War." *International Security* 21, no. 4 (Spring 1997): 49–98.

McCormick, John. *The European Superpower.* Basingstoke: Palgrave, 2005.

McGuire, Steven, and Michael Smith. *The European Union and the United States: Convergence and Competition in the Global Arena.* Basingstoke: Palgrave Macmillan, 2006.

McKay, D., and H. M. Scott. *The Rise of the Great Powers, 1648–1815*. London: Longman, 1983.

McKeown, Timothy J. "Hegemonic Stability Theory and Nineteenth-Century Tariff Levels in Europe." *International Organization* 37, no. 1 (1983): 73–91.

McLuhan, Marshall, and Bruce R. Powers. *The Global Village: Transformations in World Life and Media in the Twenty-First Century*. New York: Oxford University Press, 1989.

Mearsheimer, John J. "Back to the Future: Instability in Europe After the Cold War." *International Security* 15, no. 1 (Summer 1990): 5–56.

Mearsheimer, John J. *The Tragedy of Great Power Politics*. New York: Norton, 2001.

Medeiros, Evan S., and M. Taylor Fravel. "China's New Diplomacy." *Foreign Affairs* 82, no. 6 (November–December 2003): 22–35.

Melko, Matthew. *Fifty-Two Peaceful Societies*. Ontario: CPRI Press, 1973.

Meyer, Berthold. "Spannungsreduktion und Vertrauensbildung." In Gert Sommer and Albert Fuchs, eds., *Krieg und Frieden: Handbuch der Konflikt- und Friedenspsychologie,* 460–462. Weinheim: Beltz, 2004.

Mill, John Stuart. *On Liberty*. New York: Appleton-Century-Crofts, 1947.

Modelski, George. "The Long Cycle of Global Politics and the Nation-State." *Comparative Studies in Society and History* 20, no. 2 (April 1978): 214–235.

Moravsik, Andrew. "Taking Preferences Seriously: A Liberal Theory of International Politics," *International Organization* 51, no. 4 (Autumn 1997): 513–553.

Morgenthau, Hans J. *In Defense of National Interest: A Critical Examination of American National Interest*. New York: Knopf, 1952.

Morgenthau, Hans J. *Politics Among Nations: The Struggle for Power and Peace*. New York: Knopf, 1948 and 1978.

Moussalli, Ahmad, ed. *Islamic Fundamentalism: Myths and Realities*. Ithaca, NY: Cornell University Press, 1998.

Mueller, John. "The Catastrophe Quota: Trouble After the Cold War." *Journal of Conflict Resolution* 38 (September 1994): 355–375.

Mueller, John. *Overblown: How Politicians and the Terrorism Industry Inflate National Security Threats, and Why We Believe Them.* New York: Basic Books, 2006.

Mueller, John. *Retreat from Doomsday: The Obsolescence of Major War*. New York: Basic Books, 1989.

Müller, M. G. *Die Teilungen Polens: 1772, 1793, 1795*. Munich: C. H. Beck, 1984.

Münkler, Herfried. *Imperien: Die Logik der Weltherrschaft—Vom Alten Rom bis zu den Vereinigten Staaten*. Berlin: Rowohlt, 2005.

Nicolson, Harold. *Diplomacy,* 3rd ed. New York: Oxford University Press, 1963.

Nolan, C. J. *The Greenwood Encyclopedia of International Relations*. 4 vols. Westport, CT: Greenwood, 2002.

Norton, Augustus Richard, ed. *Civil Society in the Middle East,* vol. 2. New York: Brill, 1995–1996.

Nye, Joseph P. *Soft Power: The Means to Success in World Politics*. New York: Public Affairs, 2004.

Nye, Joseph S., Jr. *Bound to Lead: The Changing Nature of American Power.* New York: Basic Books, 1990.

Nye, Joseph S., Jr. *The Paradox of American Power: Why the World's Only Superpower Can't Go It Alone*. New York: Oxford University Press, 2002.

Odell, John. *Negotiating the World Economy.* Ithaca, NY: Cornell University Press, 2000.

O'Donnell, Guillermo, and Philippe C. Schmitter. *Transitions from Authoritarian Rule: Tentative Conclusions About Uncertain Democracies*. Baltimore: Johns Hopkins University Press, 1986.

Olson, Mancur. *The Logic of Collective Action.* Cambridge, MA: Harvard University Press, 1965.

Organski, A. F. K., and J. Kugler, *The War Ledger.* Chicago: University of Chicago Press, 1980.

Orieux, Jean. *Talleyrand ou le Sphinx Incompris*. Paris: Flammarion, 1970.

Ortega y Gasset, Jose. *The Revolt of the Masses*. New York: Norton, 1960.

Owen, John M., IV. "Transnational Liberalism and US Primacy." *International Security* 26, no. 3 (December 2001): 117–153.

Pape, Robert A. "Soft Balancing Against the United States." *International Security* 30, no. 1 (Summer 2005): 7–45.

Parasiliti, Andrew. "The Causes and Timing of Iraq's Wars: A Power Cycle Assessment." *International Political Science Review* 24, no. 1 (January 2003): 151–165.

Parker, G. *The Grand Strategy of Philip II*. New Haven, CT: Yale University Press, 1998.

Parsons, Craig, and Nicolas Jabko, eds. *With US or Against US? European Trends in American Perspective*. Oxford: Oxford University Press, 2005.

Parsons, Talcott, and Edward Shils. *Toward a General Theory of Action*. New York: Harper Torchbooks, 1951.

Pasquino, Pasquale. "Political Theory, Order, and Threat." In Ian Shapiro and Russell Hardin, eds., *Political Order: Nomos* 39, 19. New York: New York University Press, 1993.

Patrick, Stewart. "Multilateralism and Its Discontents: The Causes and Consequences of US Ambivalence." In Stewart Patrick and Shepard Forman, eds., *Multilateralism and US Foreign Policy: Ambivalent Engagement,* 1–46. Boulder, CO: Lynne Rienner, 2002.

Paul, T. V. "Soft Balancing in the Age of US Primacy." *International Security* 30, no. 1 (Summer 2005): 46–71.

Pillar, Paul. *Negotiating Peace*. Princeton, NJ: Princeton University Press, 1983.

Plato's Statesman. Translated by J. B. Skemp. London: Routledge and Kegan Paul, 1961.

Plumb, J. H. *Sir Robert Walpole*. 2 vols. Boston: Houghton Mifflin, 1956–1961.

Polanyi, Karl. *The Great Transformation,* 2nd ed. Boston: Beacon Press, 2001.

Pollins, Brian. "Global Political Order, Economic Change, and Armed Conflict: Coevolving Systems and the Use of Force." *American Political Science Review* 90 (1996): 103–117.

Pomeranz, Kenneth. *The Great Divergence: China, Europe, and the Making of the Modern World.* Princeton, NJ: Princeton University Press, 2000.

Porter, Andrew, ed. *The Oxford History of the British Empire.* Vol. 3: *The Nineteenth Century.* Oxford: Oxford University Press, 1999.

Posen, Barry. "Command of the Commons: The Military Foundation of US Hegemony." *International Security* 28, no. 1 (June 2003): 5–46.

Posen, Barry. "US Security Policy in a Nuclear-Armed World, or: What If Iraq Had Had Nuclear Weapons?" *Security Studies* 6 (Spring 1997): 1–31.

Postel, Sandra. *Last Oasis: Facing Water Scarcity.* New York: W. W. Norton, 1997.

Prendergast, John, and Colin Thomas Jensen. "Blowing the Horn." *Foreign Affairs* 86, no. 2 (March–April, 2007): 59–74.

Przeworski, Adam. *States and Markets.* Cambridge: Cambridge University Press, 2003.

Public Papers of the Presidents of the Unites States. Washington, DC: United States Government Printing Office, 1991.

Pye, Lucian. *Chinese Negotiating Style: Commercial Approaches and Cultural Principles.* New York: Quorum, 1992.

Pye, Lucian. *The Mandarin and the Cadre: China's Political Culture.* Ann Arbor: University of Michigan Press, 1988.

Quinlan, Michael. *European Defense Cooperation. Asset or Threat to NATO?* Washington, DC: Woodrow Wilson Center Press, 2001.

Rajaee, Farhang. *Globalization on Trial: The Human Condition and the Information Civilization.* Ottawa: International Development Research Centre, and West Hartford, CT: Kumarian, 2000.

Rawls, John. *The Law of Peoples.* Cambridge, MA : Harvard University Press, 1999.

Rawls, John. *A Theory of Justice.* Cambridge, MA: Harvard University Press, 1971.

Rees, Wyn. *Transatlantic Counter-Terrorism Cooperation: The New Imperative.* New York: Routledge, 2006.

Rees, Wyn. "Britain's Contribution to Global Order." In Stuart Croft, Andrew Dorman, Wyn Rees, and Matthew Uttley. *Britain and Defence, 1945–2000: A Policy of Re-evaluation.* London: Pearson/Longman, 2001.

Regelsberger, Elfriede. "Die Gemeinsame Außen—und Sicherheitspolitik der EU. Das Regelwerk im Praxistest." In Mathais Jopp and Peter Schlotter, eds., *Kollektive Außenpolitik—Die EU als internationaler Akteur.* Baden-Baden: Nomos, 2007.

Regelsberger, Elfriede. "Die vertraglichen Grundlagen der Gemeinsamen Außen—und Sicherheitspolitik der EU—Angebotsvielfalt und Wachstumstrends." In Mathais Jopp and Peter Schlotter, eds., *Kollektive Außenpolitik—Die EU als internationaler Akteur.* Baden-Baden: Nomos, 2007.

Reinhardt, Markus. "Zivil-militärische Beziehungen im Rahmen der ESVP." *Stiftung Wissenschaft und Politik-Berlin,* August 2006.

Reinicke, Wolfgang. *Global Public Policy: Governing Without Government?* Washington, DC: Brookings Institution Press, 1998.

Reno, William. "Reinvention of an African Patrimonial State: Charles Taylor's Liberia." *Third World Quarterly* 16, no. 1 (1995): 109–120.

Rhodes, Edward. "Can the United States Deter Iraqi Aggression? The Problem of Conventional Deterrence." *Columbia International Affairs Online,* 2002.

Ricks, Thomas E. *Fiasco: The American Military Adventure in Iraq.* New York: Penguin, 2006.

Riker, William. *The Theory of Political Coalitions.* New Haven, CT: Yale University Press, 1962.

Risen, James. *State of War: The Secret History of the CIA and the Bush Administration*. New York: Free Press, 2006.

Roberts, M. *The Swedish Imperial Experience, 1560–1718*. New York: Cambridge University Press, 1979.

Robinson, Ronald, and John Gallager, with Alice Denny. *Africa and the Victorians: The Official Mind of Imperialism*. London: Macmillan, 1961.

Robinson, William Alexander. *Jeffersonian Democracy in New England*. New York: Greenwood, 1916.

Rodman, Peter W. "US Leadership and the Reform of Western Security Institutions: NATO Enlargement and ESDP." In Bernhard May and Hönicke Moore, eds., *The Uncertain Superpower: Domestic Dimensions of US Foreign Policy After the Cold War*. Opladen: Leske and Budrich, 2003.

Rogowski, Ronald. *Rational Legitimacy*. Princeton, NJ: Princeton University Press, 1974.

Rose, Richard, William Mischler, and Christian Haerpfer. *Democracy and Its Alternatives: Understanding Post-Communist Societies*. Baltimore: Johns Hopkins University Press, 1998.

Rosecrance, Richard. "Bipolarity, Multi-polarity, and the Future." *Journal of Conflict Resolution* 10, no. 3 (1966): 314–327.

Rosecrance, Richard, and Arthur A. Stein. "The Theory of Overlapping Clubs." In Richard Rosecrance, ed., *The New Great Power Coalition: Toward a World Concert of Nations,* 221–236. Lanham, MD: Rowman and Littlefield, 2001.

Roseneau, James. "Global Affairs in an Epochal Transformation." In Ryan Henry and C. Edward Peartree, eds., *The Information Revolution and International Security,* 31–57. Washington, DC: Center for Strategic and International Studies, 1998.

Rosenau, James, and E. O. Czempiel, eds. *Governance Without Government*. Cambridge: Cambridge University Press, 1992.

Ross, Robert. "Navigating the Taiwan Strait: Deterrence, Escalation, and US-China Relations." *International Security* 27 (Fall 2002): 48–85.

Rotberg, Robert, ed. *When States Fail: Causes and Consequences*. Princeton, NJ: Princeton University Press, 2004.

Ruehl, Lothar. "Article." In Gustav Schmidt, ed., *A History of NATO: The First Fifty Years,* vol. 2. New York: Palgrave, 2001.

Rueschemeyer, Dietrich, Peter Evans, and Theda Skocpol, eds. *Bringing the State Back In*. Cambridge: Cambridge University Press, 1985.

Ruggie, J. G. *Constructing the World Polity*. London: Routledge, 1998.

Ruggie, J. G. "International Regimes, Transactions, and Change: Embedded Liberalism in the Postwar Economic Order," *International Organization* 36, no. 2 (Spring, 1982).

Ruggie, J. G. *Winning the Peace: America and the New World Order*. New York: Columbia University Press, 1996.

Rummel, Reinhardt. "Die zivile Komponente der ESVP." *SWP-Studie,* July 2006.

Russell, Bertrand. *The Impact of Science on Society*. London: Unwin Hyman, 1952.

Russett, Bruce, and John Oneal. *Triangulating Peace: Democracy, Interdependence, and International Organizations*. New York: Norton, 2001.

Sanderson, G. N. *England, Europe, and the Upper Nile, 1882–1899*. Edinburgh: University Press, 1965.

Saunders, Harold H. *A Public Peace Process: Sustained Dialogue to Transform Racial and Ethnic Conflicts*. New York: St. Martins, 1999.

Schatzberg, Michael. *Big Man in Africa*. Madison: University of Wisconsin Press, 1992.

Schelling, Thomas. *Arms and Influence*. New Haven, CT: Yale University Press, 1966.

Schelling, Thomas. *Strategy of Conflict*. Cambridge, MA: Harvard University Press, 1960.

Scherpenberg, Jens, and Elke Thiel, eds. *Towards Rival Regionalism?* Baden-Baden: Nomos, 1999.

Schild, Georg. *Die bedrohte Supermacht*. Opladen: Leske and Budrich, 2002.

Schindling, A. *Die Anfänge des immerwährenden Reichstags zu Regensburg*. Mainz: P. von Zabern, 1991.

Schmidt, Gustav. "Asia, Europe, North America, and the Asian Capitalist Miracle: Changing Power Cycles and Evolving Roles in Regional and International Structures." *International Political Science Review* 24, no. 3 (2003)

Schmidt, Gustav. "Getting the Balance Right: NATO and the Evolution of EC/EU Integration, Security and Defense." In Gustav Schmidt, ed., *A History of NATO: The First Fifty Years,* vol. 2, pp. 3–28. New York: Palgrave, 2001.

Schmidt, Gustav, and Charles F. Doran. *Amerikas Option für Deutschland und Japan: Die Position und Rolle Deutschlands und Japans in regionalen und internationalen Strukturen*. Bochum: Brockmeyer, 1996.

Schmidt, Peter. "Nationale Entscheidungsspielräume in der Europäischen Union und den Vereinten Nationen." In Stefan Mair, ed., *Auslandseinsätze der Bundeswehr,* 50–58. *SWP-Studie,* S 27, September 2007.

Schroeder, Paul W. "Did the Vienna Settlement Rest on a Balance of Power?" *American Historical Review* 97, no. 2 (June 1992): 683–706, 733–735.

Schroeder, Paul W. "Does the History of International Politics Go Anywhere?" In Paul W. Schroeder, *Systems, Stability, and Statecraft: Essays on the International History of Modern Europe*. New York: Palgrave Macmillan, 2004.

Schroeder, Paul W. "Iraq: The Case Against Preemptive War." *American Conservative* (October 21, 2002): 8–22.

Schroeder, Paul W. "The Mirage of Empire Versus the Promise of Hegemony?" In Paul W. Schroeder, *Systems, Stability, and Statecraft*. New York: Palgrave Macmillan, 2004.

Schroeder, Paul W. "A Papier-Maché Fortress." *National Interest,* no. 70 (Winter 2002–2003): 125–132.

Schroeder, Paul W. "The Risks of Victory: An Historian's Provocation." *National Interest* (Winter 2001–2002): 22–36.

Schroeder, Paul W. *The Transformation of European Politics, 1763–1848*. New York: Oxford University Press, 1994.

Schwarz, Benjamin, and Christopher Layne. "A New Grand Strategy." *The Atlantic,* January 2002.

Schweller, Randall. "Bandwagoning for Profit." *International Security* 19, no. 1 (Summer 1994): 72–107.

Schweller, Randall. "Domestic Structure and Preventive War: Are Democracies More Pacific?" *World Politics* 44 (January 1992): 235–269.

Schweller, Randall. "The Twenty Years' Crisis, 1919–39: Why a Concert Didn't Arise." In Colin Elman and Miriam Fendius Elman, eds., *Bridges and Boundaries: Historians, Political Scientists, and the Study of International Relations,* 181–212. Cambridge, MA: MIT Press, 2001.

Scott, H. M. *British Foreign Policy in the Age of the American Revolution*. Oxford: Clarendon, 1990.

Sen, Amartya. *Development as Freedom*. Oxford: Oxford University Press, 1999.

Sen, Amartya. *Inequality Reexamined*. New York: Russell Sage Foundation, 1992.

Seton-Watson, R. W. *Disraeli, Gladstone, and the Eastern Question*. New York: Norton, 1972.
Shambaugh, David. "China Engages Asia." *International Security* 29, no. 3 (Winter 2004): 64–99.
Shapley, L. S. "A Value for N-Person Games." *Annals of Mathematical Studies* 28, no. 3 (1953): 307–317.
Shaw, Martin. *Global Society and International Relations*. Cambridge: Polity, 1994.
Shea, Jamie. "Energy Security: NATO's Potential Role." *NATO Review*, no. 3 (Autumn 2006), www.nato.int/docu/review/2006/issue3/english/special1.html.
Sheetz, Mark, and Michael Mastanduno. "Debating the Unipolar Moment." *International Security* 22 (Winter 1997–1998): 168–174.
Singer, Max, and Aaron Wildavsky. *The Real World Order: Zones of Peace, Zones of Turmoil*. Chatham, NJ: Chatham House, 1993.
Sjöstedt, Gunnar. "Asymmetry in Multilateral Negotiation Between North and South at UNCED." In I. William Zartman and Jeffrey Z. Rubin, eds., *Power and Negotiation*, 177–198. Ann Arbor: University of Michigan Press, 2000.
Skidmore, David. "Understanding the Unilateralist Turn in US Foreign Policy." *Foreign Policy Analysis* 1, no. 2 (2005): 207–228.
Smelser, N. J., and P. B. Baltes, eds. *International Encyclopedia of the Social and Behavioral Sciences*, 6642–6650. Amsterdam: Elsevier, 2001.
Smith, M. "The European Union and a Changing Europe: Establishing the Boundaries of Order." *Journal of Common Market Studies* 34, no. 1 (1996): 5–28.
Smoke, Richard. *War: Controlling Escalation*. Cambridge, MA: Harvard University Press, 1977.
Snyder, Jack. *Myths of Empire: Domestic Politics and International Ambition*. Ithaca, NY: Cornell University Press, 1991.
Snyder, Jack. "The New Myths of Empire." *National Interest* (Spring 2003): 29–40.
Sokolsky, Richard, and Tanya Charlick-Paley. *NATO and Caspian Security: A Mission Too Far?* Santa Monica, CA: Rand Corporation, 1999.
Spector, Bertram I., and I. William Zartman, eds. *Getting It Done: Post-Agreement Negotiations and International Regimes*. Washington, DC: United States Institute of Peace Press, 2003.
Spillmann, Kurt R., Thomas Bernauer, Jürg M. Gabriel, and Andreas Wenger, eds. *Peace Support Operations: Lessons Learned and Future Perspectives*. Bern: Lang Verlag, 2001.
Spiro, David E. "The Insignificance of the Liberal Peace." *International Security* 19, no. 2 (1994): 50–86.
Sprout, Harold, and Margaret Sprout. *Environmental Possibilism*. Princeton, NJ: Princeton University Press, 1960.
Stein, Arthur A. "Introduction." In Richard Rosecrance, ed., *The New Great Power Coalition*, 1–17. Lanham, MD: Rowman and Littlefield, 2001.
Strange, Susan. "Cave! Hic Dragones." In Stephen Krasner, ed., *International Regimes*, 345. Ithaca, NY: Cornell University Press, 1983.
Strange, Susan. *States and Markets*. London: Continuum, 1988.
Strauss, Anselm. *Negotiations: Varieties, Contexts, Processes, and Social Order.* San Francisco: Jossey-Bass, 1978.
Stromseth, Jane, David Wippman, and Rosa Brooks. *Can Might Make Rights? Building the Rule of Law After Military Interventions*. Cambridge: Cambridge University Press, 2006.
Sun Tzu. *The Art of War*. Translated by Samuel B. Griffith. New York: Oxford University Press, 1963.

Sung-Joo, Han, ed. *The New International System: Regional and Global Dimensions*. Seoul: Ilmin International Research Institute, 1995.
Sutter, Robert. "Asia in the Balance: America and China's Peaceful Rise." *Current History* 103, no. 674 (September 2004): 284–289.
Tawney, R. H. *Equality*. London: Allen and Unwin, 1931.
Thibaud, J. W., and H. H. Kelley. *The Social Psychology of Groups*. New York: Wiley, 1959.
Thomas, R. Roosevelt, Jr. *Building a House for Diversity: How a Fable About a Giraffe and Elephant Offers New Strategies for Today's Workforce*. NY: American Management Association Books, 1999.
Thompson, William R. *On Global War*. Columbia: University of South Carolina Press, 1988.
Tilly, Charles. *Coercion, Capital, and European States, AD 990–1990*. Cambridge, MA: Basil Blackwell, 1990.
Tocqueville, Alexis de. *De la démocratie en Amérique*. Paris: Pagnerre, 1850.
Trachtenberg, Marc. *A Constructed Peace: The Making of the European Settlement, 1945–1963*. Princeton, NJ: Princeton University Press, 1999.
Trachtenberg, Marc. *History and Strategy*. Princeton, NJ: Princeton University Press, 1991.
Tucker, Robert. "The Radical Critique Assessed." In Robert Tucker, ed., *The Radical Left and American Foreign Policy*. Baltimore: Johns Hopkins University Press, 1971.
Tumulty, Joseph. *Woodrow Wilson as I Knew Him*. New York: Literary Digest, 1921.
Ullman, Richard H. *Securing Europe*. Princeton, NJ: Princeton University Press, 1991.
Unger, Craig. "From the Wonderful Folks Who Brought You Iraq." *Vanity Fair*, March 2007.
US Department of Defense. *The National Defense Strategy of the United States of America*. Arlington, VA: Office of the Secretary of Defense, March 2005.
US Department of Defense. *2001 Quadrennial Defense Review Report*. Washington, DC: US Government Printing Office, December 2001.
US Department of Energy, Energy Information Administration. *International Energy Outlook 1999*. Washington, DC, March 1999.
US Department of Energy, Energy Information Administration. *International Energy Outlook 2003*. Washington, DC, May 2003.
Van Evera, Stephen. "Primed for Peace: Europe After the Cold War." *International Security* 15 (Winter 1990–1991): 7–57.
Van Evera, Stephen. *Causes of War: Power and the Roots of Conflict*. Ithaca, NY: Cornell University Press, 1999.
van Oyen, R. Ch. "Der Internationale Strafgerichtshof zwischen Normativität, Machtpolitik, und Symbolik." *Internationale Politik und Gesellschaft*, no. 4 (2002): 110–123.
Vaucher, P. *Robert Walpole et la politique de Fleury*. Paris: Plon-Nourrit, 1924.
von Aretin, K. O. *Das alte Reich*. Vol. 1, *1648–1684*. Stuttgart: Klett Cotta, 1993.
von Haldenwang, C. "The State and Political Regulation: On the Legitimacy of Political Order in the Twenty-First Century." *Politische Vierteljahresschrift* 20, no. 3 (September 1999): 365–405.
von Hayek, Friedrich. *The Fatal Conceit: Errors of Socialism*. London Routledge, 1984.
von Ranke, Leopold. *Leopold Ranke: The Formative Years*. Princeton, NJ: Princeton University Press, 1950.

Wagner, Lynn. *Problem-Solving and Bargaining in International Negotiation*. Leiden: Martinus Nijhoff, 2008.

Walker, Richard L. *The Multi-State System of Ancient China*. Hamden, CT: Shoe String Press, 1953.

Wallace, William, ed. *The Dynamics of European Integration*. London: Pinter Publishers for the Royal Institute of International Affairs, 1990.

Walt, Stephen M. "Beyond bin Laden: Reshaping US Foreign Policy." *International Security* 26, no. 3 (December 2001): 56–79.

Walt, Stephen M. *The Origins of Alliances*. Ithaca, NY: Cornell University Press, 1987.

Walt, Stephen M. *Taming American Power: The Global Response to American Primacy*. New York: Norton, 2005.

Walton, Richard, and Robert McKersie. *A Behavioral Theory of Labor Negotiations*. New York: McGraw-Hill, 1965.

Waltz, Kenneth N. "America as a Model for the World? A Foreign Policy Perspective." *Political Science and Politics* 24, no. 4 (December 1991): 69.

Waltz, Kenneth N. "Contemporary Conflict in Theory and Practice." *International Security* 25 (Summer 2000): 5–41.

Waltz, Kenneth N. Letter to *Foreign Affairs* 82, no. 5 (2003): 193.

Waltz, Kenneth N. *Man, the State, and War: A Theoretical Analysis*. New York: Columbia University Press, 1959.

Waltz, Kenneth N. "A Necessary War?" In Harry Kriesler, ed., *Confrontation in the Gulf: University of California Professors Talk About the War*, 59–65. Berkeley: University of California Press/Institute of International Studies, 1992.

Waltz, Kenneth N. *Theory of International Politics*. Reading, MA: Addison-Wesley, 1979.

Weber, Max. "Politics as a Vocation." In H. H. Gerth and C. Wright Mills, eds., *From Max Weber: Essays in Sociology*. New York: Oxford University Press, 1946.

Wendt, Alexander. "Anarchy Is What States Make of It." *International Organization* 46, no. 3 (Spring 1992): 391–425.

Wendt, Alexander. *Social Theory of International Politics*. Cambridge: Cambridge University Press, 1999.

Westphal, Kirsten, ed. *A Focus on EU-Russian Relations: Towards a Close Partnership on Defined Road Maps?* Frankfurt am Main: Lang Verlag, 2005.

White House. *A National Security Strategy for a New Century*. Washington, DC: US Government Printing Office, December 1999.

White House. *A National Security Strategy of Engagement and Enlargement*. Washington, DC: US Government Printing Office, February 1995.

White House. *The National Security Strategy of the United States of America*. Washington, DC: US Government Printing Office, September 2002.

Wohlforth, William. "The Stability of a Unipolar World." *International Security* 24 (Summer 1999): 5–41.

Wolfers, Arnold. *Discord and Collaboration: Essays in International Politics*. Baltimore: Johns Hopkins University Press, 1962.

World Resources Institute. *World Resources 1996–97*. New York: Oxford University Press, 1996.

Young, Oran. *International Cooperation: Building Regimes for Natural Resources and the Environment*. Ithaca, NY: Cornell University Press, 1989.

Young, Oran. "Regime Dynamics." In Stephen D. Krasner, ed., *International Regimes*. Ithaca, NY: Cornell University Press, 1983.

Zakaria, Fareed. "Realism and Domestic Politics: A Review Essay." *International Security* 17 (Summer 1992): 177–198.

Zartman, I. William, ed. *Collapsed States: The Disintegration and Restoration of Legitimate Authority.* Boulder, CO: Lynne Rienner, 1995.

Zartman, I. William. *Elusive Peace: Negotiating an End to Civil Wars.* Washington, DC: Brookings Institution Press, 1995.

Zartman, I. William, ed. *Governance as Conflict Management: Politics and Violence in West Africa.* Washington, DC: Brookings Institution Press, 1996.

Zartman, I. William. *International Multilateral Negotiations: Approaches to the Management of Complexity.* San Francisco: Jossey-Bass, 1994.

Zartman, I. William, ed. *The Negotiation Process.* Newbury Park: Sage, 1978.

Zartman, I. William, ed. *Tunisia: The Political Economy of Reform.* Boulder, CO: Lynne Rienner, 1991.

Zartman, I. William, Daniel Druckman, Lloyd Jensen, Dean G. Pruitt, and Y. Peyton Young. "Negotiation as a Search for Justice," *International Negotiation* 1, no. 1 (1996): 79–98.

Zielonka, Jan. *Europe as Empire: The Nature of the Enlarged European Union.* New York: Oxford University Press, 2006.

Zimmermann, Andreas, and H. Scheel. "Zwischen Konfrontation und Kooperation: Die Vereinigten Staaten und der Internationale Strafgerichtshof." *Vereinte Nationen* 50, no. 4 (2002): 137–144.

Zolberg, Aristide. *Creating Political Order: The Party-States of West Africa.* Chicago: Rand-McNally, 1966.

The Contributors

Seyom Brown is Lawrence A. Wien Professor of International Cooperation at Brandeis University. He is the author of numerous books on international politics, including *The Illusion of Control: Force and Foreign Policy in the Twenty-First Century.*

Charles F. Doran is Andrew W. Mellon Professor of International Relations and director of the Center for Canadian Studies, Global Theory, and History at Johns Hopkins University's Nitze School of Advanced International Studies in Washington, DC. He is author of *Systems in Crisis,* among other works.

Francis Fukuyama is Bernard L. Schwartz Professor of International Political Economy at Johns Hopkins University's Nitze School of Advanced International Studies in Washington, DC. He is the author of *The End of History and the Last Man* and *America at the Crossroads: Democracy, Power, and the Neoconservative Legacy.*

Robert Jervis is the Adlai E. Stevenson Professor of International Politics at Columbia University; he is also past president of the American Political Science Association (2000–2001). His many published works include *Perception and Misperception in International Politics, System Effects: Complexity in Political Life,* and *American Foreign Policy in a New Era.* He is the recipient of the Grawemeyer Award for Ideas Improving World Order.

Michael T. Klare is Five College Professor of Peace and World Security Studies and director of the Five College Program in Peace and World Security Studies at Hampshire College in Amherst, Massachusetts. He is the author of *Blood and Oil: The Dangers and Consequences of America's*

Growing Dependency on Imported Petroleum and *Resource Wars: The New Landscape of Global Conflict.*

Peter Pavilionis was an editor at the United States Institute of Peace in Washington, DC, from 1995 to 2007. He has written on energy and environmental politics in the Caucasus and Central Asia.

Farhang Rajaee is professor of political science and director in the College of the Humanities at Carleton University in Ottawa, Ontario. He is the author of *Globalization on Trial: The Human Condition and the Information Civilization.*

Gustav Schmidt is professor of international politics and chairman of the department at the Ruhr-University Bochum, and coopted member of the Faculty of History. He is the editor of the three-volume *A History of NATO: The First Fifty Years.*

Paul W. Schroeder is professor emeritus of history at the University of Illinois at Urbana-Champaign, specializing in the international politics of Europe from the sixteenth to the twentieth centuries. His published works include *The Transformation of European Politics, 1763–1848* and "Historical Reality and Neo-Realist Theory," *International Security* 19, no. 2 (Summer 1994).

Kenneth N. Waltz is adjunct professor at Columbia University's Saltzman Institute of War and Peace Studies. He is also Ford Professor of Political Science emeritus at the University of California, Berkeley, and past president of the American Political Science Association (1987–1988). He is the author of *Man, the State, and War: A Theoretical Analysis* and *Theory of International Politics.*

I. William Zartman is Jacob Blaustein Professor Emeritus of International Organization and Conflict Resolution and director of the Conflict Management Program at Johns Hopkins University's Nitze School of Advanced International Studies in Washington, DC. He is the author of many books and articles on international relations, including *Cowardly Lions: Missed Opportunities to Prevent Deadly Conflict and State Collapse,* and he is the editor of *Peacemaking in International Conflict: Methods and Techniques,* revised edition.

Index

About the Book

Now that the clear delineations of the Cold War era are behind us, what are the contours of the international system? And what does the new reality mean for the United States, the acknowledged hegemon? Provocatively applying IR theory to the world of policy analysis, *Imbalance of Power* showcases current policy debates about the nature of both the international order and the role of the United States within it. The authors bring to life concepts of realism, hegemony, liberalism, and constructivism, making it clear why these ideas are so relevant to understanding the challenges of world politics today. In the process, they address thorny issues of structure versus policy, context versus content, even determinism versus choice—shedding light on the shape of a seemingly amorphous system.

I. William Zartman is Jacob Blaustein Professor Emeritus of International Organization and Conflict Resolution at Johns Hopkins University. His many publications include *Cowardly Lions: Missed Opportunities to Prevent Deadly Conflict and State Collapse*.